Winter Park Library

HOW THEY LIVED

HOW THEY LIVED

VOLUME III

*An Anthology of original documents written
between 1700 and 1815*

Compiled by

Professor Asa Briggs

BARNES & NOBLE
NEW YORK

R
9 42
H

2 England - Social life and customs.
1 Gt. Brit. - Antiquities.
3, Great Brit. - History - Sources.

Printed in Great Britain

Contents

v

List of Plates

ix

Foreword

Like the previous volumes in this series, this anthology is concerned with how people lived, worked and thought. It should be supplemented by *They Saw it Happen*, which deals with reactions to particular historical events, and *Who's Who in History*, which deals with the lives and achievements of particular people.

The period chosen for this volume is of strategic importance in modern history. The invention of steam power in the 1770s revolutionized human relations, and by 1815, when the volume ends, it was clear to contemporaries that industrialism was a *fait accompli*. Increased material wealth, unequally distributed, was associated with new factories, new towns and cities, and new ways both of thinking and of feeling. In the French traveller Misson's *Memoirs and Observations in his Travels over England* (1719), a voluble and eloquent survey, the only comment under the heading 'manufactures' is 'The *French* Refugees have brought several good Manufactures into *England*'. By 1815 it was generally recognized that Britain had established a manufacturing ascendancy which was one of its greatest assets. Indeed, British techniques were already spreading outside the country like the ideas of the French Revolution, and though the term 'industrial revolution' had not been coined, the conception behind it was commonplace.

At first, the great change had encouraged optimism. Man could control Nature and harness new forms of power to achieve unprecedented progress. Already by 1815, however, the contradictions of progress were also manifest. Scientific and technical advance carried with it new forms of social conflict and new problems of adaptation and organization. There was a clash, sometimes violent, between the pull of tradition and the pressure of innovation. Big changes were not to come until the 1830s when the political reforms of 1832 ('the Great

Reform Bill'), the first major official attempt to intervene in the management of factories in 1833 (the Factory Act), and the new Poor Law of 1834, which sought to free the labour market by introducing workhouses throughout the country and adding a new stigma to pauperism, revealed the response of politicians to some of these changes. Yet it was during the 1820s that the first changes took place and the debate about change deepened, and it was before 1815 that both 'middle-class' and 'working-class' protests against the economic and political 'system' began to multiply. The language used was often new also, although there were no sharp breaks.

The last part of this book, therefore, is concerned with the drama of these great changes and some of their immediate social implications: the continuing sequence of social and political change will provide the subject matter of the next volume. Much the bigger part of the book, however, deals with the decades before the advent of steam, with a 'traditional' society in which elegance and squalor coexisted; in which the rights of property were sacrosanct, yet in which there was serious endemic crime; in which the law was venerated, yet in which were large areas of tolerated licence in behaviour; in which traditional values propped up the social system, yet 'enlightened' ideas were always challenging it; in which most people lived in villages, yet in which the raw life of turbulent, unfashionable London attracted at least as much contemporary attention as the fashions of polite metropolitan society.

It is a curiously neglected period, although particular aspects of it—for example, the structure of aristocratic and landed politics or the rôle of politicians like Walpole—have been studied with meticulous, scholarly care. Recently, however, both professional historians and the general public have begun to look at its social history afresh. *Tom Jones* (in strictly twentieth-century mould) was an unqualified success as a film: *Culloden* was one of television's best historical recon-structions. The 'Brechtian' element in the eighteenth century seems to appeal to mid-twentieth-century tastes, just as the elegance and the polish appealed to the early twentieth-century rebels against Victorianism. As for the professional historians, they have begun to attempt to formulate and to answer leading

questions—to explain, for instance, why there was a 'take-off'
into industrialism; to show how the behaviour of eighteenth-
century crowds or 'mobs' differed from those of nineteenth-
century trade unions or labour movements; to analyse in what
ways eighteenth-century family life or village life was grounded
in attitudes and habits quite different from those of Victorian
city life; and, even more generally, and still very sketchily, to
discuss when and for what reasons people altered their basic
approaches to time, to place, to work, to play, to order, and,
above all, to scale.

Social history is directly concerned with big questions of
this kind. Some start with demography—problems of numbers,
of birth and death rates, of family size and composition, of the
impact of disease, and the frameworks both of the social and
the legal order. The eighteenth century is particularly interesting in this context, because it was the prelude to the great
modern upthrust of population. Other questions about the
eighteenth century concern quality not quantity, in so far as
the two can be separated. How did people view their own ways
of life, their sense of community, their appreciation of the past
and their anticipation of the future? To study the answers they
gave, it is necessary to turn from statistical to literary evidence,
and to pay detailed attention to the words they used (including
the new words they coined) to describe their own condition
and prospects.

Given this approach, social history forces the student of
history to speculate rather than to escape. It depends on
analysis, the kind of analysis that is stimulated by the exercise
of imagination. At the same time, the best way of starting to
deal with the big questions is often to consider the small detail
of particular instances—for example, to trace changing ways
of life in one village through its parish registers and its field
maps, its tax records and, where they exist, the diaries of its
inhabitants, above all through its buildings and its surrounding
landscape. Yet to carry out successfully such local exploration,
it is useful to know something about more general bearings,
and for this reason alone one of the main purposes of this book
is to provide a sense of historical perspective. The extracts
chosen are sometimes neither full nor representative—where

they break off, they often deserve to be continued—yet, taken together, they offer an introduction to the study of a society which, for all the neglect of historians, is far better documented than the society described in previous volumes of *How They Lived*.

Interpretations of that society tend to vary according to the angle as well as the style of approach. If you go back to the eighteenth century from the nineteenth, you look for the beginnings of those dynamic forces which became dominant in Queen Victoria's reign—urbanism, industrialism, radicalism, evangelicalism. If you go forward from the seventeenth century, you tend to begin by contrasting seventeenth-century conflict with eighteenth-century balance. In fact, the pattern of the century does not quite permit this division of the spoils. The early years of the eighteenth century, the first to be covered in this volume, were years of lively activity in economics, in politics and in society. There was a sense of movement rather than of balance. Britain's participation in European wars, the growth, sometimes hectic, of commerce, the fierce party politics of Queen Anne's reign and the emergence of new, often uncomfortable, elements in society, many of which were cogently described by Daniel Defoe, suggested that the shape of the eighteenth century might be very different from what it proved to be. There was nothing 'balanced' about the *South Sea Bubble*, though the failure of this enterprise, which was borne aloft on a European wave of confidence, brought this precocious period to a close. The gap comes between the 'commercial revolution' and the 'industrial revolution', and it is a gap characterized by a failure of inventiveness and enterprise, even of nerve, just when inventiveness and enterprise might have produced results. Politics in the age of Walpole and in the middle years of the century were less interesting than they had been earlier or than they were to be later, when war and peace provided big issues in the reign of William III or in the age of the American War of Independence. At the same time, the last years of the period should not be seen simply as a prelude to the nineteenth century. The debates on population and on poverty preceded the industrial revolution, as did the 'financial revolution'. So too did the 'Enlighten-

ment' and the emergence of 'political economy'. And many of
the most discontented groups in the late eighteenth and early
nineteenth century looked backward, like Cobbett, rather than
forward, pleading for recovery of that which was lost—
'freedom', prosperity, 'rights', even happiness. John Dyer's
poem *The Fleece* (1757) is a good half-way house book—full of
pride in Britain's commerce and industry, yet linking with the
commerce and industry of the eighteenth century not the
nineteenth-century cotton industry but the great wool trade
with its origins in the middle ages. Dyer could appreciate the
significance of modern inventions, yet he could also ask 'What
needful art is new?', and talk of a golden age which had been,
not which was to come.

The word 'debates' is a clue word to the period. There were
sharp differences of opinion in the eighteenth century—for
example, about how much wages labourers should be paid,
about the 'progress' or shortcomings of manners, about
'rational' and 'vital' religion, about literary and artistic taste.
An eighteenth-century counterpart to G. M. Young's *Victorian
England, Portrait of an Age* would bring out the light and the
shade, the subtle shifts between one generation and another,
the relationship between debate and chronology in the story of
all these and other subjects. Any serious student of the period
is struck at once by its richness and its variety. You cannot
understand the period if you concentrate on Defoe without
understanding Swift, or Adam Smith without looking also at
Cobbett. Such a student is also struck by the temptations the
period offers to new exploration, not least because life was lived
at so many different levels. Much thinking was cosmopolitan,
like fashion, yet a large part of social history was intensely
localized, like government itself. At its quietest the mood of
the period is well caught in an account by Thomas Dale,
parish constable of Little Gransden, of his duties in 1750,
'We have no Popish recusants, no common drunkards; our
Hues and Cries have been pursued; watch and ward kept;
we have not been remiss in apprehending vagrants; we have
no unlicensed ale houses or inns; we have no unlawful weights
or measures; we have no new erected cottages or inmates; we
have no young persons idle out of service; we have no ingrossers

of corn, no forestallers of markets; our town stock is employed for the relief of the poor; we have no profane swearers or cursers; we have no riots, routs or unlawful assemblies.'

Happy the parish with no history! At this point the century stands still. Yet this was only one point of calm. At many times during the eighteenth century, most English villages were troubled by the kind of people and the kind of problems Little Gransden lacked. The century saw sharp fluctuations of fortune from year to year and sharp changes of fortune from place to place. Throughout the century also there was enough foreign war to provide excitement at the margins of the British Empire—in places very different from Little Gransden—and there were enough alarms about the stability of the Hanoverian succession to ruffle years other than the famous 1745. The century began and ended in the midst of widely ranging wars which seemed to contemporaries to involve something more than simple struggles for power. As for that struggle, it was seldom stilled. Foreign commerce itself was already a complex factor in British domestic history. Moreover, alongside Thomas Dale's comments we must place Dr. John Brown's *An Estimate of the Manners and Principles of the Times*, published seven years later and running into several editions, with its complaint that 'honour' was being converted into 'vanity' and its warning, repeated so frequently since—not least during the twentieth century—that Britain was passing through an 'important and alarming crisis' from which it might not recover.

The arrangement of chapters in this volume is directly related first to my over-all view of the demands of social history as a serious subject and second to my own interpretation of the shape of the century. Although the eighteenth century is characterized by the richness of its life and the diversity of its experience, the book begins with the simplest and most basic of social facts, those relating to birth and death. Chapters follow on 'time' and 'place' and 'communication', chapters which set the limits of eighteenth-century attitudes. A chapter on 'the ranks of society' provides an introduction to the complex and changing social system of the century, and it is followed by ancillary chapters on 'work', 'play' and 'manners and styles'. 'Religion' and 'education' clearly go together, and both influenced attitudes towards 'crime and punishment'. 'Food and drink' and 'medicine' also look complementary, although contemporaries were not fully aware of all the links between them, and the all-too-brief section on medicine is reserved for the chapter on the arts and sciences. 'Going to war' could be—and sometimes has been—a book in itself, rather than a chapter, and so too could be 'the pursuit of arts and science', a big subject necessarily dealt with somewhat cursorily. The chapter on 'economic and social change' is concerned with the prelude to the nineteenth century. Again it could be doubled in size to advantage, but the themes running through it will all be dealt with more fully in the next volume. The last chapter deals with 'politics in a changing society', not because politicians should have the last word, but because politics registered, as it always does, economic and social changes, albeit slowly and inconsistently, and social history with the politics left out is not really social history at all.

The illustrations throughout the volume are as important in their way as the text: they remind us that much of social history is not abstract and that the art of seeing is a necessary quality in the social historian. The brief bibliographical note is not designed to be comprehensive, but it refers to books, some of which themselves contain valuable bibliographies. It is likely that the number of important books on the period will increase substantially during the next few years. In the meantime, it should be emphasized that the arrangement described above is not intended to place social facts in such neat and tidy categories that there is no need for a great deal of cross reference. Some of the extracts included in particular chapters might have been included just as appropriately in others. Society itself is always richer than its historians. There are also coincidental links, bringing in particular people or particular places. The best use of this book is to follow up those extracts which seem particularly interesting and to read the whole source from which they are taken. It is also valuable to add to the anthology other extracts which deal with the same or related themes. In this way historical study can push over into historical research in school, home or university.

Guide to Further Reading

J. H. Plumb's *England in the Eighteenth Century* (Penguin, 1950) is the best general introduction to the period. See also M. D. George, *England in Transition* (1953 edn.), E. N. Williams, *Life in Georgian England* (1962) and D. Jarrett, *Britain 1688–1815* (1965). Bigger books include A. S. Turberville (ed.), *Johnson's England*, 2 vols. (1933), D. Marshall, *England in the Eighteenth Century* (1962), J. S. Watson, *The Reign of George III* (1960), and Asa Briggs, *The Age of Improvement* (1959).

Two volumes in the *Historical Documents* series cover this period. The first, edited by B. D. Horn and M. Ransome is concerned with the years 1714–83; the second, edited by A. Aspinall and E. A. Smith deals with the years 1783–1832.

For the structure of politics, see J. H. Plumb, *The Growth of Political Stability in England, 1675–1925* (1967), L. B. Namier, *The Structure of Politics at the Accession of George III*, 2 vols. (rev. edn. 1957) and *England in the Age of the American Revolution* (1930); also, L. B. Namier and J. Brooke, *The House of Commons, 1754–90*, 2 vols. (1964), especially the introduction by Brooke. For other aspects of politics, see J. H. Plumb, *Sir Robert Walpole*, 2 vols. (1956, 1960), I. R. Christie, *The End of Lord North's Ministry* (1958), R. Pares, *George III and the Politicians* (1953), A. Foord, *His Majesty's Opposition, 1714–1830* (1964), S. Maccoby, *English Radicalism, 1762–1785* (1935), E. P. Thompson, *The Making of the English Working Class* (1963) and G. Rudé, *Wilkes and Liberty* (1962).

For the economic background, see T. S. Ashton, *The Industrial Revolution* (1948), *An Economic History of England: The Eighteenth Century* (1955) and *Economic Fluctuations in England, 1700–1800* (1959). See also C. Wilson, *England's Apprenticeship, 1603–1776* (1965), C. Hill, *Reformation to Industrial Revolution* (1967), P. G. M. Dickson, *The Financial Revolution in England*

(1967), and J. Carswell, *The South Sea Bubble* (1960). For aspects of social history, see J. B. Botsford, *English Society in the Eighteenth Century* (1924), R. J. Mitchell and M. D. R. Leys, *A History of the English People* (1950), M. D. George, *London Life in the Eighteenth Century* (1925), S. and B. Webb, *English Local Government*, especially the volumes on *The Old Poor Law* (1927) and *The History of Liquor Licensing in England* (1903), N. Sykes, *Church and State in England in the XVIIIth Century* (1934), D. Marshall, *English People in the Eighteenth Century* (1956), G. M. Jones, *The Charity School Movement* (1938), M. J. Quinlan, *Victorian Prelude* (1941), J. D. Chambers, *Nottinghamshire in the Eighteenth Century* (1932) and Sir Francis Hill, *Georgian Lincoln* (1966), the best of recent local histories concerned specifically with the eighteenth century. For statistics, see P. Deane and W. A. Cole, *British Economic Growth, 1688–1959* (1962).

For art, literature, science and culture, see *inter alia* C. Hussey, *The Picturesque* (1927), J. Butt, *The Augustan Age* (1950), J. Lees Milne, *The Age of Adam* (1947), E. K. Waterhouse, *English Painting, 1530–1760* (1953), J. Summerson, *Architecture in Britain 1530–1830* (1953), K. Clark, *The Gothic Revival* (Penguin edn. 1966), J. Klingender, *Art and the Industrial Revolution* (1946), A. Wolf, *A History of Science, Technology and Philosophy in the Eighteenth Century* (1938), I. Watt, *The Rise of the Novel* (Penguin edn. 1963), and B. Willey, *The Eighteenth Century Background* (1940).

Acknowledgements

The author wishes to thank in particular Clifford Musgrave and the staff of Brighton Public Library; B. S. Page, Dennis Cox and the staffs of the Libraries of the University of Leeds and the University of Sussex; Edmund Dell, formerly East Sussex County Archivist and the staff of the Records Office at Lewes; John Mitchell, Curator of the Kirkstall Museum, Leeds; E. W. Aubrook, Director of the Tolson Memorial Museum, Huddersfield; F. G. Emmison, Essex County Archivist, whose admirable publications are invaluable to social historians; W. E. Tate, helpful at every point, of the University of Leeds; E. P. Thompson of the University of Warwick; David Daiches and Hellmut Pappé of the University of Sussex; and, above all, Irina Stickland, without whose work and advice this volume could never have been completed.

The author and the publisher wish to thank the following for permission to reproduce copyright material, full details of which are given elsewhere.

The Savernake Archives, in the possession of the Marquess of Ailesbury for an extract from correspondence between Lord Bruce and Mr Beecher.

George Allen & Unwin Ltd, for extracts from *The Englishman and the Sea* by C. Lloyd, and *Equitable Assurances* by M. E. Ogborn.

Allied Ironfounders and Arthur Raistrick for an extract from *Dynasty of Ironfounders.*

Dr James Andrews for extracts from the 1934, 1935, 1936, 1937, editions of Volumes II, III, and IV of the *Torrington Diaries.*

T. Burke and B. T. Batsford Ltd for an extract from *Travel in England.*

The Bedfordshire Historical Record Society for extracts from Volume XLVII of *Some Bedfordshire Diaries.*

Ernest Benn Ltd for extracts from *Verney Letters of the Eighteenth Century*, edited by Lady Verney.

Cambridge University Press for extracts from Tate: *The Parish Chest*; Balderston: *Collected Letters of Goldsmith*; Hill: *Georgian Lincoln*, and *The Charity School Movement, 1930, 44–45*.

The Marquess of Anglesey and Jonathan Cape for an extract from *One Leg*, and Gladys Scott Thompson for an extract from *Letters of a Grandmother*.

Cassell and Co Ltd for an extract from *Dr Viper: The Querulous Life of Philip Thicknesse* edited by Philip Gosse.

The Clarendon Press, Oxford for extracts from Volumes 1 and 2 of *Johnson's England*, ed. Turberville; *Wilkes & Liberty*, by Rude; *English Men & Manners*, ed. Turberville; and Vols. III and XIV of *The Letters of Horace Walpole*, ed. Toynbee.

Country Life for an extract from their issue of October 25th 1924.

Cresset Press Ltd for extracts from *The Journey of Celia Fiennes*, ed. C. Morris.

J. M. Dent & Sons Ltd and E. P. Dutton & Co Inc, New York for extracts from the Everyman Library texts of Pope's *Collected Poems*; Smith: *The Wealth of Nations*; Defoe's *Tour Through England and Wales;* Wesley's *Journal*, and Cobbett's *Rural Rides*.

The Economic History Review for an extract from an article by Peter Mathias in their issue of 1957.

Epworth Press for an extract from *Sermons on Several Occasions* by John Wesley.

Essex Record Office for extracts from their publications: A. C. Edwards: *English History from Essex Sources 1550–1750* (out of print) and A. F. J. Brown: *English History from Essex Sources 1750–1900* (out of print).

Faber & Faber Ltd for extracts from *The Autobiography of William Cobbett*, edited by W. Reistel and *English Husbandry* by Robert Trow-Smith.

Her Majesty's Stationery Office for extracts from Sir Lewis Namier & J. Brooke: *The House of Commons, 1754–90, Volume I*, and *Mss. of the Duke of Rutland, Volume III*.

Abey Heywood & Son Ltd for extracts from Samuel Bamford's *Early Days* and *Passages in the Life of a Radical*.

The House of Commons for extracts from their Journals.

Lincoln Record Society for an extract from the *Banks Family Letters* edited by J. F. W. Hill.

Liverpool University Press for extracts from *Portsmouth Point* by C. N. Parkinson.

Longmans, Green & Co Ltd for an extract from *The Town Labourer* by J. L. & B. Hammond.

Macmillan & Co Ltd for extracts from *The Prose Works of William Wordsworth, Volume II* edited by L. Knight; *Sir Francis Burdett and His Times* by M. W. Patterson; and *Diary and Letters of Fanny Burney* by Charlotte Barratt.

Manchester University Press for extracts from *The Strutts and the Arkwrights* by R. S. Fitton and A. P. Wadsworth, and *Samuel Oldknow and the Arkwrights* by G. Unwin.

John Murray for extracts from *Wellington's Men* by W. H. Fitchett; *An Eighteenth Century Correspondence* by Dickens & Stanton; *Georgiana, Duchess of Devonshire* by the Earl of Bessborough; and *Lord Hervey and His Friends*.

Oxford University Press for extracts from E. Hughes: *North Country Life in the Eighteenth Century*; J. J. Boswell: *The Life of Samuel Johnson*; J. Woodforde: *The Diary of a Country Parson*; Josiah Tucker: *A Selection from his Economic and Political Writings*; A. E. Musson: *The Typographical Association*, and Horace Walpole: *Correspondence, Volume I*.

H. Pelling and Penguin Books for an extract from *A History of British Trade Unionism*.

The Royal Society for extracts from their *Philosophical Transactions*.

Martin Secker & Warburg for extracts from *History of Football* by M. Marples.

Society for Promoting Christian Knowledge and M. D. George for extracts from *English Social Life in the Eighteenth Century*.

Salop County Council for an extract from *Shropshire Parish Documents 189*.

Sussex Archaelogical Society for extracts from their *Collections, Volumes VI, IX and XXV*.

East Sussex Records Office, and J. D. Bickersteth, Ashburnham Place, Battle, Sussex for extracts from the Ashburnham Papers.

The author and publisher have made every effort to clear all copyright material but in spite of their efforts, it has been impossible to trace the holders of some of the extracts. In the event of any unforeseen infringements, they express their regrets, and would welcome any information which would remedy such oversight in future editions.

CHAPTER I

Birth and Death

Why is the Herse with Scutcheons blazon'd round,
And with the nodding Plume of Ostrich crown'd?
No, the Dead know it not, nor profit gain:
It only serves to prove the Living vain.
How short is Life! how frail is human Trust!
Is all this Pomp for laying Dust to Dust?

(JOHN GAY, *Trivia*, 1716)

To learn how to *die*, is beyond all doubt the most important lesson of life; it is the *great business of living*. . . . We are always on the confines of eternity; but when, to appearance, we are arrived on the very verge of it, what folly it is still to *cling* to *earth*, instead of striving to mount to *heaven*.

(J. HANWAY, *A Journal of Eight Days' Journey*, 1757)

Dec. 12, 1756. This day, died Mary Shoesmith, a child-maid, at the Rev. Mr. Porter's, after about ten days' illness. This girl was cut off in the prime of youth, not being seventeen. Oh! let mankind consider that no age or sex is exempt from death! What is it that makes men so humble at the approach of death? Only their vices.

(Diary of THOMAS TURNER, tradesman of East Hoathly, Sussex)

Dec. 29, 1782.—I saw 10 graves open in Halifax Churchyard, 9 of them for children, and was informed that 110 children had been interred in the above yard in four weeks which died of the small pox.

Jan. 19, 1783.—I saw 11 open graves in Halifax Churchyard, 8 or 9 of them for children.

(Diary of CORNELIUS ASHWORTH)

1. A FAMILY RECORD

Source: Some Bedfordshire Diaries (*Bedfordshire Historical Records Society*, 1959), pp. 35–7.

Two loose pages of entries made alternately by Edmond and Christian Williamson of Husborne Crawley have as their terse title 'An Account of the birth of my Children by my second Wife'. The document was edited by F. J. Manning.

1709

March 29. My wife fell into labour and a little after 9 in the morning was delivered of a son. Present: aunt Taylor, cousin White, sister Smith, cousin Clarkson, widow Hern, Mrs. Howe, midwife, Mr[s.] Wallis, nurse, Mrs. Holms, Eleanor Hobbs, servants.

April 4. He was baptised by Doctor Battle by the name of John. . . .

16. The child died about 1 o'clock in the morning.

1711

Sept. 17. My said wife was delivered of a son just before 4 in the morning. Present: Mrs. Thomas Molyneux's lady and maid, Mrs. Mann, midwife, Margaret Williamson, nurse, Susan Nuthall, servant.

Oct. 4. He was baptised by Mr. Trabeck by the name of Talbot after my grandmother's name. Sir John Talbot and John Pulteney esquire were gossips, with my sister Smith godmother. . . .

1713

June 9. About 8 at night my said wife began her labour.

10. Half an hour after 1 in the morning was brought to bed of a son. Present: Mrs. Molyneux, Mrs. Bisset, Mrs. Mann, midwife, Nurse Williamson, Susan Nuthall and Betty Ginger, servants.

30. Baptised by Mr. Mompesson of Mansfield by the name of Edmond. . . .

1715

March 7. My said wife was brought to bed of a daughter 10 minutes before 6 in the morning. Present: Mrs. Molyneux, Mrs. Mann, midwife, Nurse Williamson, Mary Evans, Mary Cole and Mary Wheeler, servants.

29. Was baptised by Dr. Mandivel, Chancellor of Lincoln, by the name of Christian.

1716

March 9. My wife was delivered of a daughter at 7 at night. Present: aunt Taylor, Mrs. Molyneux, Mrs. Oliver, Mrs. Man, midwife, Mary Smith, nurse, Jane Kensey, and Mary Wheeler, servants.

31. Was baptised by Mr. Widmore, the Reader of St. Margaret's, by the name of Elizanna. . . . Registered in St. Margaret's, Westminster, as all the rest were.

April 27. Died, was buried in the new chapel yard in the Broadway.

1718

Jan. 21. (C.W.) I was brought to bed of a son about 2 in the morning. Mrs. Man, midwife, nurse Chatty, dry-nurse, present; Mrs. Taylor, Mrs. White and Mrs. Molyneux, Jane Beadle; servants: Mary Wells, Jane Griffith, Edmond Kinward. He was baptised by Mr. Widmore, Reader of St. Margaret's, Westminster, by the name of Francis. . . .

1719

Feb. 21. (C.W.) I was brought to bed of a son between 6 and 7 in the evening. Mrs. Man, midwife, nurse Chatty, dry-nurse; present: aunt Taylor, Mrs. Molyneux and Jane Beadle; servants: Rebecca Shippy, Betty Hall and Mathew Dowect.

March 7. He was baptised by Mr. Widmore, Reader of St. Margaret's, Westminster, by the name of William. . . .

[N.d.] Died and buried at Hadley.

1720

June. (E.W.) My wife brought to bed of a daughter, but the child did not live a minute.

July 21. My wife died and was buried at Isleworth.

Sept. 9. [Francis] died of the smallpox at Nurse Ward's in Hampstead, and was buried at Hadley.

2. BEARING A CHILD

(a) *Source:* Letter from Sir George Lyttelton to Sanderson Miller, Feb. 1752, quoted in L. Dickins and M. Stanton (eds.), *An Eighteenth Century Correspondence* (1910), pp. 186–7.

I congratulate you and condole with Mrs. Miller on her being with child again. I know you think an Encrease of your Family an Encrease of your Blessings, but the poor little Woman who brings you those Blessings has a great deal of trouble and pain to confer them on you, and you are bound in Return *to read to her every Night*. My Wife is well and not a breeding.

(b) *Source:* Diary of Thomas Turner of East Hoathly, printed in *Sussex Archaeological Collections*, vol. VI (1859).

27 Jan. 1762. The wife of Tho. Davy was this day delivered of a girl, after being married only six months: two people whom I should the least have suspected of being guilty of so indiscreet an act. But what can be said of this passion? —how careful should we be of ourselves in this particular, when we daily see people of the strictest value apparently guilty of it?

3. PATTERNS OF LIFE AND DEATH

By modern standards eighteenth-century mortality rates were high, particularly for young children. Of total burials recorded in London in 1739 slightly more than a half were of children under eleven, and almost four out of ten were of children below the age of three. When Dr. Johnson consoled Boswell on the loss of a child he added that 'to keep three out of four is more than your share'. Yet during the late eighteenth century the death rate declined while the birth rate remained high. The extracts which follow draw attention (a) to the plight of eighteenth-century foundlings (b) to the social background of mortality rates (c) to the growing interest in the collection of relevant statistics about the chances of life and death (d) to the attempt to cover risks through insurance (e) the personal experience of death in a family which was comfortably placed.

(a) *Source:* Memorial to the Government, 1739, drawn up by Thomas Coram, a sea captain, and signed by a number of 'ladies of rank', urging the setting up of a Foundling Hospital.

No expedient has yet been found for preventing the murder of poor miserable infants at their birth, or suppressing the

inhuman custom of exposing newly-born infants to perish in
the streets; or the putting of such unhappy foundlings to wicked
and barbarous nurses, who undertake to bring them up for a
small and trifling sum of money, do often suffer them to starve
for want of due sustenance or care, or if permitted to live
either turn them into the streets to beg or steal, or hire them
out to loose persons by whom they are trained up in that
infamous way of living and sometimes are blinded or maimed
and distorted in their limbs in order to move pity or compassion,
and thereby become fitter instruments of gain to those vile
merciless wretches.

(b) *Source:* G. Crabbe, *The Parish Register* (1807). Crabbe describes
a vestry meeting held to deal with a foundling.

> Then by what name th' unwelcome guest to call
> Was long a question, and it posed them all;
> For he who lent it to a babe unknown
> Censorious men might take it for his own:
> They look'd about, they gravely spoke to all,
> And not one *Richard* answered to the call.
> Next they inquir'd the day, when, passing by,
> Th' unlucky peasant heard the stranger's cry:
> This known,—how food and raiment they might give,
> Was next debated—for the rogue would live;
> At last, with all their words and work content,
> Back to their homes the prudent vestry went,
> And *Richard Monday* to the workhouse sent.

(c) A Note made by the Vicar of Cardington, Bedfordshire, on the
pattern of births and deaths in his parish between 1780 and 1800.
Quoted in W. E. Tate, *The Parish Chest* (1960), p. 80.

It is hard to say, how many lives these cities have lost, or
how many they yet lose annually, by the poverty, filth and
vice of parents, which no public institutions in this land of
freedom can boast of, yet by being closely built, and many
living in confined places, and many too much congregated. . . .
We must not be surprized, that so great a proportion as 20232
in 43101, or near 47% die under 2 years of age: this appears
by an account now before me of 1756, 1757, and 1758. . . .

Baptisms total 482. Burials total 503. Hence there appears a diminution of Population particularly if it be considered that some Dissenters from the Established Church are buried at the Meetinghouse & are not registered: but a Consideration must be had to the number of Children interred unbaptized, which increases the Proportion of Burials to that of Baptisms, in a greater ratio than that of Burials to Births. These two circumstances being considered, I doubt not but that there has been an increase in Population for the last 21 Years, tho' the average number of Burials exceeds that of Baptisms.

(d) *Source:* An early eighteenth-century advertisement, quoted in J. Ashton, *Social Life in the Reign of Queen Anne* (1883), p. 38.

This is to give Notice, that the Office of Society for Burials, by mutual Contribution of a Halfpenny or Farthing towards a Burial, erected upon Wapping Wall, is now removed into Katherine Wheel Alley in White Chappel ... where subscriptions are taken to compleat the number, as also at the Ram in Crucifix Lane in Barnaby Street, Southwark; to which places notice is to be given of the death of any Member ... and this Thursday about 7 o'clock Evening will be buried by the Undertakers the Corpse of J. S., a Glover over against the Sun Brewhouse, in Golden Lane; as also a Child from the Corner of Scorn Alley in Bishopsgate Street. ...

(e) *Source:* A Short Account of the Society for Equitable Assurances on Lives and Survivorships (1762), quoted in M. E. Ogborn, *Equitable Assurances* (1962), pp. 47–8.

These considerations induced a number of gentlemen, in the beginning of the year 1756, to form a design of establishing a Society for equitable assurances upon lives, with a view to the sole benefit of the Persons Assured, whose interest hath been all along considered as wholly distinct from, not to say incompatible with, that of the Assurers; a society, in which the assured being at the same time mutually assurers one to the other, the interest of one might be the interest of both; in which a life might be assured for a single year, a certain number of years, or for the whole continuance of life; and in which the premiums of assurance should be no more than adequate to the chance of death attending the age of the life to be assured, and to the time the assurance was to continue. The design was received with approbation, and, with unwearied diligence and application, pursued through numerous difficulties and obstacles, for the space of almost seven years. During this time other less comprehensive societies, upon plans, indeed, something different from this, yet originally derived from this, sprung up and flourished. The promoters, however, of this design, having by perseverence surmounted all obstructions, are at length arrived (at least in this respect) at the completion of all their endeavours for the public good, the establishment of A SOCIETY FOR EQUITABLE ASSURANCES ON LIVES AND SURVIVORSHIPS.

(f) *Source:* Letter of 13 Feb. 1705, printed in J. J. Cartwright (ed.), *The Wentworth Papers, 1705–1739* (1883), p. 40.

My dearest dear childe . . . The other day Peter brought his youngist son to se me which is the fynest of all his far beyand Will. I fancy it lyke dear Paul; it has your skin and very brisk gray eye and a luvly culloar, and very plump round faic, its fyner much then the girle, whoe Bell has geven a very fyne coat to, it being her God Daughter. Its time for you to thinck of a Wife, for this will be Peter's fifth childe. I am very sorry for poor Major Larranc. I hear he is condemd to be shott to death, about a consperecy to delever up Gibletor [Gibraltar to the Spaniards] with sixteen more offecers all to dye; he was a freind of poor dear Paul's, [the writer's son] soe I am hartely sorry for him. We have fyne summer wether now, its said to be very sickly. I thanck God we are all well. Fubs [the writer's pet dog] is in sum trouble, for yesterday she parted with her last little one, but it is as great a trouble to Pug [the writer's pet monkey] for she was infenit fond of it, and soe was the puppy of her. . . .

4. TWO CHRISTENINGS

(a) *Source:* The Earl of Bessborough (ed.), *Extracts from the Correspondence of Georgiana, Duchess of Devonshire* (1955), p. 62.

Wimbledon, Tuesday the 12th (Aug. 1783),
. . . On Saturday we had the christening. Dst angelic Bess

as I know you love a detail of all concerning us I will give you of this—I had on an *habit tuve* of lace (all joining lace trim'd with Brussels) apron &c to suit, and all white. The little girl's christening suit was of one piece of Brussels lace made there on purpose, and the finest I ever saw. Harriet and her boy were very fine too, and dear little John in a frock Canis gave him, he, dear Dog, was in a very pretty grey frock. My mother, father, the D^{ss} of Portland were godfather and god-mothers to mine, who is call'd Georgiana Dorothy, and I, the D. of D. and Ld Bessboro' to my sister's, who is call'd Frederick Cavendish. . . .

(b) *Source:* Note of 20 Feb. 1762, in the *Diary* of Thomas Turner.

In the even I walked down to Tho. Davy's (by whom I had been earnestly solicited to come), his infant daughter being baptised in the afternoon . . . Came home about three minutes past twelve—sober. Oh! how comfortable does that word sober sound in my ears!

5. AN UNDERTAKER'S ADVERTISEMENT

Source: R. Steele, *The Funeral or Grief a la Mode* (1702), quoted in J. Ashton, *Social Life in the Reign of Queen Anne*, p. 36.

These are to Notice, that Mr. John Elphick, Woollen Draper, over against St. Michael's Church in Lewes, hath a good Hearse, a Velvet Pall, Mourning Cloaks, and Black Hangings for Rooms to be Lett at Reasonable Rates. He also sells all sorts of Mourning and Half Mourning, all sorts of Black Cyprus for Scarfs and Hatbands, and White Silks for Scarfs and Hoods at Funerals; Gloves of all sorts and Burying Cloaths for the Dead. He sells likewise all sorts of Woollen Cloth, Broad and Narrow, Silks and Half Silks, Worsted Stuffs of all Sorts, and Prices of the Newest Fashions, and all sorts of Ribbons, Bodies and Hose, very good Penny worths.

6. AN UNDERTAKER'S BILL

Source: Funeral bill printed in R. S. Fitton and A. P. Wadsworth, *The Strutts and the Arkwrights* (1958), pp. 129–30.

Elizabeth Strutt, widow of Jedediah Strutt, a pioneer mill-owner, was buried in a Dissenting cemetery.

For the Funerall of Mrs. Strutt

1774
May 15th

	£	s.	d.
To a Strong Elm Coffin with a Double Lid & Coverd with fine Black Cloth, Close Drove with the Best Brass Cased nails & Double Pannelld, a Double Borderd Metall Plate with Inscription, 3 Pair of the largest Patent Handles with wrought Gripes & Embellished with a Glory & an Urn & 8 Dozen of Ornamentall Drops all neatly Guilt the Inside Lined & Ruffled with Superfine Crape		6	6
To a Suit of Superfine Crape consisting of a Shroud Sheet Cap & Pillow		2	2
To 2 Men in with the Coffin & putting in the Body			3
To Screws Pitch & fixing in the false Lid & making up the Body			2
To the Use of the Best Velvett Pall			10
To 15 Plumes of the Best Black Ostrich Feathers for the Hearse & 4 Horses		1	16
To a rich Armozine Scarf for the Minister		1	14
To 3 Silk Hatbands		1	4
To 6 Pair of Mens Plain Kid Gloves			13
To 3 New Crape Hatbands			10 6
To 4 Pr of womens Plain Kid			11 11
To the Use of 3 Cloaks the Mourners			3
To the Use of 4 Hoods & Scarfes			6
To a Hearse with 4 Horses to Bunhill fields Burying Ground		1	2
To 2 Coaches with Pairs to Do		1	2
Paid for fetching Company			1
Paid for Carying the Minister to Lowlayton			6

To 2 Porters with Staves Coverd with silk Scarves & Cloaks	10	
To 2 Hatbands & 2 Pr of Gloves for Do	7	
To 3 Cloakes 3 Hatbands 3 Pr of Gloves the Coachmen	13	6
To 6 Men in Black to Bear the Body & attend as Hearse Pages with Caps & Truncheons	1 1	
To Silk favours & 6 Pr of Gloves for Do	12	
To a Hatband & a Pr of Gloves for the Men that attended the Funerall	3	6
Paid for Turnpikes	1	1
Paid for Beer for Men	2	
Gave the Grave Digger	1	
Attendance at Funerall	3	6
A Man fetching Company	1	1

7. ROYAL FUNERALS

Source: C. Morris (ed.). *The Journeys of Celia Fiennes* (1947 edn.), pp. 294–6.

This Abby alsoe is the place where the sollemnityes of the Kings interrments and coronations are performed, of which I shall give a perticular: at the Death of a Prince, which I have been a mournfull spectator or hearer of two of the most renowned that ever was, King William and Queen Marys,[1] the Queen dying before the King he omitted noe ceremony of respect to her memory and remains, which lay in State in Whitehall in a bed of purple velvet all open, the cannopy the same with rich gold fring, the middle being the armes of England curiously painted and gilt, the head piece embroyder'd richly with a crown and cyphers of her name, a cusheon of purple velvet at the head on which was the Imperiall Crown and Scepter and Globe, and at the feete another such a cusheon with the Sword and Gauntlets, on the corps which was rowled in lead, and over it a coffin cover'd with purple velvet with the crown, and gilt in moldings very curious; a

[1] Mary died in Dec. 1694 and William III in March 1702.

pall on all of a very rich tissue of gold and silver, ruffled round about with purple velvet which hung down on the ground . . . this in a roome hung with purple velvet, full of large wax tapers, and at the 4 corners of the bed stood 4 of the Ladyes of the Bed Chamber—Countesses—with vailes. . . .

The anty chamber hung with purple cloth, and there attended four of the Maids of Honnour, all in vailes, and the Gentlemen of the Bed Chamber; pages [in] another roome all in black, the staires all below the same. The Queen dyeing while the Parliament sate, the King gave mourning to them (500) and cloakes, which attended thus: their Speaker haveing his traine bore up, then the Lord Major the same, and attended by the Aldermen and officers all in black, and the Judges; then the officers of the Houshold, then the Guards, then the Gentleman Master of the Horse led the Queens led horse cover'd up with purple velvet; next came the open chariot made as the bed was . . . [and] supported by six of the first Dukes of the Realme that were not in office; this chariot was drawn by the Queens own 6 horses covered up with purple velvet and at the head and feete was laid the emblems of her dignity . . . after which the Dutchess of Summerset, as chief mourner walked being supported by these Lords, the Lord President of the Councill and the Lord Privy Seale, she haveing a vaile over her face, and her traine of 6 yards length . . . [and] after [her] two and two the Ladies followed and Lords, all long traines according to their ranke, the Bishops likewise, all on foote on black cloth strained on boards, from Whitehall to Westminster Abby where was a sermon, in which tyme the body of the Queen was reposed in a masulium [mausoleum] in form of a bed with black velvet and silver fringe round. . . .

Then after the service of burial which is done with solemn and mournfull musick and singing, the sound of a drum unbraced, the breakeing of all the white staves of those that were the officers of the Queen, and flinging in the keys of the rest of the offices devoted by that badge into the tomb; they seale it up and soe returne in same order they went.

8. A PAUPER FUNERAL

Source: A. F. J. Brown (ed.), *English History from Essex Sources*
vol. I (1952), p. 112. The list of funeral expenses is taken from the
Great Bentley Vestry Minutes, 1756.

for a quert of ould bear and a pint of gin for the widow orsbin	0. 11
for going for Mr hunt to the wid orsbin	1. 0
for fetching the nurs from wivener to the widow orsbin	1. 6
for a pint of wine and pearl barley and harts horn for the widow orsbin	1. 3½
for the Coffin for the widow orsbin	7. 0
for Carring of the widow orsbin to the ground in a tumbril	1. 0
to the minister	2. 6
for the affedave [affidavit of burial in wool]	0. 6
to the sexton	3. 0
for bear at the bering of the Widow orsbin	4. 0

9. THE DEATH OF A CRIMINAL

Source: C. Morris (ed.), *The Journeys of Celia Fiennes*, pp. 310–11.
(For crime, see below, pp. 368.)

The manner of Criminalls punishment after Condemnation:
which if it be for fellony or treason their condemnation of the
first is to be hanged, and they are drawn in a cart from their
prisons . . . with their coffin tyed to them and halters about
their necks, there is alsoe a Divine with them that is allwayes
appointed to be with them in the prison to prepare them for
their death by makeing them sencible of their crimes and all
their sins, and to confess and repent of them; these do accompany them to the place of execution which is generally through
the Citty to a place appoynted for it called Tiburn [Tyburn][1]
there after they have prayed and spoken to the people the
Minister does exhort them to repent and to forgive all the
world, the Executioner then desires him to pardon him, and

[1] For Tyburn, see below, pp. 381-3.

so the halter is put on and he is cast off, being hung on a gibbet till dead, then cut down and buried unless it be for murder; then usually his body is hung up in chaines at a cross high road in view of all, to deterre others.

For high treason they are drawn in a sledge to their execution without any coffine, for their condemnation when hang'd to be taken down before quite dead and to be opened; they take out their heart and say, this is the heart of a traytor, and so his body is cutt in quarters and hung up on the top of the great gates of the City, which are the places of their prison, some gate houses for debtors, others for fellons and traytors. . . .

10. THE DEATH OF A DOG

Source: Letter of 16 Nov. 1708, printed in J. J. Cartwright (ed.), *The Wentworth Papers*, p. 64. (For Fubs, see above, p. 7.)

My dearist and best of children . . .

I have a moste dismall story to tell you, God forgiv me for it. I cannot help being more than I ought concerned. I shall never lov anything of that kynde a quarter soe well again. I had rether lost a hundred pd., nay all the rest of my doms I would have geven to have saved poor charming Fubs, never poor wretch had a harder death. As it leved soe it dyed, full of lov leening its head in my bosom, never offered to snap at any body in its horrid torter but nussle its head to us and loock earnestly upon me and Sue, whoe cryed for thre days as if it had been for a childe or husband . . . Sure of all its kynd thear never was such a one nor never can be, soe many good qualletys, soe much senc and good nature and cleenly and not one falt; but few human creeturs had more senc then that had. . . . I could write a quier of paper in her commendations. I have buiryed her in this garden, and thear is a stoan layd at her head. . . .

11. THE DEATH OF CATTLE

The seriousness of losses of cattle in a primarily agricultural economy was plain to all writers of the eighteenth century.

Source: John Milner's account of cattle distemper, printed in E. Hughes, *North Country Life in the Eighteenth Century, 1700–1750* (1952), pp. 148–50.

The distemper first appeared in August 1714 at Islington and as soon as the Lords Justices had notice of it, the Lord Chancellor by their directions ordered four Justices to take an account of the stocks of all the Cowkeepers in or near the place who had any infected cows or calves and also to agree with them for all their cows and calves which were or should be taken ill.

This was done at 40ˢ/- a cow and 10ˢ/- a calf. On receiving information that the Distemper was chiefly propagated by the selling of infected calves, the Justices bought and killed all the calves, sick and well; they also appointed a slaughterman at 5ˢ/- a day and proper surveyors who every day visited each cowherd, killing every cow as soon as it was taken ill, burying them ten foot deep with unslaked lime and covering them well with earth to prevent infectious steames. They also every week checked the accounts of the cowkeepers' stocks to prevent their buying in new cattle or old cows of small value which practices tended to increase the Distemper.

12. EPITAPHS

Eighteenth-century epitaphs, both in their content and their style, illustrate the attitude of contemporaries to the problems of this chapter perhaps more vividly than any other source.

(a) *Source:* Alexander Pope, *Collected Poems* (Everyman edn., 1924), p. 120. (For Wordsworth's comments on this epitaph, see below, p. 17.)

On Mrs. Corbet who Died of a Cancer in her Breast.

> Here rests a woman, good without pretence,
> Bless'd with plain reason, and with sober sence:
> No conquests she, but o'er herself, desired;
> Nor arts essay'd, but not to be admir'd.
> Passion and Pride were to her soul unknown,
> Convinced that Virtue only is our own;
> So unaffected, so composed a mind;

So firm, yet soft; so strong, yet so refined;
Heaven as its purest gold, by tortures tried!
The saint sustain'd it, but the woman died.

(b) *Source:* Epitaph of 1772 in *Extant Epitaphs, Gathered by a Commercial in Spare Moments* (1870), p. 38.

Like a tender Rose Tree was my spouse to me,
Her offspring Pluckt, too long deprived of life is she,
Three went before, Her Life went with the Six,
I stay with the Three Our Sorrows for to mix,
Till Christ our only hope our Joys doth Fix.

(c) *Source:* William Hone, *The Table Book* (1827).

To the memory of my four wives, who all died within the space of ten years, but more pertickler to the last, MRS. SALLY HORNE, who has left me and four dear children: she was a good, sober, and clean soul, and may I soon go to her— A.D. 1732.

Dear wives, if you and I shall all go to heaven,
The Lord be blest, for then we shall be even.
                              WILLIAM JOY HORNE, Carpenter.

(d) *Source:* William Hone, *The Every-day Book* (1827), vol. II, col. 390. Epitaph on an Actor.

SACRED
To the memory of
THOMAS JACKSON, COMEDIAN,
who was *engaged,* 21st of Dec. 1741, to *play a comic cast of characters, in this great theatre*—the World: for many of which he was *prompted* by nature to excel.

The season being ended, his *benefit* over, the charges all paid, and his account closed, he made his *exit* in the *tragedy* of Death, on the 17th of March, 1798, in full assurance of being called once more to *rehearsal;* where he hopes to find his *forfeits* all cleared, his *cast of parts* bettered, and his situation made agreeable, by him who paid the great stock-debt, for the love he bore to *performers* in general.

(e) *Source:* Epitaph on a young smuggler caught by an excise officer, printed in *Sussex Archaeological Collections* (1857), vol. IX, p. 195.

Sacred to the Memory of Daniel Scales, who was unfortunately shot, on Thursday evening, Nov. 7th, 1796.

> Alas! swift flew the fatal lead,
> Which pierced through the young man's head.
> He instant fell, resigned his breath,
> And closed his languid eyes in death.
> All you who do this stone draw near,
> Oh! pray let fall the pitying tear.
> From this sad instance may we all
> Prepare to meet Jehovah's call.

(f) *Source:* O. Goldsmith, *The Citizen of the World* (1762), Letter CVI.

It was formerly the custom here, when men of distinction died, for their surviving acquaintance to throw a slight present into the grave. . . . This custom, however, is almost discontinued, and nothing but verses are now lavished on such occasions, an oblation which they suppose may be interned with the dead, without any injury to the living. Upon the death of the great, therefore, the poets and undertakers are sure of employment. While one provides the long cloak, black sash and mourning coach, the other produces the pastoral or elegy, the monody or the apotheosis.

(g) *Source:* L. Knight (ed.), *The Prose Works of William Wordsworth* (1896), vol. II, 'Upon Epitaphs', pp. 134, 146–7, 165–6.

As, then both in cities and villages, the dead are deposited in close connection with our places of worship, with us the composition of an epitaph naturally turns, still more than among the nations of antiquity, upon the most serious and solemn affections of the human mind; upon departed worth— upon personal or social sorrow and admiration upon religion, individual and social—upon time and upon eternity. Without being so far lulled as to imagine I saw in a village church-yard the eye or central point of a rural Arcadia, I have felt that with all the vague and general expressions of love, gratitude and praise, with which it is usually crowded, it is a far more faithful representation of homely life as existing among a

community . . . than any report which might be made by a
rigorous observer. . . . The epitaph on Mrs. Corbet [quoted
on p. 14] may be the best of Pope's Epitaphs; but if the
standard which we have just fixed is a just one, it cannot be
approved of. First, it must be observed, that in the epitaphs of
this Writer the true impulse is wanting . . . . Dr. Johnson,
making an exception of the verse 'Convinced that virtue only
is our own' praises this epitaph for 'containing nothing taken
from common places'. Now in fact, as may be deduced from
the principles of this discourse, it is not only no fault but a
primary requisite in an epitaph that it shall contain thoughts
and feelings which are in their substance commonplace, and
even trite. It is grounded upon the universal intellectual
property of man—sensations which all men have left and feel
in some degree daily and hourly.

13. THEORIES ABOUT NUMBERS

There was a protracted eighteenth-century debate about the
size of the population, and the influence on society of rising and
falling birth and death rates. The most influential book, Thomas
Malthus's *Essay on Population* was published in 1798 and went
through many editions. Malthus's theories were a direct answer
to those who believed in perpetual progress, for he pointed to the
horrors of increasing population—hunger, poverty and death—
if 'moral restraint' were not exercised within the family. His theories
were sharply contested, and were often unpopular.

(a) *Source:* T. Malthus, *An Essay on Population* (1798), pp. 18 ff.

Population, when unchecked, goes on doubling itself every
twenty-five years, or increases in a geometrical ratio.

Let us now take any spot of earth, this island for instance,
and see in what ratio the subsistence it affords can be supposed
to increase. We will begin with it under its present state of
cultivation.

If I allow that by the best possible policy, by breaking up
more land, and by great encouragements to agriculture, the
produce of this island may be doubled in the first twenty-five
years, I think it will be allowing as much as any person can
well demand.

In the next twenty-five years, it is impossible to suppose that the produce could be quadrupled. It would be contrary to all our knowledge of the qualities of land. The very utmost that we can conceive, is, that the increase in the second twenty-five years might equal the present produce. Let us then take this for our rule, though certainly far beyond the truth; and allow that by great exertion, the whole produce of the island might be increased every twenty-five years, by a quantity of subsistence equal to what it at present produces. The most enthusiastic speculator cannot suppose a greater increase than the island like a garden.

Yet this ratio of increase is evidently arithmetical.

It may be fairly said, therefore, that the means of subsistence increase in an arithmetical ratio. . . .

(b) *Source:* 1809 edition of *ibid.*, pp. 61ff.

In the former edition of this essay, I observed, that, as from the laws of nature it appeared, that some check to population must exist, it was better that this check should arise from a foresight of the difficulties attending a family, and the fear of dependent poverty, than from the actual presence of want and sickness. This idea will admit of being pursued further, and I am inclined to think, that, from the prevailing opinions respecting population, which undoubtedly originated in barbarous ages, and have been continued and circulated by that part of every community, which may be supposed to be interested in their support, we have been prevented from attending to the clear dictates of reason and nature on this subject. . . .

In the history of every epidemick it has almost invariably been observed, that the lower classes of people, whose food was poor and insufficient, and who lived crowded together, in small and dirty houses, were the principal victims. In what other manner can nature point out to us, that if we increase too fast for the means of subsistence, so as to render it necessary for a considerable part of the society to live in this miserable manner, we have offended against one of her laws. This law she has declared exactly in the same manner, as she declares that intemperance in eating and drinking will be followed by ill health; and that, however grateful it may be to us at the moment to indulge in these passions to excess, this indulgence will ultimately produce unhappiness. It is as much a law of nature that repletion is bad for the human frame, as that eating and drinking, unattended with this consequence, is good for it. . . .

After the desire for food, the most powerful and general of our desires, is the passion between the sexes, taken in an enlarged sense. Of the happiness spread over human life by this passion, very few are unconscious. . . .

The fecundity of the human species is, in some respects, a distinct consideration from the passion between the sexes, as it evidently depends more upon the power of women in bearing children, than upon the strength or weakness of this passion. It is, however, a law, exactly similar in its great features to all the other laws of nature. It is strong and general, and apparently would not admit of any very considerable diminution, without being inadequate to its object; the evils arising from it are incidental to these necessary qualities of strength and generality; and these evils are capable of being greatly mitigated, and rendered comparatively light by human energy and virtue. We cannot but conceive, that it is an object of the Creator, that the earth should be replenished, at least to a considerable degree; and it appears to me clear, that this could not be affected, without a tendency in population to increase faster than food; and as with the perfect law of increase, the peopling of the earth does not proceed very rapidly, we have undoubtedly some reason to believe, that his law is not too powerful for its apparent object. . . . It is of the very utmost importance to the happiness of mankind, that they should not increase too fast; but it does not appear that the object to be accomplished, would admit of any very considerable diminution in the desire of marriage. It is clearly the duty of each individual not to marry till he has prospect of supporting his children; but it is at the same time to be wished, that he should retain undiminished his desire for marriage, in order that he may exert himself to realize this prospect, and be stimulated to make provision for the support of greater numbers.

It is evidently therefore, regulation and direction that is required with regard to the principle of population, not diminution or alteration. And if moral restraint be the only virtuous mode of avoiding the incidental evils arising from this principle, our obligation to practise it will evidently rest exactly upon the same foundation, as our obligation to practise any of the other virtues, the foundation of utility.

14. FACTS ABOUT NUMBERS

The first decennial public Census was taken in 1801—an earlier attempt to introduce one had been turned down by Parliament in 1753—and since then the amount and variety of demographic and social information collected has greatly increased. Earlier estimates were based mainly on parish registers subject to wide margins of error, and even the Censuses of 1801 and 1811 omitted a significant proportion (as much as 5 per cent) of the population. Between 1801 and 1811 English population, according to Census information, increased by $17\frac{7}{8}$ per cent. The distribution of population by counties in 1801—by order of size—is set out below. During the eighteenth century the population of East Anglia had declined, while that of Tyneside, Yorkshire and Lancashire had increased. Surrey and Middlesex grew with the growth of London (see below, p. 54), while the population of the West Country, the South and the East Midlands had remained relatively static.

Yorkshire	858,892	Lincoln	208,557	Leicester	130,081
Middlesex	818,129	Warwick	208,190	Cumberland	
Lancashire		Shropshire	197,639		117,230
	672,731	Chester	191,751	Dorset	115,319
Devon	343,001	Cornwall	188,269	Oxford	109,620
Kent	307,624	Wiltshire	185,107	Berkshire	109,215
Somerset	273,750	Derby	161,142	Buckingham	
Norfolk	273,371	Durham	160,861		107,444
Surrey	269,049	Sussex	159,311	Hertford	97,577
Gloucester		Northumberland		Cambridge	89,346
	250,803		157,101	Hereford	89,191
Stafford	239,153	Nottingham		Bedford	63,393
Essex	226,437		140,350	Monmouth	45,582
Southampton		Worcester	139,333	Westmorland	41,617
	219,656	Northampton		Huntingdon	37,568
Suffolk	210,431		131,757	Rutland	16,356

CHAPTER II

Time

'Tis with our judgements as our watches, none
Go just alike, yet each believe his own.
(ALEXANDER POPE, *Essay on Criticism*, 1711)

She went, to plain-work and to purling brooks,
Old-fashion'd halls, dull aunts, and croaking rooks,
She went from op'ra, park, assembly, play,
To morning walks, and pray'rs three hours a day;
To part her time 'twixt reading and Bohea,
To muse, and spill her solitary Tea,
Or o'er cold coffee trifle with the spoon,
Count the slow clock, and dine exact at noon;
Divert her eyes with pictures in the fire,
Hum half a tune, tell stories to the squire;
Up to her godly garret after sev'n,
There starve and pray, for that's the way to heav'n.
(ALEXANDER POPE, *Epistle to Miss Blount*, 1717)

Mr. Pratt. My table clock stops and will not go and when it did
go the hand for the day of the month goes from 12 at noon to
12 at noon again, whereas it should go from 12 at night to 12 at
night again. I must desire you to come over on purpose to rectifie
it as soon as possible ... P.S. Pray bring your toolls and come
early enough to mend my mother's repeating watch.
(Letter from HENRY PUREFOY to a Clockmaker, 1746)

I resigned myself to the common ideas of this place [LINCOLN]
such as bells ringing, clocks striking, men drinking, women talking,
and children dancing eternally. . . .
(Letter from MARY YORKE, 19 Jan. 1771)

Whilst the engine runs the people must work—men, women,
and children are yoked together with iron and steam. The animal
machine—breakable in the best case, subject to a thousand sources

of suffering—is chained fast to the iron machine, which knows no suffering and no weariness.

(J. P. KAY, *Moral and Physical Conditions of the Operatives—employed in the Cotton Manufacture in Manchester*, 1832)

1. PERSPECTIVES

A very old man still alive at the beginning of the period had spanned great changes.

(a) *Source:* Report in *Daily Courant*, 9 April 1706.

This Day died [at Northampton] John Bales of this Town, Button Maker aged 130 and some Weeks; he liv'd in the Reigns of Queen Elizabeth, King James the First, King Charles the First, Oliver, King Charles the Second, King James the Second, King William the Third, and Queen Anne.

(b) Some old men lived through most of the period covered in this volume.

Source: Report in the *Monthly Intelligencer*, Feb. 1815.

Died at Caversham, Oxon in his 102d. year, Mr. H. Cottrell, late of Burgfield, Berks.

(c) Some old men who died much later could recall the changes described in this volume. Adam Luecock of Coalbrookdale, a centre of the early industrial revolution, died in 1831, aged 107.

Source: J. Randall, *History of Madeley* (1880), pp. 287ff.

At local festivals . . . he was brought to crown the presidential chair. Old Adam—a name truly suggestive of the past and well fitted for a village sage—was widely known. He was a specimen of archaeology in himself—the solitary link of a patriarchal chain that had fallen one by one—he the only one remaining. Old age sat as fittingly on him . . . as autumn bloom upon mellow fruit. . . . While lingering, or waiting, rather, upon the verge of another world he liked to live again the active past, and to amuse himself by talking of scenes with which he had been associated. . . . 'We used', he said, 'to bring the mine for the Dale on pack-horses. . . . We used also, to take minerals on horseback all the way to Leighton, where there was plenty of wood and charcoal, and water to blow the bellows. Strings of horses, the first having a bell to tell of their coming, used to go; they called them 'Crickers'— and a very pretty sight it was to see them winding through upland, wood and meadow, the little bells tinkling as they went. . . . Pedlars and packhorses were the means of loco- motion and the medium of news in my day; and if we travelled, it was in the four-wheeled covered waggon, over roads with three or four feet ruts, Lord, sir, I remember, in good old George the Third's time, when turnpike gates were first put up, there was a great outcry against them. . . . '

(d) By the middle of the nineteenth century most of the issues raised in this book and the ways of life associated with them had passed into history. For ordinary people the industrial revolution and the coming of railways, the greatest of all the transport changes, were the great divide. Walter Bagehot, the essayist, put the general question into historical perspective.

Source: W. Bagehot, 'Bolingbroke as a Statesman' (1863), printed in *Biographical Studies* (1881).

Who now reads Bolingbroke? was asked sixty years ago. Who now knows anything about him? we may ask now. Professed students of our history or of our literature may have special knowledge; but out of the general mass of educated men, how many could give an intelligible account of his career? How many could describe even vaguely his character as a statesman? Our grandfathers and their fathers quarrelled for two generations as to the peace of Utrecht, but only an odd person here and there could now give an account of its provisions. The most cultivated lady would not mind asking, 'The Peace of Utrecht! yes—what was that?' . . . So is history *unmade.* Even now, the dust of forgetfulness is falling over the Congress of Vienna [1815] . . . and in another fifty years 'Vienna' will be as 'Utrecht', and Wellington be no more than Marlborough.

2. MEASUREMENT

(a) For provincial men and women, the pattern of time would usually be expressed in terms of births and deaths, particularly those

within the local community. The following data refer to the parish
of Eastry in Kent.

REIGN[1]	SQUIRE[2] (at Eastry Court)	PARISH PRIEST[3]	INNKEEPER (at the Five Bells)	
1688. William III				1690
1702. Anne	Robert Bargrave	1698. Drue-Astley Cressener[4]	1693. Michael Sampson	1700
1714. George I			1707. John Cost	1710
				1720
1727. George II	1723. Isaac Bargrave born			
			1733. William Vidgeon	1730
	1744. Isaac Bargrave succeeded	1747. Culpeper Savage		1740
		1753. Samuel Herring		1750
1760. George III		1757. Richard Harvey		1760
		1772. Richard Harvey[6]	1771. William Pittock	1770
				1780
				1790
	1800. Isaac Bargrave died. Succeeded by Robert Bargrave[5]		1806. Widow Pittock	1800
				1810
				1820
1820. George IV	1825. Robert Bargrave died	1821. George Randolph (to 1841)	1822. John Wilson	
1830. William IV				1830

[1] To the old Christian festivals there had been added each year the celebration
of the Restoration of Charles II on May 29 and the martyrdom of Charles I on
30 January. On Nov. 5—to quote the Prayer Book—'the happy arrival of King
William . . . for the delivery of the church and Nation' was celebrated along
with the deliverance from Guy Fawkes.

[2] The Bargrave family, descendants of Isaac Bargrave, Dean of Canterbury
(1625–43), took up the lease of Eastry Court from the Nevinsons in 1647. They
remained at Eastry until 1858.

[3] To complete the perspectives, there were five Vicars of Eastry between 1590
and 1698 and five between 1841 and 1923.

[4] Drue-Astley Cressener presented the paten and chalice which are still used in

(b) An important new development was the rise of the newspaper press offering readers a regular flow of news. London led the way in the late seventeenth century. There was no country newspaper in existence in 1700; by 1760 130 had been started and the newspaper had become an institution. In addition to news of events they provided useful information about meetings, prices, trade returns and bills of mortality, not to speak of advertisements.

Source: Article in the *British Mercury*, 2 Aug. 1712.

About 1695 the press was again set to work, and such a furious itch of novelty has ever since been the epidemical distemper, that it has proved fatal to many families, the meanest of shopkeepers and handicrafts spending whole days in coffee-houses to hear news and talk politics, whilst their wives and children wanted bread at home, and, their business being neglected, they were themselves thrust into gaols or forced to take sanctuary in the army. Hence sprang that inundation of *Postmen, Postboys, Evening Posts, Supplements, Daily Corrants* and *Protestant Post Boys*, amounting to twenty-one every week, besides many more which have not survived to this time, and besides the *Gazette*, which has the sanction of public authority.

(c) *Source:* G. Crabbe, *The Newspaper* (1785).

I sing of NEWS, and all those vapid sheets
The rattling hawker vends through gaping streets;
Whate'er their name, whate'er the time they fly;
Damp from the press, to charm the reader's eye:
For, soon as morning dawns with roseate hue,
The Herald of the morn arises too;
Post after post succeeds, and all day long,

Eastry Church. Among his comments in the Parish Register we read, 'Astley Cressener Vicar, Inducted . . . 1698 among the Savages of Eastry, who used my Good Predecessor almost as Ill as my Self, but Death in a little time gave him a Happy Deliverance'.

[5] Robert took the name and arms of Bargrave only after Isaac's death. He was the husband of Isaac Bargrave's neice, and was previously called Tournay.

[6] Harvey came from a prosperous Eastry family who lived in one of the fine local houses which vied with Eastry Court. One of these was built by the Boteler family in 1710. Harvey's brother John was Mayor of Sandwich in 1774. He died of wounds received on the Glorious First of June, 1794.

C

Gazettes and Ledgers swarm, a noisy throng.
When evening comes, she comes with all her train
Of Ledgers, Chronicles, and Posts again. . . .

(d) In the middle of the century there were fuller chronicles of
events as well as newspapers and reviews. The *Annual Register* first
appeared in 1759.

Source: Preface to the *Annual Register* (1759).

Not confined to a monthly publication, we have an opportunity of examining with care the products of the year, and of
selecting what may appear most particularly deserving of
notice: we have from the same cause the advantage of order;
we are better able to rank the several kinds under their proper
heads . . . [Yet] we find it very difficult to trace the true
causes of events, which time only can draw from obscurity.
It is hard to find a connection between the facts upon whose
authenticity we may depend; and in the mass of materials of
a dubious authority, it is equally hard to know what ought
to be chosen to make out such a connection.

(e) For a sophisticated conception of the passage of time, see
Henry Fielding's *Tom Jones* (1749) which deliberately plays with
the time sequence of events and philosophises about the subject.

Source: H. Fielding, *The History of Tom Jones*, Book. II, Ch. I.

Though we have properly enough entitled this our work, a
history, and not a life; nor an apology for a life, as is more in
fashion; yet we intend in it rather to pursue the method of
those writers, who profess to disclose the revolutions of countries, than to imitate the painful and voluminous historian,
who, to preserve the regularity of his series, thinks himself
obliged to fill up as much paper with the detail of months and
years in which nothing remarkable happened, as he employs
upon those notable areas when the greatest scenes have been
transacted on the human stage.

Such histories as these do, in reality, very much resemble a
newspaper, which consists of just the same number of words,
whether there be any news in it or not. They may likewise be
compared to a stage coach, which performs constantly the
same course, empty as well as full. The writer, indeed, seems

to think himself obliged to keep even pace with time, whose amenuensis he is. . . .

Now it is our purpose, in the ensuing pages, to pursue a contrary method. When any extraordinary scene presents itself (as we trust will often be the case), we shall spare no pains nor paper to open it at large to our reader; but if whole years should pass without producing anything worthy his notice, we shall not be afraid of a chasm in our history; but shall hasten on to matters of consequence, and leave such periods of time totally unobserved. . . .

My reader then is not to be surprized, if, in the course of this work, he shall find some chapters very short, and others altogether as long; some that contain only the time of a single day, and others that comprise years; in a word, if my history sometimes seems to stand still, and sometimes to fly. . . .

3. THE RHYTHM OF THE SEASONS

Within each year, time was still measured by the changes of the seasons. Before the advent of 'time-tables' (it was not until the coming of railways in the nineteenth century that this term became common), work and play were closely attuned to seasonal rhythms. Many outdoor occupations were busiest in the summer and autumn, with the harvest providing a climax. Even in domestic industry there tended to be seasonal variations, with the calendar influencing business demand and work patterns. There were also special food dishes to make for each season, such as tansy pudding, simnel cakes and hopper cake.

(a) *Source:* Letter from Lord Ashburnham, 15 Oct. 1706, in the *Ashburnham Papers*, East Sussex County Record Office.

The season of the year being now well advanc'd for the cutting of underwood in Coppices and Workemen's wages more moderate than after Christmas I think it may not be amisse to discourse Mr. Kirrell the Charcoale man concerning his taking the ayre in Sussex . . . & negotiate a treaty of Sale with him in order to a bargain, and his using the present proper season to cutt the Wood.

(b) *Source: The Gentleman's Magazine* (1738), pp. 465–7.

I am now in the country, and at that Season of the Year in which Parish Feasts abound I hear of one every Sunday kept in some Village or other of the Neighbourhood, and see great Numbers of both Sexes in their Holiday Cloaths constantly flocking thither, to partake of the Entertainment of their Friends and Relations, or to divert themselves with the rural Games and athletick Exercises.

(c) *Ibid.* (1816), Part II, pp. 408–9. This passage shows the survival in Devonshire of harvest practices which already by 1816 were felt to belong to an archaic society.

The reaping and harvesting of the wheat in the county of Devon is attended with so heavy an expence, and with practices of so very disorderly a nature, as to call for the strongest mark of disapprobation, and their immediate discontinuance. . . . The wheat being ready to cut down, notice is given in the neighbourhood that a reaping is to be performed on a particular day, when on the morning of the day appointed, a gang consisting of an indefinite number of men and women assemble at the field, and the reaping commences after breakfast, which is seldom over till between eight and nine o'clock. This company is open for additional hands to drop in, at any time before the twelfth hour, to partake of the frolick of the day. By eleven or twelve o'clock the ale and cider has so much warmed and elevated their spirits, that their noisy jokes and ribaldry are heard to a considerable distance, and often serve to draw auxiliary force within the accustomed time. The dinner, consisting of the best meat and vegetables, is carried into the field between twelve and one o'clock; this is distributed with copious draughts of ale and cider; and by two o'clock the pastime of cutting and binding the wheat is resumed, and continued without other interruption than the squabbles of the party, until about five o'clock, when what is called the drinkings are taken into the field, and under the shade of a hedge row or a large tree, the panniers are examined, and buns, cakes, and all such articles are found as the confectionary skill of the farmer's wife could produce for gratifying the appetites of her customary guests at this season. After the drinkings are over, which generally consume from half to

three quarters of an hour (and even longer if such can be spared
from the completion of the field) the amusement of the wheat-
harvest is continued with such exertions as draw the reaping
and binding of the field together with the close of the evening:
this done, a small sheaf is bound up and set upon the top of
one of the ridges, when the reapers retiring to a certain
distance, each throws his reap-hook at the sheaf until one
more fortunate, or less inebriated than the rest, strikes it down.
This achievement is accompanied with the utmost stretch
and power of the voices of the company, uttering words very
indistinctly, but somewhat to this purpose—'wé hā ĭn! wé hā
ĭn!' concluding with a horrid yell resembling the war-whoop
of the Indian savages, which noise and tumult continue for
about half an hour, when the company retire to the farm-house
to supper; which being over, large portions of ale and cider
enable them to carouse and vociferate until two or three
o'clock in the morning. . . . It must be observed, that the
labourers thus employed in reaping, receive no wages; but in
lieu thereof they have an invitation to the farmer's house, to
partake of a harvest frolic, and at Christmas also, during the
whole of which time, and which seldom continues less than
four or five days, the house is kept open night and day to the
guests, whose behaviour during the time may be assimilated
to the frolics of a bear-garden.

(d) *Source:* Samuel Bamford, *Early Days* (1893 edn., ed. by H.
Dunckley), pp. 121-9, gives an account of seasonal influences on
industrial work in the North of England in the late eighteenth
century.

. . . Most of the pastimes and diversions which I shall
describe are no longer practised—some of them not even
known—by the youthful population of our manufacturing
districts at the present day. Thus we are enabled distinctly to
perceive the great change which, in a few years, has taken
place in the tastes and habits of the working classes. . . .

Some two or three weeks before Christmas it was the custom
in families to apportion to each boy or girl weaver a certain
quantity of work, which was to be done ere his or her holidays
commenced. An extra quantity was generally undertaken to
be performed, and the conditions of the performance were

such indulgences and gratuities as were agreeable to the working parties. In most families a peck or a strike of malt would be brewed; spiced bread or potato custard would be made, and probably an extra piece of beef, and some good old cheese would be laid in store, not to be touched until the work was done. The work then went on merrily. Play hours were nearly given up, and whole nights would be spent at the loom, the weavers occasionally striking up a hymn or Christmas carol in chorus. . . . Before Christmas we frequently sung to keep ourselves from sleep, and we chorused 'Christians, awake' when we ourselves were almost gone to sleep. . . . Christmas holidays always commenced on the first Monday after New Year's Day. By that day every one was expected to have his work finished. That being done, the cuts were next carefully picked and plated, and made up for the warehouse, and they having been despatched, the loom-house was swept and put in order; the house was cleaned, the furniture rubbed, and the holidays then commenced. The ale was tapped, the currant-loaf was sliced out, and lad and lass went to play as each liked best; the boys generally at football, and both boys and girls at sliding when there was ice on the ground. . . . At this season also it was the custom for the sexton of the church, and the ringers to go from house to house wishing their neighbours 'a merry Christmas', when they were generally invited to sit down, and were presented with a jug of ale and a present in money. . . .

At Shrove-tide we always had a holiday on Tuesday, when we went to each other's houses to turn our pancakes, and 'stang' such as incurred the penalty by not having eaten their cake before the next cake was ready. The person to be stanged was placed on a pole, and being held on each side, was carried by others to middin and there deposited, amid the laughter and jokes of all present. . . .

Midlent Sunday, with us called 'Cymbalin Sunday', was another of our feasts, when it was customary to eat cymbalin cake, and drink mulled ale. . . . A cymbalin is not merely round spiced cake . . . but let the maker raise a lump in the middle, like the ball of a cymbal, and turn up the edges like those of the instrument. . . .

Easter was a more important holiday time at Middleton. On Good Friday children took little baskets neatly trimmed with moss, and went 'a peace-egging', and received at some places eggs, at some places spiced loaf, and at others half-pennies, which they carried home to their mothers, who would feel proud that their children had been so much respected. On Easter Monday, companies of young men grotesquely dressed, led up by a fiddler, and with one or two in female attire, would go from house to house on the same errand. . . . At some places they would dance, at others they would recite quaint verses, and at the houses of the more sedate inhabitants, they would merely request a 'peace-egg'. Money or ale would in general be presented to them, which they afterwards divided and spent. Meantime the holiday having fairly commenced, all work was abandoned, good eating, good drinking, and new clothing were the order of the day. Men thronged to the ale-houses, and . . . on Tuesday night, some unlucky fellow who had got so far intoxicated as not to be able to take care of himself, would be selected to fill the post of lord mayor for the year ensuing. . . . On Easter Wednesday, what was called 'The White Apron Fair' was held at Middleton. It was merely an occasion for the wives and mothers, with their children, and also for the young marriagable damsels, to walk out to display their finery and to get conducted by their husbands, or their sweethearts, to the ale-house, where they generally finished by a dance. . . .

The night of the 1st of May was 'Mischief-neet', when, as 'there is a time for all things', any one having a grudge against a neighbour was at liberty to indulge it, provided he kept his own counsel. On such occasions it was lawful to throw a neighbour's gate off the angles, to pull up his fence, to trample his garden, to upset a cart that might be found at hand, to set cattle astray, or to perform any other freak. . . . The morning after 'mischief-neet' was generally prolific of gossip and some laughter, as it generally became known by breakfast-time what 'lumber' farmer So-and-so had had done. . . .

The feast of Whitsuntide was not attended by any particular local customs, except the relics of old 'Whitsun ales', which consisted in what were termed 'main brews' of ale; a number clubbing to purchase malt which was brewed by one selected from the party. . . . But the 'Rush-bearing' was the great feast of the year, and was held on the anniversary of the dedication of the church. At Middleton it is held on the third Saturday in August. . . . From tradition, as well as from custom itself, we may conclude that at first it was a simple offering towards making the church floor comfortable during the winter services . . . [yet] a rivalry as to which hamlet could bring forth the neatest formed and the most finely decorated load of rushes would ensue. . . . Music, dancing and personal finery would accompany and keep pace with the increasing display [and] the feast would become a spectacle for all the surrounding districts.

Sunday was . . . the great day for hospitality. Relations living at a distance, old friends and acquaintances, being generally invited to the wakes, considerable numbers of well-dressed people would be seen in the forenoon entering the town from all quarters. Then, the very best dinner which could be provided was set out, the ale was tapped, and the guests were helped with a profusion of whatever the host could command. It was a duty at the wakes to be hospitable, and he who at that time was not liberal according to his means, was set down as a very mean person. . . . Monday was the day for hard drinking and for settling such disputes and determining such battles as had not come off on Saturday. Tuesday was again a drinking day, with occasional race-running and more battles at night. Wednesday would be spent in similar manner. On Thursday the dregs of the wakes-keepers only would be seen staggering about. On Friday a few of the dregs of the dregs might be met with; Saturday was woful, and on Sunday all would be over, and sobered people going to church or chapel again, would make good resolutions against a repetition of their week's folly. And thus would have passed away the great feast of 'The Wakes'. From this time, as days began to shorten fast, candles were lighted up in the loom-houses, and what was called 'wakin-time' commenced—not so termed from the keeping of the wakes, but from the lighting up the waking with candles. . . .

The next holiday was the Fifth of November, the anniversary

of the discovery of Gunpowder Plot. Most people ceased from working in the afternoon, and the children went from house to house begging coal to make a bonfire. . . . In addition to these contributions gates and fences suffered, and whatever timber was obtainable from woods and plantations was considered fair game 'for King George's sake'. At night the country would be lighted up by bonfires . . . tharcake and toffy were distributed to the younger members of families, whilst the elder clubbed their pence and at night had 'a joynin' in some convenient dwelling. The lord of the manor made the young men a present of a good two-horse load of coal, with which a huge fire was lighted on The Bank near the church, and kept burning all night and most of the day following. . . . Such were the principal games, pastimes, and observances of the rural population of Middleton and its vicinity when I was a youth. . . .

4. THE DAYS OF THE WEEK

The concept of a regular working week with standard regular holidays belongs to the period after the industrial revolution. It was not only at the time of the wakes that labour slackened off. London journeymen, for example, downed tools on the eight hanging days at Tyburn (see below, pp. 381). Saint Monday was an idle day for many groups of workers. As part of the same system there were periods of incessant toil. In the third extract Adam Smith, the economist, ventured on the view that heavy work was a reason for the 'idleness': other writers related the 'idleness' to the workers' conception of 'independence'. Francis Place, the London tailor, speaks for himself in the fourth extract.

(a) *Source:* J. Houghton, *Collection of Letters* (1783 edn.), p. 177.

When the framework knitters or makers of silk stockings had a great price for their work, they have often been observ'd seldom to work on Mondays or Tuesdays but to spend most of their time at the ale-house or nine-pins. . . . The weavers, 'tis common with them to be drunk on Monday, have their headache on Tuesday, and their tools out of order on Wednesday. As for the shoemakers, they'll rather be hanged than not remember St. Crispin on Monday . . . and it commonly holds as long as they have a penny of money or pennyworth of credit.

(b) *Source:* Note by the Steward of Nocton, Lincs., in July 1765, from the *Dashwood Papers*, quoted in Sir Francis Hill, *Georgian Lincoln* (1966), p. 54.

These two feasts at (Potter) Hanworth and Dunston have so turned our labourers' heads from work, that we have not been able to get all our hay mown last week. . . . This last week has been our horse race, which has been another help to keep our heads turned from minding business, and this week is our Assize. I hope when they are all over we shall fall to business again.

Source: Evidence of Cornelius Bancroft, a Gloucestershire weaver, in *Parliamentary Papers* (1802–3), VII, p. 87.

We could work fourteen or fifteen hours a Day; in Winter we work as much by the Candle as by Daylight; I have worked from five to seven at Night in Winter, and from four to nine in Summer.

(d) *Source:* Adam Smith, *The Wealth of Nations* (1776: Everyman edn., 1910), vol. I, p. 73.

Some workmen . . . when they can earn in four days what will maintain them through the week will be idle the other three. . . . Workmen, on the contrary, when they are liberally paid by the piece, are very apt to overwork themselves, and to ruin their health and constitution in a few years. A carpenter in London, and in some other places, is not supposed to last in his utmost vigour above eight years. . . . Excessive application during four days of the week is frequently the real cause of the idleness of the other three, so much and so loudly complained of. Great labour, either of mind or body, continued for several days together, is in most men naturally followed by a great desire of relaxation, which, if not restrained by force or by some strong necessity, is almost irresistible. It is the call of nature, which requires to be relieved by some indulgence, sometimes of ease only, but sometimes, too, of dissipation and diversion. If it is not complied with, the consequences are often dangerous. . . . If masters would always listen to the dictates

of reason and humanity, they have frequently occasion rather
to moderate than to animate the application of many of their
workmen.

5. GOOD AND BAD TIMES

Fluctuations of experience were stored in the memory and
recalled, often in Biblical fashion, in terms of good and lean years.
The fortunes of farmers and workers—directly related to each
other—were subject to sharp vicissitudes. Professor T. S. Ashton
has traced the pattern of fluctuations in his *Economic Fluctuations
in England, 1700–1800* (1959). There were also long-term trends,
like the more or less continuing agricultural depression from 1730
to 1750.

(a) *Source:* Note by Henry Liddell in 1711, quoted in E. Hughes,
North Country Life in the Eighteenth Century (1952), p. 158.

Now on the best land security no money can be had; credit
is so sunk.

(b) *Source:* Letter of Matthew Ridley relating to the same part of
the country, the North East, in 1744, quoted in *ibid.*, p. 247.

We have had so terrible a summer for the Coal Trade that
we are all put to great difficulties to raise cash to carry on our
works . . . my staith is full of your coals, nor have I made a
shilling of the Colliery this year, this is the case with everybody.

(c) *Source:* Note in the *Diary* of Thomas Turner, 7 Dec. 1763.

The year 1763 was marked by a financial crisis of continental
origin. It was the year of the Peace of Paris which followed the
War of the Spanish Succession.

I think since I have lived at Hoathly I never knew trade so
dull, or money so scarce, the whole neighbourhood being
almost reduced to poverty.

(d) *Source:* Anon. *An Answer to Sir John Dalrymple's Pamphlet upon
the Exportation of Wool* (1782).

The 1780s were years of great industrial expansion, recorded
in every index of industrial growth. Yet there was depression in
many parts of the country in 1780 and 1781.

What, too, is the condition of the great body of the poor, employed in the several branches of this [woollen] manufacture? Deplorable beyond expression. Some quite destitute of employment, others half-employed, and almost all obliged to fly (where else can they fly?) to the landed interest for at least partial support. . . . It is a fact (I speak it from knowledge) that many parishes, at this instant, pay the carriage of wool, to and from the spinning houses, at the distance of twenty, thirty, and even forty miles, for the sake of obtaining some employment for their poor.

(e) Good times could be good. *Source:* Letter of S. and W. Salte, London merchants, to Samuel Oldknow, the muslin manufacturer, 23 May 1786, quoted in G. Unwin, *Samuel Oldknow and the Arkwrights* (1924), pp. 63–4.

We want as many Spotted Muslins & Fancy Muslins as you can make the finer the better. . . . You must give a look to Invention, Industry you have in abundance. Send by the Coach every day what you can. This month & the next are of the utmost consequence to you & to us. We expect to hear from you as often as possible & as the Sun shines let us make the Hay.

6. THE WEATHER

People talked and wrote a great deal about the weather, for in the country seasonal patterns varied in their effects according to the weather, thereby directly influencing the harvest and through the harvest all sectors of the eighteenth-century economy. Some trades, like building, were also directly affected by it. Periods of particularly bad weather, like 1708–10, 1725–29 and 1739–42 affected both employment and population. Weather, however, was extremely localized, and the variety added to the interest.

(a) The Wind.

Source: Note for 19 April 1715 in the *Diary* of Thomas Marchant, a Sussex yeoman, living at Hurstpierpoint, printed in *Sussex Archaeological Collections* (1873), vol. XXV.

Ned Penfold went part of the way to Lewes, but the wind

was so high it blew him off his horse. So he came back again.

[In the same year the vane and one-third of the spire of Wakefield Church in Yorkshire were blown down. Twelve years earlier in 1703 it was estimated that a 'storm of wind' in London killed several people, injured 200, and did £2 million of damage.]

(b) The Rain.

Source: Dr. Hans Sloane, 'An Account of a Storm of Rain that fell at Denbigh in Wales', printed in *Philosophical Transactions of the Royal Society* (1706), vol. XXV.

Tuesday the 16th of July 1706, about 8 o'clock in the morning, it began to rain in and about Denbigh, which continued incessantly for 30 hours, but not very violently till about 3 or 4 o'clock on Wednesday morning, when it rained somewhat faster, attended with a terrible noise like thunder, with some flashes of lightning, and a boisterous wind. About break of day the rain and wind began to abate of their violence, lessening gradually till about 1 or 2 o'clock in the afternoon, when it quite ceased, and the air became clear and somewhat calm. On the Tuesday the wind blew south west, but on the Wednesday it was come to the north west.

The effects of this great storm were dismal, for it caused the overflowing of all the rivers in Denbighshire, Flintshire, and Merionethshire, &c which spoiled a great deal of corn, and took off all the hay that was mowed, near the banks of the rivers, which was carried by the stream in such vast quantities down to the bridges that it choked the arches and inlets, so as to break down about a dozen large bridges. Great oaks and other large trees were rooted up and swept away, with several quickset hedges, and some quillets, by the side of the river Elwy were so covered with sand and gravel, that the owners cannot well tell whereabouts their hedges and landmarks stood; and the same river had altered its course in some places, so as to rob the landlords on one side of some acres, and bestowed as much on the opposite side. Two or three rivulets that conveyed water to some mills have been so choked up with stones and gravel, as to make it hardly worth the expence of clearing.

(c) Drought.

Source: J. Harland (ed.), *Autobiography of William Stout of Lancaster 1675–1752* (1851), p. 102.

1723. The summer was exceedingly droughty so that the people were straitened to keep their cattle alive, and especially for water; and the corn was burnt up, little hay got, and no sale of cattle, nor fodder to subsist them in winter. . . .

(d) Hail.

Source: Note for 13 April 1728 in the *Diary* of Thomas Marchant.

The storm on Saturday proved to be very great, especially the hail, which was prodigious; many of the stones were as big, and some bigger than hen's eggs. The windows of some houses about here were almost all broken. The corn was much injured.

(e) Frost and Snow.

Source: A contemporary pamphlet, *Contentment in God*, quoted by T. H. Baker, *Records of the Seasons* (1883), pp. 189–90.

An unheard of frost seized with extraordinary severity on the world and the elements [in 1739], so that it is scarcely possible to number or relate the many strange occurrences that took place through its violence. Men felt so oppressed that days passed by unheeded. One would and could hardly speak; one sat and thought, yet could not think; if anyone spoke a word it was with a hard, set face. Many hens and ducks, even the cattle in the stalls, died of cold; the trees split asunder. Not only beer but wine in cellars froze. Deeply sunken wells were covered with impenetrable ice. Crows and other birds fell to the ground frozen in their flight. No bread was eaten, for it was as cold and hard as a stone. In May no sign of verdure was yet to be seen; it was still cold in July, and vegetation was then still further hindered by drought. The harvest was not over till late in the autumn, and by the middle of October the frost returned before the fruit in the gardens had had time to ripen.

(f) Ice.

Source: Extracts from the Leeds Parish Church Registers.

Jan. 1739. A sheep was roasted whole upon the ice in the river . . .

Feb. 1739. The frost broke when the ice in the river was fifteen inches thick in some places. . . .

May 1740. On the 5th of this month was a great snow.

(g) Mild Weather in Winter.

Source: Note for 11 Feb. 1759, the *Diary* of Thomas Turner.

This I believe is as mild a time, considering the season of the year, as hath been known in the memory of man—everything having the appearance, and carrying with it the face of April rather than of February (the bloom of the trees only excepted); the meadows now are as verdant as sometimes they are in May, the birds chirping their melodious harmony, and the foot-walks dry and pleasant.

(h) Hot Weather in Summer.

Source: Mrs. P. J. Toynbee (ed.), *The Letters of Horace Walpole* (1903), vol. III, p. 4. Letter of 2 Aug. 1750.

While I was there [in Essex] we had eight of the hottest days that were ever felt; they say, some degrees beyond the hottest in the East Indies, and that the Thames was more so than the hot well at Bristol. The guards died on their posts at Versailles; and here a Captain Halyburton . . . went mad with the excess of it.

(i) There was a growing interest in the collection of data about the weather.

Source: T. Barker, Extract of a Register of the Barometer, Thermometer and Rain, at Lyndon, Rutland, printed in *Philosophical Transactions of the Royal Society* (1775), vol. LXV, pp. 200–1.

In the seventeen months from May 1773 to September 1774 there fell 55.890 inches of rain, which is 3.288 inches each month; and in the three years 1772, 1773, and 1774, there came 93.258 inches; that is, 31.046 inches each year. The year began very severe with a sharp frost, which was not out of the ground for seven weeks together. . . . After the frost it was windy and wet for near a month till above a week in March. . . . There was at times a good deal of fine weather in summer, yet mixed with a great deal of wet it was a great grass year, and a cool summer. The hay time and beginning of harvest were showery, yet more hindering than hurting; but the latter part of harvest in September was exceeding bad indeed. No grain could be carried for three weeks together; for it rained every day, and in great quantities. I never measured so wet a month before. . . . The weather settled just at the beginning of October, which was a very fine month, almost like summer; and it was not till then that the harvest could be finished. The wheat seed-time was good, and the rest of the year favourable upon the whole; though a frost at the end of November and beginning of December was earlier than usual, attended with snow, and threatened a severe winter; yet it grew mild again afterward, was in general fair, and the ground continued tolerably dry, and a few frosty days concluded the year.

(j) Barker watched the weather like a scientist. Dorothy Wordsworth, the poet's sister, watched it as an artist.

Source: The *Diary* of Dorothy Wordsworth, 31 Jan. 1798.

Set forward to Stowey at half-past five. A violent storm in the wood; sheltered under the hollies. When we left home the moon immensely large, the sky scattered over with clouds. These soon closed in, contracting the dimensions of the moon without concealing her. The sound of the pattering shower, the gusts of wind, very grand. Left the wood when nothing remained of the storm but the driving wind and a few scattering drops of rain. Presently all clear, Venus first showing herself between the struggling clouds; afterwards Jupiter appeared. The hawthorn hedges, black and pointed, glittering with millions of diamond drops; the hollies shining with broader patches of light. The road to the village of Holford glittered like another stream. On our return the wind high—a violent storm of rain and hail at the Castle of Comfort. All the heavens seemed in one perpetual motion when the rain ceased; the moon appearing, now half veiled, and now retired behind heavy clouds, the stars still moving, the roads very dirty.

7. CALAMITIES

There was a high degree of risk in the eighteenth-century environment, natural and man-made. Earthquakes brought out

the drama and encouraged the search for 'lessons'. At sea gales
were the main danger: in the towns fire was the great danger.
Calamities—and epidemics—served as landmarks in men's
memories.

(a) *Source:* Letter from Dover, 6 Sept. 1785, quoted in The *Annual
Register* (1785), p. 240.

This morning has been a shocking scene of distress, from the
consequence of the high wind, which blew quite a tempest.
I never saw the sea so much agitated. Several vessels attempted
the harbour without effect; at last, an English cutter came in
quite under water, but safe. A few minutes after, seeing the
cutter safe, a French vessel, with six men on board, made the
same attempt, and here a most dreadful scene appeared. After
being in an instant buried by the waves she rose again, with
the loss of a man washed overboard. In a short time another
swell quite swallowed her up. Her unfortunate crew did not
appear for some time, but at last were perceived floating on a
part of the wreck. In this situation they floated from the pier-
head, till they came opposite York-house, sometimes in view,
and at others buried by the rising waves. Though the sea rolled
mountains high, four English sailors had the temerity to strip
themselves, and ventured their lives to save two of them, who
still continued on the rafters of the vessel, and picked them
up safe. In doing this, they overset the boat, which turned
them bottom upwards; but fortunately a violent sea drove
them all on shore together, so that only four of the crew perished.

(b) R. Thoresby, Account of an Earthquake in the North of
England, reprinted in *Philosophical Transactions of the Royal Society
of London* (1809), p. 104.

This earthquake was felt at Hull, on Tuesday, the 28th of
December 1703, about 3 or 4 minutes after 5 in the evening.
It lifted up chairs and tables, and made the pewter-dishes and
windows rattle, shook whole houses, and threw down part of a
chimney. The shock came and went suddenly, and was attended
with a noise like wind, though there was then a perfect calm. . . .
It was still more violent at Lincoln, where also it raised up
the chairs people sat on, &c. It was felt pretty much at Selby,
as also near Navenby; where the sudden noise seemed to be

D

like the rumbling of two or three coaches driving furiously, and shaking the chairs on which people sat; and even the very stones were seen to move.

(c) Letter from Lady Wentworth, 4 March 1712, printed in J. J. Cartwright (ed)., *The Wentworth Papers*, pp. 275–6.

Thear was a dredfull fyer the other day in Albemal Street, Sir William Windom's hous burnt down; the Duke of Ormon stopt it from going farder, he worked as hard as any of the ordenary men and gave many ginneys about to incurradg the men to work hard. A made ran baerfoot and in her smock to Nothumbarlin hous with the strong box of jewels and most of the plate, and al his writings ar saved, yet he has lost abov twenty thoussand pd. Twoe poor maids jumpt out of the windoe, and beat thear brains out; one was very prety, and was put out only to improve her, a ritch groser's daughter in the sety. They ar much more concerned for their sarvents than for al the other lossis.

(d) *Source:* J. Macky, *A Journey Through England in Familiar Letters to a Gentleman from Abroad* (1732 edn.), p. 52.

On the 4th of *June* this Year (1731) about Noon, a Fire broke out at a Tallow Chandler's here [Blandford], which burnt with such Violence that it consum'd the whole Town (except about twenty-six Houses) together with the Church: the Consternation of the People was so great, and the Fire so quick, that few of them saved any of their Goods; the Small-pox being rife here, added to the Misfortune; for many sick of that Distemper were carry'd into the Fields, where they soon expir'd: Near three hundred Houses are laid in Ashes, and the Town is in such Confusion that 'tis difficult to find a Road through it.

(e) Epidemics were not the least of the calamities. Facts relating to them are set out in C. Creighton, *History of Epidemics* (new edn., 1965).

Typhus, described below, was not suppressed until the 'soap and water' revolution of the nineteenth century.

Source: Dr. Stranger, *Remarks on the Necessity and Means of Suppressing Contagious Fever in the Metropolis* (1802), p. 32.

When the fever has depopulated a building by death and
terror, poverty and ignorance bring new inhabitants who
sicken and die or linger and relapse, and after being carried to
the workhouse or the grave, leave the same pestilential apartment to their ill-fated successors. From these pest-houses
concentrated contagion pours into the adjacent courts and
alleys. . . . It is disseminated through the neighbourhood by
the frequent intercourse of the needy, who repeat . . . their
visits in endeavours to supply each daily want, who are frequently reduced to beg, borrow, or pawn one article to enable
them to buy another. . . . Through a medium of pawnbrokers,
old-clothes men, rag shops, and by contact in a variety of ways,
the poison is communicated where least suspected.

8. WATCHES AND CLOCKS

Measurement of time by watches, clocks and chronometers began
to be common in the eighteenth century, with London and the
big towns leading the way. Watchmakers were highly skilled
craftsmen, and as early as 1701 the London watch-making industry
was taken by a writer as an example of the division of labour.
The makers of the first clocks, like Henry Bridges, had an international reputation, and James Cox regularly exhibited his
models. Watchmakers and clockmakers later contributed to the
pool of skilled mechanics in the industrial revolution. 'Working
like clockwork' became a common expression.

(a) *Source:* M. Misson, *Memoirs and Observations in His Travels over
England* (1719), pp. 36–7.

There are now a great *many* large Clocks in London, so that
you have little Advantage by them in your Houses; but the
Art is so common here, and so much in Vogue, that almost
every Body has a Watch, and but few private Families are
without a Pendulum.

(b) *Source:* A General Description of All Trades (1747), quoted
in M. D. George, *London Life in the Eighteenth Century* (1925),
pp. 174–5.

The work of watchmaking [has been brought] to such an
exactiness that no hand can imitate it. The movement-maker
forges his wheels and turns them to the just dimensions, sends

them to the cutter, and has them cut at a trifling expense. He has nothing to do when he takes them from the cutter but to finish them and turn the corners of the teeth. The pinions made of steel are drawn at the mill so that the watchmaker has only to file down the points and fix them to the proper wheels. The springs are made by a tradesman who does nothing else, and the chains by another. These last are frequently made by women. . . . There are workmen who make nothing else but the caps and studs for watches. The watchmaker puts his name on the plate and is esteemed the maker, though he has not made in his shop the smallest wheel belonging to it.

(c) *Source:* J. Smeaton, 'Observations on the Graduation of Astronomical Instruments' in *Philosophical Translations of the Royal Society* (1786), vol. LXXVI, pp. 3ff.

In the autumn of the year 1741, I was first introduced to the acquaintance of that then eminent artist, Mr. Henry Hindley, of York, clock-maker. He immediately entered with me into the greatest freedom of communication, which founded a friendship that lasted till his death, which did not happen till the year 1771, at the age of 70. On the first interview, he showed me, not only his general set of tools, but his engine, at that time furnished with a dividing plate, with a great variety of numbers for cutting the teeth of clock wheels, and also, for more nice and curious purposes, furnished with a wheel of about 13 inches diameter, very stout and strong, and cut into 360 teeth; to which was applied an endless screw, adapted to it. The threads of this screw were not formed on a cylindric surface, but on a solid whose sides were terminated by arches of circles. The whole length contained 15 threads; and as every thread, on the side next the wheel, pointed towards the centre, the whole 15 were in contact together; and had been so ground with the wheel, that, to my great astonishment, I found the screw would turn round with the utmost freedom, interlocked with the teeth of the wheel, and would draw the wheel round without any shake or sticking, or the least sensation of inequality. How long this engine might have been made before this first interview, I cannot now exactly ascertain: I believe not more than about a couple of years;

but this I well remember, that he then showed me an instrument intended for astronomical purposes, which must have been produced from the engine, and which of itself must have taken some time in making.

(d) Epitaph in the Churchyard at Lydford, Devon.

Here lies, in a horizontal position, the outside case of George Routleigh, Watchmaker, whose abilities in that line were an honour to his profession. Integrity was the Mainspring, and Prudence the Regulator, of all the actions of his life. Humane, generous and liberal, his hand never stopped until he had relieved distress; so nicely regulated were all his movements that he never went wrong except when set a-going by people who did not know his Key. Even then, he was easily set right again, He had the art of disposing his Time so well that his Hours glided away in one continued round of Pleasure and Delight, till an unlucky moment put a Period to his Existence. He departed this life November 14th 1802, aged 57, wound up in hope of being taken in hand by his Maker, and of being thoroughly Cleaned, Repaired, and Set a-going in the World to come.

9. CHANGING THE CALENDAR

One important event in the recording of time is associated with the year 1751. In that year the old style of reckoning (O.S.) gave way to the New Style (N.S.) of the Gregorian Calendar which was already in use on the Continent. There was considerable popular resistance to the bill proposing the change which was introduced by Lord Chesterfield. 'Give us back our eleven days' was a popular cry. There was some misunderstanding of what the terms O.S. and N.S. meant (see the second extract) and even for educated people it took some time to get used to N.S. just as it takes time to get used to a new currency.

(a) *Source:* Letter of Lord Chesterfield to his Son, 18 March O.S. 1751, printed in C. Strachey (ed.), *The Letters of the Earl of Chesterfield to his Son* (1901), vol. II, p. 129.

MY DEAR FRIEND: I acquainted you in a former letter, that I had brought a bill into the House of Lords for correcting and reforming our present calendar, which is the Julian; and for adopting the Gregorian. I will now give you a more particular account of the affair. . . . It was notorious, that the Julian calendar was erroneous, and had overcharged the solar year with eleven days. Pope Gregory the Thirteenth corrected this error [in 1582]; his reformed calendar was immediately received by all the Catholic powers of Europe, and afterwards adopted by all the Protestant ones, except Russia, Sweden, and England. It was not, in my opinion, very honourable for England to remain in a gross and avowed error, especially in such company; the inconveniency of it was likewise felt by all those who had foreign correspondences, whether political or mercantile. I determined, therefore, to attempt the reformation; I consulted the best lawyers and the most skilful astronomers, and we cooked up a bill for that purpose. But then my difficulty began: I was to bring in this bill, which was necessarily composed of law jargon and astronomical calculations, to both of which I am an utter stranger. However, it was absolutely necessary to make the House of Lords think that I knew something of the matter; and also to make them believe that they knew something of it themselves, which they do not. . . . I gave them, therefore, only an historical account of calendars, from the Egyptian down to the Gregorian, amusing them now and then with little episodes. . . .

(b) Lord Macclesfield, one of Chesterfield's co-sponsors, was elected President of the Royal Society in 1752. When his son contested an election in Oxford in 1754, his opponents strongly attacked the change of calendar. Popular ignorance is satirized in the following extract.

Source: A Letter in *The Sussex Weekly Advertiser or Lewes Journal,* 16 Oct. 1752 N.S., reprinted from *The Whitehall Evening Post.*

Sir,

The following is a genuine Dialogue that passed here between a substantial Farmer and his Son, on Saturday Aug. 29, 1752, being Market Day, your inserting of which will greatly please Numbers of your Readers in this Town and Neighbourhood.

Son.   Have you heard, Father, when all the old Styles are to be changed?

Father.   Aye, Jan, they say next Week.

Son.   Are these new Styles as they talk of, to be used all over England?

Father.   Aye, they say so, and in all the King's Dominions too.

Son.   I fancy, Father, whoever has the making of them all will have a rare Job of it, as they say the King is to pay for them. But I wonder we have not heard of somebody's being about them all this while.

Father.   Why Jan, I am surprised thou shoulds't be such a Dunce; did not I explain the whole Affair to thee but the other Day. Why, lad, these New Styles are all to come from abroad; they were made there a hundred and seventy years ago, and have been used there ever since, and are now bringing over Sea to be used by us.

Son.   Aye, Father, what you say may be very true, but Parson Trout says it is all Nonsense to call them New Styles, when they have been used so many Years abroad; however he says they will be of great Service to us for all that.

Father.   What do you tell me of Parson Trout for, don't I understand as well as Parson Trout that it is Nonsense to call them New Styles: Why there is Farmer Jonathan's Styles were all made New within these thirty years to my Knowledge, and now they are all as rotten as a Pear. He'll be glad of the Alteration I'll warrant him.

Son.   Aye, Father, so I told the Parson, that Styles would not last so many years with us, but I find he knows very little of the Matter.

Father.   When Parson Trout says of the New Styles being of great Service to us, is nothing at all to the Purpose, for every Body knows that all the Styles round us are now very good, except the little one at the Bottom of our Mead, and all the Neighbours get over them very well, without boggling in the least; and let me tell thee, Jan, for all the fine Things the Parson says about them, I doubt very much whether we shall be able to get over these New Styles a bit Better than we have hitherto done over the old ones.

Here some Persons coming in to Bargain for Corn; the Dialogue ended.

10. KEEPING A DIARY

Calendar reform was a national undertaking: keeping a diary was a personal matter, which also involved special concern for time. The publishers of diaries were anxious to show that personal diaries had more than a spiritual significance; they were useful as records of transactions and engagements. Farm and gardening calendars were also beginning to be produced in considerable numbers in the late 1760s and 1770s, for example, J. Garton, *The Practical Gardener and Gentleman's Directory for Every Month of the Year* (1769).

Source: The Daily Journal or the Gentleman's, Merchant's and Tradesman's Complete Annual Account-Book for the Pocket or Desk (1782 edn), p. 2.

The use and design of this Memorandum-Book, as has been in the preceding years observed, wants no explanation to many . . . but as we find by experience (and continue to mention it with gratitude and pleasure) that we have annually a number of new purchasers, it is still necessary for their information to observe.

That every two pages in it (one on the right hand, the other on the left) one for the *appointments, memorandums,* and *business* of one entire week . . . . The other for cash receipts and payments. As for example of one day,

JANUARY, 1st Month, has xxxi Days							
	Account of Monies	Received			Paid		
7	Of Mr. Punctual, On Account	73	14	10			
	Of J. Ready, On Account	55	0	0			
	To Dr. Richardson, his Bill in full				25	9	2
	To Mr. Fitzroy, to balance his Account				7	3	
Monday	Expended on my Journey to Bath, out 14 days				10	13	9

. . . As these books may be considered as the annals of a man's life, and may be of use, even after his decease, they ought by all means to be preserved, to have recourse to, when occasion arises, to consult or prove any *receipt* or *disboursement, memorandum, account, time* or *occurrence.*

11. ADVICE ABOUT TIME

It is interesting to trace the growing emphasis on punctuality in the late eighteenth century, along with a greater stress on the virtues of using time wisely. Letters to stewards began to express this emphasis early in the century before new industrialists were forced to recognize the place of hooter and clock in the organization of factory discipline. John Wesley, the Methodist leader, made much of the need to make 'proper use of time': 'Remember', said Benjamin Franklin, 'that time is money.' The first two extracts which follow relate to rural Sussex and the attitudes of a landlord.

(a) *Source:* Letter of Lord Ashburnham to his son, 20 April 1706. East Sussex County Records Office, *Ashburnham Papers*, 4447, p. 45.

Pray my Deare to be very steddy in holding fast to keeping order and method and a very perfect account in writing dayly and hourly if need be of the House expences and of all other occurrences whatsoever in money matters and of things relating to the management of the Estate, of which allsoe a Memorandum book ought to be exactly kept and of bargains allsoe, made with all manner of people whatsoever and keep your pockett book steddy.

(b) *Source:* Letter of Lord Ashburnham to his Steward at Ampthill, 21 Aug. 1705. *Ashburnham Papers*, 4446, p. 229.

Remember to carry upp Dung, Mould, Lyme, Marle &c. for the upper Hopp ground now the weather is fitting and putt not off the good day with delays. . . . Carriage now is the word and ought to be the Deed, Winter will come, Laziness, Lying and excuses beginn to be out of fashion and ever were with wise and honest people, therefore use the time present, the past is noe more, and the future may not be in our power. Earlye in the morning is the time, the Day is short, and would be well employ'd; the Nights for rest and good hours before Sun Sett, observ'd in all matters of proceedings throughout in ye family. If servants and dayes men would perform as i say, and as justice and reason require, all would goe well on every side.

(c) *Source:* John Wesley, *Sermons on Several Occasions* (1881 edn.), pp. 708–9.

In this sermon on 'The Use of Money' Wesley himself makes it clear why Methodism as a religious system was well adapted to a period of economic growth. More important, however, than the formal system was the 'inner compulsion' which inspired 'the people called Methodists'. In another sermon he spoke of 'that invaluable talent of time with which God entrusts us from moment to moment'. (For the religious significance of Methodism, see below, p. 321.)

Whatsoever thy hand findeth to do, do it with thy might? Do it as soon as possible: no delay! No putting off from day to day, or from hour to hour! Never leave anything till to-morrow, which you can do to-day. And do it as well as possible. Do not sleep or yawn over it: put your whole strength to the work. Spare no pains. Let nothing be done by halves, or in a slight and careless manner. Let nothing in your business be left undone, if it can be done by labour or patience.

Gain all you can, by common sense, by using in your business all the understanding which God has given you. It is amazing to observe, how few do this; how men run on in the same dull track with their forefathers. But whatever they do who know not God, this is no rule for you. It is a shame for a Christian not to improve upon *them* in whatever he takes in hand. You should be continually learning, from the experience of others, or from your own experience, reading, and reflection, to do everything you have to do better to-day than you did yesterday.

12. FACTORY TIME

To run factories effectively a new code of industrial discipline had to be established. It depended on careful training in work habits, long hours (very long hours during the early industrial revolution), a working week which was not too frequently broken into by holidays, prudence, and 'diligence'. Employers' notions of how to enforce codes of behaviour were often crude, but they involved transformations in social attitudes. Time acquired a new coercive power behind it, as the following extracts show.

(a) *Source:* Evidence of R. Cookson, a hosier, before the Committee on the Woollen Manufacture of England in *Parliamentary Papers* (1806).

I found the utmost distaste on the part of the men, to any regular hours or regular habits. . . . The men themselves were considerably dissatisfied, because they could not go in and out as they pleased, and have what holidays they pleased, and go on just as they had been used to do; and were subject, during after-hours, to the ill-natured observations of other workmen, to such an extent as completely to disgust them with the whole system. . . .

(b) *Source:* Wedgwood Manuscripts, E. 19114–26, p. 27, where Wedgwood is describing the duties of the 'Clerk of the Manufactory.' He also used a factory bell in his Bell Works, and a kind of clocking-in system.

The duty of the Clerk of the Manufactory is to be at the works the first in the morning, & settle the people to their business as they come in—to encourage those who come regularly to their time, letting them know that their regularity is properly noticed, & distinguishing them by repeated marks of approbation, from the less orderly part of the work people by *presents or other marks suitable to their age etc.* Those who come later than the hour appointed should be noticed, and if after repeated marks of disapprobation they do not come in due time, an account of the time they are deficient in should be taken, & *so much of their wages stopt* as the time comes to. . . .

(c) In some factories there were elaborate works rules and instructions. The following list of fines to be imposed on 'disorderly' workers relates to a cotton mill at Tyldesley, near Manchester, where spinners worked in a temperature of 80° or more.

Source: J. L. and B. Hammond, *The Town Labourer, 1760–1832* (1917), pp. 19–20.

	s.	d.
Any spinner found with his window open	1	0
Any spinner found dirty at his work	1	0
Any spinner found washing himself	1	0
Any spinner leaving his oil can out of its place . . .	1	0
Any spinner slipping with his gas lighted	2	0
Any spinner putting his gas out too soon	1	0
Any spinner spinning with gaslight too long in the morning	2	0
Any spinner heard whistling	1	0
Any spinner being five minutes after last bell rings .	1	0
Any spinner going further than the roving-room door when fetching rovings	1	0
Any spinner being sick and cannot find another spinner to give satisfaction must pay for steam per day . .	6	0

CHAPTER III

Place

In travelling thro' England, a luxuriance of subjects presents itself to our view. Wherever we come, and which way soever we look, we see something new, something significant, something well worth the traveller's stay, and the writer's care. . . . The fate of things gives a new face to things, produces changes in low life, and innumerable incidents; plants and supplants families, raises and sinks towns, removes manufactures and trades; great towns decay, and small towns rise; new towns, new palaces, new seats are built every day; great rivers and good harbours dry up, and grow useless; again, new ports are open'd, brooks are made rivers, small rivers navigable ports and harbours are made where none were before, and the like. . . . In a word, new matter offers to new observation, and they who write next, may perhaps find as much room for enlarging upon us, as we do upon these who have gone before.

(DANIEL DEFOE, *A Tour Through England and Wales*, 1724)

Heavens! what a goodly Prospect spreads around,
Of Hills, and Dales, and Woods, and Lawns, and Spires,
And glittering Towns, and gilded Streams, till
The stretching Landscape into Smoke decays.

(JAMES THOMSON, *Summer*, 1727)

The plan I have laid down for continuing my *Tour* through *England*, is to travel as different a rout as I can from that of the former journies; so that they may in general include as many and as various tracts of country as possible: by this means the whole kingdom will be travelled, and the conclusions drawn from the particulars of the journies, come nearer to the exact averages of the whole nation.

(ARTHUR YOUNG, *The Farmer's Tour Through England*, 1771)

Cities and towns, the various haunts of men
Require the pencil, they defy the pen.

(GEORGE CRABBE, *The Borough*, 1810)

53

1. LONDON

Although England was a small country in terms of area, there were wide local variations in economic life, social structure, culture and even language. London was by far the biggest place, with an estimated population of 674,000 in 1700. In itself it was a city of contrasts, of dark alleys and elegant squares, of polite and civilized society and of rough and turbulent vitality. By 1800 its population had risen to nearly 900,000.

(a) *Source:* C. Morris (ed.), *The Journeys of Celia Fiennes* (1949), pp. 283–5.

IT CANNOT be thought amiss here to add some remarke on the metropolis of England, London, whose scituation [is] on so noble a river as the Thames, this is very comodious for shipps, which did come up just to the bridge, but from carelessness the river is choaked up that obliges the shipps to come to an anchor at Blackwall; all along this river are severall docks for building shipps of the biggest burden. . . . London joyned with West-minster, which are two great cittyes but now with building so joyned it makes up but one vast building with all its subburbs, and has in the walls ninety-seven parishes, without the walls 16 parishes, 15 subburbs, Surrey, Middlesex, 7 parishes in Westminster. London is the Citty properly for trade, West-minster for the Court.

(b) Two different Londons were described by a foreign observer in the 1780s.

Source: J. W. von Archenholtz, *A Picture of England* (1797), p. 119.

The east end, especially along the shores of the Thames, consists of old houses, the streets there are narrow, dark and ill-paved; inhabited by sailors and other workmen who are employed in the construction of ships and by a great part of the Jews. The contrast between this and the West end is astonishing: the houses here are mostly new and elegant; the squares are superb, the streets straight and open. . . . If all London were as well built, there would be nothing in the world to compare with it.

(c) The beautiful squares were often developed by the landed aristocracy, whose urban properties provided them with substantial and increasing wealth. The income of the Bedford (Russell) family from their London property more than doubled between the 1730s and the 1770s. In the East End, however, and on the fringe of the West, there was a Brechtian world, rough, raw and squalid.

Source: J. Hanway, *Citizen's Monitor* (1780), p. xvi.

One of our detachments visited Chick Lane, Field Lane, Black Boy Alley and some other such places. . . . . These places constitute a separate town or district calculated for the reception of the darkest and most dangerous enemies to society. . . . The houses are divided from top to bottom, and into many apartments, some having two, others three, others four doors, opening into different alleys. . . . The owners . . . make no secret of their being let for the entertainment of thieves.

(d) Beyond Central London were the distant suburbs, long since swallowed up in the great mass or 'Wen', as William Cobbett was to call it.

Source: Note by the Earl of Cork in *The Connoisseur*, 12 Sept. 1754.

A London tradesman is as well acquainted with Turnham-green or Kentish-town, as Fleet Street, or Cheapside, and talks as familiarly of Richmond or Hampton-Court as of the 'Change or the Custom-house. . . . [In the outer suburbs there are] elegant rural mansions, which at once shew the opulence and the taste of our principal merchants, mechanics and artificers. In these dusty retreats, where the want of London smoke is supplied by the smoke of Virginia tobacco, our chief citizens are accustomed to pass the end and the beginning of every week. Their boxes (as they are modestly called) are generally built in a row, to resemble as much as possible the streets in London. . . . A little artificial fountain, spouting water sometimes to the amazing height of four feet . . . is one of the most exquisite ornaments in [their] gardens. There are besides (if the spot of ground allows sufficient space for them) very curious statues of Harlequin, Scaramouch, Pierrot, and Columbine, which serve to remind their wives and daughters of what they have seen at the playhouse.

I went last Sunday, in compliance with a most pressing invitation from a friend, to spend a whole day with him at one of these little seats, which he had fitted up for his retirement once a week from business. It is pleasantly situated about three miles from London, on the side of a public road, from which it is separated by a dry ditch, over which is a little bridge, consisting of two narrow planks, leading to the house. The hedge on the other side of the road cuts off all prospect whatsoever, except from the garrets, from whence indeed you have a beautiful vista of two men hanging in chains on Kennington-common, with a distant view of St. Paul's cupola enveloped in a cloud of smoke. . . .

(e) The growth of London amazed and frightened contemporaries.

Source: Tobias Smollett, *The Expedition of Humphrey Clinker* (1771).

London is literally new to me; in its streets, houses, and even in its situation. . . . But notwithstanding these improvements, the capital is become an over-grown monster; which, like a despotical head, will in time leave the body and extremities without nourishment and support.

(f) *Source:* Horace Walpole, Letter to the Miss Mary Berry, 8 June 1791, printed in P. Toynbee (ed.), *The Letters of Horace Walpole* (1904), vol. XIV, p. 447.

There will soon be one street from London to Brentford; ay, and from London to every village ten miles round! Lord Camden has just let ground at Kentish Town for building fourteen hundred houses—nor do I wonder; London is, I am certain, much fuller than ever I saw it. I have twice this spring been going to stop my coach in Piccadilly, to inquire what was the matter, thinking there was a mob—not at all; it was only passengers. Nor is there any complaint of depopulation from the country: Bath shoots out into new crescents, circuses, squares every year: Birmingham, Manchester, Hull and Liverpool would serve any king in Europe for a capital, and would make the Empress of Russia's mouth water. . . .

(g) Some problems were common both to old London and new. A foreign visitor noted the smoke.

Source: P. Grosley, *A Tour to London, New Observations on England and its Inhabitants* (1772), pp. 43.

Notwithstanding the breadth and regularity of its streets, notwithstanding the free circulation of air, new London is as much buried in dirt as the old.

If we add to the inconveniency of the dirt, the smoke, which, being mixed with a constant fog, covers London, and wraps it up intirely, we shall find in this city, all those particulars which offended Horace most in that of Rome.

This smoke is occasioned, during the winter, which lasts about eight months, by the sea coals made use of in kitchens, apartments, and even the halls of grand houses; and by coals burnt in glass houses, in houses where earthen ware is manufactured; in blacksmiths' and gunsmiths' shops', in dyers' yards, &c. all which trades and manufactures are established in the very heart of London, and upon both banks of the Thames. . . . The inconveniences of the smoke gain ground every day: if the increase of London proceeds as far as it may, the inhabitants must at last bid adieu to all hopes of ever seeing the sun.

2. THE COUNTRY

As the population of London grew, so did that of the provinces. By 1760 the population of England and Wales which had stood at about 5½ million at the beginning of the eighteenth century had risen to over 6½ million. In 1801 it was nearly 9 million. For the appearance of the country, and the 'personality' of particular places, there is a vast mass of travel literature and of detailed topographical description. Since landed property was the basis of eighteenth-century society, most of this description begins with the great landed estates, social as much as economic units; and since these estates were historical products, like the great houses in the midst of them, a time dimension enters into the study of place.

(a) *Source:* J. Macky, *A Journey Through England* (1732), p. 121.

KENT is a large and noble Province; it gives Title of Duke to the Chief of the Family of *de Grays*, who . . . have neither Interest nor Estate here. There are abundance of Nobility that reside in this County: *Tufton*, Earl of *Thanet*, hath a noble Seat, and as great an Estate; Finch, Earl of *Winchelsea:* *Sackville*, Earl of *Dorset*, who was Governor of the *Cinque-Ports*,

E

and Constable of *Dover-Castle*, but just removed from that Employment as I passed there, it then being given to the Duke of *Ormond;* Sidney, Earl of *Leicester : Villiers*, Earl of *Jersey;* the Lord *Rockingham*, who has a vast Estate; Roper, Lord *Teynham*, and an infinite Number of other fine Gentry.

(b) *Source:* J. Hanway, *A Journal of Eight Days' Journey* (1757), pp. 61ff.

Let us now contemplate the charms of this world. After church we went to Wilton, the seat of the earl of Pembroke, which is distant from Salisbury three miles. . . . This palace, for so we may call it, contains a collection of the richest statues, busts, antiques or relieves, of any nobleman in England; or perhaps of any man in the world. The lower apartments are so crowded, that they appear like so many shops or magazines of marble merchandise. . . . [Yet] let us hasten from the works of men, to the more glorious works of GOD! We may here contemplate the beautiful lawns on the south-east side of the house, and the bright streams which water them. Over this river is a *palladian* bridge of exquisite architecture, much admired by all connoisseurs. Above this, to the southward, you must not forget that noble rising ground, to the summit of which is about a quarter of a mile. Here stands a very large equestrian statue, in lead, of *Marcus Aurelius*, a *Roman* emperor. . . . From this eminence there is a view of the valley below, and part of *Salisbury*, which looks very rural, the cathedral, as well as other parts of the city being embowered with trees.

(c) County life for the propertied revolved round the relationships between a number of landed families. (For social structure in the country see below, pp. 116.) There was variety, however, even in agricultural counties, with market towns, villages and landscape changing from one part of the county to another.

Source: Daniel Defoe, *A Tour Through England and Wales* (Everyman edn. 1928), vol. II, pp. 112–14.

It is remarkable of Bedfordshire, that tho' a great part of the county lies on the north side of the Ouse . . . yet there is not one market town in all that side of the Ouse, but Bedford only . . . , a large, populous, and thriving town, and a pleasant well-built place; it has five parish churches, a very fine stone bridge over the Ouse, and the High Street, (especially) is a very handsome fair street, and very well-built; and tho' the town is not upon any of the great roads in England, yet it is full of very good inns, and many of them.

Here is the best market for all sorts of provisions, that is to be seen at any country town in all these parts of England; and this occasions, that tho' it is far from London, yet the higglers or carriers buy great quantities of provisions here for London markets; also here is a very good trade down the river to Lynn.

Here is also a great corn market, and great quantities of corn are bought here, and carry'd down by barges and other boats to Lynn, where it is again shipp'd, and carry'd by sea to Holland: The soil hereabouts is exceeding rich and fertile, and particularly produces great quantities of the best wheat in England.

Indeed the whole product of this county is corn, that is to say, wheat and malt for London; for here are very few manufactures, except that of straw-hats and bone-lace, of which by itself: There are but ten market towns in the whole country, and yet 'tis not a small county neither: The towns are,

Bedford,	Ampthill,	Potton,
Biggleswood,	Shefford,	Tuddington,
Leighton,	Luton,	Wooburn.
Dunstable,		

The last of these was almost demolish'd by a terrible fire, which happen'd here just before my writing this account; but as this town has the good luck to belong to a noble family particularly eminent for being good landlords; that is to say, bountiful and munificent to their poor tenants, I mean the ducal house of Bedford.

The duke's house, call'd Wooburn Abbey, is just by the town, a good old house, but very ancient, spacious and convenient rather than fine, but exceedingly pleasant by its situation; and for the great quantity of beach woods which surround the parks and cover the hills, and also for great woods of oak too, as rich and valuable, as they are great and magnificent: The very situation of this house to promise itself another Burleigh or Chatsworth.

(d) Bedfordshire was providing wheat and manufactured goods for London. The main agricultural producing area, however, was East Anglia.

Source: Defoe, vol. I, pp. 59–60.

This county of Suffolk is particularly famous for furnishing the city of London and all the counties round with turkeys; and 'tis thought, there are more turkeys bred in this county, and the part of Norfolk that adjoins to it, than in all the rest of England, especially for sale; tho' this may be reckon'd, as I say above, but a trifling thing to take notice of in these remarks; yet, as I have hinted, that I shall observe, how London is in general supplied with all its provisions from the whole body of the nation, and how every part of the island is engaged in some degree or other of that supply; On this account I could not omit it; nor will it be found so inconsiderable an article as some may imagin, if this be true which I receiv'd an account of from a person living on the place, (viz.) That they have counted 300 droves of turkeys (for they drive them all in droves on foot) pass in one season over Stratford-Bridge on the River Stour, which parts Suffolk from Essex, about six miles from Colchester on the road from Ipswich to London.

For the further supplies of the markets of London with poultry, of which these counties particularly abound: They have within these few years found it practicable to make the geese travel on foot too, as well as the turkeys; and a prodigious number are brought up to London in droves from the farthest parts of Norfolk; even from the fenn-country, about Lynn, Downham, Wisbich, and the Washes; as also from all the east-side of Norfolk and Suffolk, of whom 'tis very frequent now to meet droves, with a thousand, sometimes two thousand in a drove: They begin to drive them generally in August, by which time the harvest is almost over, and the geese may feed in the stubbles as they go. Thus they hold on to the end of October, when the roads begin to be too stiff and deep for their broad feet and short leggs to march in. . . .

In this part, which we call High-Suffolk, there are not so many families of gentry or nobility plac'd, as in the other

side of the country: But 'tis observ'd that tho' their seats are
not so frequent here, their estates are; and the pleasure of
West Suffolk is much of it supported by the wealth of High-
Suffolk; for the richness of the lands, and application of the
people to all kinds of improvement, is scarce credible; also the
farmers are so very considerable, and their farms and dayries
so large, that 'tis very frequent for a farmer to have a thousand
pounds stock upon his farm in cows only.

3. WATERING PLACES

One of the developments outside London in the eighteenth
century which most interested both English and foreign commentators was the growth of spas and watering places.

The most famous of watering places was Bath, although there
were other spas, like Scarborough or Buxton, in many parts of the
country. Brighton emerged as a new kind of holiday resort
after Dr. Richard Russell had successfully advocated the merits
of sea water for drinking. Its merits for bathing were canvassed
later, with royal approval. The Prince Regent first visited Brighton
in 1783. Between then and 1830 it increased in size from 3,500 to
over 20,000.

Source: J. Macky, *A Journey Through England* (1732), pp. 137–40.

The *Bath* lies very low; is but a small City, but very compact; and one can hardly imagine it could accommodate near
the Company that frequents it, at least three Parts of the Year.
I have been told of 8,000 Families there at a time, some for
the Benefit of drinking its hot Waters, others for Bathing, and
others for Diversion and Pleasure; of which I must say, it
affords more than any public Place of that Kind in *Europe.*

I told you in my former Letters that *Epsom* and *Tunbridge*
does not allow visiting; the Companies there meet only on
the Walks; but here Visits are received and returned, Assemblies and Balls are given, and Parties at Play in most Houses
every Night, to which one Mr. *Nash* hath for many Years
contributed very much. This Gentleman is by Custom, a Sort
of Master of Ceremonies of the Place; he is not of any Birth,
nor Estate, but by a good Address and Assurance ingratiates

himself into the good Graces of the Ladies, and the best Company in the Place, and is Director of all their Parties of Pleasure. He wears good Cloaths, is always affluent of Money, plays very much; and whatever he may get in private, yet in publick he always seems to lose. The Town have been for many Years so sensible of the Service he does them, that they ring the Bells generally at his Arrival in Town, and, 'tis thought, pay him a yearly Contribution for his Support.

In the Morning early, the Company of both Sexes meet at the Pump, in a great Hall inrailed, to drink the Waters; and saunter about till Prayer-time, or divert themselves by looking on those that are bathing in the *Bath*. Most of the Company go to Church in the Morning in *Dishabilee*, and then go home to dress for the Walks before Dinner. The Walks are behind the Church, spacious and well shaded, planted round with Shops filled with every thing that contributes to Pleasure; and at the End, a noble Room for Gaming; from whence there are hanging Stairs to a pretty Garden, for every body that pays for the Time they stay, to walk in.

I have often wonder'd, that the Physicians of these Places prescribe Gaming to their Patients, in order to keep their Minds free from Business and Thought, that their Waters on an undisturbed Mind may have the greater Effect; when indeed one cross Throw at Play must sowre a Man's Blood more than Ten Glasses of Water will sweeten. . . .

The King and Queen's *Baths*, which have a Communication with one another, are the *Baths* where People of common Rank go into promiscuously; and indeed every body, except the first Quality.

When you enter the *Bath*, the Water seems very warm; and the Heat much increases as you go into the Queen's *Bath*, where the great Spring rises. . . . The Smoak and Slime of the Waters, the promiscuous Multitude of the People in the *Bath*, with nothing but their Heads and Hands above Water, with the Height of the Walls that inviron the *Bath*, gave me a lively Idea of several Pictures I had seen of *Angelo's* in *Italy*, of Purgatory, with Heads and Hands uplifted in the midst of Smoke, just as they are here. This *Bath* is 25 Foot long and 24 broad; but is frequented only by the Common People.

The *Cross Bath* (so call'd from a curious Cross formerly erected in it) is very gentle, and but moderately warm. On the Sides of it are 16 Stone Seats, and at the Ends Galleries for the Musick and Spectators, under which are Two Slips, one for the Gentlemen, and the other for the Ladies, the Men with all Decency keeping on the one Side, and Women on the other. This is the smallest *Bath*, being but 24 Feet and a Half long, and half as broad; but 'tis the most frequented of any by the People of the first Quality. . . .

(b) Bath continued to flourish and to grow throughout the century.

Source: E. D. Clarke, *A Tour Through the South of England, Wales, and Part of Ireland Made During the Summer of 1791* (1793), pp. 135–46.

Its numerous visitants were dispersed when we arrived. Its parades were empty, and its throng removed. But although the season was over, for pleasure and dissipation, we had the more leisure to contemplate. Its edifices, its public rooms, its baths, its streets, are beyond anything the world can parallel of a similar nature. . . . The buildings in Bath have a degree of elegance which no other city can boast. This is owing to the great plenty of stone which is found in the neighbourhood, with which the chief part of the city is built. . . .

An ingenious author observes that it far exceeds London in regularity of building, and in being proportionably a much finer city. . . . The Crescent, an elegant semicircular range of buildings, would, if Bath could boast no other edifice worth our attention, claim a particular share of attention. . . . There is, to use an expression of Gray's, something so *rus-in-urbe-ish* in the whole of it, that I would chuse a house in that edifice, when compared with one in the Circus. . . . Bath may be said to afford a universal scope for everything that is desirable. The man of pleasure may be here satiated with amusement; the philosopher may analyze its salubrious springs; the antiquarian may pursue his researches till he wearies himself with conjecture; the man of letters, will find ample repositories of genius; the poet, endless subjects to exercise his wit; the painter, may delineate the features of beauty . . . and, last of all, the dejected invalid may restore to its wonted tenour the shattered system of a broken constitution, and, by rousing his debilitated nerves to their accustomed tone, revive his health and renovate his spirits.

(c) Dr. A. Relhan, *A Short History of Brighthelmston, with Remarks on its Air and an Analysis of its Waters* (1761), pp. 31ff.

The town (June 1761) at present consists of six principal streets, many lanes, and some spaces surrounded with houses, called by the inhabitants squares. . . . The town improves daily, as the inhabitants, encouraged by the late great resort of company, seem disposed to spend the whole of what they acquire, in erecting new buildings, or improving the old ones. Here are two public rooms, the one convenient, the other not only so, but elegant, not excelled perhaps by any in England, that of York excepted.

The *endemial* or popular disorders of temperate people being the product of air and diet, the best proof of the healthfulness of the air of any place is deduced from the customary longevity of the inhabitants, and the rate of the Bills of Mortality. . . . In London there is annually a death in every 32 persons, which is nearly two to one in favour of Brighton.

With regard to the sea water at this place, it appears by experiments that in Summer (weather tolerably dry) there are in every pint of it, at least five drachms and fifteen grains of defecated salt . . . about five of bittern . . . and six grains of white calcarious earth. This proportion of clean contents . . . is as great, or perhaps greater, than is to be found in the sea water of any other port in England.

4. PORTS AND HARBOURS

The sea was a source of wealth far more than a source of pleasure, with English ports and harbours thriving and many big establishments employing large numbers of people in the naval centres.

(a) *Source:* E. D. Clarke, *A Tour Through the South of England*, pp. 7–11.

Portsmouth may, without impropriety, be called the key of England. Its noble haven, capable of containing a thousand sail of the line; its extensive fortifications, arranged and executed by engineers of the first ability; the number of its inabitants, its dock-yards, its wonderful importance to Great-Britain, render it the admiration of Europe. The entrance to the harbour does not exceed, in breadth, that of the Thames at Westminster Bridge, a circumstance, which forms a considerable addition to its strength. There is also such plenty of water within it, that a first rate man of war may always float in safety, and moreover ride secure from every wind that blows. The mouth of the harbour is defended by a . . . castle . . . fortified with a double moat, pallisadoes, ravelins, and a counterscarp, from which there are several advanced works, to cover the fort against the approach of an enemy. There is also on the same side a large platform, on which are placed pieces of ordnance; and on the opposite side, next Gosport, there is another platform, of twenty great guns, nearly level with the water. . . .

This wonderful rendezvous of the royal navy, fortified on all sides, is a striking proof of the opulence and industry of Englishmen. . . .

The dock yard contains such an astonishing quantity of every article necessary for the royal navy, and is placed in a style of such uncommon regularity that it exceeds imagination. There are seldom less than a thousand men employed within its walls, and sometimes double that number. These, in time of war, are all disciplined, and formed into a regiment, under the command of the Commissioner. . . . The dock, and other yards, now resemble a town, and may be said to form a corporation, there being large rows of dwellings, built at the public expence, for all the officers, who are obliged to reside on the spot. The rope-house, where the cables, &c. are made, is 870 feet long, and some of the cables are so large, that it requires above 80 men to work them. The labour is so excessive, that they can only continue it for four hours in the day. From one end of this remarkable room, it is not easy to discern the pigmies working at the other. . . . The smith's shop is a curious spectacle, and reminds one of Vulcan's laboratory, where we find a trio, performed by the Cyclops, upon the anvil in every corner. . . . It is impossible to convey upon paper, any idea adequate to the appearance of the immense magazines, where ships are lifted in their docks, like infants in their cradles, and the most stupendous works conducted with all that ease, and ingenuity, so peculiar to the inhabitants of this country.

(b) During the eighteenth century there was brisk economic development in the English ports of the West. Bristol, the second largest community in England (after London) in 1700, doubled its population between 1700 and 1750 to nearly 100,000; Liverpool grew from 6,000 to 35,000. African, American and West Indian trade, including the slave trade, was in the background of the picture.

Source: D. Defoe, *A Tour Through England and Wales*, vol. II, pp. 255–7.

I entered Lancashire at the remotest western point of that county, having been at West-Chester upon a particular occasion and from thence ferry'd over . . . one of the wonders of Britain. . . . The town [of Liverpool] was, at my first visiting it, about the year 1680, a large, handsome, well built and encreasing or thriving town; at my second visit, anno 1690, it was much bigger than at my first seeing it, and, by the report of the inhabitants, more than twice as big as it was twenty years before that; but, I think, I may safely say at this my third seeing it, for I was surpriz'd at the view, it was more than double what it was at the second; and, I am told, that it still visibly encreases both in wealth, people, business and buildings: What it may grow to in time, I know not.

There are no fortifications either to landward or seaward, the inhabitants resting secure under the protection of the general peace. . . .

The town has now an opulent, flourishing and encreasing trade, not rivalling Bristol, in the trade to Virginia, and the English island colonies in America only, but is in a fair way to exceed and eclipse it, by encreasing every way in wealth and shipping. They trade round the whole island, send ships to Norway, to Hamburgh, and to the Baltick, as also to Holland and Flanders; so that, in a word, they are almost become like the Londoners, universal merchants. . . .

The people of Liverpoole seem to have a different scene of commerce to act on from the city of Bristol, which to me is a particular advantage to both, namely, that though they may rival one another in their appearances, in their number of shipping, and in several particulars, yet they need not interfere with one another's business, but either of them seem to have room enough to extend their trade, even at home and abroad, without clashing with one another. One has all the north, and the other all the south of Britain to correspond in.

5. OLD TOWNS

Inland, county towns and market towns were the main centres of population, some of them, like Exeter or Norwich, with both cathedrals and specialized industries. Each town had a restricted, though ritualized and stratified, local life. Living conditions in these towns were often dirty and insanitary, yet between 1785 and 1800 211 'improvement acts' were passed dealing with measures to improve the local environment.

(a) *Source:* Letter from Charles Lyttelton, the Dean of Exeter, 1761, printed in L. Dickins and M. Stanton (eds.), *An Eighteenth-Century Correspondence* (1910), pp. 420–1.

Having in a former letter promised to give you some account of this City where I have resided with great comfort and satisfaction for a number of years, I will now fulfil my promise in as concise a manner as possible. 'Tis situated on rising ground so that from which ever way you approach it except on the east you have a steep ascent, which is an inconvenience both in going out as well as coming into the City, but this is amply made up for by the advantage of a free current of air the consequence of its high situation, which renders the City healthy, which from its close buildings and numerous Inhabitants confined in a narrow space would probably suffer greatly by infectious distempers, not to mention that every hard shower of rain performs the office of a scavenger incomparably well by the streets being very sloping, and 'tis lucky it does so, else such is the want of cleanliness among these people, that we should all be near poisoned by the filth and nastiness that every street abounds with. The Magistrates are very blameable in this respect for I have been assured that £10 per annum only is allowed for Scavengers throughout the whole City. I believe the number of Inhabitants both in City and Suburbs do not exceed 15,000. The High, or as is vulgarly called, the

Fore Street is very long and spacious, but all the Houses are old and bad within as indeed they generally are over the whole City. The most remarkable Buildings, are the Cathedral, of which more hereafter, the Doorway at the top of the steps leading to the two Courts for the Assizes, within the Castle, which is round arched and decorated in the Saxon Style, and a large Building in Water Bear St. now used as a Warehouse, but which Tradition says was formerly the Guild Hall or Town House. . . . Provision of all kinds is exceeding good (except cheese and bacon) in this City and in greater plenty than is hardly to be met with in any other Town of the bigness in the Kingdom, but tho' so very plentifull is far from cheap.

The Corporation or Chamber of Exon have a very good estate and keep up a very laudable Hospitality, the Mayor having a dinner of ten dishes at least almost every Monday throughout the year, to which all the principal Gentry, Clergy, Merchants and strangers that come to Exeter are invited in their turns, besides great and sumptious feasts on the election of the new Mayor and Sheriffs, which is indeed usual in other large Towns.

(b) Social differences in Lincoln were described by a visiting dramatist.

Source: C. Dibdin, *Observations on a Tour* (1801), vol. I, p. 377.

This city is composed of a high and a low town, which are perpetually at variance with each other. I cannot explain this better than by saying that if there were a play-house at Lincoln, it must be in one of the following predicaments. If it was situated on a hill it would be all boxes; if under the hill all gallery, and if in the midway all pit; and, therefore, as a play-house cannot subsist but by the union of boxes, pit and gallery, I should apprehend fortunes are not acquired by theatrical performances at Lincoln.

6. NEW TOWNS

Half-rural conditions existed even in new towns, like Bradford, where the urban environment was raw and tough. Bradford had a population of only 6,393 as late as 1801.

Source: Minutes of the Bradford Vestry, May and September 1798, quoted in W. Cudworth, *Historical Notes on the Bradford Corporation* (1881), pp. 8–9.

May 1798. Whereas, the order made April 20 last, 1795, respecting the turning out of pigs to run at large in the streets and highways of the township of Bradford not having been sufficiently attended to by the township men:

> *Resolved*—That public notice be given by the cryer and by handbills that, from and after the 12th of May next, the owner of such pig or pigs as are found at large will be indicted for the same by the constable of the town.
>
> *Resolved*—That John Rawnsley be appointed to get the same cry'd and handbills drawn up, printed, and distributed accordingly, and pay one shilling for every pig so found at large to any person who shall take up and get the same pounded.

Sept. 1798. The order made the 7 of May last respecting the turning out of piggs to run at large in the streets and highways within this township still continuing to be a very great nuisance:

> *Ordered*—That Robt. Wray, the beadle, with such assistance as he may procure, be appointed to carry the order made as mentioned above into execution.

7. INDUSTRIAL COMMUNITIES

Many of the great industrial cities of the nineteenth century grew rapidly during the eighteenth century. Among them were Manchester, Leeds and Birmingham. Already they were capitals of surrounding industrial regions.

(a) *Source:* W. Thompson, *Tour of England and Scotland* (1788), pp. 11–19.

May 19th. Leave Stratford. . . . In the evening arrive at Birmingham; but this being unfortunately the time of their fair, we could not see any of the manufacturers at work. Visit Clay's manufactory for making tea-boards, buttons, and other

articles pasted together and dried. Visit also Boulton's manufactory for plated articles of all sorts of steel and iron-work.
This town is very extensive, and a great part of it elegantly
built. It contains upwards of one hundred thousand inhabitants;
but the people are all diminutive in size, and sickly in their
appearance, from their sedentary employment. In Birmingham
there is one very elegant and spacious church, three chapels,
and eight meeting-houses for Dissenters . . . but the great
mass of the people give themselves very little concern about
religious matters, seldom, if ever, going to church, and spending
the Sundays in their ordinary working apparel, in low debauchery. What religion there is in Birmingham is to be found
among the Dissenters. It is well known that there are many
coiners of false money in Birmingham, a circumstance that is
easily accounted for, from the nature of the business in which
they have been accustomed to be employed. It may be added,
that there is a great deal of trick and low cunning among the
Birmingham manufacturers in general, though there are, no
doubt, some exceptions, as well as profligacy of manners. This
may be owing in part, to their want of early education; for
the moment that the children are fit for any kind of labour,
instead of being sent to school, they are set to some sort of
work or other: but it is probably more owing to their being
constantly associated together both in their labouring and in
their idle hours. It is remarkable, that society corrupts the
manners of the vulgar as much as it sharpens their understanding.

About fifty years ago, there were only three principal or
leading streets in Birmingham, which at this day is so crouded,
and at the same time so extensive a town: a circumstance
which illustrates, in a very striking manner, the rapid increase
of our manufactures and trade in steel and iron.

The manufacturers of Birmingham who are generally
accounted rich, are such as possess fortunes from five to fifteen
thousand pounds. A few are in possession of much larger capitals;
but in general, they may be said to be in easy and flourishing
circumstances, rather than very rich or affluent. The number
of carriages kept by private persons has been doubled within
these ten years: so also has that of the women of the town.

These different species of luxury seem to have advanced in proportions pretty nearly equal. The people of Birmingham have often tried to establish a coffee-house; but found this impossible, even with the advantage of a subscription. They generally resort to ale-houses and taverns. According to the size of the place, there should be several coffee-houses, taking our standard in this matter, from London. But the genius of Birmingham is not that of coffee-houses. The labouring and poor people of Birmingham fare but hardly; their chief sustenance being bread and cheese, and ale for which they pay five-pence the quart, though this measure is not so large as a quart porter-pot. There is a porter brewery at Birmingham, the liquor produced by which is equal in strength to that brewed in London; but far inferior in flavour.

It is not above seventy years since there was any great variety of metal goods fabricated here. Coarse locks and hinges, with common metal buttons and buckles, formed before that period, the whole amount of the Birmingham manufactures. But now, these coarse articles are manufactured in Wolverhampton, Walsall, Dudley, and other small towns near Birmingham. The fine and fashionable goods are manufactured in the town of Birmingham itself. In the country round about are nailers and woodscrew-makers, who work in their own cottages, and whose prices are so low, that they get but very little money by all their labour. The women and children, as well as the men, are employed in the manufacture of these articles. Sometimes the whole family will be occupied in one branch of business, which suits well enough, as the father of the family makes large nails, and the wife and children smaller ones, according to their strength. This division of labour in the same family, if studied and practised in different kinds of British manufactures, might in this country, as in India, expedite business, and also improve the articles produced by it.

The industry of the people in those parts is wonderful. They live here like the people of Spain and other hot countries, rising at three or four o'clock in the morning, going to rest for a few hours at noon, and afterwards working till nine or ten o'clock at night.

It is exceedingly remarkable, and highly worthy of observation, that industry in manufactures in the districts adjacent to Birmingham, is wholly confined to the barren parts of the country. This great town stands on the south-east extremity of a very barren region. . . . [On the] west, where the ground is fertile and well cultivated, there is scarcely a manufacturer to be found of any kind.

(b) Foreigners were particularly amazed by what they saw.

Source: B. Faujas de St. Fond, *A Journey Through England and Scotland to the Hebrides in 1784* (1907 edn.), pp. 346-9.

From the activity of its manufactures and its commerce, Birmingham is one of the most curious towns in England. If any one should wish to see in one comprehensive view, the most numerous and most varied industries, all combined in contributing to the arts of utility, of pleasure, and of luxury, it is hither that he must come. Here all the resources of industry, supported by the genius of invention, and by mechanical skill of every kind are directed towards the arts, and seem to be linked together to co-operate for their mutual perfection.

I know that some travellers who have not given themselves the trouble to reflect on the importance and advantage of these kinds of manufactures in such a country as England, have disapproved of most of these industrial establishments. I know that even an Englishman who has only taken a hasty, I would almost say an inconsiderate view of these magnificent establishments, William Gilpin, has said that it was difficult for the eye to be long pleased in the midst of so many frivolous arts, where a hundred men may be seen, whose labours are confined to the making of a tobacco box. But besides that this statement is exaggerated and ill-considered, its author has not deigned to cast his eyes over the vast works where steam-pumps are made, these astonishing machines, the perfecting of which does so much honour to the talents and knowledge of Mr. Watt; over the manufactories in constant activity making sheet-copper for sheathing ships' bottoms; over those of plate-tin and plate-iron, which make France tributary to England, nor over that varied and extensive hard-ware manufacture which employs to so much advantage more than thirty thousand hands, and compels all Europe, and a part of the New World, to supply themselves from England, because all ironmongery is made here in greater perfection, with more economy and in greater abundance, than anywhere else.

Once more, I say with pleasure, and it cannot be too often said to Frenchmen, that it is the abundance of coal which has performed this miracle and has created, in the midst of a barren desert, a town with forty thousand inhabitants, who live in comfort, and enjoy all the conveniences of life.

Here a soil, once covered with the most barren and sombre heath, has been changed into groves of roses and lilacs, and turned into fertile and delightful gardens by Mr Boulton, associated with Mr Watt, in whose work more than a thousand hands are engaged.

(c) There was a less pleasant side to industrial expansion in urban centres, as this paper on Manchester shows.

Source: Note on T. Percival, 'Observations on the State of Manchester and the Adjacent Places' in *Philosophical Transactions of the Royal Society* (1775), pp. 324–6.

Great towns are in a peculiar degree fatal to children. Half of all that are born in London die under three, and in Manchester under five years of age; whereas at Royton, a Manufacturing township in the neighbourhood of Manchester, the number of children dying under the age of three years, is to the number of children born only as one to seven; and at Eastham, a parish in Cheshire, inhabited by farmers, the proportion is considerably less.

It is a common but injurious practice in manufacturing countries, to confine children, before they have attained a sufficient degree of strength, to sedentary employments, in places where they breathe a putrid air, and are debarred the free use of their limbs. The effect of this confinement . . . is either to cut them off early in life, or to render their constitutions feeble and sickly; but the love of money stifles the feelings of humanity, an even makes men blind to the very interest they so anxiously pursue. The same principle of sound policy which induces them to spare their horses and cattle, till they arrive at a due size and vigour, should determine them to grant a proportionable respite to their children.

F

8. INDUSTRIAL DISTRICTS

It was not until the development of steam power and the rise of the factory system that industry began to be concentrated in large urban centres. Such centres for the most part, were associated with trade rather than industrial production. For most of the eighteenth century industry was dispersed and decentralized. The use of water power encouraged such dispersal, often in bleak rural areas. The extracts which follow describe particular areas at different times during the century.

(a) *Source:* D. Defoe, *A Tour*, vol. III, pp. 193–6.

From Blackstone Edge to Hallifax [sic] is eight miles . . . and the nearer we came to Hallifax, we found the houses thicker, and the villages greater in every bottom; and not only so, but the sides of the hills which were very steep every way, were spread with houses, and that very thick; for the land being divided into small enclosures, that is to say, from two acres to six or seven acres each, seldom more; every three or four pieces of land had a house belonging to it.

Then it was I began to perceive the reason and nature of the thing, and found that this division of the land into small pieces, and scattering of the dwellings, was occasioned by, and done for the convenience of the business which the people were generally employ'd in, and that, as I said before, though we saw no people stirring without doors, yet they were all full within; for, in short, this whole country, however mountainous, and that no sooner we were down one hill but we mounted another, is yet infinitely full of people; those people all full of business; not a beggar, not an idle person to be seen, except here and there an alms-house, where people antient, decrepid, and past labour, might perhaps be found; for it is observable, that the people here, however laborious, generally live to a great age, a certain testimony to the goodness and wholesomness of the country, which is, without doubt, as healthy as any part of England; nor is the health of the people lessen'd, but help'd and established by their being constantly employ'd, and, as we call it, their working hard; so that they find a double advantage by their being always in business.

This business is the clothing trade, for the convenience of

which the houses are thus scattered and spread upon the sides of the hills, as above, even from the bottom to the top; the reason is this; such has been the bounty of nature to this otherwise frightful country, that two things essential to the business, as well as to the ease of the people are found here, and that in a situation which I never saw the like of in any part of England; and, I believe, the like is not to be seen so contrived in any part of the world; I mean coals and running water upon the tops of the highest hills: this seems to have been directed by the wise hand of Providence for the very purpose which is now served by it, namely, the manufactures. . . .

Having thus fire and water at every dwelling, there is no need to enquire why they dwell thus dispers'd upon the highest hills, the convenience of the manufactures requiring it. Among the manufacturers houses are likewise scattered an infinite number of cottages or small dwellings, in which dwell the workmen which are employed, the women and children of whom, are always busy carding, spinning, &c. so that no hands being unemploy'd, all can gain their bread, even from the youngest to the antient; hardly any thing above four years old, but its hands are sufficient to it self.

This is the reason also why we saw so few people without doors; but if we knock'd at the door of any of the master manufacturers, we presently saw a house full of lusty fellows, some at the dye-vat, some dressing the cloths, some in the loom, some one thing, some another, all hard at work, and full employed upon the manufacture, and all seeming to have sufficient business.

I have dwelt so [much] upon this part [for] any one that desires a full understanding of the manner how the people of England are employed, and do subsist in these remoter parts where they are so numerous; for this is one of the most populous parts of Britain, London and the adjacent parts excepted.

(b) The Potteries provide an example of another highly distinctive area. Josiah Wedgwood started work at Burslem in 1759: by 1800 a local craft had developed into a national industry, serving an international market.

Source: C. B. Andrews (ed.), *The Torrington Diaries* (1936), vol. III, pp. 126–7.

I was now, quite undetermin'd to my purpose, whether to Stafford, to Stone, or to the left to Bromley; the fall of my stick had determin'd me: but learning here, that the pottery country began in 2 or 3 miles, which is highly flourishing, and where in is much to observe, I was resolv'd to pass thro'it, tho' it threw me considerably out of my first intention. One of the young farmers attended me thro' the grounds till I enter'd the public road. At Lane End the population of the pottery commences, (where the roads are repair'd by the fragments, 'broken in pieces like a potter's vessell',) and continues a street of many miles;—the men whiten'd with the powder, are supplied with coals to keep alive, the everlasting ovens, from every adjacent field; hundreds of horses, and asses with panniers, are incessantly taking in their lading: thro' there I pass'd along, slowly in pleasant rumination; but wonder'd much at no market being establish'd for such a multitude.

I now descended to the village of Stoke-upon-Trent, around which are numberless new buildings, and many pleasant villas for the principal merchants; and there is likewise a good inn building in this place: here I cross'd the Trent; and soon, many branches of navigation. These intersecting canals, with their passing boats, their bridges, the population, the pottery ovens, and the bustle of business, remind me of a Chinese picture, where the angler is momentarily interrupted by a boat.

The late village of Handley, now a great town, upon the hill above, cuts a flaming figure from its new church, and newly-built houses. The village of Skelton, likewise, is swell'd into great bulk.

Now I enquired for Etruria, the grand pottery establish'd by Mr Wedgwood; and putting up my horses at the adjacent inn, sent up my name and comp[ts] to Mr W., with a desire to view his manufactory: in the mean time, as the workmen were at dinner, and would be for about an hour, I saunter'd about Mr W.'s grounds; which are green, and pleasant, with some pretty plantations, views of navigation &c &c.—The house seems to be good, and is built of staring red brick; as are many in the vicinage, belonging to the principal traders. I was now sheun about the several workshops of this great pottery, wherein are employ'd 300 men; but this is a dull observation for any person who has seen China manufactories. The painting business—perform'd by females, is an hot, unwholesome, employ; the work to be painted is allways lifted up in the left hand.—Except some Irishmen, who were put in, purposely, for the intent of disertion, I did not find that any persons had attempted to carry off any secrets of the art. . . .

After an hours inspection, hunger hasten'd me away; and I thought the mile to the town of Newcastle-under-Lime, grieviously long; but as this was a large town, upon a very high road, I knew I should fare well.—

The Roe Buck, the largest inn, is one of the most savage, dirty, ale houses I ever enter'd (*Traveller, beware The Roe Buck in Newcastle*).

(c) Tin and copper mines in Cornwall and Devon were a source of interest to all travellers. Cornish tin output reached its peak in the middle of the eighteenth century.

Source: E. D. Clarke, *Tour Through the South of England*, pp. 90–6.

Soon after my arrival at Truro, I visited some of the most considerable mines in its neighbourhood, and selecting that of Poldeis, which is the oldest, the largest, and I believe the deepest in England, went to the bottom of it.

When you declare your intention to descending with the miners, the captain, as he is called, takes you into a room, and equips you in a woollen shirt, trowsers, night cap, and jacket. As for stockings, it is usual not to wear any, and agreeable to the advice of the experienced miner, we descended with our legs bare. They then tie old shoes to our feet, fit for the purpose, and having accommodated each person with a candle in his hand, and half a pound more suspended from his neck, he is declared compleatly equipped, and conducted to the mouth of the mine. It requires a good strong stomach, and a large portion of curiosity, to go through all this. For besides the fatigue and toil in the mine, the cloaths they give you are as greasy as sweat can make them, smell abominably, and are often stocked with a republic of creepers. Should any one be induced, hereafter, to explore there regions of darkness, I would advise him to prepare, at least, a woollen shirt, and a pair of trowsers, that he may avoid those unpleasant sensations which arise in every man's brest, when compelled to have recourse to a miner's wardrobe.

These preliminaries being adjusted, we began to descend. A miner went first, to serve as a guide. Jeremy followed the miner. After Jeremy, came my companion and myself; and last of all the captain, giving us this comfortable assurance, 'That if we made a slip, or a single false step, or looked either to one side or the other, we should be ground to atoms in the steam engine, or dashed to pieces in the mine.' The descent resembles a large well, with an emmense machine, for the purpose of draining the mine of water, continually in motion all the way down. Mr. Bolton, of Birmingham, receives annually some thousands from the county of Cornwall, for the use of them. . . .

We continued to descend by ladders, which were from four to five fathoms in length, and being soon wet through, weak from want of proper respiration, and half stifled with the fumes of sulphur, began to hesitate whether we should proceed or not. Curiousity got the better of our fears, and we went on. Had I known what we should endure, I never could have attempted so much as I did. I had no idea of the difficulty and danger attending such an undertaking, and only wonder that accidents are not more frequent among the miners, who run up and down these slippery places like lamp-lighters, singing and whistling all the way.

At about eighty fathoms depth we came to a vein of copper ore, where two sorry wretches were busied in the process of their miserable employment. With hardly room to move their bodies, in sulphureous air, wet to the skin, and buried in the solid rock, these poor devils live and work for a pittance barely sufficient to keep them alive; pecking out the hard ore by the glimmering of a small candle, whose scattered rays will hardly penetrate the thick darkness of the place. Those who live on earth in affluence, and are continually murmuring for additional comforts, would surely, if they saw these scenes, be happy with what they have. . . . Proceeding in our descent, we reached at length the bottom of the mine, and stood one hundred and thirty fathoms below the surface of the earth.

Thus far we had seen a mine of copper, but in this place

is contained a vein of tin also, and a communication is dug from the copper to the tin. Through this we crawled upon our hands and knees, sometimes sprawling upon our bellies, over wheel-barrows and stones, pick-axes and hammers. This we found was trifling, to that which we encountered afterwards, for we crossed over into a rapid stream whose waters rushed abundantly over us, as we crawled along in a space just sufficient to admit us upon all fours. . . .

When the ore is dug, it is conveyed up in baskets, through perpendicular shafts, to the surface. The day we went down, it happened to be a holiday for the miners, of which they have many in the year, and of course very few were at work. These holidays they call *grace days*, by which they mean surface days, as they call the surface of the earth *grace*, *graese*, or perhaps *grass*. It is very difficult to understand what they say, and our captain, who kept bawling out his precaution all the way down, might as well have held his peace, since not one of us could comprehend a syllable of his jargon.

Working our way in a direction from north to south, we came at last to the shafts of the tin mine. Here we saw, as before, two figures, that hardly wore the appearance of human beings, singing at their work. We found it exceedingly difficult to pay them a visit, as we had to descend by a single rope down a chasm, never broader than a chimney, until we reached the loade where the miners were employed.

(d) Tyneside was a highly developed industrial area, and London was dependent upon it for its coal. There were seasonal variations in the price of coal until collier-ships from the Tyne began to make journeys to London all the year round after 1760. The first 'railways' were developed in these pits. (See below, p. 107.)

Source: B. F. de St. Fond, *A Journey*, pp. 136–9.

The coal-mines, in the neighbourhood of Newcastle, are situated in so fortunate a position that the soil which covers them yields fine pasture that supports herds of horses. Under this fertile soil there is found a sandstone, of excellent quality for grind-stones. This second richness of the earth forms another extensive object of trade for the industry of the inhabitants of Newcastle: these stones have so great a reputation, that they are exported to all the ports in Europe.

The first mine I visited belongs to a private individual; it is situated about two miles from the town, and requires one hundred men to work it; thirty for the work above ground, and seventy in the pit: twenty horses live in this profound abyss, and drag the coal through the subterranean passages to the pit-bottom; four outside work the machine which raises the coal, and some more are employed in auxiliary labours. . . .

At [a] depth of one hundred and two feet the coal is found. The seam is five feet thick in some places, and varies in others; but in general it is easily wrought, and much of it is brought up in large blocks. This last circumstance is of considerable advantage, as such pieces are always easily transported, and are besides well suited for chamber-fires; which makes this coal sell at a higher price. . . .

This mine has a large steam-engine for pumping out the water, and at the same time working a ventilator to purify the air.

CHAPTER IV

Communication

Nature has set up by her own unquestionable authority certain boundaries and fences to circumscribe the discontent of man: she has effected her purpose in the quietest and easiest manner, by laying him under almost insuperable obligations to work out his ease, and to sustain his suffering at home. . . . The whole circle of travellers may be reduced to the following *heads:*

> Idle Travellers,
> Inquisitive Travellers,
> Lying Travellers,
> Proud Travellers,
> Vain Travellers,
> Splenetic Travellers,

Then follow:
> The Travellers of Necessity,
> The delinquent and felonious Traveller,
> The unfortunate and innocent Traveller,
> The simple Traveller,

And last of all (if you please) the Sentimental Traveller (meaning thereby myself). . . .

(LAURENCE STERNE, *A Sentimental Journey*, 1768)

Most Foreigners that travel into *England* content themselves with seeing *London*, the two Universities, Windsor, and the other Royal Palaces.

(M. MISSON, *Memoirs and Observations*, 1719)

Our servant came up and said, 'Sir, there is no travelling today. Such a quantity of snow has fallen in the night that the roads are quite filled up.' I told him, 'At least we can walk twenty miles a day, with our horses in our hands.' So in the name of God we set out. We kept on, on foot or on horseback, till we came to the White Lion at Grantham.

(JOHN WESLEY, *Journal*, 18 Feb. 1747)

Conversation is a traffic; and if you enter into it without some stock of knowledge to balance the account proportionally betwixt you—the trade drops at once.

(LAURENCE STERNE, *Sermons of Mr. Yorick*, 1760)

1. VILLAGE BOUNDS

For the large number of Englishmen who lived in villages, life was bounded geographically within narrow limits. The following extracts bring out different aspects both of village community and of village 'isolation'.

(a) *Source:* Note in the Parish Register of Turnworth, Dorset, 1747, quoted by W. E. Tate in *The Parish Chest* (1960), p. 74.

On Ascension Day after morning prayer at Turnworth Church, was made a publick Perambulation of yᵉ bounds of yᵉ parish of Turnworth by me Richd. Cobbe, Vicar, Wm. Northover, Churchwarden, Henry Sillers and Richard Mullen, Overseers and others with 4 boys; beginning at Church Hatch and cutting a great T. on the most principal parts of the bounds. Whipping yᵉ boys by way of remembrance, and stopping their cry with some half-pence; we returned to church again, which Perambulation and Processioning had not been made for five years last past.

(b) Strangers were strangers, and until 1795 vagrants and beggars were sent back to their own parishes if they seemed likely to be a burden on the poor rate. 'Removal Orders' were made, and 'Bills of Charges' carefully kept. Yet despite the settlement laws, there was more migration than Adam Smith suggested when he wrote that 'it was often more difficult for a poor man to pass the artificial boundaries of a parish than the arm of the sea or a ridge of high mountains'. All coastal counties, for instance, provided sailors and fishermen.

Source: Removal Order, Shelford, Notts., printed in *ibid.*, pp. 202ff.

(i) The Examination

County of Nottingham. ⎱ The Examination of Humphrey
(TO WIT). ⎰ Foulds taken upon Oath before me,

one of HIS MAJESTY's Justices of the Peace in and for the said County, this seventh Day of April 1809 touching the Place of his Settlement. This Examinant, upon Oath, saith, That he is about the Age of Thirty Eight Years, and that he was born, as he hath been informed, and verily believes, in the Parish of Old Daulbey in the County of Leicester of Parents legally settled at Shelford in the County of Nottingham, That when about seventeen years of Age he was hired to Mr. Simpson of Saxelby in the County of Leicester aforesaid for one year and served him Two years, That at Martinmas following he was hired to Henry Ellis of Shelford in the County of Nottingham for one year and served him accordingly. That at Martinmas following was hired to Mr. John Cooper of Shelford aforesaid and served him Eighteen Months. That in the Month of December following he went to Work at Grantham Canal. That in the year 1800 he went to Great Grimsby in Lincolnshire and Married Fanny his now Wife which gave him a Vote for great Grimsby aforesaid, and there Rented a House, at one Pound ten shillings a year and paid Rates or Assessments about five Shillings a year, and lived there about five or six years. That he afterwards went to live at Boston, and Rented a Room and Paid Three Shillings a week for Thirty Nine Weeks, and remainder of the year Paid 2s. 6d. per week, and was then Removed by a Warrant of Removal to the Parish of Shelford aforesaid. . . .

(ii) The Order

The Borough and Parish of Boston ⎱ Upon the Complaint of
    in the County of Lincoln ⎰ and the Churchwardens
Overseers of the Poor of the Parish of Boston aforesaid . . . in the said County of Lincoln unto us . . . that Humphrey Foulds and Frances his Wife and their three children namely Humphrey aged about six Years, Mary Ann aged about five years and Sarah aged about two years have come to inhabit in the said Parish of Boston, not having gained a legal Settlement there, nor produced any Certificate owning them to be settled elsewhere, and that the said Humphrey Foulds and Frances his wife and their said three children have become chargeable to the said Parish of Boston; we the said Justices . . .

do therefore require you the said Churchwardens and Overseers of the Poor of the said Parish of Boston, or some, or one of you to convey the said Humphrey Foulds and Frances his Wife and their said three children from and out of the said Parish of Boston to said Parish of Shelford and them to deliver to the Churchwardens and Overseers of the Poor there, or to some or one of them together with our Order or a true Copy thereof, at the same Time shewing to them the Original; and we do also hereby require you the said Churchwardens and Overseers of the Poor of the said Parish of Shelford to receive and provide for them as Inhabitants of your said Parish.

(c) In village communities, like Padworth, Berkshire, specific reference was sometimes made by providers of harvest feasts as to whether the festival included people born outside the parish.

Source: F. Turner (ed.), *A Berkshire Batchelor's Diary* (1936). The diary was kept by Francis Prior, a gentleman farmer of Ufton, Berkshire.[1]

On Tuesday the 18th of October (1768) I that day finnish my Harvest. . . . Gave all the people that work'd at Cart that day their supper and plenty of Ale and I intend if please God I live till the next harvest and remain in the same mind I now am to provide on this Occasion a large Round of Beef. . . .

Monday the 2nd of Novr. 1769 that day kill'd my bull which gave next day to the Parishioners of Padworth.

> No. 1. Wm. Wise.
> 2. Widow Saunders. . . .
> 28. Thomas Faulkner.
> 29. Thos. Hawkins.

To my day men and not of the Parish
John White the farm carter.
John Crockford Shepherd.
Edwd. Hill Thrasher. . . .

(d) Some parts of the country were notorious for their isolation.

[1] [In 1784 Prior had changed from his manuscript diary to a printed diary called 'The Daily Journal: or the Gentleman's, Merchant's and Tradesman's Complete Accompt Book, for the Pocket or Desk.' For the use of such diaries, see above, p. 48.]

Wordsworth emphasized the isolation of the Lake District, for example, before it began to be fashionable to visit it and to admire the mountains and lakes.

Source: W. Wordsworth, *A Guide Through the District of the Lakes,* written in 1810 and published in Knight (ed.), *Prose Works,* vol. II, p. 55.

From the time of the erection of these houses till within the last sixty years the state of society, though no doubt slowly and gradually improving, underwent no material change. Corn was grown in these vales (through which no carriage-road had yet been made) sufficient upon each estate to furnish bread for each family, and no more. . . . Every family spun from its own flock the wool with which it was clothed. . . . They had, as I have said, their rural chapel, and of course their minister, in clothing or in manner of life in no way differing from themselves, except on the sabbath-day; this was the sole distinguished individual among them; everything else, person and possession, exhibited a perfect equality, a community of shepherds and agriculturalists, proprietors for the most part of the lands which they occupied and cultivated. . . . Till within the last sixty years there was no communication between any of these vales by carriage roads; all bulky articles were transported on pack horses.

(e) Even in more developed parts of the country Marriage Registers reveal how many parishioners married spouses from their own or adjacent parishes within what may be regarded as the same 'group of settlements'. The procedure for registering marriages was tightened up by Hardwicke's Marriage Act of 1753. After that date information becomes more comprehensive and is set out on printed forms.

Source: Sussex Archaeological Society, *Sussex Marriage Licences,* Deanery of South Malling (1928), pp. 332–3.

1730.

Mar. 27   Thomas SNATT of Uckfield, husbandman, & Mary ALLINGHAM of same.

May   5   Richard HARLAND of Lindfield, taylor, & Hannah ALLEN of same.

May 15 Robert MOONE of Mayfield, yeoman, & Elizabeth RELF of same.

June 16 Solomon GLEED of Ashburnham, yeoman, & Sarah MEPHAM of Mayfield.

Aug. 28 Daniel KENWARD of Lewes, collermaker, & Mary TYLER of the Cliffe, widow.

Sept. 11 John DRUDGE of Edburton & Jane BURSTOW of same, spinster.

Sept. 30 John WEBB of Woodmancote & Jane HARDS of Edburton, spinster.

Dec. 23 John TOMPSETT of Newick & Jude PEIRCE of Isfield, widow.

Dec. 29 Edward COLLINS of the Cliffe, currier, & Sarah PALMER of same, spinster.

1730–1.

Jan. 18 JOHN SHARP of Lewes, bricklayer, & MARY PALMER of the Cliffe, spinster.

Feb. 1 John BUCKELL of Lewes, barber, & Elizabeth MACKFARLAND of the Cliffe, spinster.

Feb. 2 Stephen RUSSELL & Anne PIPER of Wadhurst, spinster.

Feb. 3 Zachery SYMMS of Goudhurst, barber, & Anne MATE of Wadhurst, spinster.

Feb. 15 William GILL & Elizabeth CALEY of Mayfield.

1731.

May 21 Herbert STYLES of the Cliffe, taylor, & Anne HART of same, spinster.

June 6 John CLARK of Battell, labourer, & Mary CROW-HURST, spinster.

June 8 John TYMAN of Mayfield, yeoman, & Mary MOONE of same, spinster.

July 12 Jonathan BARROWCLIFFE of the Cliffe & Martha HAMMOND, spinster.

Aug. 4 Daniel KENWARD of the Cliffe & Mary WOOD of same, spinster.

Aug. 23 John SMITH of Maresfield & Anne PRICE of Framfield, widow.

Sept. 6 William KING & Susan BACKER of Isfield.

Sept. 7 Arthur PINION of Ringmer, husbandman, & Charity TOWNSEND of Framfield.

Sept. 10 John STAPLEY of Mayfield & Sarah BROWN of Buxted, spinster.

Sept. 15 John HOLLANDS of Broadwater, yeoman, & Mary GATLAND of South Malling.

Sept. 20 Richard GOODWYN of Bexhill & Elizabeth DAY of Mayfield.

(e) Local names figure prominently in the parish records. The following example relates to the Sussex name, Elphick.

Source: Sussex Archaeological Society, *Sussex Marriage Licences, Archdeaconry of Lewes* (1928), pp. 140–1.

ELPHICK, George, of Isfield, yeoman, bachelor, & Elizabeth HARRIOTT of Tarringnevil, spinster. 14 Nov. 1801.

ELPHICK, George, of S. John's under the Castle of Lewes, bachelor, aged 22 and upds., & Ann KENNARD of S. Peter and S. Mary Westout, spinster, aged 20, and upds. 16 May 1814.

ELPHICK, James, of Kingston near Lewes, husbandman, bachelor, aged 24 and upds., & Mary IRELAND of same, spinster, aged 22 and upds. 27 Oct. 1777.

ELPHICK, John, of Framfield, yeoman, bachelor, aged 21 and upds., & Elizabeth WINTON of same, spinster, aged 21 and upds. 13 Dec. 1805.

ELPHICK, Richard, of S. Thomas in the Cliffe, labourer, bachelor, aged 22 and upds., & Jenny LOWER of Arlington, spinster, aged 22 and upds. 13 April 1782.

ELPHICK, Richard of Framfield, butcher, bachelor, aged 21 and upds., & Harriot RICHARDSON of Mayfield, spinster, aged 21 and upds.

ELPHICK, Samuel, of Willingdon, servant bachelor, aged 20 and upds., with consent of Hannah Elphick of Willingdon, widow, his mother, & Sarah GEERING of Jevington, spinster, aged 22 and upds.

ELPHICK, Walter, of Chiddingly, miller, bachelor, & Mary OLLIVER of Burwash, spinster (Chiddingly ch.). 9 Jan. 1833.

ELPHICK, William, the younger, of Meeching otherwise

Newhaven, yeoman, aged 24 and upds., & Mary LAMB of Wilmington, spinster, aged 25 and upds. 20 Aug. 1764.

ELPHICK, William, of Framfield, yeoman, bachelor, aged 21 and upds., & Susannah GADBY of same, spinster, aged 21 and upds.: bondsmen, said W. E. and Thomas Pescodd of Southover near Lewes, cordwainer. 19 Jan. 1774. [South Malling]

ELPHICK, William, of Herstmonceux, yeoman, bachelor, aged 24 and upds., & Mille MARSHALL of same, spinster, aged 21 and upds.: bondsmen, said W. E. and John Marshall of Herstmonceux, yeoman. 29 Apr. 1780.

ELPHICK, William, of Framfield, yeoman, widower, & Elizabeth HART of same, spinster, aged 19 and upds. 25 Aug. 1780. [South Malling]

ELPHICK, William, of Westham, yeoman, bachelor, aged 20 and upds., with consent of William Elphick of Westham, yeoman, & Ann GORRINGE of same, spinster, aged 23 and upds. 14 Sept. 1786.

ELPHICK, William, of All Saints, Lewes, britchesmaker, bachelor, aged 25 and upds., & Jane EGERS of same, spinster, aged 25 and upds. 1 Nov. 1791.

ELPHICK, William, of Westfirle, labourer, bachelor, aged 23 and upds., & Mary Ann REEVES of same, spinster, aged 21 and upds. 14 Dec. 1798.

ELPHICK, William, of Friston, gent., bachelor, aged 25 and upds., & Mary ARMITAGE of Eastdean, spinster, aged 21 and upds. 25 Oct. 1806.

2. POINTS OF CONTACT

Market towns were the centres of districts, and people naturally gravitated towards them. In some counties, like Herefordshire or Leicestershire, there was a strong pull towards the centre: in others, like Oxfordshire, there was not. Assize towns and petty sessional divisions were known to most people. Other points of contact were the fair, a medieval institution, and the inn, which figures prominently in almost all eighteenth-century novels, as a place where 'strangers' and 'natives' met.

(a) *Source:* D. Defoe, *Tour*, vol. I., pp. 80ff.

Sturbridge Fair . . . is not only the greatest in the nation, but in the world. . . . The shops are placed in rows like streets, whereof one is called Cheapside; and here, as in several other streets, are all sorts of trades, who sell by retale, and who come principally from London with their goods; scarce any trades are omitted, goldsmiths, toyshops, brasiers, turners, milleners, haberdashers, hatters, mercers, drapers, pewtrers, china-warehouses, and in word all trades that can be named in London; with coffee-houses, taverns, brandy shops, and eating houses, innumerable, and all in tents, and booths, as above . . . . To attend this fair, and the prodigious conflux of people, which comes to it, there are sometimes no less than fifty hackney coaches, which come from London, and ply night and morning to carry the people to and from Cambridge; for there the gross of the people lodge; nay, which is still more strange, there are wherries brought from London on waggons to plye upon the little river Cam, and to row people up and down from the town, and from the fair as occasion presents. It is not to be wondered at, if the town of Cambridge cannot receive, or entertain the numbers of people that come to this fair; not Cambridge only, but all the towns round are full; nay, the very barns, and stables are turned into inns, and made as fit as they can be to lodge the meaner sort of people: As for the people in the Fair, they all universally eat, drink and sleep, in their booths, and tents, and the said booths are so inter-mingled with taverns, coffee-houses, drinking-houses, eating-houses, cook-shops, &c. and all in tents too; and so many butchers and higglers from all the neighbouring counties come into the fair every morning . . . that there's no want of any provisions of any kind. . . . In a word, the fair is like a well fortyfy'd city, and there is the least disorder and confusion (I believe) that can be seen anywhere, with so great a concourse of people.

(b) *Source:* C. P. Moritz, 'Travels Through Various Parts of England in 1782', reprinted in W. Mavor, *The British Tourists; or Traveller's Pocket Companion* (1798), pp. 104–7.

At noon I got to Litchfield: an old-fashioned town, with

G

narrow, dirty streets, where, for the first time, I saw round panes of glass in the windows. The place, to me, wore an unfriendly appearance: I therefore . . . went straight through, and only bought some bread at a baker's, which I took along with me. At night I reached Burton, where the famous Burton Ale is brewed. . . . The houses and everything else seemed to wear nearly as grand an appearance, as if I had been still in London. And yet the manners of some of its inhabitants were so thoroughly rustic, and rude, that I saw them actually pointing at me with their fingers, as a foreigner. . . . In the afternoon I saw Derby, in the vale before me; and I was now a hundred and twenty-six miles from London. Derby is not a very considerable town; it was market day when I got there; and I was obliged to pass through a crowd of people; but there was here no such odious curiosity, nor offensive staring, as at Burton. Hereabout too, I took notice, that I began to be always civilly bowed to by the children of the villages through which I passed.

(c) *Source:* C. B. Andrews (ed.), *The Torrington Diaries* (1938), vol. IV, pp. 100–1. Lord Torrington is describing a tour in the Midlands in 1789. His many accounts of inns are always vivid and evocative. (See also, above, p. 77.)

A short Road back brought me, at 2 o'clock. to The George Inn, Silsoe, a tolerable Noon Stop, free from Noise, close to The Park, and with a neat Garden; where on a Seat in a yew-Bush, I enjoy'd the fragrance of a Sweet Briar Hedge, Shelter'd from the Rain; I but just Escaped.

The Stable here is very good, and The People very Civil.— Unluckily, I was too late for their Eggs and Bacon, So was obliged to have a bad fry'd Beef-Steak;—but I brought good Sauce with me. . . .

Wrest is a deserted Place; No Residence, now, of Nobility; or of expensive Housekeeping! I made a longish, tedious Stay here; my Horse faring better than I did, in a good Stall, and with good Food; But my charge was very cheap, and the brown Bread excellent (white I allways discard), nor was the Sage-Cheese amiss. . . . I allways think of Dinner for ½ an hour before my arrival at the Inn, which gives me an appetite, and an hurry for eating; and I never Eat with so much good will, as when I come in heated, and can have my meat quickly; for then both Body and Mind are instantly Refreshed, and Recover'd.—

			D.
Eating	. . .	Beef Steaks . . .	8
Drinking	. . .	3 glasses B. and Water	6
Horses—Hay and Corn	. . . . .		5
Feeding—two Servants	. . . . .		4

Sl. 11

I returned by Wrest-House, thro' the Park, thro' Shefford Town, and by the Meadows home. . . . My Evening Pace was very Slow, but I often look'd behind me at the lowering weather, which ended in rain, just as I return'd to my Quarters.—It is really almost cold enough for a fire and my Landlord and Landlady have one in the Bar; where I went to hold conversation; and then was obliged to light mine, and order an early hot supper;—at an hour when a genteel London Dinner is finishing, and the Opera beginning!

3. THE LURE OF LONDON

London, busy, turbulent and colourful, had an immense appeal to people from all parts of the country in the eighteenth century, although most provincials never visited it. 'When a man is tired of London, he is tired of life', exclaimed Dr. Johnson in 1777. Some of the immigrants quickly got caught up in the seamy side of London life, and for this reason guide-books and novels alike were full of warning advice both to girls and young men. Hogarth's *Rake's Progress* and *Harlot's Progress* were often played out in real life.

(a) *Source:* P. Quennell (ed.), John Cleland's *Memoirs of a Woman of Pleasure* (1963), pp. 32–3. The book was first published in 1749.

As I had nobody left alive in the village who had concern enough about what should become of me . . . I soon came to a resolution of making this launch into the wide world, by repairing to *London*, in order to SEEK MY FORTUNE, a phrase which, bye the bye, has ruined more adventurers of both sexes, from the country than it ever made or advanced. Nor did Esther Davis a little comfort and inspirit me to centure with her, by piquing my childish curiosity with the fine sights that were to be seen in *London:* the Tombs, the Lions, the King, the Royal Family, the fine plays and Operas and, in short, all the diversions which fell within her sphere of life to come at; the detail of which perfectly turn'd the little head of me. Nor can I remember, without laughing, the innocent admiration, not without a spice of envy, with which we poor girls, whose church-going clothes did not rise above Dowlass shifts and stuff gowns, beheld Esther's scowered satin gowns, caps border'd with an inch of lace, taudry ribbons, and shoes belaced with silver: all of which we imagined grew in London and entered for a great deal into my determination of trying to come in for my share of them. . . .

(b) *Source:* A Note in *Brief Description of London and Westminster* (1776), p. xxvii.

A word of advice to such young women as may arrive strangers in town. . . . Immediately on their arrival . . . and sometimes sooner, even upon their road to it, there are miscreants of both sexes on the watch to seduce the fresh country maiden, with infinite protestations of friendship, service, love and pity, to prostitution. . . . For this reason the very carriages which convey them are hunted and examined; the inns where they alight are beset by those infernal hirelings who . . . put on the demure show of modesty and sanctity for their deception. If she applies to an office of intelligence, 'tis odds but that she falls into the hands of some procuress.

(c) *Source:* Arthur Young, *The Farmers' Letters to the People of England* (1771 edn.), pp. 353–4.

Young men and women in the country fix their eye on London as the last stage of their hope; they enter into service in the country for little else but to raise money enough to go to London, which was no easy matter when a stage coach was four or five days creeping an hundred miles; and the fare and the expenses ran high. But now! a country fellow one hundred miles from London jumps on to a coach-box in the morning and for eight or ten shillings gets to town by night, which makes a material difference; besides rendering the going up and down so easy that the numbers who have seen London are increased tenfold and of course ten times the boasts are sounded in the ears of country fools, to induce them to quit their clean healthy fields for a region of dirty, stink and noise. And the number of young women that fly thither is almost incredible.

4. LONDON TRAFFIC

The bustle of London caught all its inhabitants in the same grip. It also easily turned into brawling. London had a reputation as a rough city.

(a) *Source:* John Gay, *Trivia* (1716).

Where the fair columns of *St. Clement* stand
Whose straiten'd bounds encroach upon the *Strand;*
Where the low penthouse bows the walker's head,
And the rough pavement wounds the yielding tread. . . .
Forth issuing from steep lanes, the colliers' steeds
Drag the black load; another cart succeeds,
Team follows team, crouds heap'd on crouds appear,
And wait impatient, 'till the road grows clear.
Now all the pavement sounds with trampling feet
And the mixt hurry barricades the street.
Entangled here, the waggon's lengthen'd team
Cracks the tough harness; here a pond'rous beam
Lies over-turn's athwart; for slaughter fed
Here lowing bullocks raise their horned head.
Now oaths grow loud, with coaches coaches jar,
And the smart blow provoked the sturdy war;
From the high box they whirl the thong around,
And with the twining lash their shins resound. . . .

(b) *Source:* J. J. Boswell, *The Life of Samuel Johnson* (1953 edn.), p. 608. The reference is to 2 April 1775.

I talked of the cheerfulness of Fleet-street, owing to the constant quick succession of people which we perceive passing through it. JOHNSON. 'Why, sir, Fleet-street has a very animated appearance; but I think the full tide of human existence is at Charing-Cross.'

(c) *Source:* P. Grosley, *A Tour to London* (1772), vol. I, p. 37.

Except in the two or three streets which have very lately been well paved, the best hung and the richest coaches are in point of ease as bad as carts; whether this be owing to the tossing occasioned at every step by the inequality and instability of the pavement, or to the continual danger of being splashed if all the windows are not kept constantly up. . . . The heaviest [carriages] and those that move the most slowly, directing the march of each of the files, the best carriage in London, as soon as it finds itself engaged with others, is obliged to follow the way pointed out by the file it belongs to, that is to say, to suffer itself to be tossed and jogged about for a long time, whatever reason the driver may have to be expeditious. But the English do not seem to have that eagerness to arrive at their journey's end, so general amongst people of other countries. By these delays, they rate the time they are to be upon the road, and they are seen to perform this tedious task without inquietude or impatience. However, if there seems to be any likelihood of its exceeding the time computed, they quit their coach, and mix with the crowds in the foot-path. This happens every day to persons of the first rank; who upon these occasions would find it a vain thing to attempt to avail themselves of their great names or exalted dignity to be exempted from observing this general rule.

5. TRAVEL BY ROAD

Travel to and from London for the Season or for duties in the country often posed difficult problems. So did local traffic. There is an immense literature on the state of eighteenth-century roads. Complaints grew as the century went by. The first of the Turnpike Trusts, depending for their revenue on tolls, provoked many popular protests, largely on the grounds that they raised the price of food in the agricultural areas. Yet they led (though not universally) to genuine improvements in the communications system. Attempts were also made to regulate and restrict the amount and size of traffic on the roads.

(a) *Source:* Letter from Ashburnham in the East Sussex Records Office, *Ashburnham Papers*, 841, 1697, p. 192.

Nothing but the impossibility of passing with safety through the bad ways made worse by the present Season could have hindered my being with you at the Audit but not Six horses in the Town would undertake the journey upon any account soe that we are road bound at this time without a remedy.

(b) *Source:* D. Defoe, *A Tour*, vol. II, pp. 179ff.

The Reason of my taking this Notice of this Badness of the Roads, through all the Midland Counties, is this; that as these are Counties which drive a very great Trade with the City of *London*, and with one another, perhaps the greatest of any Counties in England, and that, by consequence, the Carriage is exceeding great, and also that all the Land Carriage of the *Northern* Counties necessarily goes through these Counties, so the Roads had been plow'd so deep, and Materials have been in some Places so difficult to be had for Repair of the Roads, that all the Surveyors Rates have been able to do nothing, nay, the very whole Country has not been able to repair them. . . . This necessarily brought the Country to bring these Things before the Parliament; and the Consequence has been, that Turn-pikes or Toll-bars have been set up on the several great Roads of *England* beginning at *London*, and proceeding thro' almost all those dirty deep Roads, in the Midland Counties especially; at which Turnpikes, all Carriages, Droves of Cattle, and Travellers on Horseback are oblig'd to pay an easy Toll; that is to say a Horse a Penny, a Coach three Pence, a Cart four Pence, at some six Pence to eight Pence, a Waggon six Pence, in some a Shilling, and the like; Cattle pay by the Score, or by the Head, in some Places more, in some less. . . . Several of these Turn-pikes and Tolls had been set up of late Years, and great Progress had been made in mending the most difficult Ways. . . . It is incredible what Effect it has already had upon Trade in the Countries where it is more compleatly finished; even the Carriage of Goods is abated in some places; *6d. per* hundred Weight, in some places *12d. per* hundred . . . .

The Advantage to all other kinds of Travelling I omit here; such as the Safety and Ease to Gentlemen travelling up to *London* on all occasions. . . . Also the Riding Post, as well as the ordinary carrying of the Mails, or for the Gentlemen riding Post, when their Occasions require Speed. . . .

(c) Defoe always noted road improvements.

Source: Ibid., Appendix to the second volume. He is referring to the 'great north west road, the Watling-street Way'.

Upon this great road there are wonderful improvements made and making, which no traveller can miss the observation of, especially if he knew the condition these ways were formerly in; nor can my account of these counties be perfect, without taking notice of it; for certainly no publick edifice, almshouse, hospital, or nobleman's palace, can be of equal value to the country with this, no nor more an honour and ornament to it. . . .

From Mims to St. Albans, [it] is so well mended, the work so well done, and the materials so good, so plentifully furnish'd, and so faithfully apply'd, that in short, if possible, it out-does the Essex road mention'd before; for here the bottom is not only repair'd, but the narrow places are widen'd, hills levell'd, bottoms raised, and the ascents and descents made easy, to the inexpressible ease and advantage of travellers.

(d) That the building of turnpikes did not always lead to the improvement optimistically forecast by Defoe is well illustrated in Young's writings.

Source: A. Young, *A Six Weeks' Tour through the Southern Counties of England and Wales* (2nd edition, 1769), pp. 132–3.

The road from Witney to North Leach [Oxfordshire/ Gloucestershire] is, I think, the worst turnpike I ever travelled in; so bad, that it is a scandal to the country. They mend and make with nothing but the stone which forms the under stratum all over the country, quite from Tetsford the other side of Oxford. This stone, which rises in vast flakes, would make an admirable foundation for a surface of gravel; but by using it alone, and in pieces as large as one's head, the road is rendered most execrable. I travelled it with a very low opinion of all the counties and places it leads to: for if they were inhabited by people of fortune and spirit, I should think they would never suffer such a barbarous method of mending their capital road to subsist. . . .

(e) That improvement in Sussex was very slow can be illustrated both from Young and from John Burton, an Oxford scholar and clergyman, who journeyed into Sussex in 1751.

Source: J. Burton, Sive Iter Surrense et Sussexiense (1752)

Come now, my friend, I will set before you a sort of problem in Aristotle's fashion:—Why is it that the oxen, the swine, the women, and all other animals, are so long-legged in Sussex? May it be from the difficulty of pulling the feet out of so much mud by the stretch of the ankle, that the muscles get stretched, as it were, and the bones lengthened?

(f) Yet it was possible for Arthur Young in a more optimistic mood to extol road building as an instrument of greatly improved general communication.

Source: The Annals of Agriculture (1789), vol. XI, p. 293.

[The new road network ensured] a general impetus given to circulation; new people—new ideas—new exertions—fresh activity given to every branch of industry; people residing among good roads, who were never seen with bad ones, and all the animation and industry, which flow with a full tide through this kingdom, wherever there is free communication between the capital and the provinces.

6. MODES OF TRAVEL

Eighteenth-century inns made sharp distinctions between foot travellers, waggon travellers, travellers on public coaches and those riding either in their own coaches or on horse back. The following extracts relate to different modes of travel and the different kinds of reception different categories of travellers got.

(a) Source: M. Misson, Memoirs and Observations (1719), pp. 331–2.

They have several Ways of travelling in England. The Post is under a good Regulation throughout, and the Horses are better than those in France. There are Coaches that go to all the great Towns by moderate Journies; and others, which they call *Flying Coaches*, that will travel twenty Leagues a Day and more; but these don't go to all Places. They have no *Messagerie de Chevaux*; as in *France*; but you may hire Horses for what Time you please. The Sea and the Rivers also furnish their respective Conveniencies for Travelling; I say nothing of the *Waggons*? which are great *Carts*, cover'd in, that lumber along but very heavily; only a few poor old Women make Use of this Vehicle.

(b) *Source:* G. Farquhar, *The Beaux' Stratagem* (1707), Scene 1.

Boniface: Chamberlain! Maid! Cherry! daughter Cherry! All asleep? All dead?

Cherry: Here! Here! Why d'ye bawl so, father? D'ye think we have no ears?

Boniface: You deserve to have none, you young minx. The company of the Warrington coach has stood in the hall this hour, and nobody to show them to their chambers.

Cherry: And let 'em wait, father; there's neither red-coat in the coach nor footman behind it.

Boniface: But they threaten to go to another inn to-night.

Cherry: That they dare not, for fear the coachman should overturn them to-morrow. Coming! Coming! Here's the London coach arrived. . . . Very welcome, gentlemen. Chamberlain, show the Lion and the Rose.

(c) *Source:* T. Smollett, *Roderick Random* (1748), ch. XII.

On the sixth day, while we were about to sit down to dinner, the innkeeper came and told us, that three gentlemen, just arrived, had ordered the victuals to be carried to their apartment, although he had informed them that they were bespoke by the passengers in the waggon. To which information they had replied, 'The passengers in the waggon might be damned—their betters must be served before them—they supposed it would be no hardship on such travellers to dine upon bread and cheese for one day.' This was a terrible disappointment to us all; and we laid our heads together now to remedy it; when Miss Jenny observed that Captain Weazel, being by profession a soldier, ought in this case to protect and prevent us from being insulted. But the captain excused himself, saying he would not for all the world be known to have travelled in a waggon; swearing at the same time that, could he appear with honour, they should eat his sword sooner than his provision. Upon this declaration, Miss Jenny, snatching his weapon, drew it, and ran immediately into the kitchen, where she threatened to put the cook to death if he did not send the victuals into our chamber immediately. The noise she made brought the three strangers down, one of whom no sooner perceived her than he cried 'Ha! Jenny Ramper! what the devil brought thee hither?' 'My dear Jack Rattle!' replied she, running into his arms, 'is it you? Then Weazel may go to hell for a dinner—I shall dine with you.' They consented to this proposal with a great deal of joy; and we were on the point of being reduced to a very uncomfortable meal, when Joey, understanding the whole affair, entered the kitchen with a pitchfork in his hand, and swore he would be the death of any man who should pretend to seize the victuals prepared for the waggon. This menace had been likely to have produced fatal consequences; the three strangers drawing their swords, and being joined the servants, and we ranging ourselves on the side of Joey; when the landlord interposing, offered to part with his own dinner to keep the peace, which was accepted by the strangers; and we sat down at table without any further molestation.

(e) Buying a horse was an art in itself. *Source:* Letter of E. Poole to Sir William Lee, 20 March 1770, in the East Sussex County Records Office.

I believe you have a thorough Idea of the sort of Horse I should like from the Description I think I have given you before, & that such a one is difficult to be met with, I am but too sensible. I should wish him a gay, airy, shewy Horse, with good points, as the Jockys term it, with sufficient Life and Spirit as to appear a little alive and yet perfectly gentle & free from all vicious Habits. I would have his movements perfectly good & easy to the rider, & whose paces are such as to get on on the Road with pleasure to Himself and Rider, for I detest a slow moving Horse that labours and cannot get on and who will be as long in going a dozen or 10 Miles as another Horse shall go 20 with pleasure: such a one I have been Master of for these 16 or 17 years, as good a Mare I believe as ever was rode, sure footed, with some fashion, & yet is the dullest, heavyest moving Creature on the Road that ever was crossed; labours herself & it is really a labour to ride her, her movements are so rough and unpleasant; & with all this, you cannot push her above four or between 4 and 5 miles an Hour for the Life of you; & as a proof of this assertion, I scarsely ever traveld with any one on the Road in my Life that I could keep up with them; whilst they were stealing on, & getting [sic] ground of me every hundred yards imperceptibly as it were. A Horse I think can scarsely have too much Spirit on the Road.

(d) *Source:* C. P. Moritz, *Travels* (1798 ed.), p. 64, 74–5, 93.

I dined below with the family. . . . They could not sufficiently admire my courage, in determining to travel on foot, although they could not help approving of the motive [to see as much as possible of England and Englishmen]. At length, however, it came out, and they candidly owned, that I should not have been received into their house, had I not been introduced as I was. I was now confirmed in my suspicions, that, in England, any person undertaking so long a journey on foot, is sure to be looked upon, and considered as either a beggar, or a vagabond, or some necessitous wretch, which is a character not much more popular than that of a rogue. . . . With all my partiality for this country, it is impossible, even in theory, and much less so in practice, to approve of a system which confines all the pleasures and benefits of travel to the rich. A poor peripatetic is hardly allowed even the humble merit of being honest.

7. SPEED OF TRAVEL

The effects of distance should always be measured in terms of travel time. At the beginning of the eighteenth century a 'Flying Machine' could get from London to York in four days 'if God permits'. In the middle years of the century the quickest stage-coach journey from London to Edinburgh was said to take ten days in summer and twelve in winter. There were many signs of speeding-up on main routes in the 1780s. Certain coaches began to suspend the practice of halting at inns for the night. The 'Stage Coach and Mail', a royal mail coach introduced in 1784, did the journey from London to Bath in sixteen hours. It was not until the first thirty years of the nineteenth century, however, in the golden age of coaching, that 'Highflyers', 'Quicksilvers', 'Comets' and the like generally speeded up road travel and at the same time reduced the arbitrary element in travel times.

(a) *Source:* A York Coaching Notice of 1706, reproduced in T. Burke, *Travel in England* (1946), p. 56.

York Four Days Stage-Coach

Begins on Friday the 12th of April 1706

All that are desirous to pass from *London* to *York* or from *York* to *London* or any other Place on that Road: Let them Repair to the *Black Swan* in *Holbourn* in *London* and to the *Black Swan* in *Coney-Street* in *York*.

At both which Places they may be received in a Stage Coach every *Monday*, *Wednesday* and *Friday*, which performs the whole Journey in Four Days (*if God permits*). And sets forth at five in the Morning. And returns from *York* to *Stamford* in two days and from *Stamford* by *Huntingdon* to *London* in two days more. And the like Stages on their Return. Allowing each Passenger 10 Weight, and all above 3d a Pound. . . .

(b) *Source:* Advertisement from the *Ipswich Journal*, 14 Sept. 1754, reprinted in A. F. J. Brown (ed.), *English History from Essex Sources*, vol. I, p. 61.

Chelmsford Machine Fly sets out on Monday, Sept. 16, from the Coach and Horses at Chelmsford at Seven o'Clock in the Morning, to go every Day (except Sunday) to the Spread Eagle in Grace-church Street, and will be there at Twelve in the Forenoon; and returns the same Day at Two o'Clock in the Afternoon. Passengers will be detained no longer than to take fresh Horses at Rumford. . . .

N.B. Any Person may be furnish'd with Coaches, Hearse, or Chariot, with able Horses, to any Part of England, at reasonable Rates.

(c) *Source:* C. B. Andrews (ed.), *The Torrington Diaries* (1936), vol. III, pp. 38–9. The year is 1792.

I was thinking tonight of my own *rapidity* of riding, when compared with that of former horsemen; some of whose feats I shall recount. . . . I have taken some little trouble to find out the speed of former riders upon the road; not doubting but the strength of the men was equal to any modern exertion, and that the horses were infinitely better. When I repeat former ridings, the badness of the roads, the depth of wash-ways, and the steepness of the hill should be considered,—which are now generally done away; besides the distances being shorten'd; for the road to Dover is made nearer by two miles, than it was 50 years ago. . . . On the 17th of July 1720, Bernard Calvert, of Andover, rode from St. George's Church in Southwark to Dover; from there passed by Barge to Calice in France; and from there return'd back to St. George's Church the same day. —Setting out about 3 o'clock in the morning, and return'd at 8 o'clock in the evening, fresh and lustie.

On Monday, April 29, 1745, Mr. Cooper Thornhill, Master of the Bell Inn at Stilton in Huntingdonshire, set out from his house at 4 o'clock in the morning and came to the Queen's Arms opposite to Shoreditch Church in 3 hours, 52 minutes; and came back to London in 4 hours and 13 minutes; to a wager of 500 Guineas. He was allowed 15 hours to do it in, which is 213 miles, but perform'd it in 12 hours, 17 minutes. . . . This is deservedly reckon'd the greatest performance of its kind ever known. Several thousand Pounds were laid on this affair; and the roads for many miles lined with people to see him pass and repass.

8. ON THE ROAD

The high road was a place for adventure. Journeys could be tiring, but also dangerous, particularly to property. (See below, p. 374). There was also the problem of maintaining good relations with fellow travellers. The following extracts illustrate these themes. (a) *Source:* Poem attributed to J. Swift (1709). Swift is describing a coach journey from Aldersgate to Chester. The coach left Aldersgate at three in the morning.

Roused from sound sleep—thrice called—at length I rise,
Yawning, stretch out my arm, half close my eyes;

By steps and lantern enter the machine,
And take my place—how cordially—between
Two aged matrons of excessive bulk,
To mend the matter, too, of meaner folk;
While in like mood, jammed in on t'other side,
A bullying captain and a fair one ride,
Foolish as fair, and in whose lap a boy—
Our plague eternal, but her only joy.
At last, the glorious number to complete,
Steps in my landlord for that bodkin seat;
When soon, by every hillock, rut and stone,
Into each other's face by turns we're thrown.
This grandma scolds, that coughs, the captain swears,
The fair one screams and has a thousand fears;
While our plump landlord, trained in other lore,
Slumbers at ease not yet ashamed to snore. . . .
Sweet company! Next time, I do protest, sir,
I'd walk to Dublin ere I'd ride to Chester.

(b) *Source:* J. Woodforde, *The Diary of a Country Parson* (World Classics edn., 1949), pp. 87–9.

Jan. 31. 1774. I got up this morning at half past six in order to go to Bath. The Porter's man called me at six, for which and carrying my Portmanteau to the Cross Inn I gave him . . . 0. 1. 0. To Frank Paynes Boy this morning gave 0. 6. I went to the Cross Inn at a little after seven and the Machine was gone, however, I took a Post-Chaise immediately from the Cross Inn and overtook the Machine at Enson about 5 miles from Oxon, and there got into it.

For the Post Chaise pd.	0.	4.	0.
Gave the Driver	0.	1.	0.

There was one Passenger in it, a Gentleman of Exeter College, we stopped and breakfasted at Witney at the Bridge, and then I left the Gentleman as he came there only to meet some Company.

For my Breakfast at Witney pd.	0.	1.	0.

At Witney the Machine took up a Poor Player, a young man who is in a consumption and going to his Friends at Bath—he looked dreadful bad.

I dined at Burford by myself, pd. there   0.   4.   0.
At Burford pd. the remaining part of
  the Fare   0. 10.   6.

Dr. Bosworth of Oriel and a young lady came into the same room where I dined at Burford soon after I dined, as they were going to London in the Strand Water Machine thro Oxford. I was not long with them at the Inn at Burford as our Machine was just setting off. At Burford we took up with a young Farmer who was lame and going to try Bath Waters, and the Farmer's Sister a young Woman. The Farmer thinks his disorder to be Rheumatic. We got to Cirencester about 5 this afternoon where we supped and slept. I supped in a Room by myself and spent the evening.

Feb. 1st. I got up this morning at half past five, got into the Machine about 6 and set off before breakfast for Bath.

At Cirencester pd.   0.   3.   6.
Gave the Chamber maid and Waiter   0.   1.   6.
At Tedbury we breakfasted pd. there   0.   1.   0.

We got to Petty France about 11, where the Machine stays two or three Hours. And as I wanted to reach Ansford this evening, I took a Post-Chaise immediately at Petty France, and set forth for Bath. It snowed prodigiously all the way to Bath. . . .

I got to Bath about 1 o'clock, there I took a fresh Chaise for Old Downe.

Gave Petty France Driver   0.   1.   6.

besides a dram upon the road. I got to Old Down between 3 and 4 this afternoon where I stayed about a Quarter of an Hour, eat some Cold Rost Beef, drank a pint of Ale, and then got into a fresh Chaise for Ansford. . . . I got to Ansford, I thank God safe and well this evening about 6 o'clock.

(c) *Source:* H. Fielding, *The History of the Adventures of Joseph Andrews* (1742), Book I, ch. XII.

Nothing remarkable happened on the road till their arrival at the inn . . . ; whither they came about two in the morning. The moon then shone very bright; and Joseph, making his friend a present of a pint of wine, and thanking him for the favour of his horse, notwithstanding all entreaties to the contrary, proceeded on his journey on foot.

He had not gone above two miles . . . when he was met by two fellows in a narrow lane, and ordered to stand and deliver. He readily gave them all the money he had, which was somewhat less than two pounds; and told them he hoped they would be so generous as to return him a few shillings, to defray his charges on his way home.

One of the ruffians answered with an oath, 'Yes, we'll give you something presently; but first—"Strip," cried the other, 'or I'll blow your brains to the devil.' Joseph, remembering that he had borrowed his coat and breeches of a friend, replied, he hoped they would not insist on his clothes, which were not worth much but consider the coldness of the night. 'You are cold, are you, you rascal?' said one of the robbers: 'I'll warm you with a vengeance'; and, damning his eyes, snapped a pistol at his head; which he had no sooner done than the other levelled a blow at him with his stick, which Joseph, who was expert at cudgel-playing, caught with his, and returned the favour so successfully on his adversary, that he laid him sprawling at his feet, and at the same instant received a blow from behind, with the butt end of a pistol, from the other villain, which felled him to the ground, and totally deprived him of his senses.

9. MOVING GOODS

The movement of goods in the eighteenth century posed as many problems as the movement of people. At the beginning of the century by far the most important means of transport was shipping, either coastal or river. Surveys were made of the navigability of rivers and improvements often followed. Yet England was deficient in navigable rivers, and from the middle of the century onwards increasing attention was paid to traffic by canal. There were spurts of canal building from the 1760s to the end of the century. In each case there was a substantial fall in the urban price of coal and other commodities. The most advanced form of land transport was to be found in the North-Eastern mining areas and other districts like Coalbrookdale area in Shropshire where waggons were moved along tracks.

H

(a) *Source:* Testimony of William Taylor, a surveyor, before Parliament (1755) in the course of supporting a bill to make the Sankey Brook navigable to Liverpool, *Journals of the House of Commons,* 17 Jan. 1755.

Large Quantities of Coals are consumed in the Salt Works at Liverpoole, Dungeen, Northwich, and Winsford and by the Inhabitants of the aforesaid Towns and Places who have met great Complaints of the advanced Price which Coals have been sold for of late and of the short and uncertain Measure thereof; and that he apprehends such advanced Price is owing as well to the Difficulty of the Carriage as the Scarcity of the Coals.

(b) *Source:* J. Campbell, *A Political Survey of Britain* (1774), pp. 263ff.

A Nobleman of the First Rank [The Duke of Bridgewater] formed a Design of making a Canal from Worsley to Manchester in the County of Lancaster, for the carrying thither his Coals; which not being barely for his own but also for the publick Benefit, an Act of Parliament [was] passed [1759] to enable him to undertake this Work. . . . The Value of this Mode of Navigation came from thence to be better understood and the very extensive Uses to which it might be applied more clearly comprehended. . . . [It] very naturally excited a Spirit of Emulation in the Inhabitants of the adjacent Counties; the trading and manufacturing Part of which especially saw the Importance of this new Water-Carriage, they felt their own Wants, and after mature Consideration, conceived they might in the same Way be relieved. . . . By [new] Canals a Conjunction will be effected between the Severn and the Trent, and of both with the Mersey, so that consequently a Communication will be opened between the Ports of Bristol, Liverpool and Hull. A Scheme that would have been thought, and perhaps would have been found impracticable in the preceding Century, and which, all its Circumstances considered, must appear astonishing to our Posterity. These prodigious Works, now in a Train of Execution, shew that we ought not to despair of Things of great national Utility, though they may long dwell in the Minds, or only float upon the Tongues of Men.

(c) *Source:* Adam Smith, *The Wealth of Nations* (Everyman edn.), vol. I, pp. 167.

Six or eight men . . . by the help of water-carriage, can carry and bring back in the same time the same quantity of goods between London and Edinburgh, as fifty broad-wheeled waggons, attended by a hundred men, and drawn by four hundred horses. Upon two hundred tons of goods, therefore, carried by the cheapest land carriage from London to Edinburgh, there must be charged the maintenance of a hundred men for three weeks, and both the maintenance, and what is nearly equal to the maintenance, the wear and tear of four hundred horses as well as of fifty great waggons. Whereas, upon the same quantity of goods carried by water, there is to be charged only the maintenance of six or eight men, and the wear and tear of a ship of two hundred tons burden, together with the value of the superior risk, or the difference of the insurance between land and water carriage.

(b) *Source:* An Account by Abiah Darby of the work of her husband, Abraham Darby of Coalbrookdale in Shropshire (*c.* 1775), printed in A. Raistrick, *Dynasty of Ironfounders* (1953), p. 174. (See also below, p. 147.)

They used to carry their coal upon horse's backs, but he got roads made and laid with Sleepers and rails, as they have them in the North of England. And one waggon with three horses will bring as much as 20 horses used to bring on horse's backs. But this laying the road with wood begot a scarcity and raised the price of it, so that of late years, the laying of the rails of Cast Iron was substituted; which altho expensive, answers well for ware and duration. We have in the different works, near 20 miles of this road, which costs upward of £800 a mile. That of Iron Wheels and axle-trees for these waggons was, I believe, my Husband's invention.

10. HOW TECHNIQUES TRAVELLED

New technical developments often took considerable time to travel from one part of the country to another. This was particularly true of agricultural improvements. Eighteenth-century farming books, which received wide publicity, particularly after 1760, did much to spread knowledge of new techniques.

(a) Jethro Tull invented his drill in 1701. In 1804 Arthur Young noted that it was still not used in large parts of the tillage county of Hertfordshire.

Source: Note in the *Annals of Agriculture* (1804), quoted in R. Trow Smith, *English Husbandry* (1951), p. 135.

I passed through near one hundred miles in the county inquiring for drilled crops but neither seeing nor hearing of it.

(b) Young summed up his own influence.

Source: M. Betham-Edwards (ed.), *Autobiography of Arthur Young* (1898), pp. 53–5.

It is necessary here to pause a little in order to examine the object and the effect of the three tours I made and published. . . . Writers confined to their closets, or, at most, to a single farm, could not describe what it was impossible for them to know; . . . for a man to quit his farm and his fireside in order to examine the husbandry of a kingdom by travelling above four thousand miles through a country of no greater extent than England was certainly taking means sufficiently effective for laying a sure basis for the future improvement of the soil. To understand well the present state of cultivation is surely a necessary step prior to the proposals of improvement. This I effected; and in the opinion of some very able agriculturalists now living, the greatest of the subsequent improvements that have been made during the last forty years have, in a great measure, originated in the defects pointed out by me in the detail of these journeys.

11. HOW NEWS TRAVELLED

The advent of newspapers (see above, p. 25) led to a great speeding-up of the process of communication. By the end of the century many of the features of modern reporting had become established.

(a) *Source:* Despatch quoted in the *Bristol Post-Boy*, the earliest extant copy of a country newspaper, 12 Aug. 1704.

Whitehall, August 10. This Afternoon arrived an Express with a Letter from his Grace the Duke of Marlborough to my Lady Duchess written on Horseback with a Lead Pencil. A Copy whereof follows:

August 13 NS

I have not time to say any more than to beg of you to present my Humble Duty to the Queen, and to let her Majesty know, That Her Army has had a glorious Victory: Monsieur Tallara and two other Generals are in my Coach and I am following the rest. The Bearer, my Aid de Camp, Colonel Parkes, will give her Majesty an Account of what has passed: I shall do it in a Day or two by another more at lage. [*sic*].

Marlborough

(b) 'Proposals for Printing . . . the *Newcastle General Magazine*' (1747), quoted in G. A. Cranfield, *The Development of the Provincial Newspaper* (1962), pp. 114–15.

1. The distance of *Newcastle* from *London* rendering it impracticable for any of the MAGAZINES, or other *Monthly Performances*, to arrive here at the soonest before the 13th, and frequently the 20th Days of the succeeding Month for which they are publish'd; and the Carriers from the *Northern Counties*, and *North Britain*, not coming to this Town till the Week after their Arrival here, it frequently happens, that great Numbers of Country Readers never see any of these Pamphlets till near a Month after their Publication: by which Delay some Parts of their Contents are quite stale, and the rest less acceptable. This MAGAZINE is therefore designed to remove the said Inconveniences as much as possible; for it will be circulated in the *North* a Week or ten Days sooner than any other Pamphlet of the kind. . . .

VII. In each MAGAZINE will be inserted a regular and concise History of the most important Transactions of the Times, collected from the most authentick ACCOUNTS; to be illustrated by PLANS of such Battles, Sieges, Sea Fights, etc., in which our Arms have had any Share, or in which this Nation is particularly interested. Done by the best Hands.

(c) There was recognition later of the value of telegraphed signals.

Source: Report in *The Times*, 15 Sept. 1794.

The new mode of correspondence, by the help of which, the surrender of Quesnoy was known at Paris an hour after the entry of the French troops into that place, is a communication by signals, which are repeated from distance, to distance, by machines, stationed four, or five, leagues asunder. This may explain the celerity with which communications are made.

The telegraph, now brought into use by the French, appears to have been an invention of Dr. Hooper's, and published in his Rational Recreations, in 1774.

(d) Also in 1794 there were improvements in the London postal services.

Source: Report in *The Times*, 28 Feb. 1794.

The new Penny Post Office is likely to prove such a very great accommodation to the public, that the only wonder is, it has been so long neglected. Instead of the number of deliveries, and the hours of despatch varying in different parts of the town, as at present, there will be six deliveries each day in all parts of the town; by which means a person living at Mary-le-Bonne may send letters to, or receive letters from, Limehouse, a distance of seven miles, five times a day. . . . Persons putting in letters by nine in the morning, at the distance of ten miles from the chief Penny Post Office, and later, at less distant parts, may receive answers from London the same afternoon.

12. AT HOME AND ABROAD

There was much foreign travel for the aristocracy and the gentry, with the Grand Tour usually including France and Italy along with parts of Germany. The visit to the newly discovered ruins of Pompeii was particularly fashionable during the 1770s and 1780s, and directly influenced English tastes (see below, pp. 430), including Wedgwood's Etruria pottery. Other British travellers explored Northern and Eastern Europe and some the Eastern Mediterranean.

(a) Source: S. Jenyns, *The Fine Modern Gentleman* (1746).

Just broke from School, pert, impudent, and raw
Expert in Latin, more expert in Tawl,

His honour posts o'er Italy and France,
Measures St. Peter's dome, and learns to dance.
Thence having quick thro' various countries flown,
Glean'd all their follies, and expos'd his own,
He back returns, a thing so strange all o'er,
As never ages past produc'd before;
A monster of such complicated worth,
As no one single clime could e'er bring forth.
Half atheist, papist, gamester, bubble rook,
Half fiddler, coach man, dancer, groom and cook.

(b) Not all travellers went abroad so young or returned quite in that mood. In 1718 Lady Mary Wortley Montagu, one of the most famous of all travellers and letter writers, returned to England after a long journey abroad. Her husband was Ambassador to Turkey and she was twenty-eight years old at the time.

Source: Lord Wharncliffe (ed.), *The Letters and Works of Lady Wortley Montagu* (1837), vol. II, pp. 119/21.

I arrived this morning at Dover, after being tossed a whole night in the packet boat, in so violent a manner that the master, considering the weakness of his vessel, thought it prudent to remove the mail, and gave us notice of the danger. We called a little fisher boat, which could hardly make up to us; while all the people on board us were crying to Heaven; and 'tis hard to imagine one's self in a scene of greater horror than on such an occasion; and yet, shall I own it to you? though I was not at all willing to be drowned, I could not forbear being entertained at the double distress of a fellow passenger, . . . an English lady I had met at Calais, who desired me to let her go over with me in my cabin. She had bought a fine point-head,[1] which she was contriving to conceal from the custom-house officers. When the wind grew high, and our little vessel cracked, she fell very heartily to her prayers, and thought wholly of her soul. When it seemed to abate, she returned to the worldly care of her head-dress, and addressed herself to me:

'Dear Madam, will you take care of this point? if it should be lost.—Ah, Lord, we shall all be lost! Lord have mercy on my soul!—Pray, madam, take care of this head-dress.'

[1] A lace head-dress.

This easy transition of her soul to her head-dress, and the alternate agonies that both gave her, made it hard to determine which she thought of greatest value. But, however, the scene was not so diverting but I was glad to get rid of it, and be thrown into the little boat, though with some hazard of breaking my neck.

It brought me safe hither; and I cannot help looking with partial eyes on my native land. That partiality was certainly given us by nature, to prevent rambling, the effect of an ambitious thirst after knowledge, which we are not formed to enjoy. All we get by it is a fruitless desire of mixing the different pleasures and conveniences which are given to different parts of the world, and cannot meet in any one of them.

After having read all that is to be found in the languages I am mistress of, and having decayed my sight by midnight studies I envy the peace of mind of a ruddy milkmaid, who, undisturbed hears the sermon with humility every Sunday. And, after having seen part of Asia, and Africa, and almost made the tour of Europe, I think the honest English squire more happy, who verily believes the Greek wines less delicious than March beer; that the African fruits have not so fine a flavour as golden pippins; and the becafiguas[1] of Italy are not so well tasted as a rump of beef; and that, in short, there is no perfect enjoyment of this life out of Old England. I pray God I may think so for the rest of my life; and, since I must be contented with our scanty allowance of daylight, that I may forget the enlivening sun of Constantinople.

[1] Small birds, a favourite table delicacy.

CHAPTER V

The Ranks of Society

There are seven groups in English society
1. The Great, who live profusely.
2. The Rich, who live very plentifully.
3. The middle Sort, who live well.
4. The working Trades, who labour hard, but feel no Want.
5. The Country People, Farmers, etc., who fare indifferently.
6. The Poor, that fare hard.
7. The Miserable, that really pinch and suffer Want.

(DANIEL DEFOE, *A Review of the State of the English Nation*, 1709)

I never see Lace and Embroidery upon the Back of a Beau but my Thoughts descend to the poor Fingers that have wrought it. . . . What would avail our large Estates and great Tracts of Land without their Labours.

(Letter to the *Northampton Mercury*, 1739)

How thankful, then, the poor should be that the very circumstances in which they are placed have such a powerful tendency to cherish the divine spirit of dependence and subordination.

(WILLIAM PALEY, *Reasons for Contentment*, 1781)

The crest of noble or illustrious ancestry, has sunk before the sudden accumulation of wealth in vulgar hands. . . . Elegance of manners . . . dignity of deportment . . . pride of virtue have given way to that tide of fortune, which has lifted the low, the illiterate and the unfeeling, into stations of which they were unworthy.

(HENRY MACKENZIE in *The Lounger*, 1786)

When *master* and *man* were the terms, every one was in his place, and all were free. Now, in fact, it is an affair of *masters* and *slaves*.

(WILLIAM COBBETT in *The Political Register*, 1821)

1. SOCIAL SURVEY

Defoe's classification, one of several which he made, may be compared with the deservedly celebrated classification of Gregory

King at the end of the seventeenth century and that of Patrick Colquhoun at the beginning of the nineteenth century. King's was the most complete social description made in pre-industrial Europe. In the middle of the eighteenth century Joseph Massie made an estimate of social structure and income for the year 1759–60.

Source: P. Mathias, 'The Social Structure in the Eighteenth Century: A Calculation of Joseph Massie' in the *Economic History Review* (1957).

Rank	Annual Income or Expenses per family £	Number of Families	Total Income £m
Temporal Lords	20,000	10	.2
Spiritual Lords	10,000	20	.2
Baronets	8,000	40	.32
Knights	6,000	80	.48
Esquires	4,000	160	.64
Gentlemen	2,000	320	.64
(These categories	800	800	.64
not distinguished	600	1,600	.96
individually in	400	3,200	1.28
relation to their	300	4,800	1.44
numbers or wealth)	200	6,400	1.28
Clergy, superior	100	2,000	.2
Clergy, inferior	50	9,000	.45
Persons professing the Law	100	12,000	1.2
Persons professing liberal Arts	60	18,000	1.08
Civil Officers	60	16,000	.96
Naval Officers	80	6,000	.48
Military Officers	100	2,000	.2
Common Soldiers	14	18,000	.252

Rank	Annual Income or Expenses per family £	Number of Families	Total Income £m
Freeholders	100	30,000	3.
,,	50	60,000	3.
,,	25	120,000	3.
Farmers	150	5,000	.75
,,	100	10,000	1.
,,	70	20,000	1.4
,,	40	120,000	4.8
Husbandmen (6s. per wk.)	15	200,000	3.
Labourers, country 5s.	12.5	200,000	2.5
,,　　London, 9s.	22.5	20,000	.45
Manufacturers of Wool Silk etc., country 7s. 6d. per week	18.75	100,000	1.875
Do.　in London, 10s. 6d.	26.25	14,000	.375
Manufacturers of Wood Iron, etc., country, 9s.	22.5	100,000	2.25
Do.　in London, 12s.	30	14,000	.42
Master Manufacturers	200	2,500	.5
,,　　　,,	100	5,000	.5
,,　　　,,	70	10,000	.7
,,　　　,,	40	62,500	2.5
Merchants	600	1,000	.6
,,	400	2,000	.8
,,	200	10,000	2.
Tradesmen	400	2,500	.5
,,	200	5,000	1.
,,	100	10,000	1.
,,	70	20,000	1.4
,,	40	125,000	5.

Rank	Annual Income or Expenses per family £	Number of Families	Total Income £m
Seamen, Fishermen	20	60,000	1.2
Inn-keepers, Alesellers	100	2,000	.2
Ale-sellers, Cottagers	20	20,000	.4

2. THE TRADITIONAL SOCIAL SYSTEM

Land was the basis of social and political power in eighteenth-century England (see above, p. 57), as it was in other parts of Europe, with the landed family rather than the individual acquiring independence and standing through the possession of land. Yet there were no legal barriers to the transfer of land from one social group to another, and merchants bought estates if and when they could acquire them through the restricted land market. The social system as a whole was based on strong and extensive family ties and on accepted conventions of hierarchy, with mutual obligations and many nuances and gradations of status, but contemporaries allowed scope for individual advancement and recognized that society as a whole was changing (not necessarily for the better) even before the advent of industry. An old 'order' was being subverted by movement from within.

(a) *Source:* B. R. Haydon, painter and diarist, *Autobiography* (1927 edn.), p. 6.

Both by my father's and mother's sides I am well descended and connected; the families always residing on their own landed property.

(b) *Source:* Adam Smith, *The Wealth of Nations* (1776), Book IV, ch. 9.

M. Quesnai [a French economist], who was himself a physician, and a very speculative physician, seems to have . . .

imagined that the political body would thrive and prosper only under a certain precise regimen, the exact regimen of perfect liberty and perfect justice. He seems not to have considered that, in the political body, the natural effort which every man is continually making to better his own condition is a principle of preservation capable of preventing and correcting, in many respects, the bad effects of a political economy, in some degree, both partial and oppressive. Such a political economy, though it no doubt retards more or less, is not always capable of stopping altogether the natural progress of a nation towards wealth and prosperity, and still less of making it go backwards.

(c) *Source:* Article by H. Fielding in *The Public Advertiser*, 11 Sept. 1760.

One known division of the people in this nation is into the nobility, the gentry and the commonalty. What alterations have happened among the two former of these I shall not at present inquire; but that the last, in their customs, manners, and habits are greatly changed from what they were, I think to make appear. If we look to the earliest ages, we shall find the condition of this third part to have been very low and mean. . . . The commonalty, by degree, shook off their vassalage, and became more and more independent of their superiors. . . . Nothing has wrought such an alteration in this order of people as the introduction of trade. This hath, indeed, given a new face to the whole nation, hath in a great measure subverted the former state of affairs, and hath almost totally changed the manners, customs and habits of the people, more especially of the lower sort. The narrowness of their fortune is changed into wealth; the simplicity of their manners into craft; their frugality into luxury; their humility into pride; and their subjection into equality. . . . Now to conceive that so great a change as this in the people should produce no change in the constitution is to discover, I think, as great ignorance as would appear in the physician who should assert that the whole state of the blood may be entirely altered from poor to rich, from cool to inflamed, without producing any alteration in the constitution of a man.

(d) *Source:* H. Fielding, *Enquiry into the Causes of the Late Increase of Robbers* (1751), p. 6.

Thus while the Nobleman will emulate the Grandeur of a Prince; and the Gentleman will aspire to the proper State of the Nobleman; the Tradesman steps from behind his Counter into the vacant Place of the Gentleman. Nor doth the Confusion end here: It reaches the very Dregs of the People.

(e) *Source:* J. Hanway, *A Journal of Eight Days' Journey* (1757), vol. II, p. 263.

It seems to be one of the defects of the least imperfect form of government which has been hitherto devised, I mean our own, that the different ranks of people are too much confounded: the lower classes, as I have had occasion to observe, press so hard on the heels of the higher, if some remedy is not speedily found, the *lord* will be in danger of becoming the *valet* of his gentleman. The noble who, through idleness, trusts his *money*, if not his *secrets*, with his *servants*, and consents to their *raising contributions* on *his friends*, must often see his *footman* with more money in his purse than himself; and I suppose 'tis the case sometimes, though not so often, with your handmaids.

(f) *Source:* R. Price, *Essay on the Population of England and Wales* (1777), p. 6.

The lower ranks of the people are altered in every respect for the worse, while tea, wheaten bread and other delicacies are necessaries which were formerly unknown to them.

3. 'THE GREAT'

At the apex of the social pyramid were the landed aristocracy. There was a steady accumulation of fortunes and estates in the hands of the eighteenth-century nobility. At the end of the century there were some 400 great landlords, Burke's 'great oaks that shade a country'. (For their estates, see above, p. 57 and below, p. 194. For their manners, see below, p. 244. For their political role, see below, p. 468.)

(a) *Source:* M. Misson, *Memoirs and Observations* (1719 edn.), pp. 193–201, 216–17.

That which is commonly called Nobility. . . . is view'd under different Ideas by the several Nations of the World. . . . An *English* Nobleman is one Thing, a *French* another, a *Venetian* another, and so on. . . . France which is pleas'd to be ignorant of what they do in other Countries . . . give it [the title of Noble] to all her Gentlemen in general. . . . The Word *Noble* in English is confin'd to a more narrow Signification than it is in French. . . . They call nobody a Nobleman that is not either Duke, or Marquess, or Earl or Viscount, or Baron: A Man cannot be call'd Noble without he has one of these Titles, and all that have them are Peers of the Kingdom, and Members of the Upper House of Parliament. . . . The Quality of Peer of *England* runs in the Blood of any Body that the King is pleased to honour with it; and this Quality is indivisible and unalienable. . . . A Peer enjoys his Dignity solely, and without a Partner; his eldest Son, or other Male Successor of his Blood, shall inherit it after him. . . . No Body in *England* has the title of Prince, but the Prince of *Wales*, and he himself must be created so by Letters Patents; the other Sons of *England* have the title of Dukes. . . . There are 19 Dukes, 3 Marquesses, 72 Earls, 8 Vicounts, and 68 Barons. . . . They have divers great Privileges, among which one of the principal is, that they cannot, without very great Difficulty be forc'd to pay their Debts.

(b) The system had many eloquent defenders before it was attacked by a minority of radical writers like Tom Paine late in the century. Social stratification as such was seldom called into question.

Source: J. Boswell, *London Journal, 1762–3* (1950 edn.), p. 320.

Sir, I would no more deprive a nobleman of his respect than of his money. I consider myself as acting a part in the great system, and do to others as I would have them do to me. Sir, I would behave to a nobleman as I would expect he should behave to me were I a nobleman and he Sam Johnson. Sir, there is one Mrs. Macauley in this town, a great republican. I came to her one day and said I was quite a convert to her republican system, and thought mankind all upon a footing; and I begged that her footman might be allowed to dine with me. She has never liked me since.

4. PRIMOGENITURE

The system of titles and estates passing to eldest sons is called Primogeniture. It was the basis of the English social system, although it had voluble critics in the late eighteenth century, like Adam Smith.

(a) *Source:* Adam Smith, *The Wealth of Nations* (Everyman edn.), vol. I, pp. 341ff.

The law of primogeniture [came into existence] for the same reason that it has generally taken place . . . in monarchies. That the power, and consequently the security of the monarchy, may not be weakened by division, it must descend entire to one of the children. . . . Laws frequently continue in force long after the circumstances which first gave occasion to them, and which could alone render them reasonable, are no more. In the present state of Europe, the proprietor of a single acre of land is as perfectly secure of his possession as the proprietor of a hundred thousand. The right of primogeniture, however, still continues to be respected, and as of all institutions, it is the fittest to support the pride of family distinctions, it is still likely to endure for many centuries. In every other respect, nothing can be more contrary to the real interest of a numerous family than a right which, in order to enrich one, beggars all the rest of the children. Entails are the natural consequences of the law of primogeniture. . . . They are founded upon the most absurd of all suppositions, the supposition that every successive generation of men have not an equal right to the earth, and to all that it possesses; but that the property of the present generation should be restrained and regulated according to the fancy of those who died perhaps five hundred years ago. . . .

Compare the present condition of [entailed] estates with the possessions of the small proprietors in their neighbourhood, and you will require no other argument to convince you how unfavourable such extensive property is to improvement.

(b) Younger sons were often placed in a precarious position, and some of them went into the professions, the Church, the Law or Medicine, or even, it was said, into trade. The basic point was to secure them a 'competence'. Others, however, did much better.

Source: Misson, *op cit.*, p. 3.

The difference is likewise great between the eldest Brother and the younger; the former not only succeeds to the Honour, but carries all the real and most of the personal Estate. It is therefore *one* thing to say, that a Lord has happen'd to put his younger Son to a Trade, and *another* thing to say, it is customary in *England*, for Lords to put their Children out to Trades.

(c) Family influence counted for most, perhaps, in relation to getting younger sons into the Church.

Source: R. L. Edgeworth, *Essays on Professional Education* (1812), p. 64.

Church benefices may . . . be considered a fund for the provision of the younger sons of our gentry and nobles; and in this point of view, it cannot surely be a matter of complaint to any of the higher and middle classes in the community, that the clergy enjoy a large portion of the riches of the state.

(d) While some writers held that primogeniture assisted social mobility by placing second, third and later sons in different walks of life, others pointed to general defects of the system.

Source: Anon., *Observations on the Number and Misery of the Poor* (1765), pp. 15–16.

Land is held in England by various tenures; founded on absurd principles and obsolete usages . . . the most general entailment being from eldest son to eldest son. . . . The *second son* cannot inherit unless the first die without issue, or his issue be extinct. The *third* cannot inherit, until such failure of the first and the second; and so through the whole collateral line, daughters excluded, who, poor girls, have no other dependence than the casual personal provision their father may have made for them; or an unportioned dependence on their lordly elder brother. . . . All these excluded children, from pride of families from which they derive little but the honour of claiming kindred with them; whatever their slender means may be, emulate the rank of the elder branch. This induces a general extravagance and taste for luxury, which from this source becomes universally contagious. This must be upheld; therefore fathers and brothers, that their children and relations may not

I

disgrace them by sinking from their own rank, nor hang upon them for subsistence; are eternally gaping for places and pensions for them, which are shamefully multiplied to answer these laudable ends.

5. MARRIAGE STRATEGY

Entail was one form of legal agreement which along with other types of family settlements, trusts and mortgages, made it possible for one family to hold land for long periods of time. 'New men' of wealth and power, therefore, might find it difficult to acquire landed estates on the land market. What could not be acquired on the land market might be acquired through the marriage market. The marriage system was essentially a property system. New families could enhance their standing through marriage with aristocratic families, while aristocratic families could replenish their fortunes. For example, the grand-daughter of Sir Josiah Childe, the enormously wealthy East India merchant, became Duchess of Bedford. 'Arranged marriages' involving elaborate property settlements, including dowries, jointures, portions and trusts, were common in the eighteenth century. They kept lawyers fully and lucratively employed, but some of the arrangements put families 'at the mercy of birth and death rates'. A rapid series of successions or a large number of children could alter family history.

(a) *Source:* Letter of 19 Jan. 1736, printed in J. W. F. Hill (ed.), *Banks Family Letters* (Lincolnshire Record Society, 1936), p. 176.

Mr. Jo. Banks I hear has made his proposall to Miss Cassia. Lady Wray tells it so, they will be in town in a fortnight. Ten thousand down he desires, and twenty more at his death, which I think will just fetch him. We do nothing but marry and stuf ourselves with the turkey diet.

(b) *Source:* Letter from Sarah, Duchess of Marlborough to her grand-daughter, the Duchess of Bedford, 29 June 1733, printed in G. Scott Thomson's, *Letters of a Grandmother* (1943), p. 89.

If you think my Lord Carteret's daughter an agreeable woman, as everybody says now she is, your brother John might easily have obtained her before they thought of my Lord Weymouth, and I believe considering his debts and charges upon his estate, your brother is not a much worse match in fortune; besides the great difference in the two men. But I never heard the least word in this lady's commendations till she was disposed of. Her father is certainly a mighty agreeable man, and has better parts than almost anybody. But they don't hinder him from loving money as much as anybody that ever I knew.

Whom your brother is destined for, I can't yet see. But if it were to an agreeable and valuable woman, I should never concern myself to have a great fortune with her. And at this time, though a younger brother, he has within some pounds three thousand pounds a year in hard money. And all but the thousand pounds a year, which is for joint lives, he can dispose of.

6. THE GENTRY

The lesser landed interest was known in England as the gentry, larger, less exclusive and more diverse in origins than the aristocracy. The dividing lines between it and other social groups were difficult to draw, and it was frequently refreshed by new recruits from outside. Closely associated with the conception of the gentry was the conception of 'the gentleman'. Some of the gentry were proud of their independence from the aristocracy. Yet 'independence' did not necessarily carry with it polish or dignity. Some 'squires' were rustic and uncultivated: others men of taste and fashion. Both types have made their way into literature. All members of the gentry were concerned about taxation, and most were drawn into local politics and administration. As justices of the peace, they were concerned with the management of local affairs as well as with the law, and so important was their role in this connection that the historian Maitland rightly pointed out that 'a history of the eighteenth century which does not place the justice of the peace in the very foreground of the picture will be a caricature'.

(a) *Source:* Le Blanc, *Letters on the English and French Nations* (1747), p. 279.

He [the country squire] is naturally a very dull animal; perhaps his food is the cause of it. He eats nothing but salt beef, cold mutton, cabbage, carrots and pudding; which last is his favourite dish; and that which is heaviest he likes best. His drink is ale, coarse Portuguese wines, and now and then a little of the strongest brandy. He drinks two favourite healths at his meals, which is perhaps the only rule that he observes; the first is to all honest fox hunters in Great Britain, protestant or catholic without exception; the title of hunter reconciles them all; the second bumper is confusion to the minister.

(b) *Source:* Anon., *A Letter to a Freeholder* (1732), pp. 33–4.

The Heads and Heirs of very ancient Families . . . are obliged to live up to the nominal Value of their Estates, often beyond it, merely to support their Credit and Figure in their Counties. They have Parks and Mansion Houses, and a great Resort of Friends and Neighbours to them; which continually drains their scanty Revenues. They are obliged to serve expensive unprofitable Offices, to be High Sheriffs, Justices of Peace, Commissioners of Taxes &c. to their very great Burthen and Grievance. And when their Children are grown up, and their younger Sons are to be settled in the World and their Daughters disposed of in Marriage, then, when their Necessities are greatest, they have least Ability to bear them; they go out of the World with all their Affairs in Confusion, and leave their First-Born to inherit an insupportable Mortgage.

(c) The following extract sets out a squire's own view of the arduous nature of his commitments.

Source: Letter of Lord Fermanagh to Ralph Verney, 8 Jan. 1713, printed in Lady Verney (ed.), *Verney Letters of the Eighteenth Century* (1930), vol. I, p. 291.

'Deare Ralph,—I have now 2 Tenants come to tell me, they will leave at Lady Day unless I will abate of the Rent, tho' the present Rents have been these 50 years and above. I am very glad Christmas is Ended, for we have had every day a vast number of people, but my servants say here were 400 people and I doe believe there were rather more last Tuesday, it has been a troublesome time; Every day with the noise of Either Drums, Trumpetts, Hautboys, Pipes or Fiddles, some days 400 Guests, very few under 100, that besides the vast expense it has been very tiresome. I wish all your family a happy New

Year. This last night a Fitt of the Gout tooke me in the Foot, which confines me to my Chaire for I can't goe about the room.

7. VILLAGE SOCIETY

Eighteenth-century landowners included not only peers and gentry but 'free-holders'. The pride of the group were the independent 'yeomen', though the term is imprecise and it is not easy to distinguish between owner-occupiers and tenant farmers, since many of the owner-occupiers also rented land. During the course of the century, as large estates were consolidated, the number of small owner-occupiers declined, and by 1790 it has been estimated that three-quarters or more of English land was managed by tenants rather than by owners. Enclosure (see below, p. 190) was not the only cause of the decline in the number of small owner-occupiers, although it received most public attention. Lowest in degree in rural society were the cottagers, the hired farm labourers and the squatters on the village waste. In each village there were also a number of village craftsmen, such as thatchers, shoemakers, and, most numerous, blacksmiths. It is very difficult to generalize about the social structure of villages in different parts of the country, and much depended on the presence or absence of a squire and if there was a squire, on his personal qualities. For further details of landed society, see G. E. Mingay, *English Landed Society in the Eighteenth Century* (1962).

(a) *Source:* C. Morris (ed.), *The Journeys of Celia Fiennes* (1947), pp. 137–7.

Celia Fiennes is describing a visit to the border country of Sussex and Kent just before the beginning of the eighteenth century.

Goodhurst [Goudhurst] stands on a great hill and is seen several miles . . . its a pretty large place, old timber houses, but the extent of the parish is neare ten mile, they are a sort of yeomanly Gentry, about 2 or 3 or 400£ a year and eate and drink well and live comfortably and hospitably; the old proverb was a Yeoman of Kent with one years Rent could buy out the Gentlemen of Wales . . . and a Lord of the North Country, his Estate was so much better.

(b) The tenant farmers, in the words of Oliver Goldsmith, were 'equal strangers to opulence and poverty'. All such judgements should be treated cautiously, particularly judgements of people of one social group on another.

Source: O. Goldsmith, *The Vicar of Wakefield* (1766), ch. IV.

As they had all the conveniences of life within themselves, they very seldom visited the towns or cities in search of superfluities. Remote from the polite, they still retained the primeval simplicity of manners; and frugal by habit, they scarcely knew that temperance was a virtue. They wrought with cheerfulness on days of labour, but observed festivals as intervals of idleness and pleasure. They kept up the Christmas carol, sent true love-knots on Valentine morning, ate pancakes on Shrovetide, showed their wit on the 1st of April, and religiously cracked nuts on Michaelmas eve.

(c) Much of the information about better-off people in the villages comes from inventories, records of the goods villagers left when they died. A study of 1,400 East Sussex inventories drawn up between 1705 and 1722 provides a good glimpse of social structure. 41% showed assets valued between £10 and £59 and the same percentage assets valued over £100. 12% fell between £60 and £100. A third of the persons leaving inventories were 'yeomen', farmers and husbandmen. Of the three hundred persons whose occupations lay outside farming there were 23 blacksmiths, 23 carpenters, 13 millers, 25 butchers and 5 victuallers. See E. M. Gardner, 'East Sussex Inventories' in *Sussex Notes and Queries* (1959). The following extracts from an inventory of 1734 relate to Thomas Brown of Rotherfield, East Sussex, a husbandman. The inventory is in the East Sussex Record Office.

Item: His Weareing Apparrel and Money in   £ s. d.
      Pockett   2 10 0

ITEM IN THE KITCHEN

Two Payer of Andirons Two Firepans one Payer
    of Tongs one Payer of Potthangers one Payer
    of Bellis Three Spitts Two Iron Candelsticks
    Two Iron Dripingpans one old Grigiron one
    Chopingknife one old Cleavour one old Clock
    one old Warming pan one Payer of Stylliards

one old Gunn Nyne Dishes of Pewter And A
Pewter Tanker Two old Tables and Fine Old
Joynd stools Fine old Chairs one Large Iron
Skillet And one Small Brass Skillet one Old
Iron kettle Three old Iron Porridgpotts one
Old Settle And One old Buntinghutch And
other Small Things 4 18 6

ITEM IN THE PARLOR £ s. d.
One Table and Form and one Old Cubbard 0 8 0

£ s. d.
ITEM IN THE CILLER
Fine Old Barrels Two Powderingtubbs One
Longe Keeller Two Old Stalders one Wood-
den Funnel and one Duz. of Glass Bottles 1 6 0

ITEM IN THE KITCHEN CHAMBER
One Featherbed and Bolster and Two Blanketts
and Steddle and Matt 2 10 0
One old Featherbed and Bolster one Pillow
And Two Blanketts and Steddle and Matt 1 17 6
One old Flockbed and Bolster and Two Blan-
ketts and Steddle and Matt and one old
Trunkelbed and Steddle and Matt and one
old Trunkelbed and Bolster And one Blankett
and Steddle 1 5 0
One Joynd Chest and Fine old Boarded Chestes
Two Old Trunks and one Old Box 0 11 0

ITEM IN THE PARLOR CHAMBER
One old Flockbed and Bolster one Coverlet
one Steddle and Matt and Curtains and
Vallents and Curtain Rods 1 1 0
Six Chairs one old Payer of Bellis and one Payer
of Andirons one Boarded Chest and One old
Table 0 15 0
One Payer of fine Sheets Nyne Payer of Course

Sheets Foure Tablecloaths and Two Pillow-
bears   3 6 0

ITEM FOR HUSBANDRY TACKLEN

For Two Old Waggens	5	5	0
For One Old Timbertugg	4	0	0
For Three Old Courts and One Old Plough	2	0	0
For One Old Oxharrow and Five Small Horsharrows and Three old Ploughs And One Whibbletree	2	18	0
For Six Yoakes Six Tyths and Two Chains And Foure Horsharnesses	2	3	0
For foure Corn Sincs and one Payer of old Swips and one Halfbushell and Three Shalls Foure Old Prongs and one old Spad and One Old Radsaddle	1	10	0
ITEM: Two Matthooks one Shovel and Three Old Spades and one Hoppitcher And one Ax and Two Old Hanbills and Two Payer of Hedging Gloves	0	10	0
ITEM: 13 Sacks And Two Old Mealebaggs And Two Old Waggenrops	1	5	0
ITEM: For Old Hoppoles	0	15	0
ITEM: For one Hundred of New Hopps	4	10	0
ITEM: For one Sack of Cloverfeede	2	8	0
ITEM: For Old Iron	0	5	0
ITEM: For Book Debts	8	12	6
ITEM: For Desparate Debts	4	15	0
ITEM: For Things out of Sight and Forgott	0	15	0

(d) The Sussex figures should be compared with figures from other parts of the country. Land ownership patterns varied also. In Wigston, a Leicestershire village, figures of land holdings show that by 1765 only 3 families in 10 owned or occupied any land. The following list excludes occupiers of less than 2 acres (another 40 occupiers). It demonstrates, however, that 37% of the acreage of the parish was being farmed in large farms of 200 acres or more.

Source: W. G. Hoskins, *The Midland Peasant* (1957), p. 218.

Occupier	Acreage	Occupier	Acreage
Oliver Fox	46	Patience Abbot	8
Mr. Buszard	4	Daniel Ward	6
William Freer	18	John Pawley	4
Mrs. Holms	8	Henry Johnson	8
Luis Russell	88	William Gibbons	66
Richard Pochin	112	William Richardson	4
Thomas Coltman	4	Widow Darker	4
Mrs. Russell	32	Thomas Langton	4
Wm. Goodrich	12	Thomas Hurst	4
Armston Pochin	128	Mr. Burgess	44
Samuel Davenport	83	Thomas Wilson	208
Tithe and glebe	–	Henry Branson	160
John Dand	2	Widow Langton	8
John Astill	8	Alban Aynge	14
Thomas Blockley	104	Widow Johnson	12
James Bingley	8	Joseph Johnson	10
Thomas Johnson	4	Thomas Goode	16
John Johnson	4	Thomas Horner	132
John Freer	200	Cornelius Darker	16
Simeon Brewin	88	John Phipps	8
Francis Johnson	4	Thomas Goodwin	28
Richard Abbot	4	George Boulter	16
Mr. Clarke	148	John Burdet	4
Mr. Ragg	44	Abram Hach	208
Robert White	4	Mr. Ragg	172
William Brewin	64	Joseph Langham	8
Sarah Simons	4	William Johnson	260
William Langton	6	Thomas Jackson	136
William Coltman	4	George Ross	117
Richard Coltman	20	John Cooper	8
William Blaksley	4	Richard Branson	4

(e) Catalogues do not provide the only evidence. Crabbe, the Suffolk poet, has painted a convincing picture of the yeoman turned gentleman farmer. Compare the picture in Oliver Goldsmith's *The Deserted Village* (1770), with its account of a traditional society undermined by 'agricultural improvers'.

Source: G. Crabbe, *The Village* (1783).

> Gwyn was a farmer, whom the farmers all,
> Who dwelt around, the *Gentleman,* would call;
> Whether in pure humility or pride,
> They only knew and they would not decide.
> Far different he from that dull plodding tribe,
> Whom it was his amusement to describe;
> Creatures no more enlivened than a clod,
> But treading still as their dull fathers trod;
> Who lived in times when not a man had seen
> Corn sown by drill, or threshed by a machine;
> He was of those whose skill assignes the prize
> For creatures fed in pen, or stall or sties;
> And who, in places where improvers meet,
> To fill the land with fatness had a seat;
> Who in large mansions live like petty Kings,
> And speak of farms but as amusing things
> Who plans encourage, and who journals keep
> And talk with lords about a breed of sheep.

(f) At the other end of the social scale were the cottagers and the squatters who often found life hard, were badly hit by enclosure (see below, p. 193), and formed a large substratum of rural poor. Some of them were hired as cowmen, haymakers, threshers and hedgers for bigger farmers (hirings were social occasions with their own rituals); others left for the towns; others were forced to subsist on the poor rate (see below, p. 163). During the early part of the century Defoe contrasted the rural labourer's lot with that of work-people in manufacturing areas. He called the agricultural counties 'unemployed counties'.

Source: D. Defoe, *A Plan of the English Commerce* (1728), pp. 89ff.

Where the poor are full of work they are never empty of wages; they eat while the others starve, and have a tolerable plenty; while in the unemployed counties it goes hard with them. And whence is all this? Look to the lands, and consequently to the estates of the gentry, the manufacturing counties are calculated for business, the unemployed for pleasure; the first are thronged with villages and great towns, the last with parks and great forests; the first are stored with people, the last with game. . . . The reason of the thing answers for itself; a poor labouring man that goes abroad to his day's work and husbandry, hedging, ditching, threshing, carting, etc., and brings home to his wife his week's wages, suppose at eightpence to twelvepence a day or in some counties less, if he has a wife and three or four children to feed, and get little or nothing for themselves, must fare hard and live poorly: 'tis easy to suppose it must be so.

(g) *Source:* David Davies, the Rector of Barkham, Bucks., *The Case of the Labourers in Husbandry Stated and Considered* (1795), p. 5.

In visiting the labouring families of my parish, as my duty led me, I could not but observe with concern their mean and distressed condition. I found them in general but indifferently fed; badly clothed; some children without shoes and stockings; very few put to school; and most families in debt to little shopkeepers. In short there was scarcely any appearance of comfort about their dwellings, except that the children looked tolerably healthy. Yet I could not impute the wretchedness I saw either to sloth or wastefulness. For I knew that the farmers were careful that the men should not want employment; and had they been given to drinking, I am sure I should have heard enough of it. And I commonly found the women, when not working in the fields, well occupied at home; seldom indeed earning money; but baking their bread, washing and mending their garments, and rocking the cradle.

(h) The growth of enclosure robbed the rural poor of many of their remaining rights (see below, p. 163).

Source: Letter from Henry Purefoy to W. Hughes, a London attorney, 26 Oct. 1746, printed in G. Eland (ed.), *Purefoy Letters* (1931), vol. I, pp. 4–5.

The poor people of Bidlesdon importune mee so strongly that I can't forbear writing to you to acquaint you that one Flowers of Bidlesdon detains from the Poor of the Parish 12 of their 14 Cows Commons, w.ch Arthur, Lord Grey of Wilton ab.t the year 1590 gave to seven ancient cottages of that parish, & to the Vicar of Bidlesdon hee gave a mare & colt and Bull common. The Vicar & poor folks occupiers of these 7 ancient cottages enjoyed these Commons ever since, till a few years ago M.ʳ Sayer pulled down 6 of the ancient cottages & erected 6 new ones in another place, & took 12 of the poor folk's commons from them, but was kind to them in other Respects in Lieu of it. Now when M.ʳ Sayer went beyond sea the poor people, having then no benefit from M.ʳ Sayer, had their Cows Commons again & sett all of them but two to ffflowers for 5s. a year apiece, for w.ᶜʰ ffflowers paid them for (sic) till a year due last Michas, w.ᶜʰ hee says hee will not pay unlesse yᵉ Law compells him to it. They are poor & not able to contest it at Law, & I hope it will be in your power to releive them, & fflowers to this day pays the Vicar for his mare & colt & bull common, & as the Vicars commons stand on the same foundation as to right & Title with the poor's Commons it is plain they have as good right to it as the Vicar, & as to the other Cows commons belonging to the House not pulled down M.ʳ Sayer never took them from that house, but they enjoyed them all along to this day without Interruption. I desire you will lay this before S.ʳ Robert Cotton in a proper light & your ffavour & assistance will be a great Charity for I think it a pity the Poor should be deprived of their Right only because they are poor, & that any Charity should be abused. Your good offices in this affair will be esteemed a signal favour to

Your unknown hle serv.ᵗ
H.P.

8. MERCHANTS

At the pinnacle of urban life were the great London merchants with interests scattered throughout the world. 'Our merchants are Princes', wrote Defoe, 'greater, richer and more powerful than some sovereign Princes.' Many of them aspired to become country gentlemen, and some succeeded. They were flattered by admirers who claimed that they were the true source of England's greatness. Mercantile wealth was associated not only with London, but in lesser degree with ports like Bristol and Liverpool. Throughout the provinces, however, there were lesser merchants, men of the 'middling sort', some of them with limited ambitions, all with limited fortunes.

(a) *Source:* E. Young, *The Merchant* (1725).

> Are there, then, men of lofty brow,
> Who think trade mean, and seem to bow
> So far beneath the state of noble birth?
> Alas these chiefs but little know
> Commerce how high, themselves so low:
> The sons of Nobles are the sons of Earth . . .
> Trade, Art's Mechanic, Nature's Stores
> Well weighs; to starry Science soars . . .
> Who studies Trade, he studies all.

(b) *Source:* R. Campbell, *The London Tradesman* (1747), pp. 284ff.

Commerce, the Sphere of the Merchant, extends itself to all the known World, and gives Life and Vigour to the whole Machine. . . . The Merchant draws his honest gain from the distant Poles, and every Shilling he returns more than he carried out, adds so much to the National Riches and Capital Stock of the Kingdom. Wherever he comes, wherever he lives, Wealth and Plenty follow him: the Poor is set to work, Manufactures flourish, Poverty is banished, and Public Credit increases. . . . Before we were a Trading People, we . . . lived in a kind of Penury . . . but we no sooner became a Trading People, than the Arts and Sciences began to revive, and polished us out of our rustic Simplicity and Ignorance. . . . The Trade of Britain may be divided into Inland and Foreign: Inland Trade is the transporting of the Commodities of one Part of the Kingdom to another, and especially to the grand Mart of Trade, the City of *London*. . . . The Foreign Merchant exports the Goods of the Growth or Manufacture of this Kingdom to the proper Markets, and imports the Commodities of other Countries in Exchange. The Merchants are distinguished one from another either by the Goods they traffic in, or by the Countries wherewith they have the greatest Correspondence; Thus a Merchant dealing in Tobacco is termed a Tobacco-Merchant, or a *Virginia* Merchant. . . . The best way then to distinguish the several Classes of Merchants is to take a View of our Imports and Exports. We export to *Jamaica* [for example], and the rest of the Sugar Colonies, all manner of Materials for Wearing Apparel, Household Furniture of all

Sorts, Cutlery and Haberdashery Wares, Watches, Jewels and Toys, *East-India* Goods of all sorts, some *French* wines, *English* Malt Liquor, Linen Cloths of the Growth of *Scotland, Ireland* and *Germany*, and our Ships generally touch in *Ireland*, and take in Provisions such as Beef, Pork, and Butter. The Returns from thence are Rums, Sugars, Cottons, Indigo, some fine Woods, such as Mahogany, Lignum Vitte, &c, and some Dying Woods, particularly Logwood. . . .

(c) Not everyone was so impressed by mercantile virtues.

The South Sea Bubble, which reached its climax in 1720, left a nasty taste. Legitimate trade and reckless speculation had been difficult to separate from each other.

Source: Poem in *The Weekly Journal or British Gazette*, 13 May 1721.

> Go on, vile Traders, glory in your Sins,
> And grow profusely Rich, by Wicked Means . . .
> Impoverish Thousands by some Publick Fraud,
> And worship Interest as your only God;
> Though you may gain in Time, a South Sea Coach,
> And ride through London, loaded with Reproach,
> Become a proud Director, and at last,
> Be bound to render what you got so fast;
> Perhaps be punish'd when your All is lost;
> With Gallows, Pillory or Whipping-Post,
> Or if you have your Gold, be doom'd to float,
> To Hell, in this infernal Ferry-boat.

(d) The traders were, of course, not the only people to blame. 'Never was such a time to get money as now', one society lady had written enthusiastically in 1720, when 'South Sea' was all the talk and fashion.

Source: Report in *Applebee's Journal*, 5 Aug. 1720.

Our South-Sea Equipages increase every day; the City-ladies buy South-Sea jewels; hire South-Sea Maids; and take new country South-Sea Houses; the Gentlemen set up South-Sea Coaches, and buy South-Sea Estates, but they neither examine the Situation, the Nature or Quality of the Soil, or Price of the Purchase.

(e) For a comment in retrospect, note the following extract from a speech in the House of Commons.

Source: Report in *The Gentleman's Magazine* (1733), vol. 3, pp. 673–4.

The many bad consequences of stock-jobbing are well-known, and it is high time to put an end to that infamous practice. It is a lottery, or rather a gaming-house, publicly set up in the middle of the city of London, in which the heads of our merchants and tradesmen are turned from getting a livelihood by the honest means of industry and frugality, and are enticed to become gamesters by the hope of getting an estate at once. It is not only a lottery, but one of the very worst sort, because it is always in the power of the principal managers to bestow the benefit tickets as they have a mind. The broker comes to the merchant and talks to him of the many fatigues and dangers, the great troubles and small profits that are in his way of trade; and after having done all he can to put him out of conceit with his business, which is often too easily affectuated, he proposes to dig for him in the rich mine of Exchange Alley, and to get more for him in a day than he could get by his trade in a twelvemonth. Thus the merchant is persuaded. He engages; he goes on for some time; but never knows what he is a doing, till he is quite undone.

(f) Until the last decades of the century the slave trade was one of the most successful 'legitimate' sources of income for the great merchants. It was described by Postlethwayt, for instance, as 'the first principle and foundation of all the rest, the mainspring of the machine which sets every wheel in motion'. West Indian planters were familiar figures in English eighteenth-century society. This is how one of them was briefly and conclusively described by a playwright.

Source: R. Cumberland, *The West Indian, A Comedy* (1775).

He's very rich, and that's sufficient. They say he has rum and sugar enough belonging to him, to make all the water in the Thames into punch.

(g) *Source:* J. Matthews, *A Voyage to Sierra-Leone on the Coast of Africa* (1791).

When the adventurer arrives upon the coast with a suitable cargo—which for this place consists of European and Indian cotton and linen goods, silk handkerchiefs, taffities, coarse blue and red woollen cloths, scarlet cloth in grain, coarse and fine hats, worsted caps, guns, powder, shot, sabres, lead bars, iron bars, pewter basons, copper kettles and pans, iron pots, hardware of various kinds, earthen and glass ware, hair and gilt leather trunks, beads of various kinds, silver and gold rings and ornaments, paper, coarse and fine check, and linen ruffled shirts and caps, British and foreign spirits and tobacco— he dispatches his boats properly equipped to the different rivers. On their arrival at the place of trade they immediately apply to the head man of the town, inform him of their business, and request his protection; desiring he will either be himself their landlord, or appoint a respectable person, who becomes security for the person and goods of the stranger, and also for the recovery of all money lent, provided it is done with his knowledge and approbation. This business finished, and proper presents made (for nothing is done without) they proceed to trade either by lending their goods to the natives, who carry them up into the country, or by waiting till trade is brought to them. The former is the most expeditious way, when they fall into good hands; but the latter is always the safest.

When the country people come down themselves to trade with the whites, they are obliged to apply to the inhabitants of the villages where the factories are kept, to serve as brokers and interpreters.

When a slave is brought to be sold he is first carefully examined, to see that there is no blemish or defect in him; if approved, you then agree upon the price at so many bars, and give the dealer so many flints or stones to count with; the goods are then delivered to him piece by piece, for which he returns so many stones for each, agreeably to their denominated value; and they always take care to begin with those articles which they judge most essentially necessary.

Exclusive of this method of dealing directly with the natives, transient ships, or those who only come for a small number, generally barter with the white traders resident on the coast, or with the factories established there, who take their whole cargo at once, and deliver them slaves, camwood, ivory, etc. according to their agreement, in a certain time.

From the great number of slaves which are annually exported, and which, from this place and the parts adjacent, including Sherbro' and the Riomoonas, amounts to about three thousand annually, one would be led to imagine the country would, in time, be depopulated; instead of which no diminution of their numbers is perceived; and, from every account we have been able to acquire from the natives themselves, who travel into the interior country, it is extraordinarily populous.

9. THE PROFESSIONS

Entry to the professions depended usually on family influence—examinations were usually perfunctory—but success depended on ability. The Master of the Rolls, Lord Kenyon (1732–1802), made £80,000 in 16 years through the practice of the law: Sir Henry Halford, the physician, earned an income of £10,000 a year for many years. (For doctors, see also below, pp. 458ff.) Such great men were to be distinguished from lesser professional folk, and they moved in the society of the great.

(a) William Hickey, whose memoirs are well-known, described how he became an attorney in 1775.

Source: William Hickey, *Memoirs* (1913 edn.), vol. I, pp. 331–2.

At the time appointed I attended, and in a terrible fright I was at the ordeal I imagined I had to pass through, and the probable loss I might be in at answering some of the many questions I understood would be put to me upon points of practice. Being conducted into his [the Judge's] parlour . . . in five minutes the Judge entered. We sat down, and he recommended his French rolls and muffins as of the best sort, but so predominant were my fears about the dreaded examination that I had no inclination to eat. Breakfast being over, he asked me how I liked the Law, how long I had been out of my clerkship, and two or three other questions equally unimportant, when a servant entered to announce the carriage being at the door, whereupon he desired his clerk to be called,

K

upon whose appearance he enquired whether Mr. Hickey's certificate was ready. The clerk having it and other papers in his hand, the Judge took it from him, and after perusal subscribed his name, and then said, 'Now, Mr. Hickey, if you will be so good as to accompany me to Westminster Hall, I will get you sworn, and the business concluded.' I accordingly stepped into his coach which conveyed us to Westminster. . . . The Judge ordered the oaths to be administered to me, after which, and my subscribing my name to each, I was entered upon the Roll as an attorney, and making a respectful bow to the Bench and the Bar, I retired, most agreeably relieved from my apprehensions respecting the various interrogatories I had expected would be put to me on the subject of my qualifications.

(b) Many writers treated professional men as parasites.

Source: H. Fielding, *Pasquin* (1736).

Religion, law, and physic, were designed
By Heaven the greatest blessing on mankind;
But priests, and lawyers, and physicians made
These general goods to each a private trade,
With each they rob, with each they fill their purses,
And turn our benefits into our curses.

(c) *Source:* G. Peacock, *Life of Thomas Young, M.D., F.R.S.* (1855), p. 216.

I was dining at the Duke of Richmond's one day last winter, and there came in two notes, one from Sir W. Farquhar, and the other from Dr. Hunter, in answer to an enquiry whether or no His Grace might venture to eat fruit pies or strawberries. I trembled for the honour of the profession, and could not conceal my apprehensions from the company; luckily, however, they agreed tolerably well, the only difference of opinion being on the subject of the pie crust.

(d) More humble provincial virtues are commemorated on many local tombstones.

Source: A Tablet in Hulme Church, described in J. Crabtree, *A Concise History of Halifax* (1836), pp. 123–4.

Near this place, in the grave of the late Richard Taylor,

Esq. are deposited the remains of JOSEPH HULME, M.D. who departed this life on the 2nd day of February, 1806, aged 92 years. He practised Physic in this town, with great success, about 63 years. To his patients he was very attentive and humane; to the poor, benevolent and charitable. He was ready in lending pecuniary assistance, to most who applied to him, but slow in calling in debts. He was a man of few words, yet affable and pleasant with his friends. From his medical abilities, his general knowledge, and gentle manners, he was much respected by all who knew him. He was a rare instance of temperance and sobriety, water being his common drink from his youth, and for many years he never tasted animal food. This strict regimen did not prevent his taking much exercise, and undergoing great fatigue: for he was almost daily on horse-back, over the neighbouring hills, in every season and in all weather. Though so far advanced in life, yet his hand continued steady, and his judgement clear, so that he died not of old age, but of an acute disease: and in the blessed hope that he should not dwell for ever with corruption.

10. DOMESTIC SERVANTS

There was a steadily increasing demand for domestic servants throughout the eighteenth century, with their conditions of employment varying immensely from household to household and within each household according to rank in an elaborate occupational hierarchy. The greatest landlords might employ as many as thirty to forty manservants, and even the gentry might have 'numerous establishments'. Lower down the social scale it was noted in Smollett's *Humphrey Clinker* (1771) how 'at present, every trader in any degree of credit, every broker and attorney, maintains a couple of footmen, a coachman, and a postillion'.

(a) *Source:* An Article in the *Westminster Journal*, reprinted in *The Gentleman's Magazine* (1745), pp. 544–5.

I have always thought of the great interest a nobleman, or gentleman of large estate, might always secure by only the proper choice of his *domestics*. Such a one cannot be without a great number of tenants, who might think their children honoured in the *service* of his lordship, and whose tenures would be a sort of *security* for the honesty and good behaviour of the servant.

(b) *Source:* An article in *The Gentleman's Magazine* (1743), p. 433.

When I see four or five able Fellows swinging behind a gilt Chariot, and reflect, that they have no other Business to do than what, perhaps, might be better undone; that they are . . . of so little Use to Society, that in the Course of their whole Lives not one of them adds a *Shilling* to the publick *Stock*, I am grieved to see *Englishmen* in such a Situation.

(c) *Source:* R. Dodsley, *Servitude* (1728), p. 18.

> NEXT, as we're Servants, Masters at our Hands
> Expect Obedience to all just Commands;
> Which, if we rightly think is but their Due,
> Nor more than we in Reason ought to do.
> Purchas'd by annual Wages, Cloaths and Meat,
> Theirs is our Time, our Hands, our Head, our Feet:
> We think, design and act at their Command,
> And, as their Pleasure varies, walk or stand;
> Whilst we receive the covenanted Hire,
> Active Obedience justly they require. . . .

(d) *Source:* Note on the recruitment of servants in the *Morning Post*, 20 June 1777.

Suppose . . . a man gets one hundred pounds a year by trade . . . and that he has four or five sons, is it in his power to make mechanics or tradesmen of them all? I will answer no;—the sums that must be given as apprentice fees with them would ruin him, was he to do it with more than one or two of them; the consequence is that he has no other resource than to make them servants, to get their living.

(e) The Steward was the most important servant. He controlled domestic staff and regulated household economy.

Source: G. Jacob, *The Country Gentleman's Vademecum* (1717), p. 45.

[It is the Steward's duty] to take and state all Accompts, receive and pay all Monies, buy in the Provision for the

Family, hire all Livery-men, buy all Liveries, pay all Wages, direct and keep in order all Livery-men (except the Coachman and Groom) to be at his Master's Elbow during Dinner, and receive all Orders from him relating to Government; to oversee and direct the Bailiff, Gardener, etc. in their Business; and also the Clerk of the Kitchen, Cook, Butler, etc. to whom he delivers the Provision, Wine, Beer, etc. who give him an Account of the spending it, Weekly or otherwise.

(f) Letter from John Ashburnham to his Steward, 19 Jan. 1705.

Source: East Sussex County Records Office, *Ashburnham Papers,* Letter Book, MSS. 846.

I shall now soone be with you in Bedfordshire, if God permitt and therefore doe admonish you to gett the house in order for my Reception, that is ayred and cleane. I shall bring downe with me two freinds besides my son Jack soe that accommodation must be found and the Beds extream drye and wholesome. I expect to find the gardens in good Condition in every particular and the fontaines perfected. . . . Remember about getting inn a sufficient stock of Oates and Beanes for the service of the stables as you did the last yeare and lett me find you loose noe time in this soe necessary a worke. I thinke you send upp but very few sparagrasse. lett me know your proceedings in all manner of businesse. your freind John Ashburnham.

(g) In large and medium-sized households testimonials for other servants usually passed through the Steward's hands.

Source: Letter from Blundell to Oldfield, 10 Dec. 1704, printed in *Blundell's Diary and Letter Book,* p. 26.

Honoured Sir,

Tho I have not the Honour to be Acquainted with you, yet I Presume to send these few Lines being your Stuard told me you were in want of a Chamber Maid. I am now Parting with mine. She is a Catholic and a brisk mettled Workwoman, gets up Linnen both fine and corse very well, rubs well and is a neat Cleanly Lass. I shall be glad to have your Speedy answer whether you will have her or noe, as if you will, please to let Her know what her Work must be and what Waiges.

I think she will expect something above 40s. If I can be provided at Christmass she will then be at liberty.

(h) Servants did not always find themselves in a position where they were seeking employment, as the following two extracts show.

Source: Letter quoted in Lady Mary Jennings, *A Kentish Country House, or the Records of Hall House, Hawkhurst* (1894), p. 73.

Sir, I shall take your warning from this day. . . . I see there is no such thing as pleasing you, I knew what business was before I came to you and more than what you have to do, and though I cant please you, I dont doubt but I shall please other people very well, I never had the uneasiness anywhere, as I have here, and I hope never shall again; for you are never easy [MS. torn] let one do never so much for you, and you can get Mrs. Buck or any body else as may do your work better for I will not stay with you, to be found fault with for nothing; when I am in fault, I desire to be told of it, but not to be told of other peoples, Betty is too good a servant for you, you never had a better, nor will have again, she understands business, better than you can teach her; and I expect to be paid for the half year I have been without cloaths. . . .

(i) *Source:* J. Mandeville, *The Fable of the Bees* (1723).

. . . A parcel of Footmen are arriv'd to that Height of Insolence as to have enter'd into a Society together, and made Laws by which they oblige themselves not to serve for less than such a Sum, nor carry Burdens or any Bundle or Parcel above a certain Weight, not exceeding Two or Three Pounds, with other Regulations directly opposite to the Interest of those they Serve, and altogether destructive to the Use they were design'd for. If any of them be turn'd away for strictly adhering to the Orders of this Honourable Corporation, he is taken care of till another Service is provided for him, and there is no Money wanting at any time to commence and maintain a Law-suit against any Master that shall pretend to strike or offer any other Injury to his Gentleman Footman, contrary to the Statutes of their Society.

(j) There was a sharp rise in servants' wages between 1763 and 1791 as the following Essex extract shows.

Source: Note in the Audley End Archives, printed in A. F. J. Brown, *English History from Essex Sources*, vol. II, p. 42.

	1763			1791		
	£	s.	d.	£	s.	d.
House Steward and Butler (Butler, 1763)	20.	0.	0	63.	0.	0
Game Keeper				59.	4.	0
Cook	12.	0.	0	50.	0.	0
Bailiff				50.	0.	0
Valet				30.	0.	0
Groom of Chambers				30.	0.	0
Coachman	21.	0.	0	26.	5.	0
House Keeper	16.	0.	0	25.	0.	0
Kitchen Gardener				25.	0.	0
Porter				21.	0.	0
Lady's Footman (Upper Footman, 1763)	10.	0.	0	18.	0.	0
2nd Coachman (Upper Postillion, 1763)	15.	0.	0	16.	16.	0
Groom	15.	0.	0	16.	0.	0
Under Butler	10.	0.	0	16.	0.	0
Lord's Footman (Upper Footman, 1763)	10.	0.	0	12.	7.	0
Lady's Woman	8.	0.	0	12.	0.	0
1st Laundry Maid				10.	10.	0
Kitchen Maid				10.	0.	0
Housemaid (Upper)	7.	0.	0	9.	9.	0
Do.				9.	9.	0
2nd Laundry Maid				9.	9.	0
Postillion	7.	0.	0	9.	9.	0
Houseboy	7.	0.	0	9.	9.	0
Dairy Maid				9.	0.	0
House Maid	5.	0.	0	8.	8.	0
Pantry Boy				8.	8.	0
House Maid	3.	0.	0	7.	0.	0
Stillroom Maid	3.	16.	0	7.	0.	0

(k) A special problem in domestic service is revealed in the following extract.

Source: Newspaper advertisement, quoted in M. D. George, *London Life in the Eighteenth Century* (1925), pp. 136–7.

Run away on Wed. the 28th ult., and stole money and goods from his master, John Lamb, Esq., an indentured black servant man about twenty-four years of age named William, of a brown or tawney complexion; had on when he went off, a parson's greay coat, blue breeches, white Bath flannel waistcoat, yellow gilt shoe buckles, and a beaver hat with a white lining.

Whoever apprehends him and brings him to his master at the Rookery House in Lewisham, Kent, shall have ten guineas reward and ten more on conviction in court of any persons harbouring or concealing him either on board ship or on shore.

N.B.—He is also the property of his master, and has a burnt mark L.E. on one of his shoulders (1770).

11. INDUSTRIALISTS

The word 'industry' was not used in its modern sense to denote a sector of economic life until the late eighteenth century. Industry was thought of as a human quality, not as a branch of business. Yet there was a growth of industrial activity in the eighteenth century preceding the spectacular developments of the 1780s (see below, pp. 203). Both the iron industry and the textiles industry saw significant new developments: the latter in particular—with its overseas connections—was the nursery of inventions. Fortunes could be made not only out of enterprise, but out of the exploitation of mineral rights.

(a) Old forms of industrial organization survived into the eighteenth century. For example, a company of framework knitters founded in 1657 continued to regulate the trade until the middle of the eighteenth century. Its code of regulations was re-drafted in 1745.

Source: W. Felkin, *A History of the Machine-Wrought Hosiery and Lace Manufactures* (1867), pp. 75–8.

1. The court of assistants shall yearly, on Midsummer day, choose out of the assistants, one master and two wardens.

2. And at the same time choose three persons to audit the master and wardens' accounts. . . .

3. The master and wardens shall, within one week, be sworn into their offices.

4. The court shall as often as they think fit, admit such members as are free of the city and of the livery, to be assistants; upon refusing to serve, to forfeit £10.

5. And may admit into the livery, so many of the members of the company as they may think fit. . . .

6. The court may elect two or more members to be their deputies, to rule and govern all persons exercising the trade of framework-knitting, according to the powers of the charter, within such district as may be assigned them apart from their habitations.

7. The court may elect yearly, on the second Tuesday in April, two members as stewards, within forty miles of London, who shall provide a dinner on Midsummer day, for the master, wardens and assistants, at their own charge, or forfeit £6; such dinner not to exceed the value of £12. . . .

8. The court may choose a clerk. . . .

9. The company shall have a chest with three locks for the custody of their treasure; the keys of which shall be kept by the master and two wardens.

10. Four quarterly courts shall be held every year, for every member that will attend, to hear the ordinances read. . . . Every member neglecting to appear, to forfeit for the first offence 1s., the second 2s., and for every other default 5s.

11. It shall be lawful for the master and wardens, or any two of them, with two or more assistants, and also for their sworn deputies, four times in every year or oftener, in the presence of a constable, to enter into shops, etc. to view, search, and prove all framework-knitted goods, frames, etc., and if found defective, to seize the same, and produce them at their hall of meeting on their next court day; to be fined at the discretion of the court, not exceeding 10s. Every person obstructing the master, etc. to be fined £5. The master on searching any house may demand 4d; any person refusing to pay, to forfeit 3s. 4d.

12. No member to hire frames, but of such as are members, on pain of paying 1s. per week for every frame.

13. No member shall teach and instruct any person in the art of frame-work-knitting, other than his male child, or children or apprentices, unless bound according to the ordinances of the company, upon forfeiture of £50 for every offence.

14. No member shall retain an apprentice until, for trial of his skill, he shall have wrought in the presence of the master and wardens, or some persons appointed by them, a pair of silk stockings, and upon finishing thereof, if approved, he shall be allowed as a work-house keeper, upon pain of forfeiting £5.

15. No person shall exercise the trade of frame-work-knitting, unless he shall have served seven years' apprenticeship, and shall first be admitted a member of the company; and neglecting to be a member for three months, to forfeit 30s. for every neglect.

16. No person shall employ an alien or foreigner, under penalty of £10 for every offence.

17. Every member residing within forty miles of London, who shall be minded to take an apprentice, shall present him within one month at the hall; or, if at a greater distance, to the deputies to be bound by the clerk of the company, on pain of forfeiting 40s. Any member, free of the City of London, who shall cause an intended apprentice to be bound to a freeman of any other company, shall forfeit £5.

18. No member shall turn over his apprentice, without license of the master and wardens, on pain of forfeiting 40s. for every offence.

19. No journeyman shall depart his service, without a month's warning, except for non-payment of wages, or by mutual agreement; and no master shall turn away such journeyman, without the like warning, and paying him what shall be due to him, under a penalty of £5.

20. No journeyman shall work with any, but such as are members of the company, under a penalty of 20s.

21. No master shall set any person on work but such as are members, except his male children or apprentices, under a penalty of £5. . . .

22. The master and wardens, or any person appointed by them, shall receive of every member using the trade as a master, 6d. per quarter; and from every journeyman 3d. per

quarter. Every member refusing to pay the same when demanded, to forfeit 6s. 8d.

23. Every member shall contribute proportionably to the necessary expences of the company, upon pain of paying double what he shall be rated at for that purpose.

24. Every member free of the City of London, who shall neglect to enrol his apprentices before the chamberlain, within one year after the binding, shall pay 20s.

25. Widows, on being admitted members, may exercise the trade during widowhood.

26. The court of assistants may moderate, or wholly remit, any penalties, provided such persons pay such sum, without suit at law.

27. All fines and penalties to be sued for in the name of the company, by action of debt, in any of His Majesty's Courts of Record.

The following are fees paid to the company:

Admittance 10s., clerk 2s. beadle 1s. stamp 2s. total 15s.

Apprentice bound 3s. stamp 3s., clerk 2s., beadle 1s., total 9s.

Work-house keeper's proof piece 3s., clerk 2s., beadle 1s., total 6s.

Apprentice turned over, 3s. 6d.

(b) This kind of corporate organization gave way in the eighteenth century to greater business individualism. A new kind of business enterprise was represented by Abraham Darby, who discovered how to smelt iron ore with coke instead of charcoal.

Source: A letter written by Mrs. Abiah Darby (*c.* 1775) and reprinted in A. Raistrick, *Dynasty of Ironfounders* (1953), pp. 38–9.

It was my Husband's Father, whose name he bore (Abraham Darby who was the first that set on foot the Brass Works at or near Bristol) that attempted to mould and cast Iron pots &c., in sand instead of Loam (as they were wont to do, which made it a tedious and more expensive process) in which he succeeded. This first attempt was tryed at an Air Furnace in Bristol. About the year 1709 he came into Shropshire to Coalbrookdale, and with other partners took a lease of the works, which only consisted of an Old Blast Furnace and some

Forges. He here cast Iron Goods in sand out of the Blast Furnace that blow'd with wood charcoal; for it was not yet thought of to blow with Pit Coal. Sometime after he suggested the thought, that it might be practable to smelt the Iron from the ore in the Blast Furnace with Pit Coal; Upon this he first try'd with raw coal as it came out of the Mines, but it did not answer. He not discouraged, had the coal coak'd into Cynder, as is done for drying Malt, and it then succeeded to his satisfaction. But he found that only one sort of pit Coal would suit best for the purpose of making good Iron—These were beneficial discoveries, for the moulding and casting in sand instead of Loam was of great service, both in respect to expence and expedition. And if we may compare little things with great —as the invention of printing was to writing, so was the moulding and casting in sand to that of Loam. He then erected another Blast Furnace, and enlarged the Works. The discovery soon got abroad and became of great utility.

(c) New industrialists came from many different sections of society—small tradesmen and mechanics, yeomen and even Oxford dons, as the following extracts show.

Source: Letter of Thomas Ridgeway to the son of Richard Arkwright, the great textile entrepreneur (1799), printed in R. S. Fitton and A. P. Wadsworth (eds.), *The Strutts and the Arkwrights* (1958), pp. 61–2. Arkwright's business power also depended on the holding of strategic patents.

My first knowledge of your Father, was about the year 1750 when he came to reside in Bolton and was I think then about the Age of 18. He entred into the employment of one Edward Pollit, A peruke maker there, on whose death he remained with his widow for Sometime—He then married your Mother, and began business for himself; which he pursued with most indefatigable industry and with some success. He might now be considered in a comfortable situation; he had a decent House, a cleaner one could not be and his friends and acquaintance always found in it a cordial reception from him. These were persons of no mean consideration in the town, but such as were in Superior Stations to himself. To these he recommended himself by his character for neatness, sobriety,

industry, and good Sense. The Latter part of his time at
Bolton was not so pleasant as it had been. He became necessitous in consequence of taking a public house, which did not
answer his purpose and upon which he expended much money
in alterations. He was obliged to leave the house and had a
many interruptions caused by an inveterate asthma, which
brought him very low in every sense of the word. Notwithstanding this, I believe there was only one Person to whom
he owed Money, when he left the town, and his credit [was]
otherwise good. His customers that had employed him in his
business were generally of the better sort, he might probably
have done better could he have Stooped to the vulgar, but
his spirit was much superior to it, And always seemed to have
something better in view. His genius for Mechanics was
observed, it was perceived in his common conversation, which
often turned on subjects of that kind. I well remember we had
often great fun with a Clock he put up in his shop, which had
all the appearance of being worked by the smoke of the chimney
and we have caused a many to believe it was so; I have often
seen him cut pasteboard into different shapes such as forming
squares from oblongs without adding or diminishing, and a
Hundred curious knackey things that one cannot find words
to explain. He was always thought clever in his peruke making
business and very capital in Bleeding & toothdrawing and
allowed by all his acquaintance to be a very ingenious man.

(d) *Source:* Letter from S. Salte to Samuel Oldknow, 5 Nov. 1787,
printed in G. Unwin, A. Hulme and G. Taylor, *Samuel Oldknow
and the Arkwrights* (1924), pp. 99–100. Oldknow was a master
spinner and Salte his London agent. Cartwright invented a power
loom.

. . . It often happens both Hope and Expectation meet with
cheats like common Mortals in their passage through Life.
Mr Cartwright was once Professor of Poetry at Oxford &
really was a good Poet himself. But it seems he has left the
Barren Mountain of Parnassus & the fountain of Helicon, for
other mountains & other Vales & Streams in Yorkshire &
he has left them to work in the Wild large & open Field of
Mechanics—be it so, and may his schemes prosper & fill his

purse with Gold. You say not a word about the probability of success, likely to attend his weaving Invention. Can this new Automaton perform the wonders in weaving so Confidently & so flatteringly held out to the World. . . .? Mr. Arkwright was a happy Mechanic. In his Life time he has received the reward of his Ingenuity—It does not happen so in general. We think Mr Cartwright will not be equally fortunate.

(e) Salte gave good advice to Oldknow about the best way to organize his enterprise.

Source: Letter of 1 Dec. 1786, printed in *ibid.*, p. 83.

How true it is, I know not, but there is an old proverb, that Fortune favors the Bold—This I know, that she generally favors the prudent & the wise. I think in your declining the late Conexion, you will in your own mind be much happier, independence is seated there, & not in the regions of fancy & imagination. . . . I apprehend Mr A[rkwright] to be what he has proved a Gentleman & I think he will assist you at any time in the pecuniary way. But pray above all do not involve yourself in too many Schemes, & too much business—it will defeat the very purpose you was born for, to live happy, & become independent. Drop the Chk Trade, & all the branches that a common Manufacturer can do better. Keep & confine yourself to the improvement of Muslins particularly. You will have rivals enough to contend with—& your Work must be superior.

(f) British manufacturers often prided themselves on the fact that their goods were sold not only to the rich but to a cross-section of society. They took pride also in salesmanship.

Source: Dean Tucker, *Instructions for Travellers* (1758), printed in R. L. Schuyler (ed.), *Josiah Tucker, A Selection from his Economic and Political Writings* (1931), pp. 245ff.

Q. Are the Men of England, those especially in the Toy, Jewellery, Cabinet, Furniture and Silk Trades chiefly adapted for high or middling Life and what Species of People make up the Bulk of the Customers?

A. England, being a free Country, where Riches got by

Trade are no Disgrace, and where Property is also safe against the Prerogative either of Princes or Nobles, and where every Person may make what Display he pleases of his Wealth . . . the Manufacturers of the Kingdom accommodate themselves, if I may so speak, to the Constitution of it: That is they are more adapted to the Demands of Peasants and Mechanics . . . for Farmers, Freeholders, Tradesmen and Manufacturers in middling Life and for Wholesale Dealers, Merchants, and all Persons of Landed Estates, to appear in genteel Life; than for the Magnificence of Palaces, or the Cabinets of Prices. Thus that is, according to the very Spirit of our Constitution, that the *English* of these several Denominations have better Conveniences in their Houses, and appear to have more in Quantity of clean neat Furniture, and a greater Variety (such as Carpets, Screens, Window Curtains. . . . Bells polished Brass Locks, Fenders etc. Things hardly known among Persons abroad of such a Rank) than in any other Country in Europe, Holland excepted.

(g) The manufacturers had other responsibilities: these were well described by Robert Owen, who was to establish his reputation as the founder of co-operative socialism. He began work as a manufacturer in Manchester in 1791. Later he moved to New Lanark.

Source: R. Owen, *Life* (1857), p. 36.

When I arrived at the mill . . . I found myself at once in the midst of five hundred men women and children who were busily occupied with machinery much of which I had scarcely seen. . . . I had to purchase the raw material—to make the machines, for the mill was not nearly filled with machinery—to manufacture the cotton into yarn—to sell it—and to keep the accounts—pay the wages—and in fact to take the whole responsibility for the first fine cotton spinning establishment by machinery that had ever been erected. . . . I looked grave—inspected everything very minutely—examined the drawings and calculations of the machinery. . . . I continued this silent inspection and superintendence day by day for six weeks saying merely yes or no to the questions of what was to be done or otherwise. . . . But by the end of that time I felt . . . ready to give directions in every department.

(h) By the 1780s and 1790s the number of manufacturers had greatly increased (see below, pp. 203ff.) and Josiah Wedgwood and others were anxious that they should co-operate together and bring pressure to bear upon the government. The General Chamber of Manufacturers was set up in 1785.

Source: Sketch of a Plan of the General Chamber of Manufacturers of Great Britain in the Wedgwood Archives.

The Manufacturers of Great Britain constitute a very large, if not a principal part of the community; and their industry, ingenuity and wealth, have contributed no small share towards raising this kingdom to the distinguished and envied rank which she bears amongst the European nations. But their importance to the state, and the relation which they bear to the rest of the community, have been perhaps misunderstood by some, who have considered them as a mere source of revenue, and by others, who have deemed them to be of little, if any advantage to the nation at large; neither has their importance to each other made an impression strong enough to induce them hitherto to act in concert, and there by to obtain that assistance, of which their respective situations have often stood in need, and which nothing but united counsels and exertions can afford. . . . Common danger having at length brought together a number of Manufacturers in various branches, and from various places, and these having felt the advantages resulting to each other from unreserved conferences, and mutual assistance, they are now persuaded, that the prosperity of the Manufacturers of this kingdom, and of course that of the kingdom itself, will be promoted by the formation of a general bond of union, whereby the influence and experience of the whole being collected at one common centre, they will be the better enabled to effect any useful purpose.

12. CRAFTSMEN, MECHANICS AND LABOURERS

Before the development of the factory system, there were many gradations among craftsmen and artisans. Working standards were established through apprenticeship and maintained by regulation. Yet 'domestic workers' in home industry were subject to many problems, including great hardship in lean years and 'incessant toil' when times were good. The factory system produced a new kind of labour force and ultimately a new brand of working-class consciousness. (See below, p. 500.)

(a) *Source:* Adam Smith, *The Wealth of Nations* (1776), Book I, ch. X.

The wages of labour vary with the ease of hardship, the cleanliness or dirtiness, the honourableness or dishonourableness of the employment. Thus in most places, take the year round, a journeyman tailor earns less than a journeyman weaver. His work is not always easier, but it is much cleaner. A journeyman blacksmith, though an artificer, seldom earns so much in twelve hours as a collier, who is only a labourer, does in eight. . . . Secondly, the wages of labour vary with the easiness and cheapness, or the difficulty and expense of learning the business. When any expensive machine is erected, the extraordinary work to be performed by it before it is worn out, it must be expected, will replace the capital laid out upon it. . . . A man educated at the expense of much labour and time to any of these employments which require extraordinary dexterity and skill, may be compared to one of those expensive machines. . . .

(b) Skilled labourers were anxious to protect their skills, and apprenticeship ceremonies were often highly ritualistic.

Source: Note in *The Craftsman*, 24 May 1740, quoted in A. E. Musson, *The Typographical Association* (1954), p. 12.

When a Boy is to be bound Apprentice, before he is admitted a Chappellonian, it is necessary for him to be made a Cuz, or Deacon; in the Performance of which there are a great many Ceremonies. The Chappellonians walk three Times round the Room, their right Arms being put thro' the Lappets of their Coats; the Boy who is to be made a Cuz carrying a wooden Sword before them. Then the Boy kneels and the Father of the Chapel, after exhorting him to be observant of his Business, and not to betray the Secrets of the Workmen, squeezes a Spunge of strong Beer over his Head, and gives him a Title, which is generally that of some Duke of some Place of the least Reputation near which he lives or did live before. . . . Whilst the

L

Boy is upon his Knees, all the Chappellonians, with their right arms put through the Lappets of their Coats, as before, walk round him, singing the Cuz's Anthem, which is done by adding all the Vowels to the Consonants in the following Manner.

Ba-ba; Be-be; Bi-bi; Ba-be-bi; Bo-bo; Ba-be-bi-bo; Bu-bu; Ba-be-bi-bo-bu-

And so through the rest of the Consonants.

(c) Attempts were also made to protect skilled wages. Colchester weavers, for example, asked Essex Quarter Sessions in 1749 to lay down wage rates.

Source: Essex Quarter Sessions Bundle (1749) in the Essex County Record Office, printed in Brown (ed.), *English History From Essex Sources,* vol. II, p. 5.

And your petitioners further shew unto your Worships that from the reign of Queen Elizabeth the woollen manufacture hath been largely carried on in the town of Colchester and many thousands of families creditably maintained thereby, and from that motive your petitioners have been induced to bring, teach and instruct their wives [and] children to employ their lifetime in weaving, spinning, combing, carding, beating and the several other branches necessary to that manufacture, so that at present there are by computation more than 3000 hands employed therein who are not able, on account of their habitual sedentary way of life, to maintain themselves or get their bread in any other way of business. That within these 20 years last past, by the death of several eminent baymakers and their policy in not taking of apprentices, the trade of baymaking is come into [the] hands of a few who . . . have by degrees so reduced our wages that we are not able to support ourselves and families with the wages they give us. And they have in that interval acquired to themselves large fortunes.

That your petitioners humbly conceive that the aforesaid pretences and suggestions for lowering our wages ought to carry no weight, the same, or rather more, labour being required now than when they paid 15s. 6d per bay. Besides whatever the maker pays his workmen, he makes the Spaniard, the consumer, repay him double, and the lowering our wages is an additional profit to him only. For the Spaniard must have the sort of bay and no place but Colchester can furnish them with merchandise so good of the sort.

(e) The following Colchester weaver's inventory of 1744 should be compared with the rural inventories printed above (pp. 126–8).

Source: St. Nicholas, Colchester, Overseers' Accounts, printed in *ibid.*, p. 7.

An Invatory of Eliz. Finch's Goods Remov'd into the Workhouse Two Bedsteads 2 Beds 1 pair of Curtains 7 Sheets 3 Blanketts 2 Coverlids 4 pillows 4 pair of Cases 2 Bolsters 2 Pair of Drawers 3 Tables 1 Copper Saucepan and Cover 1 small Boyler 1 Iron pot 1 Iron Kettle 2 Box Irons and heaters 2 Iron Candlesticks 1 Looking Glass 3 Jugs 1 pair Bellows 12 pictures 3 glass Ditto 1 pair Tongs Sifter poker and Fender 1 Frying pan 2 Chamber pots 1 Iron Tramell 3 Basketts 2 Earthern pots 1 Wash tub 1 pail 2 Bowl dishes 9 Glass Bottles 3 Dishes 16 plates 9 Basons 4 Tea pots 16 Cups and Saucers 2 Silver Spoons 3 Quart pots 1 Trunk 1 Sweeping Brush 3 pewter Measures half pint Quar^r D^o and ½ quar^r Ditto 1 Bird Cage 14 Gallon Cask 1 Bay Loom Quill wheel pedon Block and Blades.

(f) As the century went by, statutory regulation of wages and hours of labour became exceptional, and bargaining procedures sometimes took over. As late as 1770, however, an act was passed to fix the wages of London coal-heavers. Workers continued to ask for such protection in many parts of the country, and there was also bitter criticism of 'truck'-wages being paid not in cash but in kind.

Source: Charles Peard, *The Woollen Labourer's Advocate* (1733), pp. 3–6.

. . . The Masters of the Woollen Manufactory of the Western Parts of this Kingdom . . . not only [reduce] their Labourers poor diminutive Wages by Abatements, but in compelling them by their Necessities to accept of their Woollen Manufactories as Money for their Labour: that when sold, they receive but half their Charges for them; and not only Woollen, but Linnen, &c., and some Masters impose upon their Servants all manner of Hucstery Wares, which they esteem as Cash;

others obtrude Malt of a very bad Quality upon their Labourers at the Price of the best, and yet accounted as ready Money.

There are others of these Masters who purchase Houses, when the Overtures of a cheap Bargain presents, and lets them to their Servants at a hard Rent. Others again impower their Labourers with Tickets of Credit, their Value to be received in Liquor, from such Publick-Houses as they supply with Malt; and what Payments they make with Cash is generally in Gold, which their Servants exchange for Silver at such Publick-Houses . . . and each of them are obliged to spend the Value of a pint of Liquor for drawing the Money, which is often a Snare to further expences; And in the Season of the Year some Masters oblige their servants to make their Hay, without a recompence; and some sell their cast-off Cloathes to their Servants at very exorbitant Prices.

(g) Journeymen and masters were often at loggerheads with each other, and journeymen 'combined' together separately from their employers. In 1721 the London master tailors petitioned Parliament against their journeymen.

Source: The outline of the petition is printed in H. Pelling, *A History of British Trade Unionism* (1963), p. 12.

To the number of seven thousand [they had] lately entered into a combination to raise their wages and leave off working an hour sooner than they used to do; and for the better carrying on their design have subscribed their respective names in books prepared for that purpose, at the several houses of call or resort (being publick houses in and around London and Westminster) where they use and collect several considerable sums of money to defend any prosecutions against them.

(h) For an example of strike activity in the West country in 1776, the following account of evidence given to a House of Commons Committee is revealing.

Source: Journal of the House of Commons, vol. XX, pp. 647–8.

Mr. *John Vowler* . . . said, That the Weavers have many Clubs in several Places in the West of *England*, particularly at *Exeter*, where they make Bye-laws; some of which he has seen; which Bye-laws are, among divers other things, to

appoint Places of Meeting, fix their Officers, make Allowances
to travelling Workmen and to ascertain their Wages:

That several Weavers have brought home their Work, and
durst not go on to serve their Masters, for fear of other Weavers
of the Club, who have deterred them therefrom: And he
believes, one of the Occasions of the late Riots, that have
happened, has been, that the Masters have refused to raise
the Workmen's Wages to what Price they pleased:

That he was present at a great Mob in the Town of *Crediton*,
in *Devonshire*, consisting of Weavers, and others concerned in
the Woollen Manufacture; who were headed by a Captain,
who threatened their Masters, if they refused to raise their
Wages; and carried about with them a Chain of Serge cut off
from a Loom; and declaring they would do the like to the
Pieces of Serge of the other Masters, who refused to comply
with their Demands: That, when the Constables had seized
some of the Ringleaders, and brought them before Two Justices
of Peace, the Mob beset the House, insulted the Justices,
threw Stones at them, and forced them to fly, and rescued the
Prisoners: That at *Callington*, on another Riot, he has seen
a Master carried about on a Coolstaff, for refusing to comply
with their Demands; and that others have been threatened with
the like Usage:

That most of the Masters do pay their Workmen in Money;
but some of them do pay by way of Truck; which is not so
satisfactory; however, he believes, the Masters would all
willingly be obliged to pay the Whole in Money.

Mr. *William Pike* said, That he has seen the Weavers at
their Clubs, where none but Weavers are admitted; and that
they have their Ensigns and Flags hung out at the Door of
their Meetings:

That they go about, in Parties, to Looms; and demand
Twelve Pence, or some other Sum of Money, towards supporting such of their own Gangs as are now in Prison; and has
seen several Looms cut within these Eight Months past, and
the Work carried away for the Non-payment of the Money,
and because some would work cheaper than others; and that
Pieces of Serge are frequently cut on the Racks:

That the Weavers complain of paying them in Truck; but

believes, that is not the Cause of their Riots; for that they generally begin in the Spring, when there is the greatest Demand for Goods, and most Plenty of Work:

That his own Weavers would willingly have worked for him at the Wages he gave; but that the Club threatened, if they did so, to pull them out of the House, and coolstaff them; upon which, he was forced to pay them the Price demanded, to save his Work from being cut; and has known several that have been coolstaffed:

That he is willing to pay his Workmen in Money; and, believes, all the other Masters would willingly be obliged to do the same.

(i) With the development of new inventions and the application to the textiles industry of water power and 'mill' production, advertisements for workers of the following kind began to appear in local papers.

Source: Derby Mercury, 13 Dec. 1771.

Cotton Mill, Cromford, 10th Dec. 1771.

WANTED   immediately, two Journeymen Clock-Makers, or others that understands Tooth and Pinion well: Also a Smith that can forge and file.—Likewise two Wood Turners that have been accustomed to Wheel-making, Spole-turning, &c. Weavers residing at the Mill, may have good Work. There is Employment at the above Place, for Women, Children, &c. and good Wages.

N.B. A Quantity of Box Wood is wanted: Any Persons whom the above may suit, will be treated with by Messrs. Arkwright and Co. at the Mill, or Mr. Strutt, in Derby.

(j) Much was made of the improved conditions in some of the factories. There was, of course, a quite different side to the picture (for factory discipline, see above, pp. 50ff.: for later conditions in factories, see below, pp. 207ff.).

Source: A Ballad sung at the Cromford mill and printed in R. S. Fitton and A. P. Wadsworth, *The Strutts and the Arkwrights*, p. 100.

Tune: Roast Beef of Old England
Ye num'rous Assembly that make up this Throng,
Spare your Mirth for a Moment, and list to my Song,

The Bounties let's sing, that our Master belong,
At the Cotton Mills now at Cromford,
The famous renown'd Cotton Mills.

Our number we count seven Hundred or more,
All cloathed and fed from his bountiful Store,
Then Envy don't flout us, nor say any's poor, &c.

Ye know we all ranged in Order have been,
Such a Sight in all Europe sure never was seen,
While Thousands did view us to complete the Scene, &c.

Likewise for to make our Procession more grand,
We were led in the Front by a Musical Band,
Who were paid from the Fund of that bountiful Hand, &c.

Ye Hungry and Naked, all hither repair,
No longer in Want don't remain in Despair,
You'll meet with Employment, and each get a Share, &c.

Ye Crafts and Mechanics, if ye will draw nigh,
No longer ye need to lack an Employ,
And each duly paid, which is a great Joy, &c.

To our noble Master, a Bumper then fill,
The matchless Inventor of this Cotton Mill,
Each toss off his Glass with a hearty Good-will,
With a Huzza for the Mills now at Cromford
All join with a jovial Huzza.

(k) The different kinds of organization of workers were summed up
in an interesting official report of 1806.

Source: Select Committee of the House of Commons, *Report on
the State of the Woollen Manufacture of England* (1806).

It may be expedient for Your Committee to state that there
are three different modes of carrying on the woollen Manufacture; that of the Master Clothier of the West of England,
the Factory, and the Domestic system.

In all the Western Counties as well as in the North, there
are Factories, but the Master Clothier of the West of England,
buys his Wool from the Importer, if it be foreign, or in the
Fleece, or of the Woolstapler, if it be of Domestic growth;
after which, in all the different processes through which it
passes, he is under the necessity of employing as many distinct

classes of persons; sometimes working in their own homes, sometimes in those of the Master Clothier, but none going out of their proper line. Each class of Workmen, however, acquires great skill in performing its particular operation. . . .

In the Factory system, the Master Manufacturers, who sometimes possess a very great capital, employ in one or more Buildings or Factories, under their own or their Superintendent's inspection, a number of Workmen or fewer according to the extent of their Trade. Both in the system of the West of England Clothier and in the Factory system . . . . the work, generally speaking, is done by persons who have no property in the goods they manufacture. . . .

In the . . . Domestic system, which is that of Yorkshire, the manufacture is conducted by a multitude of Master Manufacturers, generally possessing a very small, and scarcely ever any great extent of Capital. They buy the Wool of the Dealer; and in their own houses, assisted by their wives and children, they dye it (when dyeing is necessary) and through all the different stages work it up into undressed Cloth.

(1) It took time for the social consequences of assembling workers together in factories to be fully appreciated.

Source: R. Guest, *A Compendious History of the Cotton-Manufacture* (1823), pp. 32ff.

The progress of the Cotton Manufacture introduced great changes into the manners and habits of the people. The operative workmen being thrown together in great numbers, had their faculties sharpened and improved by constant communication. Conversation wandered over a variety of topics not before essayed; the questions of Peace and War, which interested them importantly, inasmuch as they might produce a rise or fall of wages, became highly interesting, and this brought them into the vast field of politics and discussions on the character of their Government, and the men who composed it. . . . The facility with which the Weavers changed their masters, the constant effort to find out and obtain the largest remuneration for their labour, the excitement to ingenuity which the higher wages for fine manufactures and skilful workmanship produced, and a conviction that they depended on their own exertions, produced in them . . . a spirit of freedom and independence.

(m) This was only one side of the picture, however. Some workers felt that they lost their independence when they left their homes for the factories. Others saw new machinery as a threat to their well-being.

Source: A Gloucestershire letter of 1802, printed in D. M. Hunter, *The West of England Woollen Industry under Protection and Free Trade* (1910), p. 21.

Wee Hear in Formed that you got Shear in mee sheens and if you Dont Pull them Down in a Forght Nights Time Wee will pull them Down for you Wee will you Damd infernold Dog. And Bee four Almighty God we will pull down all the Mills that heave Heany Shearing mc Shens in We will cut out Hall your Damd Hearts as Do Keep them and We will meock the rest Heat them or else We will Searve them the Seam.

(n) Opposition to the introduction of machinery reached its peak in the secret Luddite agitation of 1811 to 1812. Nottingham was a Luddite centre: so too was the West Riding of Yorkshire.

Source: A copy of a letter sent to a Huddersfield manufacturer in the *Home Office Papers*, 1812.

Sir, Information has just been given in, that you are a holder of those detestable Shearing Frames, and I was desired by my men to write to you, and to give you fair warning to pull them down. . . . If they are not taken down by the end of next week, I shall detach one of my lieutenants with at least 300 men to destroy them, and further more take notice that if you give us the trouble of coming thus far, we will increase your misfortune by burning your buildings down to ashes, and if you have the impudence to fire at any of my men, they have orders to murder you and burn all your Housing. You will have the goodness to go to your neighbours to inform them that the same Fate awaits them if their Frames are not taken down. . . . We will never lay down our arms till the House of Commons passes an act to put down all the machinery hurtfull to the Commonality and repeal that to the Frame

Breakers—but we petition no more, that wont do, fighting must,

Signed by the General of the Army of Redressers,

NED LUDD, Clerk.

(o) Despite attempts to put down workingmen's combinations to protect wages, there were many examples of what we would now call strike action.

Source: Letter from the Rev. Charles Prescot and John Philips of Stockport to Lord Hawkesbury, 28 May 1808, in the *Home Office Papers.*

As magistrates acting for this and the adjoining County of Lancaster, we think it a duty we owe to Government to acquaint your Lordship with the state of this town and neighbourhood, which, since the Bill, lately before the House of Commons for fixing the price of the labour of the cotton weavers, was thrown out, have been under continual alarm and terror, owing to great bodies of the weavers having assembled for the purpose of obliging the manufacturers to raise their wages, and in the meantime neither working themselves, nor suffering others to work, and of course their families starving.

13. PAUPERS

Below the craftsmen and artisans, there were large numbers of poor people throughout the eighteenth century who were compelled to rely for their livelihood on poor relief administered by the parish (see above, p. 82). Attitudes towards both the poor and the poor law changed throughout the century and from place to place. They were often a matter of debate. The extracts which follow deal both with attitudes and procedures. They also show how some of the poor were 'recruited into industry'.

(a) *Source:* Letter of Daniel Baker to R. Verney, 7 Jan. 1710, printed in Lady Verney (ed.), *Verney Letters of the Eighteenth Century* (1930), vol. I, p. 278.

'. . . Peas never bore such a price as they doe now for a great many yeares; and also all other grain rises with us; especially Barley and Wheat, notwithstanding the late Act of

Parliamt. which was made on the poor's behalf; for wheat with us is 12s. 6d. a bushell, I mean old Wheat, and Barley is 35s. per qr., soe tis very hard with poor people and they are ready to famish, & so many Sessions have been harping upon it, I marvell no Act passes about erecting workhouses; or for the better employing soe many hands for the good of the Kingdom. Otherwise the nation must sink under the burthens & the Parishes will hardly be able to keep 'Em. In some places near us tis 4 shillings in the pound already as to their Rates. Not that God forbid I should speak this out of Envy, but I believe expedients might be found out for the Easing of one and the other. I do hope Sir you will escuse this tedious digression which must partly help to fill up a letter, for otherwise wee have little or no news in the country.

(b) *Source:* Memorandum of the Vestry, Bradford, Yorkshire, 1714, printed in W. Cudworth, *Historical Notes on the Bradford Corporation* (1887), p. 4. Overseers of the Poor were selected by Justices of the Peace from names submitted at the Easter Vestry. Some parishes had a rota system.

We do order and agree that none of the poor persons in this town shall, for the future, be relieved by us or any other of the inhabitants of this town, at our or their respective houses, by way of alms. But that in lieu thereof a month's additional poor assess shall from henceforth be annually collected in this town by the Overseers of the Poor for the time being, whereof one twenty-sixth part shall, every fortnight be bestowed in oat-bread, to be by such overseers distributed every other Sunday, or Lord's Day, at the Parish Church of Bradford, immediately after divine service and sermon there in the morning, to and amongst such poor persons of this town as shall resort to the said church on those days to hear divine service there, or being impotent and unfit to repair to the said church shall send some other person thither on his, her, or their behalf.

(c) *Source:* Note for 24 March 1763 in the *Diary* of Thomas Turner.

I went to Jones's, there being a vestry holden there to make a poor rate. We staid till near one o'clock, quarreling and bickering about nothing. The design of our meeting was to have made a poor rate, every one to be assessed to the racked rent. But how do I blush to say, what artifice and deceit, cunning and knavery was used by some to conceal their rents. I look upon that man, be he who he will, that endeavours to evade the payment of his just share of taxes, to be a robbing every other member of the community that contributes his quota.

(d) The amount spent on the poor varied considerably from year to year. It rose sharply late in the century and during the Napoleonic Wars.

Source: Expenditure on the Poor at Wigston, Leicestershire, 1735–55, as set out in W. G. Hoskins, *The Midland Peasant* (1957), p. 230.

1735–6	£57	7s.	9d.	1745–6	missing		
1736–7	£77	5s.	6¾d.	1746–7	£74	13s.	10½d.
1737–8	£75	6s.	10½d.	1747–8	£59	9s.	9d.
1738–9	£57	1s.	0½d.	1748–9	£71	5s.	7¼d.
1739–40	missing			1749–50	£75	18s.	3d.
1740–1	missing			1750–1	£91	14s.	3½d.
1741–2	£52	2s.	7d.	1751–2	£73	18s.	0½d.
1742–3	£94	2s.	4¼d.	1752–3	£107	6s.	1½d.
1743–4	£81	12s.	8½d.	1753–4	£91	13s.	10¾d.
1744–5	£65	5s.	2d.	1754–5	£95	3s.	10d.

(e) Attitudes towards responsibilities towards the poor varied also. Some Overseers of the Poor paid particular attention to distress caused by ill-health or injury.

Source: The *Accounts* of the Overseers of Bury, Lancs, 1707.

It gives help to Susan Kaye to get help for her distemper	£1
It pd to one Whitworth the one half of the cure of Roger Greenall	£1 13s.
It pd to Tho. Schofield about the birth of his child	1d.
It given to six persons about the birth of their children 1709.	6d.
It pd to John Shepherd in tymes in their sickness by order	1s. 11d.
It pd for physics for Jonothon Schofield, and some other things before his death	3s. 4d.

(f) *Source:* Note of 21 Nov. 1773 in the Minutes of the Mainstone Vestry, Shropshire, printed in *Shropshire Parish Documents*, p. 222.

Agreed in publick Vestry held on this day in the Parish Church of Mainstone that John Jones a poor boy maintained by the parish is to be settled as here followeth, viz.:—that every householder shall keep this boy for half a year according to Lotts—first half year to be allowed fifteen shillings second half year twelve shillings and six pence and for every half year after two shillings and six pence less till he shall be able to gett his living; only ye Parish to keep him in whole clothing and 'reasonably to be alowd if ye boy shall be sick.

(g) Many writers generalized about the poor.

Source: J. Townsend, *A Dissertation on the Poor Laws* (1786).

It seems to be a law of nature, that the poor should be to a certain degree improvident, that there may always be some to fulfil the most servile, the most sordid, and the most ignoble offices in the community. The stock of human happiness is thereby much increased, whilst the more delicate are not only relieved from drudgery, and freed from those occasional employments which would make them miserable, but are left at liberty, without interruption, to pursue those callings which are suited to their various dispositions, and most useful to the State. As for the lowest of the poor, by custom they are reconciled to the meanest occupations, to the most laborious works, and to the most hazardous pursuits; whilst the hope of their reward makes them cheerful in the midst of all their dangers and their toils. The fleets and armies of a state would soon be in want of soldiers and of sailors if sobriety and diligence universally prevailed: for what is it but distress and poverty which can prevail upon the lower classes of people to encounter all the horrors which await them on the tempestuous ocean, or in the field of battle? Men who are easy in their circumstances are not among the foremost to engage in a seafaring or military life. There must be a degree of pressure, and that which is attended with the least violence will be the best. When hunger is either felt or feared, the desire of obtaining bread will quietly dispose the mind to undergo the greatest hardships, and will sweeten the severest labours.

(h) *Source:* William Blake, *Songs of Experience* (*c.* 1794).

> Is this a holy thing to see
> In a rich and fruitful land,
> Babes reduc'd to misery,
> Fed with cold and usurous hand?

> Is that trembling cry a song?
> Can it be a song of joy?
> And so many children poor?
> It is a land of poverty!

> And their sun does never shine,
> And their fields are bleak and bare,
> And their ways are fill'd with thorns:
> It is eternal winter there.

(i) *Source:* G. Howlett, *The Insufficiency of the Causes to which the Increase of the Poor and of the Poor's Rates have been commonly Ascribed* (1788), p. 118.

Our general system of Poor Laws is a venerable pile, raised by the hands of skilful architects and stands a distinguished monument of the wisdom and humanity of the British Nation. Like every other edifice, it is liable, indeed, to the injuries of time and seasons, and must want occasional repairs and occasional improvements; but if pulled entirely down, we might stand a chance of either being buried in its ruins, or, at best, of never raising anything in its stead of equal grandeur, utility or beauty.

(j) *Source:* Sir William Temple, *Essay on Trade and Commerce* (1770), p. 106.

Our poor laws are at present a snare to the poor, and leave them loose to idleness, debauchery and insolence; because they depend on these laws for support in necessity; and knowing that a justice of the peace will relieve them, they despise parish officers, insult the inhabitants, and do not feel themselves obliged to their benefactors for what they receive. It is upon the poor laws that the poor rely and not upon their own behaviour and conduct; and this tends to destroy all subordination as well as gratitude and mutual esteem.

(k) *Source:* Sir F. M. Eden, *State of the Poor* (1797), vol. I, pp. 667–8.

It is impossible to provide a national fund for setting the Poor to work in any species of employment, without in some degree injuring those who are engaged in similar undertakings. If, for instance, a parish work-house undertakes the manufacture of mops, ropes, and sacking; those who before subsisted by means of these trades are sure to be the sufferers. Whether the mops are made by the private manufacturer, or by the parish children, no more will be sold than the Public have occasion for. The managers of the work-house, however, without being able to increase the demand, can generally obtain a preference and a certain sale for their goods, by selling them rather below the market price. The concern, though a losing one, is carried on by the contributions of the parishioners; and a poor industrious manufacturer will, perhaps, often have the mortification to reflect, that, in contributing his portion of Poor's Rate, he is helping the parish to undo him. . . . Projects, which, without increasing the demand for any article of consumption, interfere with established manufactures, and oblige the fair trader (whose capital is limited), to enter into competition with the parish, (whose capital can, upon any emergency, be recruited by an order of Justices), are, it may well be supposed, as injurious to the general interests of the community, as the monopolizing speculations of Governments in foreign commerce.

(1) *Source:* A fascinating account of a particular case given by Eden in *ibid.,* vol. I, p. 579.

Anne Hurst was born at Witley in Surrey: there she lived the whole period of a long life; and there she died. As soon as she was thought able to work, she went into service; there, before she was twenty she married James Strudwick; who, like her own father, was a day-labourer. With this husband she lived a prolific, hard-working, contented life, somewhat more than fifty years. He worked more than threescore years on one farm; and his wages, summer and winter, were regularly a shilling a day. He never asked more; nor was ever offered less. They had between them seven children; and lived to see six daughters married, and three of them the mothers of sixteen children; all of whom were brought up, or are bringing up, to be day-labourers. Strudwick continued to work till within seven weeks of the day of his death: and at the age of fourscore, in 1787, he closed, in peace, a not inglorious life; for, to the day of his death, he never received a farthing in the way of parochial aid. His wife survived him about seven years; and though bent with age and infirmities, and little able to work, excepting as a weeder in a gentleman's garden, she also was too proud either to ask or receive any relief from her parish. For six or seven of the last years of her life, she received twenty shillings a year from the person who favoured me with this account, which he drew up from her own mouth. With all her virtue, and all her merit, she yet was not much liked in her neighbourhood: people in affluence thought her haughty; and the Paupers of the parish, seeing, as they could not help seeing, that her life was a reproach to theirs, aggravated all her little failings. Yet, the worst thing they had to say of her was, that she was proud; which, they said, was manifested by the manner in which she buried her husband. Resolute, as she owned she was, to have the funeral, and every thing that related to it, what she called decent, nothing could dissuade her from having handles to his coffin, and a plate on it, mentioning his age. She was also charged with having behaved herself crossly and peevishly towards one of her sons-in-law, who was a mason, and went regularly, every Saturday evening, to the ale-house, as he said, *just to drink a pot of beer.* James Strudwick, in all his life, as she often told this ungracious son-in-law, never spent five shillings in any idleness; luckily, (as she was sure to add) he had it not to spend. A more serious charge against her was, that, living to a great age, and but a little able to work, she grew to be seriously afraid, that, at last, she might become chargeable to the parish, (the heaviest, in her estimation, of all human calamities;) and that thus alarmed, she did suffer herself more than once, during the exacerbations of a fit of distempered despondency, peevishly (and, perhaps, petulantly,) to exclaim that God Almighty, by suffering her to remain so long upon earth, seemed actually to have forgotten her.— Such are the simple annals of Dame Strudwick.

(m) Many overseers sent pauper children into industry. Indentures were drawn up.

Source: Indenture in the *Tibbitts Collection,* Sheffield Public Library.

This Indenture made the Fourteenth Day of September in the Year of our Lord 1784 between John Lee, Michael Dent and John Gray Churchwardens and Overseers of the Poor . . . and Thomas Wilson a poor Child of the said Township on the one Part, and Timothy Bolsover of the Township of Sheffield in the said Riding on the other Part, WITNESSETH, That the said Church-Wardens and Overseers of the Poor Have, by and with the Consent, Allowance, and Approbation of two of his Majesty's Justices of the Peace for the said Riding put, placed, and bound the said Thomas Wilson as an Apprentice to and with the said Timothy Bolsover with him to dwell and remain from the Day of the Date hereof, until the said Apprentice shall attain the Age of Twenty one years according to the Form of the Statute in that Case made and provided. During all which said Term the said Apprentice his said Master well and truly shall serve, his Secrets shall keep, his Commands (being lawful and honest) at all Times willingly shall perform; and in all Things, as a good and faithfuly Servant, shall demean him, self towards his said Master and all his Family. And the said Timothy Bolsover for himself, his Executors, Administrators and Assigns, doth Covenant, Promise and agree to and with the said Church-Wardens, Overseers, and his said Apprentice, that he will educate and bring him up in some honest and lawful Calling, and in the Fear of God; and that he will find, provide for, and allow unto his said Apprentice sufficient wholesome, and competent Meat, Drink, Washing, Lodging, Apparel, and all other Necessaries meet for such an Apprentice, during all the said Term.

In Witness whereof the said Parties to these Presents have hereunto interchangably set their Hands and Seals the Day and Year first above-written.

(n) Opponents of the poor law extolled the virtues of charity.

Source: J. Townsend, *op. cit.,* pp. 107–8.

To relieve the Poor by voluntary donations is not only the most wise, politic, and just: is not only most agreeable both to reason and to revelation; but it is most effectual in preventing

M

misery, and most excellent in itself, as cherishing, instead of
rancour, malice and contention, the opposite and most amiable
affections of the human breast, pity, compassion, and benevolence in the rich, love, reverence, and gratitude in the poor.
Nothing in nature can be more disgusting than a parish pay-
table, attendant upon which, in the same objects of misery, are
too often found combined, snuff, gin, rags, vermin, insolence,
and abusive language; nor in nature can any thing be more
beautiful than the mild complacency of benevolence, hastening
to the humble cottage to relieve the wants of industry and
virtue, to feed the hungry, to cloath the naked, and to sooth
the sorrows of the widow with her tender orphans; nothing
can be more pleasing, unless it be their sparkling eyes, their
bursting tears, and their uplifted hands, the artless expressions
of unfeigned gratitude for unexpected favours. Such scenes will
frequently occur whenever men shall have power to dispose of
their own property. When the poor are obliged to cultivate
the friendship of the rich, the rich will never want inclination
to relieve the distresses of the poor.

(o) The following extract is one example out of a vast 'charity'
literature.

Source: J. Crabtree, *A Concise History of Halifax* (1836), pp. 222–3.

Frances Thornhill by will, dated July 31st, 1718, gave and
bequeathed nine hundred pounds to be laid out to pious and
charitable uses in the manner following; the sum of one hundred and fifty pounds, and the interest thereof, into the hands
of the heir and chief of her family of Fixby, her nephew,
Thomas Thornhill, Esq; to be the first trustee. And her will
was, that his heirs, being the principals of her name and family
of Fixby aforesaid, should successively for ever be trustees to
see the said one hundred and fifty pounds laid out in a purchase,
for building or making a proper habitation for teaching and
improving ten poor girls in spinning wool, knitting, sewing,
reading, and writing, and to be taught the catechism of the
church of England, and private prayers for them every morning
and night. And for the continuance of that her good intention
for ever, she devised four hundred pounds, being further part
of the said nine hundred pounds, to rest in the heir of Fixby's

hands for the time being, whom she desired to consult with the minister of Elland for the time being, to chuse a proper master and dame to teach and instruct the said ten poor girls; the interest of which said sum of four hundred pounds to be annually laid out, and paid for the salaries of the said master and dame, and maintenance of the said poor girls, in such manner and proportion as the said heir of Fixby, or trustee for that her charity for the time being, should see proper and convenient. And the said testatrix's desire was that the said poor girls might, from time to time, be chosen out of the greatest objects of charity which should then be living in Fixby, and the town and parish of Elland, so as the said school may be preserved and kept up for ever for the purpose aforesaid; and that the heir and owner of Fixby for the time being, should take great care in his choice of a master and dame as aforesaid, for the good teaching and looking after these ten poor girls, so that they may have all necessaries provided for them, and that the said master might read unto them the prayers of the church of England every night after the girls gave over work. And the said testatrix also devised two hundred pounds more . . . to rest in the heir or owner of Fixby land for the time being, for ever, to the end that the minister of Elland, for the time being, might receive the interest thereof, as an augmentation for his better subsistence: and that in consideration of the said interest to be paid to the said minister, he should read every morning, in the church of Elland, the common prayers of the church of England at six o'clock in the morning in summer, and at eleven o'clock in the morning in winter, and the charity girls, with their master and dame, might attend and be present at the said times and hours of devotion: and in case the minister of Elland refused to attend and read prayers, according to this request and intent, then the said interest of the said two hundred pounds, designed for the minister aforesaid, should go to the said poor girls, for their better maintenance and subsistence. Also, her will and mind was, that that part of her will only that related to the charity school of Elland . . . should be read every Christmas day in the morning, between prayers and sermon, in the parish church of Elland.

(p) The inadequacies of charity became apparent in particularly hard times when there was general distress. Many magistrates, after 1795, followed the pattern set out Speenhamland, Berkshire, of supplementing wages as food prices rose. The system had its critics from the start.

Source: Sir F. M. Eden, *The State of the Poor* (1797), vol. I, pp. 575–6.

Instead of an advance in wages, proportion'd to the increased demand for labour, the labourer has received a considerable part of that portion of his employer's capital, which was destined for his maintenance, in the form of the Poor's Rate (the very worst that it could assume), instead of being paid it as the fair, well earned recompence of equivalent labour. This is a deplorable evil, which has fallen heaviest on the Poor than on the Rich; and it has been considerably aggravated by the very injudicious steps which have been adopted for administering relief to those whom the pressure of the late scarcity had incapacitated from supporting themselves and families, in the way to which they had been accustomed. Many instances might be adduced, of the ill-effects of the indiscriminating charity of individuals, and of the no less ill effects of the discriminating interference of magistrates and parish-officers. . . . The very great price of the necessaries of life, but more particularly of bread-corn during the whole of last year, produced numberless extraordinary demands for parochial assistance. In many parishes in the county of Berks, relief from the Poor's Rate was granted, not only to the infirm and impotent, but to the able-bodied and industrious, who had, very few of them, ever applied to the parish for relief; and then only during temporary illness or disability. There was no doubt, but that the circumstances of the times required an increase in the income of the labourers in husbandry. . . . But there existed a different of opinion, respecting the mode of making such increase. . . .

14. OUTSIDERS

No account of eighteenth-century society would be complete without reference to the 'outsiders'. Vagrants fell into this category.

So too, although they were often locally tolerated, did smugglers and poachers. Smugglers were often organized on 'professional' lines. Gipsies formed a category of their own.

(a) *Source:* Hertfordshire Quarter Sessions Book, vol. XV, Epiphany Session, 1786.

[Special Order addressed to all Constables, instructing them to be more assiduous and severe in enforcing the Vagrancy Laws.]

And for the better information of such High Constables, Petty Constables, Headboroughs, and Peace Officers, they are to take Notice that all Persons going about as Alms-gatherers for Losses by Fire or other Casualties, or as Collectors for Gaols or Hospitals, or Fencers, or Bear Wards, or exhibiting Shews, or players of Interludes, Comedies, Tragedies, Operas, or Farces without Authority, or Minstrels, Jugglers, or Gypsies wandering in Form or Habit of Egyptians, or Persons telling Fortunes or using subtile Crafts to deceive the King's Subjects, or playing at unlawful Games, or that run away from their Families and leave them chargeable to their Parishes, and all Petty Chapmen and Pedlars not licensed, or Persons lying abroad or lodging in Outhouses and not giving a good Account of Themselves, or wandering and begging as Soldiers or Seafaring Men not having License so to do, or pretending to go to Work in Harvest and wandering abroad and begging, are deemed Vagrants by the Laws of this Realm. . . . This Court doth earnestly recommend to every acting Magistrate in this County to put the said Act strictly into Execution, first searching their Bundels and Parcels to see if they are able to pay for their Passing and, if they shall be found returning again, then treating them as incorrigible Rogues and Vagabonds.

(b) *Source:* G. Bridges, *The Smugglers Defeated* (1739), pp. 5–7.

That having been bred from my Youth among the Clandestine Exporters of Wool and Yarn from Ireland to France, whither he made Nine Voyages on that illicit Trade, which hath given me all the opportunities that could be desired, of discovering every Particular thereof.

I. He knows and is perfectly well acquainted with most of

the Creeks and Harbours on the Coast, and most of the Private and By-Roads which are made up for that purpose.

II. He knows the Names and Places of Abode of lots of the particular Men which are concerned in the Exportation, as aforesaid.

III. As also the Names of some of the Merchants in France, to whom the Wool and Yarn is consigned, likewise some of the Insurers and their Correspondents in *London*; with almost every one's particular Address.

IV. Also he knows most of the Estated Gentlemen and Magistrates who have built Warehouses by the Sea Side, one of which is a Member of Parliament, and do receive the said Wool and Yarn into them, and Ship the same on Vessels bound to *France* for 4s. *per* Peck.

V. The very Owners and Captains of the Vessels he knows also, who receive 20s. *per* Peck from *Ireland* to *France*. . . .

VI. He knows also a Justice of the Peace, who kept two Ships constantly employed on the same illicite Trade. . . .

VII. He also remembers and saw seven Vessels loaden in less than 24 Hours on that illicite Trade, besides what were loaden in other places out of his sight, and by Night in other Parts.

VIII. Also he is well acquainted with Mr. *China* and Mr. *Dawson*, both Riding and Coast officers, who attempted a Seizure of the said Wool, but were obliged to fly in the jeopardy of their lives, when showers of Stones followed them, and one of their servants were stoned to Death.

IX. Besides many other Things he knows along with these, which he names in a Schedule, ready to produce, when Time and proper Opportunities requires a further Discovery of Names and Places.

(c) *Source:* Letter from Thomas Watterton, gamekeeper to Lord Irwin, 1736, from the *Temple Newsam Archives*, Leeds.

My Lord,
    heare is such a number of Poachers & Coarsers in this Lordshipe. This winter, more than ever has bin since I new Temple newsam. These poachears noes that I can't Bussell amoungst them as I could a have don. This wicke Wm Moore,

Halton, John Simpson of Rounder, David Sayner, Seacroft was in ye Liberty & kild a brace of Haers neverry one of them quallified. John Clark & two or three Cunterry with him killd a brace more ye last wick which Parsson Hopkins told me. As for Clark he never misses going 3 daies a wick either with Mr. Fran. Millner, or sum cunterry fealows he surches all round the Park. . . .

(d) *Source:* Chap Book, *An Account of the Life and Death of Tobias Smith* (1793), pp. 3–5.

Tobias Smith was born at Southwell in Bedfordshire, in 1773. His parents, James and Jemima Smith, are of that class of vagrants called *Gipsies*, who procure a wretched livelihood by selling small articles from place to place, fortune telling, fiddling, and such kind of loose and unlawful practices.

His mother, it seems, had some education in her youth; she lived several years in service, and afterwards took up with a gypsy. Some of her younger children can read and repeat the Lord's prayer, creed, and ten commandments; but she complained that Tobias was of so untractable a disposition, that he would never learn one letter or prayer.

The first thing Toby mentioned to me, as the cause of his misfortunes, was the unhappy state his father and mother lived in, quarrelling and fighting. His father, several times, turned him off, and forced him into other companies, where he was further corrupted, and persuaded to steal and plunder for a living. The first time I saw him was in the prison at Bedford, where he was committed in Nov. 1791, for stealing a mare out of a pasture at Staysden, the property of Mr. William Curtise, a farmer. He was tried at the Lent assizes 1792, before Sir William Ashurst, and being found guilty, was condemned to be hanged; which was executed upon him April the third near Bedford.

But as it pleased God to make him an object of his tender mercy, in so singular a manner, he repeatedly requested me, (and many others who visited him,) to make it public, for the information of gipsies, and as far as possible to reclaim all ranks of offenders.

His parents had sixteen children, eight of whom are still

living, and wandering as vagabonds over the earth. Toby was rather low in stature, but one of the neatest, proportionate made men I ever saw. He was admired by all who knew him for his uncommon agility, in leaping, running, fighting, &c. From his infancy he never knew any other way of life, but wandering from place to place, fairs, feasts, races and other places of public concourse and diversions: he was early taught to play on the fiddle, for the purpose of getting money at those times when people are intoxicated. Many persons greatly hurt themselves and their families by falling a prey to such companies of depredators.

Toby deeply lamented the unhappy disagreement between his parents. His father broke his mother's arm by beating her, had fractured the bone of her leg, and much injured her otherwise. He frequently left her with all her children, and took up with other women, and other gangs of gipsies. Sometimes he turned out his children to provide for themselves. . . .

He [Toby] told me also of his breaking into his uncle's house at Great Stourton, as he was returning from Thrapstone fair, being very hungry, but only found a bottle of wine which he drank: this he acknowledged to his uncle, asked his pardon, and obtained forgiveness. Many other petty thefts he was guilty of too tedious to mention. Fighting was a practice he greatly delighted in and generally was victor; he was so nimble that he thought no men could ever hurt him, except on his arms by fencing. He challenged the great Mendoza, and believed he could have beat him, said he had beat several better men than the Jew. But he sorely lamented that he had been guilty of manslaughter twice, having so bruised his combatants that they never recovered of the blows he gave them. The temptation to steal horses continued with him, at times, for above two years, before he committed the crime. He had been drinking, it being a very rainy day, and by coming to Stagsden got very wet; as he was going by the pasture, he saw Mr. Curtis's mare and resolved to take her; he went to the White Horse, where he got more liquor. He left the public house a little after dark, much intoxicated, and went to the field, stole the mare, and rode her to Safron Walden in Essex, but had forgot the fair-day being the week before. He rode back to Potton, where he offered her to sale, but could not sell her. Being much afraid less he should be found out, he went to the pasture where he had left her, and stabbed her in two places with his knife. The account of her being killed in such a manner made a great rumour in the country. Many talked to him about her, as it was well known he had brought her to Potton, asking him whose she was, how he came by her, &c. He said he was so frightened he could not stir a step to run away; and having told many lies about the matter, he was entangled in his talk, and suspected that he had stole her. Being taken into custody, and brought before Sir Philip Monoux of Sandy, he confessed his crime, and was sent to Bedford prison.

14. NEW VIEWS OF SOCIETY

By the beginning of the nineteenth century, old ideas of society based on 'ranks, orders and degrees' were giving way to new views of society based on class. There was also a vigorous assertion of the values of self-help, coupled with warnings from social critics, like Cobbett, that society was now becoming divided between 'masters' and 'slaves'.

(a) *Source:* Robert Owen, *Observations on the Effect of the Manufacturing System* (1815).

Those who were engaged in the trade, manufactures, and commerce of this country thirty or forty years ago formed but a very insignificant portion of the knowledge, wealth, influence or population of the Empire. Prior to that period, Britain was essentially agricultural. But, from that time to the present, the home and foreign trade have increased in a manner so rapid and extraordinary as to have raised commerce to an importance, which it never previously attained in any country possessing so much political power and influence. . . . This change has been owing chiefly to the mechanical inventions which introduced the cotton trade into this country. . . . The wants which this trade created for various materials requisite to forward its multiplied operations, caused an extraordinary demand for almost all the manufactures previously established, and also for human labour. . . . Hitherto, legislators have appeared to regard manufactures only in one point of view, as a source of national wealth. . . . Yet the political and moral effects . . . well deserve to occupy the best faculties of the greatest and wisest statesmen. The general diffusion of manufactures throughout a country generates a new character in its inhabitants, and as this character is formed upon a principle quite unfavourable to individual or general happiness, it will produce the most lamentable and permanent evils, unless its tendency be counteracted by legislative interference and direction. . . . This alteration is still in rapid progress, and ere long, the comparatively happy simplicity of the agricultural peasant will be wholly lost among us. . . . The employer [now] regards the employed as mere instruments of gain, while these acquire a gross ferocity of character, which, if legislative measures shall not be fully devised to prevent its increase, and ameliorate the condition of this class, will sooner or later plunge the country into formidable and perhaps inextricable state of danger.

(b) *Source:* P. Colquhoun, *A Treatise on the Wealth, Power, and Resources of the British Empire* (1814), ch. IV.

It becomes an interesting object to discover . . . in what manner and in what proportions . . . property is divided among the various classes of society. . . . With a view to this object [a] Table . . . has been constructed, It may be considered as a map of civil society, exhibiting in one view the proportions of created wealth which is allotted annually to every class of the community, from the Sovereign in regular gradation down to the pauper. . . . It will, through this medium, be discovered what classes of the community by their labour in different pursuits tend to increase the national capital, and what other classes diminish it. . . . [The Table] shews the distinction between the productive and unproductive labourers, according to their different pursuits in society. . . . It distinguishes the useful from the noxious members of the body politics. . . .

The population of the United Kingdom of Great Britain and Ireland including the army and navy, admits of the following division into classes, viz.

	Heads of Families.	Total persons, comprising their Families.
HIGHEST ORDERS		
1st. The Royal Family, the Lords Spiritual and Temporal, the Great Officers of State, and all above the degree of a Baronet, with their families . . .	576	2,880
SECOND CLASS		
2d. Baronets, Knights, Country Gentlemen, and others having large incomes, with their families	46,861	234,305
THIRD CLASS		
3d. Dignified Clergy, Persons holding considerable employments in the State, elevated situations in the Law, eminent Practitioners in Physic, considerable Merchants, Manufacturers upon a large scale, and Bankers of the first order, with their families .	12,200	61,000
Carried forward	59,637	298,185
FOURTH CLASS		
4th. Persons holding inferior situations in Church and State, respectable Clergymen of different persuasions, Practitioners in Law and Physic, Teachers of Youth of the superior order, respectable Freeholders, Ship Owners, Merchants and Manufacturers of the second class, Warehousemen and respectable Shopkeepers, Artists, respectable Builders, Mechanics, and Persons living on moderate incomes, with their families . . .	233,650	1,168,250

	Heads of Families.	Total persons, comprising their Families.
FIFTH CLASS		
5th. Lesser Freeholders, Shopkeepers of the second order, Inn-keepers, Publicans, and Persons engaged in miscellaneous occupations or living on moderate incomes, with their families	564,799	2,798,475
SIXTH CLASS		
6th. Working Mechanics, Artisans, Handicrafts, Agricultural Labourers, and others who subsist by labour in various employments, with their families .	2,126,095	8,792,800
Menial Servants		1,279,923
SEVENTH, OR LOWEST CLASS		
7th. Paupers and their families, Vagrants, Gipsies, Rogues, Vagabonds, and idle and disorderly persons, supported by criminal delinquency . .	387,100	1,828,170
	3,371,281	16,165,803
THE ARMY AND NAVY		
Officers of the Army, Navy, and Marines, including all Officers on half-pay and superannuated, with their families . . .	10,500	69,000
Non-commissioned Officers in the Army, Navy, and Marines, Soldiers, Seamen, and Marines, including Pensioners of the Army, Navy, &c. and their families .	120,000	862,000
Total . .	3,501,781	17,096,803

. . . There is however another and, perhaps, a more interesting statistical view of this important and curious subject, as it relates to the productive and unproductive labourers in the United Kingdom, which it may be useful to explain,—as a means of more fully elucidating the state of society, which, in this country, differs in many respects from every other civilized nation, and will account for its superiority in arts and arms (when its population is considered) to every nation in the world.

It has been already shewn, that in this as indeed in all other kingdoms, states, and empires, the communities, of which they are composed, consist of *productive* and *unproductive* labourers. In the United Kingdom of Great Britain and Ireland, as far as approximating facts could be obtained, they seem to admit of the following classification.

Productive Labourers, by whose exertions a new Property is created every year.

	Families.	Persons.	Income.
Agriculture Mines, &c. }	1,302,151	6,129,142	£107,246,795
Foreign Commerce, Shipping, Trade, Manufactures, Fisheries, &c. }	1,506,774	7,071,989	183,908,352
Fine Arts . .	5,000	25,000	1,400,000
Total . .	2,813,925	13,226,131	£292,555,147

Unproductive Labourers, whose exertions do not create any new Property.

	Families.	Persons.	Income.
Royalty Nobility Gentry }	47,437	416,835	£58,923,590

	Families.	Persons.	Income.
State and Revenue Army Navy Half-pay Pensioners	152,000	1,056,000	34,036,280
Clergy Law Physic	56,000	281,500	17,580,000
Universities Schools Miscellaneous	45,319	567,937	17,555,355
Paupers . .	387,100	1,548,400	9,871,000
Total . .	687,856	3,870,672	£137,966,225

Thus it would appear, that more than ⅛th part of the whole community are unproductive labourers, and that these labourers receive from the aggregate labour of the productive class about ⅓d part of the new property created annually. But it does not follow, as has been already observed, that a very great proportion of these unproductive labourers are not highly useful in their different stations in society. On the contrary, with a few exceptions, in addition to the benefits derived from personal exertions, they eminently tend to promote, invigorate, and render more productive the labour of the creating classes.

Such is the structure of civil society, that the classes, whose minds are enlarged and their intellects and faculties improved by a superior education, are indispensably necessary as master-springs in the great machine; not only for the purpose of giving energy to the efforts of the productive labourers by means of capital furnished by every member of the community possessing real or personal property, from which they derive an income, but from the skill and superior knowledge of those who give employment to the labouring classes in agriculture, manufactures, trade, commerce, and navigation, and other objects of productive industry. But this is not the only advantage resulting from the labour of the higher and middling classes of the community; particularly in the British dominions, where they are called upon as legislators, judges, magistrates, jurors, managers of the poor, and peace-officers, to execute the functions which are required for the purpose of preserving the harmony and order, which are necessary to the existence of civil society. . . .

CHAPTER VI

Work

Shalstone,
Saturday, Septemb^r ye 23^d 1738

Master Parker
This is the third day you have been from my worke, tho you promised faithfully you would never leave it till you had finished it; if you don't come on Monday next I will set somebody else to worke upon it. I think you are a very unworthy man to neglect it so this fine weather & am

Your freind to serve you
Henry Purefoy
(from the *Purefoy Letters*)

Use all possible diligence in your calling. . . . Every business will afford some employment sufficient for every day and every hour.
(JOHN WESLEY, *Sermon L*)

If a person can get sufficient in four days to support himself for seven days, he will keep holiday the other three; that is, he will live in riot and debauchery.
(J. POWELL, *A View of Real Grievances*, 1772)

Is not the creation of wants the likeliest way to produce industry in a people?
(Bishop BERKELEY, 1755)

The hours of work are from seven to twelve, and from one to between five and six. Even in summer when at day-work, the labourer is frequently seen on his way home with his tools upon his back thus early in the evening. This does not arise so much from absolute idleness, as the custom of the country, the day's work being generally admitted to consist of a certain stint or portion of labour.
(CHARLES VANCOUVER, *General View of the Agriculture of Devon*, 1808)

PLATE 1

BIRTH AND DEATH

The Foundling Hospital, London

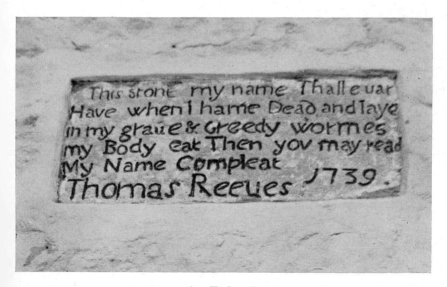

An Epitaph

PLATE 2

TIME

Eighteenth-century Watches

PLATE 3

TIME

A Time Recorder from Wedgwood's Etruria Factory

PLATE 4

PLACE

London—Charing Cross

PLATE 5

PLACE

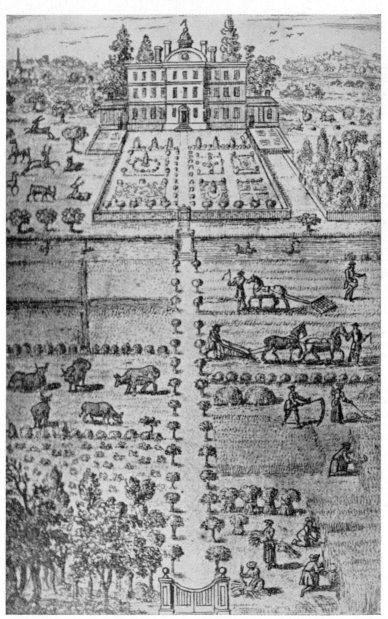

A Place in the Country

PLATE 6

PLACE

Nottingham as it was

Bath as it still is

PLATE 7

COMMUNICATIONS

A Parochial Perambulation

Inn Yard with Stage Coach

PLATE 8

THE RANKS OF SOCIETY

High Degree

PLATE 9

THE RANKS OF SOCIETY

'The City 'Prentice at his Master's Door'

'The Honest English Farmer's Wife'

PLATE 10

THE RANKS OF SOCIETY

'The Fashionable Mamma'

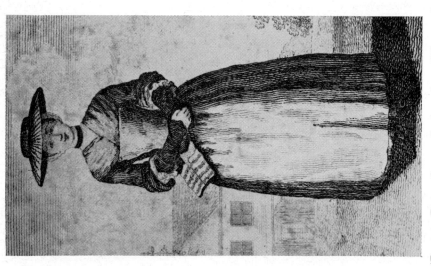

'Proper Dress for an Industrious Woman'

PLATE 11

WORK

In the Country

PLATE 12

WORK

This Four Wheel Drill Plow, with a Seed and a Manure Hopper, was first Invented in the Year 1745 and is now in Use with Wm Ellis at Little Gaddesden near Hempstead in Hertfordshire, where any person may View the same. It is so light that a Man may Draw it, but Generally drawn by a pony or little Horse...

At the Plough

PLATE 13

WORK

Spinning and Weaving

PLATE 14

WORK

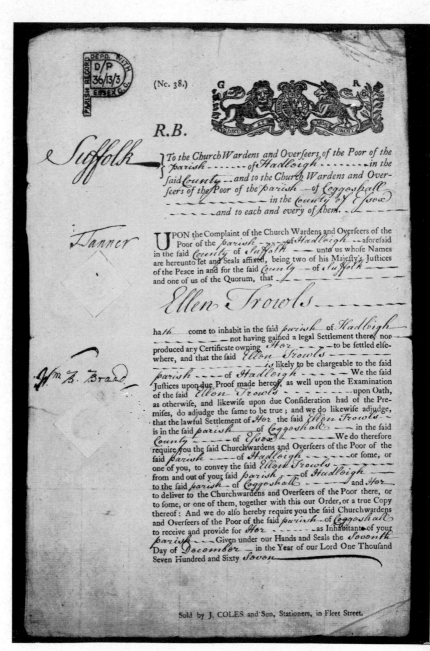

A Settlement Order

PLATE 15

PLAY

May Fair

Cock Fighting

PLATE 16

PLAY

Bear Baiting

'Italian Theatre'

inclosed by each of them at their own expense. . . . Further agreed that the Bailiff of the Manors and Richard Sorrell farmer shall be appointed to allot the commons and waste, and the tenants covenant to take up and be admitted to their several proportions at the next court by the yearly rent of 3 pence per acre and pay a fine of 1 shilling an acre on every death or alienation.

[Sixteen signatures, 4 by mark, and signature of the lord of the manors.]

(b) *Source:* Note on 3 Feb. in the *Journal of the House of Commons* (1766), vol. XXX.

Mr. *Chalmley* presented to the House, according to Order, a Bill for inclosing and dividing the Common Waste Grounds, Open Fields, Open Meadows, Grounds and Ings, within the Parish of *Stillington*, in the County of *York:* And the same was received; and read the First Time. *Resolved,* That the Bill to read a Second Time.

(c) *Source:* W. Marshall, *The Rural Economy of Yorkshire* (1788) vol. I, pp. 48ff.

There has no doubt been a time (and not perhaps many centuries past) when the entire country lay open. . . . In the present century [however], more especially within the last fifty years, inclosure has made a rapid progress. . . . The garden is the highest state of cultivation; open fields and pastures the lowest; separate inclosures a middle state which seems to be well adapted to the present population of this country. Be that as it may, the spirit of inclosure continues to be such, that in half a century or more an open field, or an undivided common may be rare, and the remembrance of them will of course soon wear away.

(d) *Source:* Anon., *An Inquiry into Bills of Inclosure* (1780), pp. 22ff.

If it appears, that no reason can defend, no advantage can justify the injury committed by inclosing bills, for even large sandy wastes and wide boggy moors, which are so beneficial to the community, what then shall we say, when the same objection equally applies to those for the inclosure of small circumscribed commons; by which therefore, the same private injustice is committed, without the alleviation of any public benefit? For no one advantage is conferred by them, which may not be obtained by rating the commons, without them. Nay further, where not only no additional benefit accrues, but even certain and considerable detriment, and that, not only arising from the cause I have already assigned, but from another, I shall now mention. For where all the commons in a parish are entirely inclosed, and distributed into several small allotments, all who are skilled in rural affairs will acknowledge, that sheep, that valuable animal to the farmer, and that inexhaustible source of wealth to the public, can not thrive. It being a position generally admitted; that sheep require at least, a fenceless scope of fifty acres, for their due, and proper range. This is a circumstance, of the utmost moment to the community; which in the late frequent paroxysms of rage for the indiscriminate inclosing of commons has been entirely neglected, or overlooked. . . . At the time the rage of inclosing first spread its fury, and scattered its pestilence about the nation, great and inestimable advantages accrued from the growth of corn, both to individuals and to the public. The profits resulting from this, were then so great and so immediate, to landlord as well as tenant, that every other species of produce was not only diminished, but as it were sacrificed, to the design of reaping the superior advantages, resulting from the increase of this commodity. For this purpose, the farmer converted every nook and corner of his land into arable;— and even the cottager forsook his one little ewe lamb, and turned his scanty orchard into tillage. For this likewise, the farmer could then brook, without murmuring, the loss of pasture upon the common almost wholly without recompence; because he received an accession of land for his plough, which he at that time thought, that even gold could not buy too dear.

But what is the case now of many of those very farmers, who once thought thus? The wisest of them, are so far from wishing for an addition of arable land, that they are re-converting part of their present, into pasture. The richest amongst them, are bowed down by the burthen of a rent lain upon them by the former high price of corn, which on account of the diminished value of that commodity, they now know not how to bear. As to the rest,—call but for any of the country news-papers,—look at the numerous advertisements for the sale of farming stocks and implements of husbandry, and—in them—you will read their history. Most of them, are no longer able to occupy, either arable or pasture land. Some of them, are working as hired servants, in those very fields, of which they were before the masters. Others, instead of beholding, as formerly, the smiles of plenty and of chearfulness at home;— are ruminating upon their own, and the distress of their wives and little ones, amidst the horrors of a jail.

Is this then the time, for . . . MEN, nay for those who call themselves GENTLEMEN,—rapaciously to seize from their tenants, the benefit of the commons they had before leased to them, and thus render their little morsel still more bitter? Can they wear the garb of humanity, and instead of lightening the burden, which more prosperous times lay upon their fellow-creatures, add now still greater weight to their afflictions? Heaven and earth forbid it! Both piety and humanity revolt at the idea! . . .

(e) *Source:* Arthur Young, *Annals of Agriculture* (1804), vol. XLII, p. 27. The reference is to Maulden, Cambridgeshire, enclosed in 1779.

The common very extensive. I conversed with a farmer, and several cottagers: one of them said, inclosing would ruin England; it was worse than ten wars: Why, my friend, what have you lost by it? *I kept four cows before the parish was inclosed, and now I do not keep so much as a goose. And you ask me what I lose by it!* Their accounts of advantages, especially when they are gone, are not to be credited.

(f) Young attempted a balance sheet.

Source: Note in *Ibid.*, pp. 38–40. The reference is to Eaton, Bedfordshire, enclosed in 1796.

Before a great deal of old pasture land was constantly mowed; now, that is turned to pasturage by means of mowing clover and tares, which yields four times as much: and this proves a great advantage to those grounds. . . .

Farms.—The open field farmers were generally very poor

and backward, and many against the inclosure; but are now converted, and admit the benefit of the measure. . . .

Sheep.—Every man might have had a flock, and many had flocks; but some of the little farmers none. Mr. W. had only 200 sheep before; now he has clipt 500. . . .

Cows.—The farmers never kept more than for their own use: they do the same now; but the cottagers' cows are lessened: they have, however, allotments in lieu. . . .

The persons who were most affected and hurt, were higlers —fish, gingerbread, apples, carting for hire, etc.: these kept horses, and turned without any right on the commons: these men have been hurt, and these only; and they complain, but with no right to do it. Now they hire bits of land, and feed better. . . .

General advantage. On the whole, the measure has been very beneficial to every party: the land produces more corn; the farmers are coming into better circumstances; the rent is raised; the poor are better employed; and every thing advancing; and an emulation raised which must do good.

4. ESTATE WORK

(a) *Source:* Notes in *Blundell's Diary and Letter Book*, pp. 115–6. (For Blundell, see above, p. 141.) Squire and workmen were associated in common tasks, working side by side, as the following brief extracts show.

Philip Syer began to lay a Cundit across ye way between ye Long Garden and ye Bleaching-Ground. I helped to carry a Great many of ye Stones. . . . I was most of ye Afternoone in ye Next North Hey, helping ye Workmen up with two great Roots of trees out of ye new Moss pits. . . . I helped to Winnow some of ye worst wheat with ye Fann. . . . I was in ye Winter Heys with my Workfolk. There was a great thunder Shower and all or most of us took Shelter. Thence I went to see John and Jane Bryanson who were ill. . . . I went betymes in ye Morning to my Burners in ye Winter Heys and after Dinner I stayed with them till Night and gave them a Sillibube. I had

32 Hands working for me at my Water-Cours. . . . I went to them in ye Morning and brought them some strong Drink and Biskett, and went againe after dinner and brought some more strong Drink. . . . I was most of ye Afternoone with my Burners in ye Winter Heycs. I sent them two large Pailes of Whey which was very acceptable.

(b) *Source:* Letter from Lord Irwin to Robert Hopkinson, Attorney of Wakefield, 10 June 1736, in the *Temple Newsam Papers,* Leeds. This letter shows what factors had to be taken into account when a small estate changed hands.

I intend being down towards the end of the summer, but in the meantime would you look after everything and do whats necessary as if I was there, and if any particular instructions may be wanting you'l write to me at Hills. As soon as you receive this you must pay all the servants their wages due from the late Lord . . . those that I would have continued in my service are my old friend Arthur Copperwaite, the groom, the 2 housemaids, the gardener and the old woman to look after the poultry. As I don't know what land my Lord had in his hands, but suppose he had some, I take it for granted that a husbandman will be wanting. . . . I would have the gardener lay in the house and charge him to take the best care possible of all the Plantations and of the gardens and you will allow him what help you think requisite by way of day labourers or otherwise. Take the keys of all the cellars into your possession and let no one under any pretence have them but when you are with them. You'll keep the servants at board wages or otherwise as you think best. If you have an opportunity of going to Leeds yourself make my compliments to Mr. and Mrs. Milner and family and tell them that if there is anything in the gardens that they have not, they will oblige me in sending for it, for they are heartily welcome to it. . . . My Lady desires that for the present you would remove all the plate to yours or your father's house till further orders. . . . Give the keeper a strict charge that he preserves the game in as full a manner as ever he did in the late Lords time, for shooting is my diversion and let him send me a true state of his deer and what he can spare this year. . . . Let all the spaniels be taken care of and let the keeper take care to air them. My service to your father. If he or you think it worth your while to have anything out of the garden you may. Keep my letters on a file. . . .

5. BUILDINGS AND REPAIRS

The immense amount of building in the late seventeenth and first half of the eighteenth century was mainly associated with the life of the great and small estates, although in the second half of the eighteenth century urban, commercial and industrial building began to assume great significance. Landed proprietors were often keenly interested in building problems, which sometimes involved large initial outlays on new structures as well as costs of adaptation and improvement of older structures which were difficult to predict. Active supervision was usually necessary. The noble houses in Horace Walpole's phrase were 'dispersed like great rarity plums in a vast pudding of country'; in the first industrial buildings a 'functional tradition' was perpetuated.

(a) *Source:* Letter from the Duchess of Marlborough to her grand-daughter, the Duchess of Bedford, 2 April 1732, printed in G. Scott Thomson (ed.), *Letters of a Grandmother* (1943).

I am come at this moment from Cheam. . . . The house was full of workmen. . . . What is doing to the house will make it mighty convenient and large enough, and though there is no great beauty in the situation of the house, considering 'tis within half a mile of the finest downs and best air in England and within two hours driving from London, I think it is a very pleasing habitation. And when you have quite finished it, I am sure you will like it better than anything that is done now by such as call themselves architects. I observed that the bricks were extremely good, better than I have seen anywhere, except those at Marlborough House. . . . I think the stables stand in a mighty proper place, will hold as many horses and all that belongs to them as can ever be of any use to you. And I like the walls extremely. I never saw any before of that sort, and though I think they look as well as is necessary for that use, they told me they did not cost so much as brick walls. To conclude, I think there is sense and reason in this place.

(b) *Source:* Letter from Colonel Liddell to William Cotesworth, 4 March 1718, printed in E. Hughes, *North Country Life in the Eighteenth Century* (1952), pp. 26–7. The house described is Park House, Gateshead.

Ventured to the Parke yesterday morning tho' the wind was so high it had almost blown off my head. See the worst plastering my eyes ever beheld and, what is worse, I doubt there can be no cure for it. I ordered Grey to be discharged and Wm Teward to go on with that work. I would advise you to latt and plaster to your boards first which will keep all dry and warm and the joints of the boards close and not only so but will take off a great deal of noise and the charge will not be above 15s/- a room. I have ordered them to do one after this manner but to do no further without your directions.

The timber in the Rooms over the one which was the kitchen is extremely mean so that I have ordered them to put one new baulk there to support the partition which is to be betwixt Madam's room and the other. They tell me you have given orders for a sash window to be put in the North Gavell end over the brew house. We have, one and all, agreed to suspend it till further orders. The wall is very mean, being much shaken and has a great weight upon it so that it will be very hazardous. That room will not want light so that without you have any perticular reason for it, think it advisable to run no risque. Besides, if you build a kitchen where the brew house now is, as probably you will, then that window will be stopt up. I design to step over now and then tho' perhaps you will not thank me for it, but I will do my best.

(c) The minimum cost of building a country mansion during the first half of the century was between £3,000 and £4,000, although some houses might cost thirty times as much. Public building, however, was often carefully costed. Hertfordshire Quarter Sessions decided in January 1769 to build a new Shire Hall by Michaelmas 1770. It was to cost £4,950, and to include an Assembly Room costing £550.

Source: W. Le Hardy (ed.) *Hertfordshire County Records* (1935), vol. VIII, Quarter Sessions Book, vol. 12, 9 Jan. 1769.

The said Committee, having produced to this Court several

propositions for the Strength and Ornament of the Building, have rejected those which appeared to be merely Ornamental and have returned the following Articles to the consideration of the Justices at the next Quarter Sessions:—

	£	s.	d.
If His Majesty's Justices . . . chuse to have a Stone Cornice and Blocking Course to go round the Building instead of Wood, the Difference will be	173	13	2
If it should be thought proper to put Stone Sills to all the Windows of the House instead of Lead, the Difference will be	19	10	0
And if the Justices chuse to have Stone Steps and Landings to the Great Stairs, with an Iron Rail and a Wainscot Hand Rail, instead of Wood Steps, Landings, String, and Balustrade, the Difference will be	73	12	0
If the said Justices incline to have Stone Plinths and Capings to the piers front of the Corn Market, the additional Expense will be	41	9	4
. . . if in front of the Hall, the additional Expense will be	13	11	0

(d) *Source:* Advertisement for the sale of an early industrial building in *Aris's Birmingham Gazette*, 14 April 1777.

Iron Works

To be sold, New Mills and Mackenay Forges in the Parish of Duffield and County of Derby, most beautifully and conveniently situated upon each side the River Derwent; consisting of two Iron Forges; Hammersman's Forge with a Scrap Furnace, and divers Workmen's Houses, Gardens, and a spacious Yard, lying on the East Side of the River, Also a Slitting and Rowling Mill, for Iron and Copper, and a Through adjoining, with a large Building, used as a Paper or Tin Mill, a large Warehouse, an handsome Dwelling-House, with necessary Conveniences; several Workmen's Houses and other Buildings, with Gardens, Orchard, and Croft, most delightfully situated on the Side of the River, and worked by Wears made at vast Labour and Expence, and executed with great Judgment. The Situation of these Works, with the constant Power of the Water, and all their Conveniences renders them capable of being vastly improved, and altered or changed to any other Purpose or Business whatever, where a continual Supply of Water is necessary. . . .

(e) *Source:* Letter from Sir Robert Williams to Michael Hughes, 1 Feb. 1805, printed in T. C. Barker and J. R. Harris, *A Merseyside Town in the Industrial Revolution* (1954), p. 152.

I have never altered my opinion on the point that you have acted wisely in building when you can, for a thousand reasons —and now my good Sir allow me to give you my poor advice, of all things make your new house snug and comfortable, instead of attending to great uniformity in the building, a good water closet contiguous to your Bed Chambers—and one out of your house, your rooms high, but small as you please— Carpets to take up in your bedrooms and dressing rooms; and good fire-places—these are luxuries that all the World like.

(f) Owner occupiers who built their own houses often did better than people who bought houses designed by speculative builders.

Source: Report on the Mecklenburgh Square Estate, London, begun in 1807, printed in J. Summerson, *Georgian London* (1945), p. 152. The houses in this estate provided urban accommodation of a carefully graded kind for all classes.

The State and General conduct of the Buildings are much upon a par with the state and general conduct of Buildings erected by speculators in various parts of the metropolis and its vicinity. Those who build for their own occupation may reasonably expect such Buildings as we fear it is not practicable to obtain from speculative Builders for however prudent or desirable it may be to restrain and regulate the conduct of the work by Agreements founded on the most minute description of the dimensions and quality of every part of the Building yet experience has shewn that such restrictions would materially impede the letting of the ground.

6. EXPERT WORK

While much eighteenth-century estate work could be carried out by domestic staff, experts sometimes had to be employed.

(a) *Source:* Notes in Blundell's *Diary and Letter Book,* p. 122. Notice how the millwrights who were summoned to repair Blundell's mill worked as a family team.

Dec. 3rd 1710. I sent for my Miller for ye Mill Rights, my Mill having suffered great damage in ye Sales and Shalft this last Night by ye Winde.

Dec. 5th. Rich Dauber came to repair ye great Loss I have suffered in my Mill.

Dec. 6th. Henry Dauber ye Mill Right and his Nephew James came to mend my Mill, and ye two Sawyers Richard and Joseph came to do ye Sawing Work for it. I helped Henry Dauber to see whether I had any Tree growing about ye House proper for a Mill Shaft.

Dec. 7th. I felled an Oak Tree between ye New Orchard & the new Grounds for a Mill Shaft.

Dec. 11th. Charles Howerd brought me Home two Fir Ballks for my Mill from Thomas Hurst.

Dec. 21st. I put up a new Mill Shaft.

Dec. 23rd. I paid off ye Sawers, and ye Mill Rights went hence.

Jan. 9th 1711. My Mill was set a-going, it being ye first Time it went since it was so ill Brocken.

(b) *Source:* Letter from Edward Purefoy to Zachary Jordan, 30 March 1736, printed in *Purefoy Letters,* vol. I, p. 45.

Master Zachary/

I can't find by the people of Shalstone what your other name is, I understand by them you make their ploughs. I desire you will make mee a very good plough & bring it over as soon as possible you can. If you come soon in the morning you may do something to a plough that I have already.

from

Your freind to serve you

E. P.

ffor/
    Goodman Zachary a
    ploughmaker at Helmdon

7. GENTEEL WORK

At the opposite end of the scale to expert work was work carried on by wives and daughters to while away time in leisurely households. It ranged from needlework (and in the late eighteenth century the making of samplers) to keeping a diary.

(a) *Source:* Letter from Isabella Ingram to Mrs. Charles Ingram, 26 Sept. 1758, in the *Temple Newsam Papers*, Leeds.

I work comme quatre and to be sure my chair is beautiful (I mean a little bit of the back that is done) tea green and purple, all my own ingenious conceit and I really think (tho' comparisons are odious) they will be much handsomer than Gobelin Tapestry, but I am *modest* and therefore shall say no more about it.

(b) The governess, Miss Weeton, filled seven quarto volumes between 1805 and 1825 with copies of letters she had sent and letters she had received.

Source: Note in E. Hall (ed.), *Miss Weeton, Journal of a Governess* (1936), p. xiii.

It has been a great amusement during many a solitary hour when I had no other employ, when I should only have been engaged in some fine tedious piece of needlework or other.

8. HOUSE WORK

In the household of the propertied, big or small, 'real' housework was carried out by domestic servants. (See also, above, p. 139.)

(a) *Source:* Instructions to a house maid in T. Balston (ed.), *The Housekeeping Book of Susanna Whatman 1776–1800* (1956), pp. 17ff.

To use as little soap as possible (if any) in scowering rooms. All the rooms to be dry scrubbed with white sand.

To take the papers off the tops of the beds twice a year.

To whisk all the window curtains every Saturday. Shake mats, carpets, etc. every Saturday. To use a painter's brush to all the ledges, window frames and furniture, and then the duster. Never to use a hard brush to any mahogany carving that has been neglected and the dust suffered to settle in it.

o

To keep a small mop in the cupboard in the Water Closet, and use warm water every day to keep the inside clean. In frosty weather not to pour it too hot, only just warm. . . .

To rise on Tuesday morning to wash her own things and the dusters, and help wash stockings. To iron her own things of an evening. To mend the towels and her Master's common stockings of an evening.

To work in [the] Storeroom every day after her house work is finished, except Saturday, when every thing must be looked to that wants doing weekly. Housemaid folds with the Laundry-maid every Wednesday.

To take turns of going to Church every other Sunday with the Laundrymaid.

Never to dust pictures, nor the frames or anything that has a gilt edge. . . .

To force back all the window shutters: otherwise they get warped, and will not go into their place, which makes a room look very bad indeed. To sweep the steps in front of the house every morning when necessary.

When a floor cloth wants washing, not to use a brush or soapsuds, but a soft linen and some fresh milk and water. A steel should be used round the hearth and in all dirty corners.

Venetian blinds. When let down, to pull the longest string to turn or close them quite. Otherwise the sun will come through the laths.

(b) Things did not always run smoothly in the domestic work of a household.

Source: Letter from Lady Fermanagh to her husband, 1 Dec. 1710, printed in *The Verney Letters*, p. 284.

. . . The Keeper is such a dredfull fellow that for my part I can't immagin what the maids will doe with him, for he went in the Beer Seller and he is more drunk than yesterday, for above three hours with small Beare, as there won't be a drop left when I goe away; & because the Cooke lock'd the Seller Doore in the afternoon, as I order'd her, Roberts being gon out, he nail'd up all the Larders & the Cook's Chamber doore, & indeed you never saw so strange a fellow in your life, & the gardener is as bad; I really think the maid would not stay

behind, only that I tell her she will be in towne in a little
while. I think you would doe well to write to Mr. Challoner
strictly what you would have don about the House; that he
himself must not be out on your business if the Keeper is out
late or comes in drunk, that he must be keep't out of the
House and Mr. Challoner should take care about the Gardener,
& let you know how he goes on.

9. MANUFACTURING

Manufacturing, assisted by technical invention, became an
increasingly important national activity as the century went by.
(See above, p. 144.) Conditions of work (size of establishment;
use of machines, patterns of human relations) varied from place
to place.

(a) Dean Tucker looked at the manufacturing distribution of work
thirty years after Defoe.

Source: Dean Tucker, *Instructions to Travellers* (1758).

In many Provinces of the Kingdom, particularly *Staffordshire, Lancashire,* and certain districts of *Yorkshire,* with the
Towns of *Manchester, Norwich,* and some others, the Labour . . .
is very properly proportioned . . . so that no Time shall be
wasted in passing the goods to be manufactured from Hand to
Hand, and that no unnecessary Strength should be employed.
For an instance of both Kinds, take one among a Thousand
at *Birmingham,* viz. When a Man stamps a metal Button by
means of an Engine, a Child stands by him to place the Button
in readiness to receive the Stamp, and to remove it when
received, and then to place another. By these Means the
Operator can stamp at least double the Number, which he
could otherwise have done, had he been obliged to have
stopped each Time to have shifted the Buttons: And as his
Gettings may be from 14d to 18d and the Child's from a Penny
to 2d. *per* Day for doing the same Quantity of Work, which
must have required double the Sum, had the Man alone been
employed; this single Circumstance saves alone 80, or even
100 *per cent* at the same Time that it trains up Children to an
Habit of Industry, almost as soon as they can speak. And hence

it is that the *Bijoux d'Angleterre,* or the Birmingham Toys, are rendered so cheap as to astonish all *Europe*; and that the Roman Catholic countries are supplied with such vast Quantities of Crucifixes, Agnus Dei's, &c from *England.* . . . The good Effects of this Proportioning of Labour to different Strengths and Sexes is still more extensive than at first appears. For in *Birmingham* the Numbers of poor Women on the Pay-Bill, compared to those of Poor Men, are hardly three to two, whereas in *Bristol,* the Numbers are upwards of four to one; and in many parts of *London,* it is still worse: So great is the Difference, and such is the Expensiveness and heavy Burdens of a Wrong Conduct even in this Respect; not to mention that Prostitution and Debauchery seem to be an unavoidable Consequence in the Female Sex of Poverty and Idleness, when they are young; and when they grow old, what Refuge can they have, if they do not soon rot with their Diseases, but the Parish pay. . . .

(b) A Yorkshire ballad gives a close-up account of the variety of family jobs involved in domestic manufacture. A clothier tells the members of his household what to do while he is away buying wool.

Source: The manuscript of the ballad is in the Leeds Reference Library, and parts of it have been quoted by H. Heaton in *Yorkshire Woollen and Worsted Industry* (1920), pp. 344–6.

MASTER: Lads, work hard I pray,
　　　　　Cloth mun be pearked [examined for faults]
　　　　　　next Market day.
　　　　　And Tom mun go to-morn to twi' spinners,
　　　　　And Will mun seek about for t' singers;
　　　　　And Jack, to-morn by time be rising,
　　　　　And go to t' sizing mill for sizing.
　　　　　And get you web and warping done
　　　　　That ye may get it into t' loom.
　　　　　Joe, go give my horse some corn,
　　　　　For I design for t' Wolds to-morn.
　　　　　So mind and clean my boots and shoon,
　　　　　For I'll be up i' t' morn right *soon!*
　　　　　Mary—there's wool—tak thee and dye it. . . .

[His wife protests]

MISTRESS: So thou's setting me my wark,
I think I'd more need mend thy sark. [Shirt]
Prithie, who mun sit at bobbin wheel?
And ne'er a cake at top o' th' creel!
And me to bake, and swing, to blend,
And milk and barns to school to send,
And dumplings for the lads to mak,
And yeast to seek, and 'syk as that!
And washing up, morn, noon and neet,
And bowls to scald, and milk to fleet,
And barns to fetch again at neet.

MASTER: When thou begin thou's never done!
Bessie and thee mun get up soon,
And stir about and get all done;
For all things mun aside be laid,
When we want help about our trade.

(c) Domestic work encouraged feelings of 'independence', but there was often a big gulf between master clothier and worker (see above, p. 156). Bitterness is expressed in a contemporary ballad.

Source: Lines put into a clothier's mouth from *The Clothier's Delight, or the Rich Man's Joy,* printed in J. Burnley, *History of Wool and Woolcombing* (1883), pp. 161–3.

We'll make the poor weavers work at a low rate,
We'll find fault where there is none, and so we will bate;
If trading goes dead, we will presently show it,
But if it grows good, they shall never know it;
We'll tell them that cloth beyond sea will not go,
We are not whether we keep clothing or no . . .
By poor people's labour we full up our purse
Although we do get it with many a curse.

(d) Machinery could take some of the drudgery out of work. (Yet for its harmful effects, see also below, p. 212.)

Source: J. Kennedy, 'Observations on the Rise and Progress of the Cotton Trade in Great Britain' in *Memorials of the Manchester Literary and Philosophical Society* (1819), p. 130.

In the year 1797 a new machine for cleaning cotton was

constructed by Mr. Snodgrass, and first used at Johnston near Paisley by Messrs. Houston and Co. This is called a scutching or blowing machine. Its merits were but little known till 1808 or 1809, when it was introduced into Manchester. It is now generally adopted for cleaning cotton. The labor of that operation, formerly performed by women, in a most fatiguing manner, and always considered as degrading; has been reduced by this machine to about one twentieth of what it used to be.

(e) The real transformation in manufacturing came with the development of steam power. Thomas Newcomen had built the first steam engine in 1712, but it was James Watt, who joined Matthew Boulton of Birmingham in 1775, who introduced the strategic new techniques. Boulton and Watt's order book is a guide to the spread of the 'industrial revolution'. The following letter from Samuel Walker, a progressive ironfounder of Rotherham, Yorkshire, is typical of many they received.

Source: Letter of 15 May 1781, printed in A. H. John, *The Walker Family* (1951), pp. 56ff.

of S. Yorkshire, Rotherham, May 15th, 1781.
Gentn.
We have some works upon a river, wh. in general supplies us well with water; but in dry seasons we are much retarded for want of water. In order to make up this defect in some measure, we are intending to build a fire engine, either in the old or common manner, or under the sanction of your patent. We should therefore be glad to know on what terms we can be permitted to go on under the latter. We have coal of our own getting laid down at the Work at about 2¾d. cwt. and are thinking of a cylinder with 36 or 43 in. diamr., and eight foot stroke, and suppoee we may work the engine 3 to 6 months in the year, according as the seasons are wet or dry.—Quere, on what terms we can be permited to go on with either of the above cylinders, as to time, & sum, or what sum in hand you will give us a commission to go on without further interruption.

We hope you will be moderate in your demands, which may be a means of introducing your engines into this country, & without which I imagine you can not expect any thing scarce from this neighbourhood. Your reply *as soon as you can* will oblige Gentn.

Your etc.

N.B. We can have small coal which is got very near to us laid down at our works at about 1½d cwt.

(f) Backed by power, machinery could also do much that men could not easily do.

Source: Note added by W. Brownrigg to J. Dalton, *Descriptive Poem to Two Ladies at their Returning from Viewing the Mines near Whitehaven* (1754).

It appears from pretty exact calculation that it would require about 550 men, or a power equal to that of 110 horses, to work the pumps of one of the largest fire engines now in use. . . . And that as much water may be raised by an engine of this size kept constantly at work, as can be drawn up by 2,250 men with rollers and buckets, after the manner now daily practised in many mines. . . . So great is the power of the air in one of these engines.

(g) By the end of the century not everyone agreed with Defoe's assessment of the relative merits of work in the country and in industry.

Source: C. B. Andrews (ed.), *The Torrington Diaries* (1935), vol. II, p. 118. The passage comes from an account of 'a tour of the North' in 1792.

Oh! That the wastes of this land were cultivated; and that the property of the land was properly sub-divided for the support, and encouragement of the honest kind; and that it were not thought usefull, (nor necessary,) that vicious unwholesome trades should be encouraged to the immense gain of a few, by the loss of the lives of thousands.—Amidst all the crew of artisans, you may search in vain for healthy looks;—for, alas! they are all sqalid from unwholesome toil, and relaxing debauchery.—At Liverpool the importation of wheat from America is very great; for this great cotton trade cannot support itself; consequently as their husbandry keeps pace with our manufactories, who, think ye, will last longest; the ground work, or the cotton work?—The one fix'd as the Globe; the other as precarious as the wind:—The one rearing hardy honesty: the other supporting enervating debauchery—. Now were five hundred of either of such men to come to combat; what could the sons of the shuttle perform against the followers of the plough? Why—they would fall before the latter.—

10. WOMEN'S WORK

As some of the extracts quoted above reveal, women were employed in the eighteenth century not only on farms and estates or as domestic servants but in a wide variety of industrial occupations, sometimes alongside men and children, often within their own family, at other times in groups of their own under separate supervision. Conditions were sometimes appalling and the work dangerous. Sometimes too, as extract (e) shows, attempts were made during times of trade depression to exclude women from 'the better classes of work'.

(a) *Source:* D. Davies, *Care of Labourers in Husbandry* (1787).

These [Gloucestershire] women commonly begin the world with an infant, and are mere nurses for ten or twelve years after marriage, being always either with child, or having a child at the breast, consequently incapable of doing much other work besides the necessary business of the families, such as baking, washing, and the like. . . . If in the summer they are able to go to harvest work, they must pay some person a shilling a week out of their earnings for looking after their children.
Their earnings would be

Bean or pease setting for 3 weeks at 7d a day	10s. 6d.
Fruit picking for 2 weeks at 4d.	4s.
Haymaking for 2 weeks at 4d	4s.
Gleaning, or leasing 6 bushels at 5s. 6d. pr. bushel	£1 13s.

(b) *Source:* W. Hutton, *History of Birmingham* (1783 edn.), p. 84.

When I first approached Birmingham, from Walsall in

1741, I was surprised at the prodigious number of blacksmiths' shops upon the road; and could not conceive how a country, though populous, could support so many people of the same occupation. In some of these shops I observed one or more females, stripped of their upper garments, and not overcharged with the lower, wielding the hammer with all the grace of their sex. The beauties of their faces were rather eclipsed by the smut of the anvil. . . . Struck with the novelty, I inquired 'Whether the ladies in this country shod horses?' and was answered with a smile, 'They are nailers'.

(c) *Source:* C. B. Andrews (ed.) *The Torrington Diaries*, vol. II, p. 59.

Turning to the right over mossy commons with much fatigue to ourselves, and horses, arrived at 12 o'clock at the Ecton Mines [Derbyshire], the most valuable property of the Duke of Devonshire.—Our horses were led forward by T. B. to the village of Warsell, where dinner was to be provided for us.—One of the managers of the mine conducted us up the shaft to the water engine, which drains the mine; and a dirty and tedious walk it was; the manager, a miner, P— and myself, with each a lighted candle in our hands. In this infernal region one cart of ore passed by us. At the water engine we were stunn'd by the noise, and astonish'd at the body of water; one river flowing above, and one below us. Next, we were carried to the smeltings of the copper, and lead, saw several siftings, and the many children employ'd in the laborious pounding of the stone, by which hand work they *may* gain 6d. per day. The women wash the ore. In the several branches are employ'd many hundred labourers.

(d) *Source:* R. Ayton, *Voyage Round Great Britain* (1813), vol. II, p. 155. Although this account is late in time, it refers to conditions at Whitehaven, Cumberland, which were not new.

We were frequently interrupted in our march by the horses proceeding in this manner with their cargoes to the shaft, and always driven by girls, all of the same description, ragged and beastly in their appearance, and with a shameless indecency in their behaviour, which awe-struck as one was by the gloom and loneliness around one, had something quite frightful in it, and gave the place the character of a hell. All the people whom we met with were distinguished by an extraordinary wretchedness; immoderate labour and a noxious atmosphere had marked their countenances with signs of disease and decay; they were mostly half-naked, blackened all over with dirt, and altogether so miserably disfigured and abused, that they looked like a race fallen from the common rank of men and doomed, as in a kind of purgatory, to wear away their lives in these dismal shades.

(e) *Source:* A List of Prices in Branches of the Spitalfields Weaving Manufacture (1769), quoted in M. D. George, *London Life in the Eighteenth Century* (1925), p. 182. Note how dilution of labour in war-time was expressly permitted.

No woman or girl to be employed in making any kind of work except such works as are herein fixed and settled at 5½d per ell . . . or under for the making and those not to excell half an ell in width. . . . And no woman or girl is to be employed in making any sort of handkerchief of above the usual or settled price of 4*s*. 6*d*. per dozen for the making thereof PROVIDED always . . . that in case it shall hereafter happen that the Kingdom of Great Britain shall engage in war . . . that then every manufacturer shall be at liberty to employ women or girls in the making of any sort of works as they shall think most fit and convenient without any restraint whatsoever. . . .

(f) Some women had a reasonable degree of independence in their work, and some widows tried to continue in their late husbands' footsteps.

Source: Notice in the *Newcastle Courant*, 13 Feb. 1779.

M. Hawthorn, Widow of the late John Hawthorn, Watchmaker of this town, tenders her grateful thanks to the friends of her late husband; and begs to acquaint them and the public, that she will carry on the said Business (having engaged able workmen therein) and hopes for the continuance of their favours, which she will at all times studiously endeavour to merit.

Jewelry, Trinkets, Watches, Music and Musical Instruments.

11. CHILD LABOUR

Child labour was taken for granted within this economic and social system: it was supported even by moral arguments. An American visitor to Halifax in 1777 spoke of child labour which 'not only keeps their little minds from vice . . . but takes a heavy burden from their poor parents'. [See also Defoe's view, above, p. 75.] Apprenticeship was the most highly organized system of dealing with child labour: it sometimes involved very fierce discipline, particularly for pauper apprentices (see above, p. 169).

(a) *Source:* Note in the *Annual Register* (1775).

Every design which tends to promote the commercial interest of a country is worthy of observation; but that, which at the same time that it strengthens the hands of industry, advances the temporal and eternal welfare of our fellow-creatures in an especial manner merits attention. . . . The employing of female infants, especially those of the poor, from five years old and upwards, will introduce an early familiar habit of industry among the most indigent of the community, and lay a foundation for preserving them from those dangers and misfortunes to which—from their sex and situations, they are so peculiarly exposed.

(b) *Source:* Anon., *Enquiry into the Causes of the Increase of the Poor* (1738), p. 43.

A most unhappy practice prevails in most places to apprentice poor children, no matter to what master provided he lives out of the parish; if the child serves the first forty days we are rid of him for ever. The master may be a tiger in cruelty; he may beat, abuse, strip naked, starve, or do what he will to the poor innocent lad. . . . I knew a poor old weaver . . . who some time ago took a poor apprentice from another parish; he covenanted, as is usual, to teach him his trade, to provide and allow him meat, drink, apparel, etc. to save harmless and indemnify the parish whence he took him, and to give him two good new suits of wearing apparel at the end of his apprenticeship. This master had several times been convicted of theft, and had then actually left off his trade through weakness and old age, and as soon as the money he had with the boy was spent threw himself, apprentice and all, upon the parish.

(c) *Source:* W. Radcliffe, *Origin of the New System of Manufacture* (1828).

My Mother taught me (while too young to weave) to earn my bread by carding and spinning cotton, winding linen or cotton weft for my father and elder brothers at the loom, until I became of sufficient age and strength for my father to put me on to a loom.

(d) Samuel Crompton, the inventor of the mule, recollected how his mother helped him to prepare cotton when he was a child.

Source: G. T. French, *The Life and Times of Samuel Crompton,* (1859).

I recollect that soon after I was able to walk I was employed in the cotton manufacture. My mother used to bat the cotton wool on a wire riddle. It was then put into a deep brown mug with a strong ley of soap suds. My mother then tucked up my petticoats about my waist, and put me into the tub to tread upon the cotton at the bottom. When a second riddleful was batted, I was lifted out, it was placed in the mug, and I again trod it down. This process was continued until the mug became so full that I could no longer safely stand in it, when a chair was placed besides it and I held on by the back. When the mug was quite full the soap suds were pored off, and each separate dollop of wool well squeezed to free it of moisture. They were then placed on the bread rack under the beams of the Kitchen loft to dry. My mother and my grand-mother carded the wool by hand, taking one of the dollops at a time or the single hand cards. When carded, they were put aside in separate parcels ready for spinning.

(e) The place of child labour in the new factory system was satirized by Robert Southey, the poet and essayist.

Source: R. Southey, *Letters from England* (1807).

Mr.— remarked that nothing could be so beneficial to a country as manufactures. 'You see these children, sir,' said he. 'In most parts of England poor children are a burthen to their

parents and to the parish; here the parish, which would else
have to support them, is rid of all expense; they get their
bread almost as soon as they can run about, and by the time
they are seven or eight years old bring in money. There is no
idleness among us:— they come at five in the morning; we
allow them half an hour for breakfast, and an hour for dinner;
they leave work at six, and another set relieves them for the
night; the wheels never stand still.' I was looking, while he
spoke, at the unnatural dexterity with which the fingers of these
little creatures were playing in the machinery, half giddy
myself with the noise and the endless motion; and when he
told me there was no rest in these walls, day or night, I thought
that if Dante had peopled one of his hells with children, here
was a scene worthy to have supplied him with new images of
torment.

12. INCENTIVES

Some account has been given previously of eighteenth-century
conceptions of business and industrial discipline (see above, p. 50).
There was a running debate in the eighteenth century as to whether
high or low wages provided the more adequate incentive to work.

(a) *Source:* J. Smith, *Memoirs of Wool* (1747), vol. II, p. 308.

It is a fact well known . . . that scarcity, to a certain degree,
promotes industry, and that the manufacturer who can subsist
on three days' work will be idle and drunken the remainder of
the week. . . . We can fairly aver that a reduction of wages
in the woollen manufacture would be a national blessing and
advantage, and no real injury to the poor. By this means we
might keep our trade, uphold our rents, and reform the people
into the bargain.

(b) There are many concrete examples of this philosophy. Yet
there were other writers who were concerned about low wages.
The following comes from Melksham, Wiltshire.

Source: Letter from an anonymous 'Englishman' to Lord Harring-
ton (1738 or 1739) in the Public Record Office, SP 36/47, folio 37.

Most of [the discontent] proceeds from the Contrivances and
Pride of the Clothiers, as living in luxury, neglecting their

Business, trusting Servants with the care of their Affairs; and beating down the Wages of the Poor, & paying them in bread, cheese, meat, linnen, & Woolen Cloth and so forth att a price att least one third more than the real value. . . . The poor workman is starved into frenzy & then is guilty of rash decisions by which he forfeits his life to the Law (if a Lunatick can forfeit it).

(c) Adam Smith took the same point of view.

Source: The Wealth of Nations (1776), Book I, ch. VIII.

The liberal reward of labour as it encourages the propagation, so it increases the industry of the common people. The wages of labour are the encouragement of industry, which, like every other human quality, improves in proportion to the encouragement it receives. A plentiful subsistence increases the bodily strength of the labourer, and the comfortable hope of bettering his condition, and of ending his days in ease and plenty, animates him to exert that strength to the utmost. Where wages are high, accordingly, we shall always find the workmen more active, diligent, and expeditious than where they are low: in England, for example, than in Scotland; in the neighbourhood of great towns than in remote country places.

(d) *Source: Select Committee of the House of Commons, Report on the State of the Woollen Manufacture of England* (1806).

An evil in itself abundantly sufficient to accomplish the ruin, not only of any particular branch of Trade, but even of the whole commercial greatness of our country is the progressive rise of Wages.

CHAPTER VII

Play

28 June 1763. In the even, Joseph Fuller and myself plaid a game of cricket with Mr. Geo. Bannister and James Fuller, for half a crown's worth of punch, which we won very easy, but it being hot and drinking a pretty deal of punch, it got into my head, so that I came home not sober.

(from the *Diary* of THOMAS TURNER, 28 June 1763)

That disease of indolence, which you and my other companions used to laugh at, grows stronger and stronger upon me; my symptoms, indeed, are mortal; for I begin now to lose the power of struggling against the malady, sometimes to shut my ears against self-admonition, and admit of it as a lawful indulgence.

(Letter in *The Mirror*, 1 March 1779)

BOSWELL: But if we could have pleasure always, should not we be happy? The greatest part of men would compound for pleasure.

JOHNSON: Supposing we could have pleasure always, an intellectual man would not compound for it. The greatest part of men would compound, because the greatest part of men are gross.

(BOSWELL's *Life of Johnson*, 1778)

In the estimation of many people, the Duke of Dorset is the most extraordinarily accomplished nobleman we have—at cricket, tennis and billiards his Grace has hardly any equal.

(*Whitehall Evening Post*, 8 July 1783)

The amusements of the people have changed with their character. Athletic exercises of Quoits, Wrestling, Foot-ball, Prison bars and Shooting with the Long-bow are becoming obsolete and almost forgotten; and it is to be regretted that the present pursuits and pleasures of the labouring class are of a more effeminate cast. They are now Pigeon-fanciers, Canary-breeders and Tulip-growers.

(RICHARD GUEST, *A Compendious History of the Cotton-Manufacture*, 1823)

1. DIVERSIONS

Rough sports remained favourite pastimes of the British throughout the century, although increasing order and regulation were apparent. The Jockey Club, for instance, which regulated racing, was founded in 1750.

(a) *Source:* M. Misson, *Memoirs and Observations* (1719), pp. 304ff.

Besides the Sports and Diversions common to most other *European* Nations, as Tennis, Billiards, Chess, Tick-Tack, Dancing, Plays etc., the *English* have some which are particular to them, or at least which they love and use more than any other People. Cock-fighting is a Royal Pleasure in *England*. Their Combates between Bulls and Dogs, Bears and Dogs, and sometimes Bulls and Bears, are not Battals to Death, as those of Cocks: Anything that looks like Fighting is delicious to an *Englishman*. If two little Boys quarrel in the Street, then Passengers stop, make a Ring round them in a Moment, and set them against one another, that they may come to Fisticuffs. When 'tis come to a Fight, each polls off his Neckcloth and his Waistcoat (some will strip themselves quite naked to their Wastes), and give them to hold to some of the Standers-by; then they begin to brandish their Fists in the Air; the Blows are aim'd all at the Face, they kick one another's Shins, they tug one another by the Hair etc. He that has got the other down, may give him one Blow or two before he rises, but no more; and let the Boy get up ever so often, the other is oblig'd to box him again as often as he requires it. During the Fight, the Ring of By-standers encourage the Combatants with great Delight of Heart, and never part them while they fight according to the Rules: and these By-standers are not only other Boys, Porters and Rabble, but all Sorts of Men of Fashion; some thrusting by the Mob that they may see plain, others sitting upon Stalls; and all would hire places if Scaffolds could be built in a Moment. . . . These Combats are less frequent among grown Men than Children, but they are not rare. . . . Wrestling too is one of the Diversions of the English, especially in the Northern Counties. . . . In Winter *Footballs* is a useful and charming Exercise: it is a Leather Ball about as big as one's Head, fill'd with Wind: This is kick'd about from one to t'other in the Streets, by him that can get at it, and that is all the Art of it. Setting up a Cock in some open Place, and knocking it down with a Stick, at forty or fifty Paces Distance, is another Sport that affords no little Pleasure; but this Diversion is confin'd to a certain Season. . . .

2. COUNTRY SPORTS

Leisure patterns were as highly stratified as work patterns. Partridge shooting was 'the genteelest sport we have' (1777) and cockfighting the most popular. In the country fox-hunting became a national sport only after the middle of the eighteenth century. The first fox-hunting classic, Peter Beckford's *Thoughts on Hunting*, was not published until 1781. Property qualifications limited participation in many sports.

(a) *Source:* Inscription on a hunting horn, quoted in The Duke of Beaufort and M. Morris, *Hunting* (1891), p. 28. The attribution has been questioned, and certainly many country squires kept hounds early in the eighteenth century. (See below, extract (d).)

Thomas Boothby, Esq., Tooley Park, Leicester. With this horn he hunted the first pack of fox-hounds then in England 55 years: born 1677, died 1752.

(b) *Source:* J. S. Gardiner, *The Art and Pleasure of Hare-Hunting* (1750).

A lover of hunting almost every man is, or would be thought; but twenty in the field after an hare find more delight and sincere enjoyment than one in twenty in a fox-chase, the former consisting of an endless variety of accidental delights, the latter little more than hard riding, the pleasure of clearing some dangerous leap, the pride of bestriding the best nag, and showing somewhat of the bold horseman; and (equal to anything) of being first in at the death, after a chase frequently from county to county, and perhaps above half the way out of sight or hearing of the hounds, So that, but for the name of fox-hunting, a man might as well mount at his stable-door, and determine to gallop twenty miles an end into another county.

P

(c) Deer hunting was an older sport. The duties of a park-keeper are set out in the following extract.

Source: G. Jacob, *The Compleat Sportsman* (1718), p. 67.

He must daily take a Turn round his Park, and keep a constant Account of the Number of his Deer, and oftentimes watch them at Night, for their Preservation against unlawful Hunters, especially in Moonshiny Nights and the Rutting Season. He must take care to calculate an exact Number of Bucks and Does proper to be kill'd in each Season. . . so as not to make any Destruction, or lessening of his Park, and at the same Time not to over-stock the same, preserving a proper number of young Fawns to be bred up in the steads of those he kills; and having always a Regard to Casualties, which some will happen in the Winter, unavoidably.

(d) Sir Roger de Coverley was a keen sportsman—without too much formality. Fox-hunting was far more formally organized by the end of the century.

Source: Article in *The Spectator*, No. 116. 13 July 1710/11.

In his youthful days [he had] taken forty coveys of partridges in a season and tired many a salmon with a line consisting of a single hair. The constant thanks and good wishes of the neighbourhood attended him on account of his remarkable enmity towards foxes: having destroyed more of these vermin in one year than it was thought the whole country could have produced. . . . His hunting horses were the finest and best managed in all these parts: his tenants are still full of the praises of a grey stone-horse that unhappily staked himself several years since, and was buried with great solemnity in the orchard.

Sir Roger, being at present too old for fox-hunting, to keep himself in action, has disposed of his beagles and got a pack of stop-hounds. What these want in speed, he endeavours to make amends for by the deepness of their mouths and the variety of their notes, which are suited in such manner to each other, that the whole cry makes up a complete concert. . . .

(e) Cockfighting (along with badger-baiting and bull-baiting) was carried on throughout the century, often, but not always, with all sections of society present.

Source: Advertisement in the *Chelmsford Chronicle*, 11 May 1787.

Cocking—This is to acquaint all Gentlemen Cockers, That there will be a Main of Cocks fought at the King's Arms, at Burnham, on the 21st of May, between the gentlement of Dengie Hundred and the gentlement of Rochford Hundred— To fight eleven battles for Two Guineas a battle, and Five the Main. Dinner at One O'Clock.

(f) Boxing fitted into this range of sports. Contests were with bare fists and sometimes ended in death. There were often several thousand spectators, particularly in the last decades of the century. They included members of the aristocracy and the royal family. London had its first boxing booth in 1719. There were no rules until 1867.

Source: Report in the *Ipswich Journal*, 19 July 1788.

Wednesday se'nnight a pitched battle was fought at Tillingham, in this county, between R. King of Southminster, and Noah Church of Bradwell; they met about 5 in the afternoon. The contest lasted about an hour and 5 minutes, during which time, it is supposed, more hard fighting was never known. Church being a strong powerful man, not less than 6 feet 2 inches high, and King only 5 feet 9 inches and a half, betts ran much in favour of him; but King gained a complete victory over his antagonist, amidst a concourse of nearly 3000 spectators.

(g) *Source:* Report in the *Morning Post*, 18 April 1788.

On Friday, a battle was fought at Blackheath between Crabbe, a Jew, and Oliver, commonly called *Death*; in which the former was victorious. All the great patrons, and distinguished professors of this *fine art* were present, and many bets were laid. The battle was honoured, in particular, by the attendance of his ROYAL HIGHNESS THE PRINCE OF WALES.

(h) Boxing gloves had been invented, but were seldom used.

Source: Note in the *Advertiser*, 16 Feb. 1747.

Mr. Broughton proposes with proper assistance to open an Academy at his house in the Haymarket for the instruction of those who are willing to be initiated in the mystery of boxing ...

where that truly British art, with all the various blows, stops,
cross buttocks, etc., incidental to the combatants will be fully
taught and explained; and that persons of quality and distinction may not be debarred from entering into a course of
these lectures, they will be given with the utmost tenderness
and regard to the delicacy of the frame and constitution of
the pupil, for which reason muffles will be provided that will
effectually secure them from the inconveniency of black eyes,
broken jaws and bloody noses.

(i) *Source:* J. Freeth, Stage Boxing in *The Political Songster* (1790),
p. 161.

The true art of BOXING—the old English game,
Of late to so fond an attention lays claim;
JOHN BULL seems resolv'd to throw bullets aside
And let by the Fist future contests be try'd.

This art if we turn about forty years back,
Was taught by old BROUGHTON, and practic'd by SLACK . . .
SLACK's reign was not long—with his match soon he met,
GEORGE TAYLOR, the Barber, who never was beat;
By plunges well aim'd, in John Bull's crowded pit,
The swaggering Butcher soon made to submit.

Cross-buttocks caus'd laughter, the whole was a treat,
A feast for the VULGAR, and fun for the GREAT;
And CUMBERLAND WILL was as fond of the sport,
And any PRINCE now is that graces the COURT.

(j) Horse racing was popular in Queen Anne's reign, and there
was a sporting paper at Newmarket as early as 1704. The Oaks
was first run in 1779 and the Derby a year later.

Source: Notice in *The Gazette,* 18/21 June 1705.

These are to give Notice, That his Royal Highness the Prince
is pleased to give a Gold Plate, value One Hundred Guineas,
to be run for at Black Hambleton in Yorkshire, over the four
miles long Beacon course, the last Thursday in July, by any
Horse five years old last Foaling time; no Horse to be admitted
to run but such as bring a Certificate from the Breeder of his
Horses Age . . . each Horse to carry ten Stone weight, and
start at the usual hours.

(k) *Source:* Notes for 12 and 22 Aug. 1756 in the *Diary* of Thomas Turner.

This day being the first race-day at Lewes, my sister Ann Slater and I, upon a horse borrowed of Mr. French, rode to Lewes, where we arrived just as the people came from the hill. We went to see the ball, which, in my oppinion, was an extremely pretty sight. The King's plate of 100 sovereigns was run for by Mr. Warren's horse Careless, and Mr. Rogers's horse Newcastle Jack, which was won by Careless, the other being drawn after the first heat. 'Tis said there were £100 laid by the grooms. . . .

22 August 1756. I sett off for Piltdown, where I saw Charles Diggens and James Fowle run twenty rod for one guinea each. I got never a bet, but very drunk.

3. GAMES

Both cricket and football were played in the eighteenth century. They were adaptations of older games, with marked local variations. Cricket became much more highly organized during the eighteenth century, with money stakes, betting on the results, and a considerable popular appeal. All classes participated. In a famous match at Finsbury when Kent beat All England by one run, Lord John Sackville was a member of the Kent team which was captained by Rumney, his head gardener. The M.C.C. was formed in 1787.

(a) *Source:* An account by John Nyrenone of the famous matches between the Hambledon Club, a remarkable Hampshire village club, and All England, which Hambledon won, taken from his *Young Cricketer's Tutor* (1833).

There was high feasting held on Broad Halfpenny during the solemnity of one of our grand matches. Oh! it was a heart-stirring sight to witness the multitude forming a complete and dense circle round that noble green. Half the county would be present and all their hearts with us. Little Hambledon pitted against All England was a proud thought for the Hampshire men. Defeat was glory in such a struggle—Victory, indeed, made us only 'a little lower than angels'. How those brawny-faced fellows of farmers would drink to our success!

There would this company, consisting most likely of some thousands, remain patiently and anxiously watching every turn of fate in the game, as if the event had been the meeting of two armies to decide their liberty. And whenever a Hambledon man made a good hit, worth four or five runs, you would hear the deep mouths of the whole multitude baying in pure Hampshire—'Go hard!—Go hard!—Tich and turn!—Tich and turn.' To the honour of my countrymen, let me bear testimony upon this occasion also, as I have already done upon others. Although their provinciality in general, and personal partialities individually, were naturally interested in behalf of the Hambledon men, I cannot call to recollection an instance of their willfully stopping a ball that had been hit out among them by one of our opponents. Like true Englishmen, they would give an enemy fair play.

(b) *Source:* Report in the *Chelmsford Chronicle*, 20 July 1787.

On Tuesday last the long impending match of Cricket, between Essex and Kent, was decided at Swanscombe, when the former gained a complete victory over their adversaries in that noble game, at only one innings, and had 44 notches to spare. This so exasperated the gentlemen of Kent, that they would not so much as drink with their competitors.

(c) Kent was not always so unfortunate.

Source: Report in *The Times*, 4 Sept. 1795.

The grand match of Cricket, for one thousand guineas, between Kent and All England, was some days since terminated at Margate, in favour of Kent.

(d) *Source:* E. Chamberlayne, *Angliae Notita* (1694 edn.), p. 52.

The Natives will endure long and hard labour insomuch, that after twelve hours hard work, they will go in the Evening to Foot-ball, Stool-ball, Cricket. . . .

(e) *Source:* A Report of 1722 in W. Andrews, *Old Church Lore* (1891), p. 96, quoted in M. Marples, *History of Football* (1954), p. 79.

They write from Eastlow, that at a neighbouring Village,

on Sunday seven-night, during the usual time of Divine
Service there happened such a violent Hurricane, that a great
part of the steeple of the Church was blown down; which
would have done very considerable Damage to the Parishioners
had they been at Church: But they happened to be luckily at
a Foot-ball Match, by which means their Lives were probably
spared.

(f) *Source:* J. Freeth, *The Political Songster* (1790), p. 83.

> Some years ago the rustic game
> Of FOOTBALL was the fashion,
> And broken shins to merit fame,
> Would frequently occasion;
> Variety diverts the mind,
> And fancy will be straying,
> Else why at present do we find
> This rage for Marble playing.
>
> Of children's play for men to share,
> The scene however novel;
> MECHANICS meet and many are,
> As beggars in a novel;
> They laugh and sing—and round the RING,
> By turns take off a bumper,
> Then eye the spot—and give the SHOT,
> From TAW a deadly PLUMPER.

4. TOWN PLEASURES

People in the eighteenth century drew contrasts between the
'rustic' and the 'civilized'. These contrasts were based on concrete
facts about city and countryside. (See above, p. 57.) London life,
in particular, had a definite round of its own associated with the
'season'. It rested on the existence of a number of social institutions,
including clubs, coffee houses, theatres and gaming houses, and the
acceptance of social conventions and the influence of fashion.

(a) *Source:* J. Macky, *A Journey Through England* (1714), vol. I,
pp. 190ff.

I am lodged in the Street called *Pall Mall* . . . where the
best Company frequent. If you would know our manner of

Living, it is thus: We rise by Nine, and those that frequent
great Men's Levees find Entertainment at them till Eleven, or,
as in *Holland*, go to Tea-Tables. About Twelve the *Beau-Monde*
assembles in several Chocolate and Coffee Houses: The best
of which are the *Cocoa-Tree* and *White's* Chocolate-Houses,
St. *James's*, the *Smyrna*, and the *British* Coffee-Houses; and all
these so near one another, that in less than an Hour you see the
Company of them all. We are carried to these Places in Chairs
(or Sedans) which are here very cheap, a Guinea a Week, or a
Shilling *per* Hour, and your Chairmen serve you for Porters to
run on Errands as your *Gondoliers* (Watermen) do at *Venice*.

If it be fine Weather, we take a Turn in the *Park* till two,
when we go to Dinner; and if it be dirty, you are entertain'd at
Picket or *Basset* at *White's*, or you may talk Politicks at the
Smyrna and St. *James's*. I must not forget to tell you, that the
Parties have their different Places, where, however a Stranger
is always well received; but a *Whig* will no more go to the
Cocoa-Tree or *Ozinda's*, than a *Tory* will be seen at the Coffee-
House of St. *James's*.

The *Scots* go generally to the *British*, and a mixture of all
Sorts to the *Smyrna*. There are other little Coffee-Houses much
frequented in this Neighbourhood, *Young-Man's* for Officers,
Old-Man's for Stock-Jobbers, Pay-Masters, and Courtiers, and
Little-Man's for Sharpers. I never was so confounded in my
Life, as when I enter'd into this last: I saw two or three Tables
full at *Faro*, heard the Box and Dice ratling in the Room above
stairs, and was surrounded by a set of sharp Faces, that I was
afraid would have devoured me with their Eyes. I was glad to
drop two or three Half-Crowns at *Faro*, to get off with a clear
Skin, and was overjoy'd I was so got rid of them.

At Two we generally go to Dinner: Ordinaries are not so
common here as abroad; yet the *French* have set up two or
three pretty good ones, for the Conveniency of Foreigners, in
Suffolk-Street, where one is tolerably well served; but the general
way here, is to make a Party at the Coffee-House to go dine
at the Tavern, where we sit till Six, that we go to the Play;
except you are invited to the Table of some Great Man, which
Strangers are always courted to, and nobly entertain'd.

(b) *Source:* A letter to *The Times*, 31 Dec. 1795.

London is certainly an eligible place for persons who have nothing but their labour to depend on, to get forward in life, provided they steer clear of the many snares, and temptations, which hover in every alley, street, winding, and corner.

The mischief is, however, that the generality of young men, the moment they set foot in town, or, if brought up in the Metropolis, directly they enter the world on their own account, are hurried away, thoughtlessly, with the stream of error, and dissipation. If he happens to be a young man possessed of a moderate independence, without the suggestion of prudence, the caution of experience, the councils of wisdom or the restraint of authority, his whole conduct is then influenced by the passion with which he is actuated, which becomes at once, whether good or bad, his impulse, and his guide.

The Play-house is the first place of resort, which from the frequency of his visits, instead of being an instructive amusement, or a moral lesson, turns out a rendezvous of intrigue, and intemperance, where he soon acquires an intimacy with the idle, the profligate, the gambler, and the prostitute, who eye him as their lawful prey, and with all that ease, dexterity, and artifice, which a knowledge of the town, and its vicissitudes, has furnished them with, they imperceptibly lead him from one crime to another, till at length he becomes extravagant, and irregular, callous, and abandoned. Bagnios, gaming-tables, horses, and black-legs, are now his only wish, theme, and delight, and so long as his pocket will endure the burden, so long, and no longer, is he duped, flattered, caressed, and encouraged, by those who surround him. But everything must have an end, and enormous expenditures cannot keep pace with that income which should be managed with care and frugality. The young Gentleman runs short, as it is termed, and, on his first embarrassment, is advised to apply for the assistance of some friendly advertising money lender, who, upon proper security, has the modesty to procure him from time to time, sums of money, at the equitable premium of 100 per cent. A repetition so involves him, that, by degrees, his estate falls into the hands of Mr. Usurer, who takes an absolute assignment of his estate, for a consideration less than half its true value: . . . he gets [deeper] into debt, is arrested, carried to a spunging house, and from thence is removed to the King's Bench, or Fleet Prison.

Far be it from me to throw any odium on an unfortunate class of people immured in the walls of either of those places, there are no doubt, imprisoned, as worthy, and as good a set of people, as any in society. But the young spark I am speaking of, being mortified at his late companions standing aloof, and resigning him to his fate, becomes loaded with obloquy, associates with characters equally as vicious as himself, smoaks, swears, and carouses, and, all at once, is wholly lost, as it were to himself, and to the world.

(c) *Source:* Report in *The Times,* 5 March 1794.

The entertainment given by the Manager of the Opera House, on Monday night, was the best attended of any we have seen for many years, and fully answered the expectations that had been formed of it. The space allotted, however, large as it was, with the addition of the new room, and another above stairs, was by no means sufficient for so large a company: and the pressure of the crowd rendered the rooms insufferably hot, as well as prevented the masks from appearing to advantage. For so large an assembly, there were fewer masks than usual, but the hilarity of the company made amends for this deficiency. The Prince of Wales was in a black domino, arm-in-arm with Captain Churchill, and Lord George Conway; the Duke of Clarence was the whole evening with Mrs. Jordan in a private box upstairs. Michael Angelo Taylor was dressed in women's cloaths, but was less talkative than usual. The supper was extremely well conducted, and the provisions better than usual. The refreshments were also liberally supplied. There were about 2700 persons in the rooms, and among them some of the prettiest women in town.

5. COFFEE HOUSES

The coffee house reached the zenith of its popularity in the early eighteenth century. It provided a centre of news (see above, p. 25), and a meeting place for business men and politicians, as well as a place for the 'idlers'.

(a) *Source:* T. Brown, *Amusements Serious and Comical* (1700), vol. III, p. 65.

Every coffee-house is illuminated both without and within doors. . . . At the bar the good man always places a charming Phyllis or two, who invite you by their amorous glances into their smoaky territories. . . . This is the place where several *knights errant* come to seat themselves at the same table without knowing one another, and yet talk as familiarly together as if they had been of many years acquaintance: They have scarce look'd about them, when a certain liquor as black as soot is handed to them, which being soppishly sum'd into their noses, eyes and ears, has the virtue to make them talk and prattle together of every thing but what they should do. Now they tell their several adventures by sea and land; how they conquer'd the giant, were overcome by the lady, and bought a pair of waxed boots at *Northampton* to go a wooing in. One was commending his *wife*, another his *horse*, and the third said he had the best *smoak'd beef in Christendom*. Some were discoursing of all sorts of government, *Monarchical, Aristocratical* and *Democratical*; some about the choice of *mayors, sheriffs* and *aldermen*; and others of the transcendant virtues of *vinegar, pepper* and *mustard*. . . . To the charms of *coffee* the wiser sort join'd *spirit of clary* . . . and *brandy*, which completely enchants the knights. By the force of these *soporiferous enchantments* you shall find one snoaring heartily on a *bench*, another makes love to beautiful *Phyllis* at the bar, and the third, as valiant as *Orlando Furioso*, goes to signalise his valour in scouring the streets.

6. CLUBS

The name 'club' derives from the practice of 'clubbing' the expenses of entertainment. All foreign visitors to Britain were impressed by English 'clubbability'. During the eighteenth century some clubs in London evolved from coffee or chocolate houses (notably White's) and by the end of the century there were some with a political orientation, others entirely social. In the provinces 'clubs' were found among many strata of society. In the meantime, some coffee houses had evolved into restaurants.

(a) *Source:* P. Grosley, *A Tour to London*, Vol. I (1772), pp. 146–7.

The establishment of these clubs is owing to the English character, which must perpetuate the customs. They are held amongst friends, who, having contracted an intimacy in their early days, and experienced each other's fidelity, are united by a conformity of tastes, schemes of life, and way of thinking. These meetings fully gratify that desire, which every man has to associate with his equals. . . .

Affairs of interest and religion are considerably interwoven with their private connexions, which Addison has admirably described in his Spectator, where we find clubs of hump-backed men, stammerers, &c. Their fundamental statutes turn upon all the most important duties of friendship. I have been assured, that when the members of some of these clubs happen, upon a sudden emergency, to be distressed for money, the purse of every individual of the society is immediately opened to them. . . .

There are regular clubs, which are held in coffee-houses and taverns, at fixed days and hours; wine, beer, tea, pipes, and tobacco help to amuse them at these meetings. There are others kept at the houses of persons of fortune: they meet in turn at the apartments of the several members, if they are bachelors; and even if they are married, in case their wives have no objection to it. He, at whose house the club is kept, supplies the members with refreshments.

Most of the public societies have a president, who is chosen either by plurality of votes or by ballot, for a limited time; at the expiration of which, they proceed to a new election. The president's seat is at the upper end of the table; and his chair, somewhat more elevated than those of the other members, is adorned with some embossed figure, relative most generally to those objects, which engage the attention of the members.

(b) *Source:* Edward Gibbon, *Journal*, Entry for 24 Nov. 1762.

I dined at the Cocoa-Tree with Holt. . . . We went from thence to the play (the Spanish Fryar); & when it was over, returned to the Cocoa-tree. That respectable body, of which I have the honour to be a member, affords every evening a sight truly English. Twenty or thirty, perhaps, of the first men in the kingdom, in point of fashion and fortune, supping at little tables covered with a napkin, in the middle of a Coffee-room, upon a bit of cold meat, or a sandwich, & drinking a glass of punch. At present, we are full of Privy Counsellors and Lords of the Bedchamber; who, having jumped into the Ministry, make a very singular medley of their old principles and language, with their modern ones.

(c) At the other end of the social scale there were craftsmen's and farmers' social clubs, like the following at Aveley, Essex.

Source: M.S. Articles of Aveley Lunatick Clubb, printed in Brown (ed.), *English History from Essex Sources*, vol. II, p. 160.

1st It is hereby agreed that we whose names are under written do meet Monthly at The Sign of the Harrow in Aveley, there to Expend One Shilling, and be Subject to such Rules and Orders as are hereafter Express'd.

2[ndly] It is likewise agreed that the said meeting shall be on the First Monday after every full Moon in the Year.

3rd That some one Member of the said Body, be Chosen President or Chairmen for one whole year and no longer, unless Re'elected into the said Trust by a Majority of Voices.

4th That Every Member shall on his Admission pay Two Shillings and Sixpence, which shall goe towards the Publick fund for the use hereinafter mention'd,—And the Night of his Admission he shall be Exempt from any further payment.

5th That Every Member or Members after Signing his Name, shall on absenting himself or Themselves, forfeit the Sum of One Shilling, which forfeit or forfeitures, shall on the next night of their coming be deposited into the hands of the President or Chairman; There to be kept untill there is a Sufficient fund for a Dinner, which Day is to fixed by a Majority of Voices—The Two Shillings and Sixpence paid by a New Member to be apply'd to the same use as the forfeit Money.

6th That Every Member on his coming into the Clubb Room do pay Obeisance to the President or Chairman, and Imediately pay his Shilling & forfeit Money if any due; If a New Member his Two Shillings and Sixpence.

7th That no Member do presume on any pretence Whatsoever to use ill Manners to a Brother Member. Such as saying, You Lye Sir! or Swear or Curse on pain of being Mulch in the Sum of One Shilling, This to take effect during Clubb Hours only.

8th If any Member or Members do come into the said Clubb Room, Fuddled, Disguis'd in Liquor, or Vulgarly Speaking Drunk, him or them shall forfeit One Shilling. . . .

7. THEATRES

There were four London theatres in Queen Anne's reign, each with places for different sections of the population. The audience was often boisterous. Later in the century plays like Sheridan's *The Rivals* (1775) hit off most of the fashionable pursuits of the day. The audience, however, was not interested exclusively in what happened on the stage.

(a) *Source:* A comment in *The Tricks of the Town Laid Open* (1747)

We have three . . . different and distinct Classes; the first is called the *Boxes*, where there is one peculiar to the King and Royal Family, and the rest for the Persons of Quality, and for the Ladies and Gentlemen of the highest Rank, unless some Fools that have more Wit than Money, or perhaps more Impudence than both, crowd in among them. The second is call'd the *Pit*, where sit the *Judges*, *Wits* and *Censurers*, . . . in common with these sit the *Squires*, *Shapers*, *Beaus*, *Bullies* and *Whores*, and here and there an extravagant *Male* and *Female Cit*. The third is distinguished by the Title of the *Middle Gallery*, where the Citizens Wives and Daughters, together with the *Abigails*, Serving-men, Journey-men and Apprentices commonly take their Places. . . .

(b) *Source:* Letter in *The Mirror*, No. 9, 23 Feb. 1779.

Some weeks ago I was called from my retreat in the country, where I have passed the last twenty years in the enjoyment of ease and tranquillity. . . .

Last Thursday I was solicited by an old friend to accompany him to the Playhouse, to see the tragedy of King Lear. . . . As the theatre had been always my favourite amusement, I did not long withstand the entreaties of my friend; and when I reflected that Mr. Garrick was now gone to 'that undiscovered country, from whose bourn no traveller returns,' I felt a sort of tender desire to see even a copy of that great original, from whose performances I had often, in the earlier part of my life, received such exquisite pleasure.

As we understood the house was to be crowded, we went at an early hour, and seated ourselves in the middle of the pit, so as not only to see the play to advantage, but also to have a full view of the audience, which, I have often thought, is not the least pleasing part of a public entertainment. When the boxes began to fill, I felt a secret satisfaction in contemplating the beauties of the present times, and amused myself with tracing in the daughters, those features, which, in the mothers and grandmothers, had charmed me so often. . . .

Whilst I was amusing myself in this manner, I observed, that some of the upper boxes were filled with ladies, whose appearance soon convinced me that they were of an order of females more desirous of being distinguished for beauty than for virtue. I could not refrain from expressing some disgust at seeing those unfortunate creatures sitting thus openly mingled with women of the first rank and fashion. 'Poh!' said my friend, 'that is thought nothing of now-a-days'. . . .

As I was going to reprove my friend for talking with such levity of a matter that seemed to be of so serious a nature, the curtain drew up, and the play began. It is not my design, Sir, to trouble you with any remarks on the performance; the purpose of this letter is to request of you to take some notice of a species of indecorum, that appeared altogether new to me, and which, I confess, it hurt me to observe.

Before the end of the first act, a number of young men came in, and took their places in the upper boxes, amidst those unhappy females I have already mentioned. I concluded that these persons were as destitute of any pretension to birth or fashion, as they were void of decency of manners; but I was equally surprised and mortified to find, that many of them were of the first families of the kingdom. You, Sir, who have lived in the world, and seen the gradual and almost imperceptible progress of manners, will not, perhaps, be able to judge of my astonishment, when I beheld these very gentlemen quit their seats, and come down to pay their respects to the ladies in the lower boxes. The gross impropriety of this behaviour raised in me a degree of indignation which I could not, without difficulty, restrain. I comforted myself, however, with the hopes, that those unthinking youths would meet with such a reception from the women of honour, as would effectually check this indecency; but I am sorry to add, that I could not discern, either in their looks or manner, those marks of disapprobation which I had made my account with perceiving. Both the old and the young, the mothers and the daughters, seemed rather pleased when these young men of rank and fortune approached them. I am persuaded, at the same time, that were they to think but for a moment of the consequences, they would be sensible of the impropriety of their behaviour in this particular. I must therefore intreat of you, Sir, to take the earliest opportunity of giving your sentiments on the subject.

(c) *Source:* Report in the *Morning Post*, 27 Oct. 1798, quoted in J. Ashton, *Old Times* (1885), pp. 192–3.

Two men in the pit at Drury Lane Theatre, last night, were so turbulent, and riotous, during the last act of Henry the Fifth, that the performance was interrupted upwards of a quarter of an hour. The audience, at last, asserted their power, and turned them disgracefully out of the Theatre. This should always be done to crush the race of disgusting puppies that are a constant nuisance at the playhouse every night.

8. PLEASURE GARDENS

Two of the most fashionable places of entertainment in eighteenth-century London were Ranelagh Gardens and Vauxhall Gardens.

Source: C. P. Moritz's account of Vauxhall and Ranelagh in 1782, reprinted in *The British Tourists* (1798).

One evening I visited Vauxhall. I had not far to go from my lodgings, in the Adelphi Buildings, to Westminster Bridge, where you always find a great number of boats on the Thames, which are ready, on the least signal, to serve those who will pay them, according to the distance. . . .

Vauxhall is, properly speaking, the name of a little village, in which the garden, now almost exclusively bearing the same name, is situated. You pay a shilling on entrance.

On entering it, I really found, or fancied I found, some resemblance to our Berlin Vauxhall; if, according to Virgil, I may be permitted to compare small things with great ones. The walks at least, with the paintings at the end, and the high trees, which here and there, form a beautiful grove, or wood, on either side, were so similar to those of Berlin. . . . Here and there you are pleasingly surprised by the sudden appearance of the statues of the most renowned English poets and philosophers; such as Milton, Thomson, and others. But what gave me most pleasure, was the statue of the German composer, Handel, which, on entering the garden is not far distant from the orchestra.

This orchestra is among a number of trees, situated as in a little wood, and is an exceedingly handsome one. As you enter the garden, you immediately hear the sound of vocal and instrumental music. There are several female singers constantly hired to sing here.

On each side of the orchestra are small boxes, with tables and benches, in which you sup. The walks before these, as well as in every other part of the garden, are crowded with people of all ranks. I supped here with Mr. S***r, and the Secretary of the Prussian ambassador; besides a few other gentlemen from Berlin; but what most astonished me, was the boldness of the women of the town, who often rushed in upon us by half dozens, and in the most shameless manner importuned us for wine. Our gentlemen thought it either unwise, unkind or unsafe, to refuse them so small a boon.

When the evening was pretty far advanced, we were entertained with a sight, that is indeed singularly curious and interesting. In a particular part of the garden, a curtain was drawn up, and by means of some mechanism, of extraordinary ingenuity, the eye and the ear are so completely deceived, that it is not easy to persuade one's-self it is a deception; and that one does not actually see and hear a natural waterfall from a high rock. As every one was flocking to this scene in crowds, there arose all at once a loud cry of 'Take care of your pockets'.

Q

This informed us, but too clearly, that there were some pick-pockets among the crowd, who had already made some fortunate strokes.

The rotunda, a magnificent circular building, in the garden, particularly engaged my attention. By means of beautiful chandeliers, and large mirrors, it was illuminated in the most superb manner; and every where decorated with delightful paintings and statues, in the contemplation of which, you may spend several hours very agreeably, when you are tired of the crowd and the bustle, in the walks of the garden. . . . But enough of Vauxhall! . . .

I had often heard Ranelagh spoken of. On the evening of the 12th I took a walk, in order to visit this famous place of amusement; but I missed my way and got to Chelsea; where I met a man with a wheelbarrow, who not only very civilly shewed me the right road, but also conversed with me the whole of the distance, which we walked together. . . . At length I arrived at Ranelagh; and having paid my half-crown, on entrance, I soon enquired for the garden door, and it was readily shewn to me; when to my infinite astonishment, I found myself in a poor, mean-looking, and ill-lighted garden, where I met but few people. I had not been here long, before I was accosted by a young lady, who also was walking there, and who, without ceremony, offered me her arm, asking me why I walked thus solitarily? I now concluded, this could not possibly be the splendid, much-boasted Ranelagh; and so, seeing not far from me a number of people entering a door, I followed them in hopes either to get out again, or to vary the scene.

But it is impossible to describe, or indeed to conceive, the effect it had on me, when coming out of the gloom of the garden, I suddenly entered a round building, illuminated by many hundred lamps; the splendor and beauty of which surpassed every thing of the kind I had ever seen before. Every thing seemed here to be round; above, there was a gallery divided into boxes; and in one part of it an organ with a beautiful choir, from which issued both instrumental and vocal music. All around, under this gallery, are handsome painted boxes for those who wish to take refreshments: the

floor was covered with mats; in the middle of which are four
high black pillars; within which there are neat fire places for
preparing tea, coffee, and punch: and all around also there
are placed tables, set out with all kinds of refreshments. Within
these four pillars, is a kind of magic rotundo, where all the
beau-monde of London move perpetually round and round.

I at first mixed with this immense concourse of people, of
all sexes, ages, countries and characters: and I must confess,
that the incessant change of faces, the far greater number of
which were strikingly beautiful, together with the illumination,
the extent and majestic splendor of the place, with the continued sound of the music, makes an inconceivably delightful
impression on the imagination.

Being, however, at length tired of the crowd, . . . I sat
down in one of the boxes, in order to take some refreshment,
and was now contemplating at my ease, this prodigious
collection and crowd of a happy, cheerful world, who were
here enjoying themselves devoid of care, when a waiter very
civilly asked me what refreshment I wished to have, and in a
few moments returned with what I asked for. To my astonishment, he would accept no money for these refreshments; which
I could not comprehend, till he told me that every thing was
included in the half-crown I had paid at the door; and that I
had only to command, if I wished for any thing more; but
that, if I pleased, I might give him as a present a trifling
douceur.

I now went up into the gallery, and seated myself in one of
the boxes there: and from thence, becoming all at once, a
grave and moralizing spectator, I looked down on the concourse of people, who were still moving round and round in
the fairy circle; and then I could easily distinguish several
stars, and other orders of knighthood. An Englishman, who
joined me during this my reverie, pointed out to me, on my
enquiring, princes and lords with their dazzling stars, with
which they eclipsed the less brilliant part of the company. . . .

At Ranelagh, the company appeared to me much better,
and more select than at Vauxhall; for those of the lower class,
who go there, always dress themselves in their best; and thus
endeavour to copy the great. Here, even the poorest families

are at the expence of a coach, to go to Ranelagh, as my landlady assured me. She always fixed on some one day in the year, on which, without fail, she drove to Ranelagh. On the whole, the expence at Ranelagh is nothing near so great as it is at Vauxhall, if you consider the refreshments; for any one who sups at Vauxhall is likely, for a very moderate entertainment, to pay at least half-a-guinea.

9. POPULAR ENTERTAINMENTS

(a) *Source:* J. Marchant (ed.), *Sophie in London* (1933), p. 155.

From Somerset House we set out over Blackfriars Bridge to the Royal Circus, where trick riders, tumblers and plays can be seen. Actually it is large circular building.

Children from seven to twelve years ride there, and perform a hundred and one tricks. A dear little girl eight years of age was particularly entertaining: first dismounting from her horse, she proceeds to the stage, where she amuses the spectators with her by-play. Then it was the adults' turn to ride, and an operetta followed, after this rope-walkers, then a handsome boy raced the girl on horseback, next came tumblers, and finally three grown-ups in a group galloped with the four children balanced on their hands and shoulders. This pyramid, fraught with art and danger, rode past us a few times, changing places as it went. The scenes with these children grieved me, though I could not but admire their skill, energy, and the infinite flexibility of our body. What cannot human nature accomplish by straining every sinew, using all the power of its intellect and every minute of its time.

(b) *Source:* Note for 9 July 1760 in the *Diary* of Thomas Turner.

In the afternoon my wife walked to Whitesmith, to see a mountebank perform wonders, who has a stage built there, and comes once a week to cozen a parcel of poor deluded creatures out of their money, by selling his packets which are to cure people of more distempers than they ever had in their lives, for 1s each, by which he sometimes takes £8 or £9 of a day.

(c) *Source:* Report in the *Ipswich Journal*, 12 May 1753.

To be seen at the King's Arms in Harwich, the surprising Dancing Bears, Late arrived from Abroad, who by an infinite deal of Labour and Trouble are brought to foot it to a Violin, both in Comic Dances and Hornpipes, even beyond Imagination. The largest of them is eight Foot high, and dances to the Admiration of all Beholders. They have had the honour twice to perform before his Majesty King George, his Royal Highness the Prince of Wales, the Duke of Cumberland, and all the Royal Family, and upwards of 300 of the Nobility in London. They perform many other Particulars as expressed in the Bills; and are separated by a Partition that Gentlemen and Ladies may see their Performances without Fear.

(d) *Source:* J. Macky, *Journey Through England* (1714 edn.), vol I, p. 153.

The hunting of a PIG there [at Ewel] every *Monday* Morning, when the only knack consists in catching and holding him up by the Tail, is infinitely more becoming the Boys that perform it, than the Spectators that employ them.

(e) *Source:* Report in the *Ipswich Journal*, 26 Oct. 1754.

Dedham, October 23, 1764.
Our Peal of Eight Bells being now compleated; Friday the First of November is fixed for Ringing them, when we believe they will be esteemed good Bells.
John Saunders, William Cross, Churchwardens.
N.B. In the Long Room at the Sun, in the Evening, will be Country Dancing; proper Musick is provided.

(f) *Source:* C. B. Andrews (ed.), *The Torrington Diaries* (1935), vol. II, p. 22. The passage refers to a visit to Yorkshire in 1789.

By a country of much beauty, hill, dale and wood, we enter'd the town of Rotherham. . . . The master of the inn has got a patent (a very odd one) for making marbles for children, which he can do of all descriptions, so well and expeditiously, that he will soon supply all the schoolboys of the world.

(g) *Source:* W. Cowper, *Tirocinium* (1784).

The little ones, unbutton'd, glowing hot,
Playing our games, and on the very spot,
As happy as we once, to kneel and draw
The chalky ring, and knuckle down at taw;
To pitch the ball into the grounded hat
Or drive it devious with a dextrous pat.

10. GAMBLING

Throughout the century gaming was one of the most active national pastimes. Wagers were laid on all kinds of contingency, and there were large numbers of gaming houses, particularly in London.

(a) *Source:* Passage from *The Works of Thomas Brown* (1705), quoted by J. Ashton, *Social Life in the Reign of Queen Anne* (1883), pp. 82–3.

Gaming is an Estate to which all the World has a Pretence, tho' few espouse it that are willing to keep either their Estates or their Reputations. . . . In some Places they call Gaming Houses *Academies*; but I know not why they should inherit that honourable Name, since there's nothing to be learn'd there, unless it be *Slight of Hand.* . . . One idle day I ventur'd into one of these *Gaming Houses*, where I found an *Oglio of Rakes* of several Humours, and Conditions met together. Some that had left them never a Penny to bless their Heads with. One that had played away even his Shirt and Cravat, and all his Clothes but his Breeches, stood shivering in a Corner of the Room, and another comforting him, and saying, *Damme*, Jack, who ever thought to see thee in a State of Innocency?

(b) *Source:* Note in *Luttrell's Diary*, 21 Jan. 1710, quoted in *ibid.*, p. 87.

Yesterday books were opened at Mercer's Chappel for receiving subscriptions for the lottery, and 'tis said, above a Million is already subscribed. . . .

(c) *Source:* Note in the *Post Boy*, quoted in *ibid.*, 6/8 Jan. 1713, p. 88.

Yesterday was drawn No. 22858 [in the Public Lottery], which entitles the Bearer to £36,000.

(d) *Source:* Note in *The Every-Day Book* (1827), vol. II, col. 1344.

In October, 1735, a child of James and Elizabeth Leesh, of Chester-le-Street, in the County of Durham, was *played for at cards*, at the sign of the Salmon, one game, four shillings against the child, by Henry and John Trotter, Robert Thomson, and Thomas Ellison, which was won by the latter, and delivered to them accordingly.

(e) *Source:* Report in *The Times*, 25 Sept. 1797.

To such a height has the spirit of gambling arisen, that at some of the great Tables it is not uncommon to see the stake consist wholly of property *in kind*. A house of furniture was last week lost to a Lady in the neighbourhood of Pall Mall. The successful party had played against it, the stock of a farm in the County of Essex.

(f) *Source:* Report in *ibid.*, 2 Nov. 1797.

At some of our Boarding Schools, the fair pupils are now taught to play whist, and cassino. Amongst their *winning* ways, this may not be the least agreeable to Papa and Mamma.

It is calculated, that a clever child, by its cards, and its novels, may pay for its own education.

(g) State Lotteries were in operation until 1826.

Source: Report in *ibid.*, 19 March 1798.

The £20,000 prize, drawn on Friday, is divided amongst a number of poor persons: a female servant in Brook St., Holborn, had a sixteenth; a woman who keeps a fruit-stall in Gray's-Inn-Lane another; a third is possessed by a servant of the Duke of ROXBURGHE's; a fourth by a Chelsea carrier of vegetables to Covent Garden. . . .

(h) Charles Lamb protested against the eventual abolition.

Source: C. Lamb. 'The Illustrious Defunct' in the *New Monthly Magazine* (1825).

Never can the writer forget when, as a child, he was hoisted upon a servant's shoulder in Guildhall, and looked down upon the installed and solemn pomp of the then drawing Lottery. . . . The grave and reverend faces of the commissioners eyeing the announced number; the scribes below calmly committing it to their huge books; the anxious figures of the surrounding populace, while the giant figures of Gog and Magog, like presiding deities, looked down with a grim silence upon the whole proceeding. . . .

11. AT THE SPA

The growth of spas and watering places (see above, pp. 61 ff.) encouraged organized 'idleness' in congenial surroundings away from London.

(b) *Source:* Letter from William Mildmay to his cousin, 1749, printed in Edwards (ed.), *English History from Essex Sources*, vol. I, p. 160.

I was persuaded to stay at this place [Spa in Germany] longer than I first intended, by being assured of the greatest services these waters perform, in removing the cause of the nervous complaints I have heretofore been afflicted with; and now I am induced to stay yet longer, since I have been informed that your Lordship and Lady Fitzwalter are taking the benefit of the waters at Tunbridge, which I heartily wish may have as good an effect as these have had on Lady Holderness, who is surprisingly recovered in her strength, appetite and spirits, which has been in some measure owing to her persevering in the regimen to be observed at this place. But Mr. Tindal, who desires to have no appetite raised that he can't gratify, is much enraged at being told, that though the waters make him sleepy, he must not sleep; and though they make him hungry, he must not eat; so he has forsaken the spring, but is very regular in drinking the Burgundy. Your Lordship, I presume, is apprised that there are four fountains belonging to this place, and one in the town, the others about a league distant, and though these are severally recommended according to their different medicinal virtues for various disorders, yet Fashion gives the preference alternately to go either to the one or the other.

I wish the passage hither was but as easy as a journey to Bath or Tunbridge, being persuaded they would yield great benefit to my Lady Fitzwalter; but the spirit of none of the waters, except the Pohun, will remain, if bottled to be carried into England, or even to be brought down in the town, and so much the better for those that are here, since the rising early in the morning, and the exercise of going up and returning back, greatly help towards the cures which are attributed to the waters. . . .

At present the Season is near over with the foreigners, who not being able to afford staying here a long time, drink as much in a fortnight as should suffice for a month. This particularly is the Dutch frugality, who will drink 20 or 30 glasses in a morning, and thus drench and wash their insides, without giving time to the blood to imbibe and correct itself with the mineral virtues. The English by being better advised, drink gently and stay longer, so that within a week, we shall be left to ourselves.

12. AT THE SEASIDE

(a) *Source:* Advertisement in the *Ipswich Journal*, 25 April 1761.

WIVENHOE in Essex, April 21, 1761.

The Wivenhoe Sea Water Bath is continued by Tho. Tunmer, Surgeon and Apothecary, as usual. He letts and procures Lodgings, Board, etc, at a reasonable Rate; and by him Dresses and a Guide, with proper Attendance, are provided.

Wivenhoe is admired for these Reasons; being situated on the Banks of the Coln, about eight Miles from the open Sea, it is free from those noxious Exhalations that are consequent on a nearer Situation, while it enjoys all that can be reasonably expected from Sea-Water; the Density of which, as proved by Evaporation, is little or nothing inferior to that in the open Sea. The Town is entirely free from all contagious Disorders, and the Country round hilly, healthful, and pleasant, abounding with Gentlemen's Seats.

(b) *Source:* Report in the *Brighton Morning Herald*, 28 August 1806.

The Beach this morning was thronged with ladies, all anxious to make interest for a dip. The machines, of course, were in very great request, though none could be run into the ocean in consequence of the heavy swell, but remained stationary at the water's edge, from which Martha Gunn and her robust female assistants took their fair charges, closely enveloped in their partly coloured dresses, and gently held them to the breakers, which not quite so gently passed over them. The greatest novelty, however, that this part of the coast exhibited this morning, was in a gentleman's undressing himself on the Beach, for the purpose of a ducking, in front of the town, attended by his lady, who *sans diffidence*, supplied him with napkins, and even assisted him in wiping the humid effects of his exercise from his brawny limbs, as he returned from the water to dress.

CHAPTER VIII

Manners and Styles

This is the only pleasant Hour
Which I have in Twenty-four;
For whilst I unregarded stand,
With ready Salver in my Hand . . .
I hear and mark the courtly Phrases,
And all the Elegance that passes . . .
The Laws of true Politeness stated,
And what Good-breeding is, debated.

(ROBERT DODSLEY, *The Footman*, 1732)

Good company is composed of a great variety of fashionable people, whose characters and morals are very different, though their manners are pretty much the same.

(LORD CHESTERFIELD, *Letters*, 1748)

There never was a period since the creation of man when crimes and vices were less atrocious and shocking than in the present age. Manners, now polished and softened, have improved morals. Self-interest was always the ruling passion of all mankind; the old way of gratifying it was by murdering and poisoning; the new fashion by deceit.

(THE ANNUAL REGISTER, 1761)

An elegant manner and easiness of behaviour are acquired gradually and imperceptibly. No man can say 'I'll be genteel'. There are ten genteel women for one genteel man, because they are more restrained.

(SAMUEL JOHNSON, as quoted by BOSWELL, 1776)

Everything about this farm-house was formerly the scene of *plain manners* and *plentiful living*. . . . [Now] there were the decanters, the glasses, the 'dinner-set' of crockery ware, and all just in the true stock-jobber style.

(WILLIAM COBBETT, *Rural Rides*, 1830)

1. ADVICE ON MANNERS

Source: B. Dobrée (ed.), *Letters of Lord Chesterfield* (1932), vol. 4, p. 1240.

The letter was written by Chesterfield to his son in the autumn of 1748. The letters as a whole are full of advice both about the norms of acceptable social behaviour and the leading political and social personalities in England and Europe.

The company of professed wits and poets is extremely inviting to most young men, who, if they have wit themselves, are pleased with it, and if they have none, are sillily proud of being one of it; but it should be frequented with moderation and judgment, and you should by no means give yourself up to it. A wit is a very unpopular denomination, as it carries terror along with it; and people in general are as much afraid of a live wit in company as a woman is of a gun, which she thinks may go off of itself, and do her a mischief. Their acquaintance is, however, worth seeking, and their company worth frequenting; but not exclusively of others, nor to such a degree as to be considered only as one of that particular set.

But the company which of all others you should most carefully avoid, is that low company, which, in every sense of the word, is low indeed; low in rank, low in parts, low in manners, and low in merit. You will, perhaps, be surprised that I should think it necessary to warn you against such company; but yet I do not think it wholly unnecessary, from the many instances which I have seen of men of sense and rank, discredited, vilified, and undone, by keeping such company. . . .

Depend upon it, you will sink or rise to the level of the company which you commonly keep: people will judge of you, and not unreasonably, by that. There is good sense in the Spanish saying, 'Tell me whom you live with, and I will tell you who you are'. Make it therefore your business, wherever you are, to get into that company which everybody in the place allows to be the best company next to their own; which is the best definition that I can give you of good company. . . .

As I make no difficulty of confessing my past errors, where I think the confession may be of use to you, I will own, that when I first went to the university, I drank and smoked, notwithstanding the aversion I had to wine and tobacco, only because I thought it genteel, and that it made me look like a man. When I went abroad, I first went to the Hague, where gaming was much in fashion; and where I observed that many people of shining rank and character gamed too. I was then young enough, and silly enough, to believe that gaming was one of their accomplishments; and as I aimed at perfection, I adopted gaming as a necessary step to it. Thus I acquired, by error, the habit of a vice which, far from adorning my character has, I am conscious, been a great blemish in it.

Imitate then, with discernment and judgment, the real perfections of the good company into which you may get; copy their politeness, their carriage, their address, and the easy and well-bred turn of their conversation; but remember that, let them shine ever so bright, their vices, if they have any, are so many spots, which you would no more imitate, than you would make an artificial wart upon your face, because some very handsome man had the misfortune to have a natural one upon his: but on the contrary, think how much handsomer he would have been without it.

2. THE ROUGH AND THE SMOOTH

Eighteenth-century contrasts can never be evaded. Violence and good manners coexisted, with areas and times of tolerated licence for the first.

(a) London crowds were rough and zenophobic.

Source: P. Grosley, *Observations on England* (1772), pp. 85–5.

Inquire of them [the people] your way to a street: if it be upon the right, they direct you to the left, or they send you from one of their vulgar comrades to another. The most shocking abuse and ill language make a part of their pleasantry upon these occasions. To be assailed in such manner, it is not absolutely necessary to be engaged in conversation with them: it is sufficient to pass by them. My French air, notwithstanding the simplicity of my dress, drew upon me, at the corner of every street, a volley of abusive litanies, in the midst of which I slipt on, returning thanks to God, that I did not understand English. The constant burthen of these litanies was, French dog, French b——: to make any answer to them, was accepting a challenge to fight; and my curiosity did not carry me so far. I saw in the streets a scuffle of this kind, between a porter and a Frenchman, who spit in his face, not being able to make any other answer to the torrent of abuse which the former poured out against the latter without any provocation. . . .

Happening to pass one day through Chelsea, in company with an English gentleman, a number of watermen drew themselves up in a line, and attacked him, on my account, with all the opprobrious terms which the English language can supply, succeeding each other, like students who defend a thesis: at the third attack, my friend stepping short, cried out to them, that they said the finest things in the world, but unluckily he was deaf: and that, as for me, I did not understand a word of English, and that their wit was of consequence thrown away upon me. This remonstrance appeased them, and they returned laughing to their business.

(b) There was delight in rough spectacles (for cruel sports, see above, p. 216), like the sight of prisoners in procession on their way from Newgate Prison to Tyburn Gallows. (See below, pp. 381 ff.) Sympathy was often expressed for criminals, but the crowds could take affairs in their own hands.

Source: Note in the *Gentleman's Magazine*, September 1735.

[After a sailor found guilty of murdering his wife had poisoned himself] the people about *Bristol* were so incensed at his hardened Wickedness, that they dug up his Body, after it had been buried in a Cross Road near that City, dragg'd his Guts about the Highway, poked his Eyes out, and broke almost all his Bones.

(c) Most foreign visitors, including Grosley, saw redeeming features, however, even in crowd behaviour.

Source: J. W. von Archenholz, *A Picture of England* (1790), p. 210.

On any public commotion, when the people run into the

streets, and assemble in crowds, the greatest care is taken lest any accident should happen to the women and children, whom they either make room for, or carry in their arms, that they may be better seen.

(d) At least one French observer noted the relationship between 'roughness' or 'fierceness', as he called it, and English love of liberty. This relationship has been taken up by recent historians.

Source: B. L. de Muralt, *Lettres sur les Anglais et les Français* (1725), p. 25.

I would not have you any way offended at this Word [fierceness]; it insinuates, no doubt, something very odious to Strangers, but at the same time, it produces a great many good Effects among the *English*. 'Tis to this Fierceness, which can bear nothing, and is jealous of everything, that they owe their chief Happiness, their Liberty. 'Tis by this that the People, tho' divided and plunged in Prosperity and Idleness, recover in a Minute all their Strength and forget their Disputes, to oppose unanimously every thing that tends to subdue them.

(e) In high life also, behind the elegance there was often a touch of squalor—in big and little things. There was also frankness about the coexistence of elegance and squalor.

Source: Letter from the Duchess of Leinster, 1 June 1792, in B. Fitzgerald, *Emily, Duchess of Leinster, A Study of Her Life and Times* (1951), p. 198. The scene is a masked ball.

We had no crowd either in going in or getting out, and our coachy and footman managed very well. Ciss looked very pretty when she took off her mask, dress'd like a little Savoyarde, and was very much entertained and very happy & delighted, tho' Ld. C—— was not there; and when we first went in her supper which she had hurried down made her sick. But we got her to an open window behind a curtain, where she threw it up, and then she was perfectly well. We were very lucky, for no mortal saw it or suspected it, but Robert, Henry and me; for dr good-natured Arabella had run for a glass of water as quick as lightening, and brought it back just as it was all come up, which recover'd her entirely; and she was as well as if nothing had happen'd. . . . I always feel a little nervous among masks; but this really went off vastly well, and I was even diverted with some of the comical masks. Charles Fox was there and sat by me a good while, but it was no place to talk.

Ciss is fast asleep and it is three o'clock. I got up very well and refresh'd. I am an excellent rake.

(f) Prostitution (see above, pp. 91ff.) was commonplace and generally accepted throughout the country.

Source: M. Misson, *Memoirs and Observations on England* (1719), p. 60.

COURTEZANS, ALIAS WHORES. Mr. Monconys wrote above 33 or 34 Years ago in his Little Voyage into E. that he had been through one of the Streets (about Lincolns Inn Fields) which were wholly inhabited by professd Courtezans. At present theres a great Alteration in this Point, for now those Ladies are distributed all the Town over.

(g) Duelling also persisted, although Steele described it early in the century as 'a custom which all men wish exploded, though no man has courage enough to resist it'. Codes of honour still held.

Source: Report in *The Times*, 13 March 1794.

On Sunday morning a duel was fought in Hyde Park between Mr. PARKHURST and LIEUT. KELLY of the Navy. The dispute originated in some difference about places at the Opera Pit on the preceding night. A brace of pistols was discharged, and the latter gentleman wounded in the shoulder. The seconds then interfered, and brought the matter to a termination.

3. FASHION

Throughout the century both tastes and conduct were regulated by fashion. Chesterfield was a judge not only of behaviour, but of fashion, and in the elegant social world Paris clearly set the fashion.

(a) *Source:* The Earl of Chesterfield, *Letters to his Son* (1901), vol. II, p. 48.

Fashion is more tyrannical at Paris than in any other place in the world; it governs even more absolutely than their king, which is saying a great deal. The least revolt against it is punished by proscription. You must observe, and conform to all the *minutiæ* of it, if you will be in fashion there yourself; and if you are not in fashion, you are nobody. Get therefore, at all events, into the company of those men and women *qui donnent le ton;* and though at first you should be admitted upon that shining theatre only as a *persona muta,* persist, persevere, and you will soon have a part given you. . . .

(b) Paris felt, as usual, however, that it had the advantage.

Source: P. Grosley, *Observations on England* (1772), p. 106.

A mode begins to be out of date at Paris, just when it has been introduced at London by some English nobleman. The court and the first-rate nobility immediately take it up: it is next introduced about St. James's, by those that ape the manners of the court; and, by the time it has reached the city, a contrary mode already prevails at Paris, where the English, bringing with them the obsolete mode, appear like the people of another world.

(c) Fashions percolated through society—with tradesmen and servants as intermediaries.

Source: Vicesimus Knox, *The Works of Vicesimus Knox* (1824), vol. I, p. 374.

The vanity of the great and opulent will ever be affecting new modes, in order to increase that notice to which it thinks itself exclusively entitled. The lower ranks will imitate them as soon as they have discovered the innovation. . . . The pattern is set by a superior; and authority will at any time countenance absurdity.

(d) Coach travel gave ample opportunity for discussion of fashion: it also spread news of fashion in the provinces.

Source: C. B. Andrews (ed.), *The Torrington Diaries* (1934), vol. II, pp. 154–5. The passage refers to a change of coach at Northampton.

Whilst a change of coaches was preparing, the older ladies revell'd in tea, and the Islingtons sipp'd coffee, who were reproved by me for being all new dress'd; 'Your old worst

R

cloaths, (I told them,) were fittest for travelling'. Resuming the coach, the tea (which caused *strong* perspirations) set the ladies tongues a-wagging, and developed their characters; for now the younger four (the cook and I taking no part) began an elaborate discourse about fashions, feathers, robes, bodies, French backs, &c. &c. and then Miss H— proclaim'd herself a mantuamaker, told them for whom, and at what prices she work'd; (meaning to serve the Miss Islingtons;) and brag'd of her getting silver'd muslins; and that she had equipp'd, last year, the Sheriff's lady going to *a consort* at Leicester:—The old-blue also spake so scientifically, that I should think they were of the same business, and that they had been up to town to see, and study fashions; and to view (as they said) 'The *Qualaty* . . . and who walk'd in St. James's Park of a Sunday evening, and who were dressed so *fancically*'.

(e) Sometimes there could be sudden switches in fashion. In the 1790s, for instance, buckles (whether made of cheap metal or of silver) suddenly went out of fashion as part of a simplification of styles (see below, p. 254) and 'effeminate shoe-strings' took their place. Despite furious petitions from Birmingham manufacturers, the change in fashion proved permanent.

Source: Petition to the Prince of Wales, January 1792, printed in J. A. Langford, *A Century of Birmingham Life* (1871), vol. II, p. 14.

. . . With minds strongly agitated by the alarming decline of our Trade, we approach your ROYAL HIGHNESS, not without hope, being abundantly convinced that you will rejoice in an opportunity of displaying at the same time, your goodness, public spirit and humanity.

It will stand, instead of a thousand arguments, simply to state to your ROYAL HIGHNESS, that the Buckle Trade gives employment to more than Twenty Thousand Persons, numbers of whom, in consequence of the prevalency of Shoe-strings and Slippers, are at present without employ. . . . It is in great measure owing to the two valuable Manufactures of Buckles and Buttons, that Birmingham has attained her present importance in the map of Great Britain. . . .

We beg leave to observe that when Fashion, instead of foreign or unprofitable ornaments, wears and consumes the

Manufactures of this Country, she puts on a more engaging form and becomes Patriotism. When Taste, at the same time and by the same means that she decorates the Persons of the Rich, cloaths and feeds the naked Poor, she deserves a worthier appellation and may be styled Humanity. We make no doubt but your ROYAL HIGHNESS will prefer the blessings of the Starving Manufacturer to the enconiums of the Drawing Room.

We know it is to no purpose to address Fashion herself; she is void of feeling and deaf to argument; but fortunately she is subject to your control; She has been accustomed to listen to your voice and obey your commands.

We, therefore, most earnestly implore your ROYAL HIGHNESS, as our present Hope and future Sovereign, attentively to consider the deplorable situation of our trade, which is in danger of being ruined by this mutability of Fashion.

(f) Women's fashions were, of course, a source of interest to the press as well as to women.

Source: Note in *The Times,* 27 Aug. 1796.

Fashion would be its own murderer, if it were to be constant and permanent. The last year's dress seems to abdicate entirely; even the waist is walking down towards the hip; and three straps, with buckles in front, have abridged so much of the usurpation of the petticoat. One cannot see so many Ladies of high ton with the straps over the bosom, without thinking how much better they might have been employed over the shoulders.

(g) Some fashions were designed to shock.

Source: Letter from Caroline Cornwallis to Signora Sara Forti, 6 April 1806 in the *Sismondi Papers,* Pescia, Italy.

The part of this letter which will first take your attention will show you that I have not been inattentive to your wishes— I have then endeavour'd to give you as good an idea as I could upon so small a scale of the dress and fashion of English women but I must beg you at the same time to remember that in looking at them you do not see me, as I should be very sorry to be dressed exactly in the style of any of those ladies— A *decent* compliance with fashion is certainly proper and so far

I do comply, but I have not yet reconciled to my eyes or my conscience that *indecency* which I am sorry to say is but too prevalent in the dress of the English Ladies at present—the fashion in general I must call detestable and it grieves me to see many of my best friends and who would not do a wrong thing for the world suffering themselves to be led into a mode of dress so extremely reprehensible—That you may judge to what a pitch it is carried tho' for the honour of my country-women I should wish to conceal it would they make a secret and fit themselves I will tell you what a friend of mine saw herself at a ball she was at last year there were two young Ladies reckon'd beauties who had literally no covering on the upper part of their bodies but a worked muslin strap over the shoulders to support the gown and a piece of lace put across the breast just above the petticoat! ! Thank heaven the minds of those present were not enough corrupted to approve such a mode of appearing in public and every one show'd as far as possible their contempt for those silly girls—the instance of such immodesty is I hope infrequent.

(h) Yet great attention was paid also to men's fashions both at the beginning and end of the period.

Source: M. Misson, *Memoirs and Observations* (1719), pp. 15–16.

It must be own'd there are more Gascoons in *Gascony* than in any other Part of the World; but then it must be own'd, there are many of them everywhere. The same may be said of those smart Fellows, or *He-Coquets*, who are not rare in any part of *France*, and who abound at *Paris*. England also has a competent Share of these Animals, and the City of *London*, particularly is thoroughly stock'd with 'em. These Gentlemen in *English* are called *Fops* and *Beaux*. The Playhouses, Chocolate-houses, and Park in Spring, perfectly swarm with them: Their whole Business is to hunt after new Fashions. They are Creatures compounded of a Perriwig and a Coat laden with Powder as white as a Miller's, a Face besmear'd with Snuff, and a few affected Airs; they are exactly like *Molière's* Marquesses, and want nothing but that Title which they would infallibly assume in any other Country but England. . . . A Beau is so much the more remarkable in *England*, because, generally speaking, the *English*-Men dress in a plain, uniform Manner.

(i) *Source:* Note in the *Morning Post*, 18 Sept. 1788.

The fashionable bathing dress, at Brighton, is chiefly a pair of buff trousers, with a slight jacket. This is adopted by all the young men of the place, and a number of idle, sauntering land lubbers meet the eye every morning on the STEYNE, that one cannot help wishing for a sturdy pressgang to give them useful employment, or at least keep them out of mischief. After breakfast they are accoutred for the sports of the field. The sporting dress is a brown jacket, with a multiplicity of pockets, on each side, that reaches from the bottom to the top, so that, from this appearance, it is somewhat difficult to determine which the fashionable tribe most resemble—a set of grooms, or a company of smugglers.

When the dinner hour arrives, . . . they then attire themselves in order to enjoy the pleasures of the table, and, however deranged they may afterwards be by convivial excess, they march or stagger away to the Rooms, as circumstances may determine and entertain the Ladies with elegant and decent gallantry.

(j) Fashions also influenced phrases as well as clothes. One phrase —'That accounts for it' was commented on in the press in 1798. On this occasion, the theatre was the medium of communication.

Source: Note in *The Times*, 14 Dec. 1798.

Our Dramatic Authors have lately amused themselves, and the Public, with cant phrases, instead of character, 'That's your fort'—'Keep moving'—&c. Young Dibdin, in his Jew and Doctor, seems to have hit upon the happiest cant, imaginable; 'That accounts for it,' which seems applicable in almost all cases.

'There is no opposition to Government, in the House of Commons—for a change of Ministry would ruin the country— that accounts for it.'

'A very great Personage pays no regard to Lovers' Vows: he has been disgusted with a German translation—that accounts for it.'

'Buonaparte wishes to return to Paris, though he should go

thither as naked as the back of his hand; he prefers soup-maigre to water melons—that accounts for it.'

'Women complain of the want of Gallantry in men, though the modern dress shows more than enough to excite passion, but—that accounts for it.'

This cant phrase would comprehend all the science of Logic, if properly used, and appropriately designed. It might be amplified, in the present instance, to any length of space, but exemplification breaks off because *ne quid nimis*—that accounts for it.

4. DRESS

Dress reflected social class far more than it reflected fashion. There were also differences in making and buying habits. Yet there was little scope for regional variation in styles in England, and, unlike most other European countries, England had no 'national dress'. As far as fashionable clothes were concerned, the basic design of men's dress, which had been set in the 1680s, lasted until the 1790s—three-cornered hats, periwigs (though there were complaints by wig makers in 1765 that gentlemen were beginning to prefer their own hair), lace ruffles, long waistcoats, skirted coats, tight breeches, stockings and buckled shoes (for the fate of buckles, see above, p. 250). Women's dress changed more. Hoops for example, returned in early eighteenth century and lasted until its third quarter, and hair styles changed in the 1760s, when hair, often powdered, began to be worn in enormous and elaborate 'edifices'.

(a) Most poor people made their own clothes. What Eden wrote of the North of England was true of most parts of the country earlier in the eighteenth century. Yet by the 1790s the South was different.

Source: Sir F. M. Eden, *The State of the Poor* (1797), vol I, pp. 554–5.

In the midland and southern counties, the labourer, in general, purchases a very considerable portion, if not the whole, of his cloaths, from the shop-keeper. In the vicinity of the metropolis, working-people seldom buy new cloaths: they content themselves with a cast-off coat, which may be usually purchased for about 5s. and second-hand waistcoats and breeches. Their wives seldom make up any article of dress, except making and mending cloaths for the children. In the

North, on the contrary, almost every article of dress worn by farmers, mechanics, and labourers, is manufactured at home, shoes and hats excepted. . . . Although broad cloth, purchased in the shops, begins now to be worn by opulent farmers, and others, on Sundays; yet there are many respectable persons, at this day, who never wore a bought pair of stockings, a coat, nor waistcoat in their lives.

(b) Local landed families would often order clothes direct from London.

Source: Letter from Henry Purefoy, 26 March 1740 in G. Eland (ed.), *The Purefoy Letters* (1931), vol. I, p. 304.

I desire you will send mee ffive and thirty yards of Irish holland of about three Shillings a yard to make mee night shirts, it must be yard wide cloath & very good of the price. Pray send with it seven ells [an ell was 45 inches] of Irish Holland at 6s. 6d. a yard, or thereabouts, if as fine and as white as Dutch Holland, if not send Dutch Holland of about 7s. an ell. And send two yards of Cambrick for shirt Rufles; the Last you sent was too thin. Send these by the Buckingham carrier. . . .

(c) There are many surviving account books for clothes, like the following from Fitzwalter's account book in the Mildmay Archives, Essex.

Source: Edwards (ed.), *English History from Essex Sources* (1952), vol. I, p. 161–2.

1734		£ s. d.
Jan.	6 Mathews, the periwig-maker, for a tied wig . . .	7. 1. 0
Jan.	6 Matthews, also for three wigs and bags for my Lord Holderness . . .	6. 18. 0
Jan.	7 Hawson, the stocking-maker, his bill in full	2. 14. 0
Jan.	13 Mr. H. Smart, lace-man, for a broad silver trimming, etc., for my Lady Caroline's petticoat when she held up the train of the Princess Royal at her marriage with the Prince of Orange, March 1733	78. 17. 6

Jan.	6	Melchior Wagner, the hatter . . .	11.	3.	6
Jan.	6	To do. for a hat for Lord Holderness . . .		18.	6
Feb.	6	Mr. Boney, periwig-maker, for a bob-wig . . .	3.	13.	6
Mar.	17	Wm. Garret, his bill for 7 pairs of leather breeches, and in full of all accounts, Chandos Street	7.	7.	0
Mar.	17	Thos. Garnham, my coachman, for 3 white frocks he bought last week, viz. one for himself and two for the other two people in his table, and one for one of my footmen to powder my periwigs in	1.	8.	0
Mar.	18	H. Mertens, the German periwig-maker, for a tied periwig, and in full	6.	6.	0
Apr.	17	Mr. Mann, woollen-draper, his bill delivered Feb. 10 1731, and is in full to Jan. 8 1734	62.	6.	7
May	7	To Wm. Platon for 2 pairs of leather breeches viz. for the groom and his boy . . .	2.	2.	0
May	31	To Mr. Cutler for five Barcelona silk-snuff handkerchiefs	1.	2.	6
June	4	Wm. Hawson . . . stockings	3.	7.	0
July	23	Mr. Vickers this day in part of a bill this day given in for mercery goods of £188. 5. 11	100.	0.	0
Aug.	23	Claude Dubois, in full for six pairs of blue gloves		12.	0
Aug.	28	For a blue velvet morning cap now bought		16.	0
Nov.	17	Mr. Basnet, lace man, for a white silk waistcoat flowered and embroidered with gold for the Earl of Holderness for my Lady Ancram's wedding	16.	16.	0
Nov.	19	Townsend and Holford at the Golden Fleece, Cheapside, their bill in full for stockings	6.	17.	6

Dec. 10 John Hume, for a pair of boots for my
postillion, not yet used   18. 0
Dec. 10 John Hume for a pair of boots for my
Lord Holderness to ride in at Mons.
Toobart's Academy. Nov. 27 first put
on   1. 5. 0

(e) There are many descriptions of dress at court.

Source: Report in *The Times*, 4 June 1794.

Yesterday, being the anniversary of the King's birthday . . .
a DRAWING-ROOM was held in the afternoon, and, at night, a
Ball at St. James's. The GENTLEMEN's dresses were in general
embroidered silks and silk cloths: but one half were dressed in
REGIMENTALS.

HIS MAJESTY, as usual on his own Birthday, was in a plain
suit of clothes. The best dressed Gentlemen whom we saw at
Court, and indeed their dresses were very generally noticed
for their taste and splendour, were—

Mr. Skeffington.

A brown spotted silk coat and breeches, with a white silk
waistcoat richly embroidered with silver, stones, and shades
of silk: the design was large baskets of silver and stones, filled
with bouquets of roses, jonquilles, &c., the ensemble producing
a beautiful and splendid effect.

The Hon. Thomas Anson.

A striped silk coat and breeches, with a white silk waistcoat,
richly embroidered with white silk and dentelle: the waistcoat
embroidered to match the coat. . . .

Lord Willoughby de Broke.

A dark olive spotted silk coat, and breeches, with a white
silk waistcoat, the suit richly embroidered in silver, coloured
stones, and shades of silk.

(f) At the holiday resorts, in particular, not all dress met with
general approval.

Source: Report in the *Morning Post*, 18 Sept. 1788.

The Ladies have no particular dress for the morning, but
huddle away to the bathing place, in close caps, and gipsey

bonnets, so that they look like a set of wandering fortune-tellers, who have just had the opportunity of pillaging the contents of a frippery warehouse, with which they had bedecked themselve in haste.

It is to be remarked, that the ladies do not atone for the negligence of the morning, by neatness, and elegance, during the rest of the day, but shuffle on something by dinner time, covering themselves with an enormous nondescript bonnet, which, to the confusion of all order, they afterwards think a proper garb for the Assembly.

5. THE SOCIAL ROUND

The sharp distinction drawn in the eighteenth century between town and country (see above, p. 57) involved different conceptions of manners and styles in each, not least for women.

(a) *Source:* A Mock Journal of a Lady of Fashion, printed in *The Adventurer*, 23 Jan. 1753.

ENGAGEMENTS	OCCASIONAL MEMORANDUMS
January.	
1. Monday. To call at Deards in the morning, To dine with my husband's uncle, the city merchant.	City politeness intolerable! Crammed with mince pies, and fatigued with compliments of the season. . . .
2. Tuesday. In the morning with the Miss Flareits, to drive to the Silk mercer's, &c. At night to go to the opera.	A beautiful new French Brocade at Silver Tongues on Ludgate Hill. Mem. To teaze my husband to buy me a suit of it.
3. Wednesday. Expect Mademoiselle La Toure to try on my French head. In the evening to pay forty-three visits.	Mademoiselle the milliner tells me that Lady Z is in love with Captain X. Told it as a great secret at Lady F's, the Countess of L's, etc. etc.
4. Thursday. My own day. At home. To have a drum major and 17 card tables.	Miss Sharp is a greater cheat than her mamma. Company went before five. Stupid creature Mrs. Downright.

5. Friday. To go to the auction with Lady Nicknack. To dine at home with a parcel of my husband's city relations.

Lady Nicknack finely taken in. The whole day a blank. Head ache. Could not dress. Went to bed horrid soon; —before one. Lay alone, maid sat by me.

6. Saturday. Monsieur le Frise all the morning to dress my head. At night (being Twelfth Night) at court. To dance if I can with the handsome Bob Brilliant.

My left temple singed with the Curling iron. Sir John Dapperwit whispered me that Miss Bloom was almost as charming as myself. She must paint I am certain.

7. Sunday. If I rise soon enough St. James Church. Lady Brag's in the evening.

Not up till two. Bad luck at night. Never could win on Sundays. Miss Serious, who hates cards, says it is a judgement.

(b) *Source:* S. Richardson, *Pamela* (1740–4). Pamela is describing the round of life in the country.

The two ladies insisted upon it that I would take them with me in my benevolent round which I generally take once a week among my poor and sick neighbours, and finding I could not avoid it I set out with them.

The coach set us down by the side of a large common about five miles distant from our house, and we alighted and walked a little way, choosing not to have the coach come nearer that we might be taken as little notice of as possible, and they entered with me into two mean cots with great condescension and goodness; one belonging to a poor widow, with five children, who had all been down in agues and fevers; the other to a man and his wife, bed rid with age and infirmities, and two honest daughters, one a widow with two children, the other married to a husbandman, who had also been ill, but now by comfortable cordial, and good physic, in a hopeful way.

Now you must know that I am not so good as the old ladies of former days who used to distil cordial waters, and prepare medicines, and dispense them themselves. But this is my method. I am upon an agreement with Mr. Barrow, who is

deemed a very skilful and honest apothecary, and one Mr.
Simmonds, a surgeon of like character, to attend all such cases
and persons as I shall recommend. . . .

My Lady Davers observed a Bible, a Common Prayer Book,
and a *Whole Duty of Man* in each cot, in leathern outside cases,
to keep them clean, and a Church Catechism or two for the
children, and was pleased to say it was right.

The ladies left tokens of their bounty behind them to both
families, and all the good folks blessed and prayed for us at
parting.

[After further visits] after we had just looked in upon a
country school, where I pay for the learning of eight children,
we went home.

And here, my dear Miss Darnford, is a cursory account of
my benevolent weekly round, as the two ladies will call it.

(c) English Sundays were thought by most foreigners to be dull.
Here is an account of 'a citizen's Sunday' in 1754.

Source: Article in *The Connoisseur*, 25 July 1754.

SUNDAY. Overslept myself—Did not rise till nine—Was a full
hour in pulling on my new double-channell'd pumps—Could
get no breakfast, my wife being busy in dressing herself for
church.

At ten—Family at church—Self walked to Mother Redcap's
—Smoked half a pipe, and drank a pint of the Alderman's.
N.B. The beer was not so good as at the Adam and Eve at
Pancras.

Dined at one—Pudding not boiled enough, suet musty—
Wife was to drive me in a one-horsed chair to see Mother Wells
at Enfield Wash, but it looked likely to rain—Took a nap, and
posted seven pages from my day-book till five. . . .

At six—Mrs Deputy to drink tea with my wife—I hate their
slip-slops—Called on my neighbour the Common-council man,
and took a walk with him to Islington.

From seven to eight—Smoked a pipe at the Castle, ate a
heart-cake, and drank two pints of cider. N.B. To drink cider
often, because neighbour tells me it is good for the stone and
gravel.

At nine—Got to town again, very much fatigued with the

journey—Pulled off my claret coloured coat and blue satin waistcoat—Went to club, smoked three pipes, came home at twelve, and slept very soundly. . . .

6. MANNERS, TABLE AND GENERAL

Table manners were crude at the beginning of the century, when Defoe thought it necessary in *The Compleat Gentleman* to warn diners not to pick their teeth with a fork and to use a napkin. By the end of the century they had greatly improved. (See also below, p. 275.) There were frequent toasts, and men and women separated after dinner.

(a) *Source:* Le Blanc, *Letters on the English and French Nations* (1747), vol. I, p. 326.

A good butler is more esteemed here than a confectioner would be. . . . Even at tables where they serve desserts, they do but just show them and presently take away everything, to the very tablecloth. By this the English, whom politeness does not permit to tell the ladies their company is troublesome to them, give them notice to retire, when they are weary of them, and school-boys don't show more joy, when their master goes out of school, than the guests do when they take leave of them. The satisfaction that appears in their looks shows the pleasure they feel on finding themselves freed from the restraints the company of the women laid them under. . . . The table is immediately covered with mugs, bottles and glasses, and often with pipes and tobacco; and all things thus disposed, the ceremony of toasts begins.

(b) To some writers there was 'effeminacy' in the new manners.

Source: J. Brown, *An Estimate of the Manners and Principles of the Times* (1757), pp. 29, 35–6. This book went into seven editions in a year.

The Character of the Manners of our Times . . . on a fair Examination, will probably appear to be that of a *'vain, luxurious* and *selfish* EFFEMINACY. . . . The first and capital Article of Town-Effeminacy is that of *Dress:* which, in all its Variety of modern Excess and Ridicule, is too low for serious

Animadversion. Yet in this, must every Man of every Rank and Age employ his Mornings, who pretends to keep good *Company*. The wisest, the most virtuous, the most polite, if defective in their exterior and unmanly Delicacies, are avoided as *low People*, whom *Nobody knows*, and with whom one is asham'd to be seen. How would he have been derided in the Days of ELIZABETH, when a great Queen rode on Horseback to *St. Paul's*, who should have foretold, that in less than two Centuries no Man of Fashion would cross the Street to Dinner, without the effeminate Covering and Conveyance of an easy *Chair?* Yet thus accountred the modern Man of Fashion is *conveyed* to Company. Wherever he goes the same false Delicacy in all: Every Circumstance of modern Use conspires to soath him into the Excess of Effiminacy: Warm carpets are spread under his Feet; warm Hangings surround him: Doom and Windows nicely jointed prevent the least rude Encroachment of the external Air.

VANITY lends her Aid to this unmanly Delicacy: Splendid Furniture, a sumptuous sideboard, a long Train of Attendants, an elegant and costly Entertainment, for which Earth, Air and Seas are ransacked, the most expensive Wines of the Continent . . . the most inflaming Foods. . . . To this every Man of Taste now aspires, as to the true *sçavoir vivre*.

7. SHOPPING

Shops, with imposing windows and bright lighting, were one of the great attractions of London.

(a) *Source:* T. Baker, *The Female Tatler* (1709).

This afternoon, some ladies, having an opinion of my fancy in clothes, desired me to accompany them to Ludgate-Hill. . . . The shops are perfect gilded theatres, the variety of wrought silks so many changes of fine scenes, and the mercers are the performers. . . . As people glance within their doors they salute them with—'Garden silks, ladies; Italian silks; very fine mantua silks; any right Geneva velvet, English velvet, velvet embossed?' And to the meaner sort—'Fine thread satins, both

striped and plain; fine mohair silks; satinnets, burdets; Per-
sianets; Norwich crapes; anterines; silks for hoods and scarves;
hair camlets, druggets; gentlemen's nightgowns ready made;
shalloons; durances; and right Scotch plaids'.

We went into a shop which had three partners; two of them
were to flourish out their silks . . . and the other's sole business
was to be gentleman usher of the shop, to stand completely
dressed at the door, bow to all the coaches that pass by, and
hand ladies out and in. We saw abundance of gay fancies. . . .
'This, madam, is wonderful charming. This, madam, is so
diverting a silk. This, madam, My stars! how cool it looks!
But this, madam—ye Gods! would I had 10,000 yards of it!'
Then gathers up a sleeve, and places it to our shoulders. 'It
suits your ladyship's face wonderful well.' When we had
pleased ourselves, and bid him ten shillings a-yard for what he
asked fifteen: 'Fan me, ye winds, your ladyship rallies me!
Should I part with it at such a price, the weavers would rise
upon the very shop. Was you at the Park last night madam?
Your ladyship shall abate me sixpence. Have you read the
Tatler today?'

(b) *Source:* P. Grosley, *Observations on England* (1772), p. 35.

The finest shops are scattered up and down in these courts
and passages. The grand company which they draw together,
the elegant arrangement and parade made by the shops,
whether in stuffs exposed to sale, fine furniture, and things of
taste, or the girls belonging to them, would be motives sufficient
to determine those that walk, to make that their way in preference to any other, even if they had not neatness and security
to recommend them.

The shops in the Strand, Fleet-street, Cheapside, &c. are
the most striking objects that London can offer to the eye of a
stranger.

(c) *Source:* H. Meister, *Letters Written During a Residence in England*
(1799), pp. 16–18.

The variety, the neatness, and the rich shew made by such
numbers of shops of every kind, formed a spectacle of so delightful and astonishing an appearance, as to conceive must
needs be seen. There are so many things laid open to view,

and spread forth with so much art and attention, that till the eye is accustomed to sights so various and brilliant it must needs be weary. You are not ignorant that London alone transacts two thirds of the trade of the three kingdoms; the splendour and activity of its retail trade will not therefore surprise you. . . . I confess that such a view of the glorious consequences of civilisation affect my mind equally with the striking beauties of unadorned nature, and that this sight has filled me with wonder and admiration.

8. SERVICE

The place of domestic servants in the social hierarchy has already been examined (see above, p. 139). The following extracts reveal the dependence of eighteenth-century people of property on domestic service and the kind of attitudes that were engendered.

(a) *Source:* J. Moore, *A View of Society and Manners in France, Switzerland and Germany*, Vol. I. (6th edn., 1786), p. 15.

Many of our acquaintances seem absolutely incapable of motion, till they have been wound up by their valets. They have no more use of their hands for any office about their own persons, then if they were paralytic. At night they must wait for their servants, before they can undress themselves, and go to bed: In the morning, if the valet happens to be out of the way, the master must remain helpless and sprawling in bed, like a turtle on its back upon the kitchen table of an alderman.

(b) *Source:* Letter from the Duchess of Leinster, August 1761 in B. Fitzgerald, *Emily, Duchess of Leinster*, p. 87.

This morning I had a long conversation with Mrs Clarke, our new housekeeper. She seems a sensible, notable, genteel sort of woman; not fine, but just the manner to create a little respect from the under-servants, and enters perfectly into our schemes. We are to give her £25E. the first year, and £30E. if we approve of her afterwards. I told her the allowance for tea and sugar, & that for strangers' servants when at Carton. I like her vastly, and so will you, I am certain. She has quite persuaded me to have a housekeeper's maid and shew'd me the necessity of it. She is to take one over with her from hence. . . .

(c) *Source:* C. B. Andrews (ed.), *The Torrington Diaries* (1935), vol. II, p. 70.

. . . Instead of a nasty, dirty wench, watching you all the time, picking her nails, blowing her nose upon her apron, and then wiping the knives and glasses with it; or spitting and blowing upon the plates. Surely with a great fortune, there is nothing so comfortable for a small company as dumb waiters; as for myself, I am uneasy when a fellow stands behind me, watching me, running away with my plate and winking at his fellows.

9. LOVE AND MARRIAGE

'Affairs of the heart' were much discussed, and there were even magazines giving good advice to the lovelorn. Manners were stratified in this as in other forms of behaviour.

(a) *Source:* Mock letters to the *Spectator* asking for advice, 28 Dec. 1711, 25 Feb. 1711–12.

Mr. SPECTATOR, Here is a gentlewoman lodges in the same house with me, that I never did any injury to in my whole life; and she is always railing at me to those that she knows will tell me of it. Do you not think she is in love with me? or would you have me break my mind yet, or not? Your servant, 'T.B.'

MR. SPECTATOR, I am a footman in a great family, and am in love with the house-maid. We were all at hot cockles last night in the hall these holidays; when I lay down and was blinded, she pulled off her shoe and hit me with the heel such a rap, as almost broke my head to pieces. Pray, Sir, was this love or spite? T**.

MR. SPECTATOR. I am a certain young woman that love a certain young man very heartily; and my father and mother were for it a great while, but now they say I can do better, but I think I cannot. They bid me not love him, and I cannot unlove him. What must I do? Speak quickly. 'BIDDY DOW-BAKE.'

(b) *Source:* An Account in *The Guardian*, 20 June 1713.

S

I happened the other day to pass by a gentleman's house, and saw the most flippant scene of low love that I have ever observed. The maid was rubbing the windows within side of the house, and her humble-servant the footman was so happy a man as to be employed in cleaning the same glass on the side towards the street. The wench began with the greatest severity of aspect imaginable, and breathing on the glass, followed it with a dry cloth; her opposite observed her, and fetching a deep sigh, as if it were his left, with a very disconsolate air did the same in his side of the window. He still worked on and languished, until at last his fair one smiled, but covered herself, and spreading the napkin in her hand, concealed herself from her admirer, while he took pains as it were, to work through all that intercepted their meeting. This pretty contest held for four or five large panes of glass, until at last the waggery was turned into an humourous way of breathing in each other's faces, and catching the impression. The gay creatures were thus loving and pleasing their imaginations with their nearness and distance, until the windows were so transparent that the beauty of the female made the man-servant impatient of beholding it, and the whole house besides being abroad, he ran in, and they romped out of my sight.

(c) *Source:* Letter from Emily, 3 Dec. 1745, printed in B. Fitzgerald, *Emily, Duchess of Leinster,* p. 14.

Goodwood,
3rd December 1745

Prince Lobkowitz, who I believe you remember, a giddy, good-natured, wild young man as any in the world, was coming and has had a fall off his horse, so that I fancy he won't be here this good while. Apropos to him, I must make you laugh and tell you what the Town says—*He is in love with me, I very much so with him. But his relations don't care he should marry a Protestant, tho' as he is his own master that would be no objection; but that Papa and Mama, great as he is, won't part with me; and besides have other views for me.* Is not this a pretty story? I assure you 'tis told for certain all over the town and several of my friends have told me of it. The truth of the matter is that he is vastly fashionable, and as I happen to speak French and to know most of his acquaintances in Holland, he takes it into his head to talk a good deal to me; and you know in London two people can never talk together a quarter of an hour but they must immediately either be in love or to be married.

They say also that the Venetian Ambassadrice is in love with him, and I believe with rather more foundation, for she really behaves very ridiculously about him.

(d) *Source:* Fanny Burney, *Diary*, 10 July 1770.

We have just had a wedding—a public wedding, and very fine it was I assure you. The bride is Miss Case, daughter of an alderman of Lunn, with a great fortune; the bridegroom Mr. Bagg. Our house is in the churchyard, and exactly opposite the great church door—so that we had a good view of the procession. The walk that leads up to the church was crowded —almost incredibly a great mob indeed—I'm sure I trembled for the bride—oh what a gauntlet for any woman of delicacy to run! How short a time does it take to put an eternal end to a woman's liberty! I don't think they were a quarter of an hour in the church altogether. . . . [When] the bell began to ring so merrily, so loud, and the doors opened—we saw them walk down the Isle, the bride and bridegroom first—hand in hand—the bridegroom looked so gay, so happy! She looked grave, but not sad—and, in short, all was happy and charming. Well of all things in the world, I don't suppose anything can be so dreadful as a public wedding—my stars! I should never be able to support it.

(e) Thomas Turner was married twice, and has left a frank account in his *Diary* of his marital vicissitudes.

30 April 1756

This morn my wife and I had words about her going to Lewes tomorrow; oh, what happiness must there be in the married state, when there is a sincere regard on both sides, and each partner truly satisfied with each other's merits! But it is impossible for tongue or pen to express the uneasiness that attends the contrary! . . .

Oh, was marriage ever designed to make mankind unhappy?

No, unless by their own choice it's made so by both partners being not satisfied with each other's merit. But surely this cannot be my own affair, for I married, if I know my own mind, intirely to make my wife and self happy; to live in a course of virtue and religion, and to be a mutual help to each other. Oh! what am I going to say? I have almost made, as it were, a resolution to make a sepparation by settling affairs and parting in friendship. But is this what I married for? . . . Oh, were I endowed with the patience of Socrates, then mt. I be happy; but as I am not, I must pacify myself with the cheerful reflection that I have done my utmost to render our union happy, good and comfortable to ourselves and progeny. . . .

6 Oct. 1756. This day how are my most sanguine hopes of happiness frustrated!—I mean the happiness between myself and wife. . . . I think I have tryed all experiments to make our life's happy, but they have all failed. The opposition seems to be naturally in our tempers. . . .

26 Oct. (Sunday) 1756. This day, the holy sacrament being administered, my wife, self, and maid, all staid—my wife and I taking up a resolution . . . to become better Christians, and to bear with each other's infirmityes, and live in peace with all mankind. . . .

2 Nov. 1756 . . . I who, on Sunday last, was all calm and serenity in my breast, am now nought but storm and tempest. Well might the wise men say, 'It were better to dwell in a corner of the house-top than with a contentious woman in a wide house.' . . .

23 June 1761. About five o'clock on the afternoon, it pleased Almighty GOD to take from me my beloved wife, who poor creature, has laboured under a severe tho' lingering illness for these thirty-eight weeks, which she bore with the greatest resignation to the Divine Will. In her I have lost a sincere friend, a virtuous wife, a prudent good economist in her family, and a very valuable companion.

5 August 1761. Almost distracted with trouble: how do I hourly find the loss I have sustained in the death of my dear

wife! What can equal the value of a virtuous wife? . . . I am left as a beacon on a rock, or an ensign on a hill.

[Turner often lamented the death of his wife in this Diary, but in 1765 he married again—Molly Hicks, the daughter of a Chiddingly yeoman—after a somewhat tiring courtship.]

28 March 1765. In the afternoon rode over to Chiddingly, to pay my charmer or intended wife, or sweetheart, or whatever other name may be more proper, a visit at her father's, where I drank tea, in company with their family. . . . I supped there on some rasures of bacon. It being an excessive wet and windy night, I had the opportunity, sure I should say the pleasure, or perhaps some might say the unspeakable happiness, to sit up with Molly Hicks, my charmer, all night. I came home at forty minutes past five in the morning—I must not say fatigued; no, no, that could not be, it could be only a little sleepy for want of rest. . . .

Good Fryday—In the evening I met with Molly Hicks, by appointment, and walked home with her, where I staid with her, the weather being excessive bad, till past five in the morning, and then came home.

7 April 1765—In the even very dull and sleepy; this courting does not well agree with my constitution, and perhaps it may be only taking pains to create more pain.

Sunday 15 April—After dinner I set out to Malling, to pay Molly Hicks, my intended wife, a visit. . . . Now, perhaps, there may be many reports about in the world of my present intentions, some likely condemning my choice, others approving it. . . . I will take the trouble to relate what really and truly are my intentions. . . . First, I think marriage is a state agreeable to nature, reason, and religion. . . . As to my choice I have only this to say—the girl, I believe, as far as I can discover, is a very industrious, sober woman, and seemingly endowed with prudence and good nature, with a serious and sedate turn of mind. She comes of reputable parents, and may perhaps, one time or other, have some fortune. As to her person, I know it's plain (so is my own) but she is cleanly in her person and dress. . . . She is, I think, a well-made woman. As to her education, I own it is not liberal; but she has good sense, and a desire to improve her mind. . . .

3 July 1765 . . . Married, at our church . . . and for about fourteen days was very ill with a tertian ague, or rather an intermitting fever . . . however, thank God, I begin to once more be a little settled, and am happy in my choice. I have, it's true, not married a learned lady, nor is she a gay one; but I trust she is good-natured, and one that will use her utmost endeavour to make me happy. As to her fortune, I shall one day have something considerable, and there seems to be rather a flowing stream. Well, here let us drop the subject, and begin a new one.

10. BABIES

(a) *Source:* An Account by Richard Steele in *The Tatler*, 1706, of what a baby might expect on being introduced to the world.

I lay very quiet; but the witch, for no manner of reason or provocation in the world, takes me and binds my head as hard as she possibly could; then ties up, both my legs and makes me swallow down an horrid mixture. I thought it an harsh entrance into life, to begin with taking physic. When I was thus dressed, I was carried to a bedside where a fine young lady (my mother, I wot) had like to have hugged me to death. . . . Crowds of relations came every day to congratulate my arrival; amongst others, my cousin Betty, the greatest romp in nature; she whisks me such a height over her head, that I cried out for fear of falling. She pinched me and called me squealing chit, and threw me into a girl's arms that was taken in to tend me. The girl was very proud of the womanly employment of a nurse, and took upon her to strip and dress me anew, because I made a noise, to see what ailed me; she did so and stuck a pin in every joint about me. I still cried, upon which, she lays me on my face in her lap; and, to quiet me, fell to nailing in all the pins, by clapping me on the back and screaming a lullaby. . . .

(b) *Source:* Letter from Emily, Duchess of Leinster, 10 Dec. 1762, printed in B. Fitzgerald, *Emily, Duchess of Leinster*, p. 107.

I have a pleasant and cheerful prospect before my eyes within doors. The dear little brats are, thank God, so well, so merry, so riotous, so hardy and so full of play from morning till night that it would enliven the dullest of mortals to see them. The two nurses . . . are the best playfellows for children I ever saw. They invent some new diversions every night. . . . Henry naked is the dearest little being on earth.

(c) Letter from John Wesley's mother, 24 July 1732, quoted in J. Wesley, *Journal* (Everyman edn., 1906).

According to your desire, I have collected the principal rules I observed in educating my family; which I now send you as they occurred to my mind. . . . When turned a year old (and some before) they were taught to fear the rod, and to cry softly; by which means they escaped abundance of correction they might otherwise have had; and that most odious noise of the crying of children was rarely heard in the house. As soon as they were grown pretty strong, they were confined to three meals a day. At dinner, their little table and chairs were set by ours, where they could be overlooked; and they were suffered to eat and drink (small beer) as much as they would, but not to call for anything. They were never suffered to choose their own meat, but always made to eat such things as were provided for the family. Mornings they always had spoon meat; sometimes at night. But whatever they had, they were never permitted to eat, at those meals, of more than one thing, and of that sparingly enough. Drinking or eating between meals was never allowed, except in case of sickness, which seldom happened. At six, as soon as family prayer was over, they had their supper; at seven, the maid washed them; and, beginning at the youngest, she undressed and got them all to bed by eight: at which time she left them in their several rooms awake; for there was no such thing allowed of in our house, as sitting by a child until it fell asleep. They were so constantly used to eat and drink what was given them, that when any of them was ill, there was no difficulty in making them take the most unpleasant medicine; for they durst not refuse it, though some of them would presently throw it up. None of them were taught to read till five years old, except Kezzy in whose case I was over-ruled; and she was more years learning than any of the rest had been months. . . . There was no such thing as loud talking or playing allowed of; but every one was kept close to their business for the six hours of school. Rising out of their places, or going out of the room was not permitted except for good cause; running into the yard, garden, or street, without, leave, was always esteemed a capital offence.

11. CHILDREN

Not all regimes were like Mrs. Wesley's. For families that could afford toys and presents, there was ample choice. Treatment of children owed much to social position. There was also considerable change from generation to generation.

(a) *Source:* Disbursements for children of the aristocracy listed in in G. Scott-Thomson, *The Russells in Bloomsbury* (1940), pp. 197ff.

November 5 1751	Paid at the Playhouse with Lord Tavistock	10s. 0d.
December 2 1751	Paid for seeing the rhinoceros and alligator with Lord Tavistock	2s. 2d.
December 2 1751	Paid for battledores and shuttlecocks	9s. 6d.
February 12 1752	Gave the dog doctor for coming to Bounce	5s. 0d.
February 27 1752	Paid for seeing the Russia man for Lord Tavistock	3s. 0d.
	Paid at the Playhouse, ditto	5s. 0d.
May 29 1752	Paid Isaac Smith a bill for bird cages for Lord Tavistock and Lady Caroline	£1 14s. 0d.
July 19 1752	Paid for three peewits for Lord Tavistock	2s. 6d.
February 25 1753	Paid for paint and prints for Lord Tavistock and Lady Caroline	6s. 1d.
March 28 1753	Paid for a book of drawings for Lady Caroline	5s. 0d.

April 3 1753	Paid for a new door to the doormouse's cage		6d.
May 5 1753	Paid Richard Bynion for fireworks for Lord Tavistock	£1	0s. 4d.
May 6 1753	Paid for the print of Miss Bellamy and Mr. Garrick for Lady Caroline		7s. 6d.
November 24 1753	Paid for battledore and shuttlecocks for Lord Tavistock		4s. 6d.
	Paid for whips and top for Lord Tavistock		6d.
	Paid for five cups and balls		5s. 2d.

(b) *Source:* Earl of Carnavon (ed.), *Letters of the Fourth Earl of Chesterfield to his Godson* (1890), vol. I, pp. 15–16. The letter was written in 1762 and the recipient was seven years old.

As I know that you desire to be a well bred gentleman, and not a two-legged Bear . . . I send you some general rules for your behaviour . . . whoever you speak to, to whoever speaks to you, you must be sure to look them full in the face. . . . You must call every gentleman, Sir, or My Lord, and every Woman, Madam. You must never on any account put your fingers in your nose, for that is excessively ill-bred, very nasty, and will make your nose bleed and be very sore. What is your handkerchief for? When you are at dinner you must sit upright in your chair, and not loll. . . . When you first come into a room you must not fail to make a bow to the company, and also when you go out of it you must never look sullen or pouting, but have a cheerful, easy countenance. Remember that there is no one thing as necessary for a gentleman as both [to be] perfectly civil and well bred.

(c) By the end of the century there were many 'improving' books for children.

Source: Abbé Gaulthier, *Amusing and Instructional Conversations for Children of Five Years* (1803), pp. 69ff.

Have you ever seen Thomas Violent? He is a very fine boy (if it is possible to be a fine boy without being good); but he is capricious, and so naughty, that nobody likes to see him.

If he is hungry, and wishes for bread, instead of speaking properly . . . he says rudely, Give me some bread—I want it: and if it is not given to him immediately, he cries, he grunts like a little hog.

But, yesterday, he received a lesson, which, I believe, he will for a long-time remember. He took it into his head, not to suffer himself to be washed, nor dressed.

The poor maid, whose patience was at an end, perceived in the street Mr. Reform.

Ah, good day, Mr. Reform, cried she at the window: where have you been to-day sir? You seem much displeased. Is it because you have heard my little Thomas crying? He makes a terrible noise.

Yes, Madam, said Mr. Reform, I came on purpose to ask you what noise this is? I hear that little master is often naughty, and that he is not quiet when he is washed nor when he is dressed. . . . Lead me to him, and I will make him a good boy.

Then he goes himself to where master Thomas was still in bed, and as he hears him crying, while yet on the staircase, I will not be washed—I will not—I will remain dirty—I will remain naked.—You will, said Mr. Reform, you will?—Say you so, master Thomas? You are then master here. Ah! little boy, you have your own way; we shall soon see if I cannot teach you better than this.

He takes him in his arms, carries him to the garden, and then plunges him into a large tub.

Now, says he to him, what do you think of the matter, master Thomas? Do you still say that you will not be washed? If ever that comes into your head again, I will leave you a long while in this tub; and if you will not be dressed, in the morning I will come and whip you well. . . . See, I have here very good rods, and I have always found them hurt little children much. Take care of yourself.

Little Thomas then promised that he would be sure, for the future, never to say; I will not be washed;—I will not be dressed;—I will remain as I am.

I am sure that he will keep his word, and that he will always be very tractable.

This Mr. Reform is a very terrible man. O, if you were to see how stately he walks along! with what a deliberate pace! and how ready he always is to do to little naughty untractable children, just what he did yesterday to little Thomas!

12. THE IMPROVEMENT OF MANNERS

The attempt to 'improve' the manners of adults as well as children was a feature of eighteenth-century life both at the beginning and end of the period. The influence of women was one factor; religion another. There was particular concern, however, for the manners (and morals) of the poor.

(a) Societies for the Reformation of Manners were prominent in the 1690s and the early years of the century.

Source: An account of this period in *An Address from the London Society for the Suppression of Vice* (1703), p. 79.

We are told that many thousands have been brought to punishment for swearing and cursing; that a multitude of drunkards and profaners of the Lord's Day, some of whom kept, as it were, open markets within a few years past, have been made examples of . . . that hundreds of disorderly houses, which were little better than sowes, and nests for thieves, clippers, and coiners, etc., have been rooted out and suppressed . . . public disorders are remarkably cured; and, in short, vice is afraid and ashamed to show its head, where within a few years past it was daring and triumphant.

(b) By the middle years of the century, there had been big changes, though the earlier societies disappeared.

Source: J. Brown, *An Estimate of the Manners and Principles of the Times* (1757), p. 20.

Let us now trace the spirit of liberty through as its effects. The first that occurs in *Humanity*. By this is not meant that smoothness and refined polish of external manners, by which the present age affects to be distinguished [but] that pity for distress, that moderation in limiting punishments or even the general humanity of our highwaymen and robbers compared with those of other countries.

(c) *Source:* Joseph Farington, *Memoirs of the Life of Sir Joshua Reynolds* (1819), p. 55.

At this time [about 1770] a change in the manners and habits of the people of this country was beginning to take place. Public taste was improving. The coarse familiarity so common in personal intercourse was laid aside, and respectful attention and civility in address gradually gave a new and better aspect to society. The profane habit of using oaths in conversation no longer offended the ear, and bacchanalian intemperance at the dinner-table was succeeded by rational cheerfulness and sober forbearance.

(d) Hannah More, the Evangelical (for Evangelical attitudes, see below, p. 332) seized on the change with pleasure.

Source: Hannah More, *Works* (1853), vol. V, pp. 316–17.

> Long was society o'er run,
> By whist, that desolating Hun;
> Long did quadrille despotic sit,
> That Vandal of colloquial wit;
> And conversation's setting light
> Long half-obscur'd in Gothic night;
> At length the mental shades decline,
> Colloquial wit begins to shine,
> Genius prevails, and conversation
> Emerges into reformation.

(e) The civil power sometimes backed up the efforts of the Evangelicals.

Source: Report in the *Bristol Gazette*, 10 April 1788.

In the town of Stroud a great diminution of irregularity and misbehaviour has of late been observed, to the comfort and satisfaction of the inhabitants. Such a change shews what may be effected in time by the uniform but gentle perseverance of a worthy minister, when supported by a few active and exemplary characters. The present High Constable has proved that our laws give full power for the suppression of every enormity, when the execution of them is consigned to men of spirit and integrity.

(f) William Cobbett and his first 'tory' mentor, William Windham, disliked many of the changes, as they disliked both Evangelicals and Utilitarians. Windham, for example, opposed a bill to abolish bull baiting in 1800. They accused the Evangelicals and Utilitarians of robbing the poor of their pleasures.

Source: T. Aymot (ed.), Speeches in Parliament of the Rt. Hon. William Windham (1812), vol. I, pp. 332ff.

In my whole life, I have never been present but at two Bull-Baitings, and they happened while I was a schoolboy; but I cannot say that I experienced any bad effects from the gratification of my curiosity. I did not find myself the worse for it, nor could I suspect that the other spectators were contaminated by the spectacle. . . . Whatever may be the habits of the more luxurious climates of the continent, the amusements of our people were always composed of athletic, manly, and hardy exercises, affording trials of their courage, conductive to their health, and to them objects of ambition and of glory. In the exercise of those sports they may, indeed, sometimes hurt themselves, but they could never hurt the nation. . . . Some little time since it was thought matter of reproach for gentlemen to be present at any of these athletic trials; and even *boxing* was cried down as an exercise of ferocity. It is time to resist these unnecessary restraints . . . [for] it is idle to declaim against savage manners or dispositions in this country. The character of the people is directly the reverse; their sports are robust and hardy, but their tempers are not ferocious. . . . Has not the butcher as much right to demand the exercise of his sport, as the man of fortune to demand that of hunting? Is not the latter as painful to the horse, as the former to the bull? Might not the butcher say, 'have no coaches, horses, balls, masquerades, nor even books, which afford so much delight to those in higher stations, and who have more leisure time; do not therefore deprive me of the amusement I feel in setting the propensities of one animal against those of another'. The common people may ask with justice, why abolish bull-baiting and protect hunting and shooting? What appearance must we make, if we, who have every source of amusement open to us, and yet follow these cruel sports, become rigid censors of the sports of the poor, and abolish them on account of their cruelty, when they are not more cruel than our own?

CHAPTER IX

Food and Drink

The *Pudding* is a Dish very difficult to be describ'd, because of the several sorts there are of it. . . . They bake them in an Oven, they boil them with Meat, they make them in fifty several Ways: BLESSED BE HE THAT INVENTED PUDDING, for it is a Manna that hits the Palates of all sorts of People.

(M. MISSON, *Memoirs and Observations*, 1719)

At Castleford, the starving inhabitants seized a vessel laden with corn, and did not give her up till the riot act was read, and the military on the spot had captured twelve of their leaders.

(J. MAYHALL, *The Annals of Yorkshire*, on the year 1795)

While their Majesties were at Drury Lane Theatre to see the Winter's Tale, as Garrick was repeating the lines
'For you, my hearts of oak, for your regale
Here's good old English stingo, mild and stale'
a fellow cried out of the gallery: 'At threepence a pot, Master Garrick, or confusion to the brewers.'

(Quoted by R. V. FRENCH, *Nineteen Centuries of Drink in England*, 1884)

Will the *sons* and *daughters* of this happy isle, this reputed bode of *sense* and *liberty*, for *ever* submit to the bondage of so tyrannical a custom as drinking tea?

(JOSEPH HANWAY, *Journal*, 1757)

We had an old English menu: a large fish, boiled mutton, pudding, boiled cabbage with butter, and a roast. Punch was made at table.

(SOPHIE V. LA ROCHE, 1786)

1. STANDARDS OF LIVING

Social differences were as marked in relation to food and drink as in relation to any other aspect of life. There were also marked fluctuations, as far as the common people were concerned, from year to year. Given the difficulty of generalizing, it is likely that the standard of living improved for most sections of the community during the first half of the century, and that after a rise in prices in the 1760s wages more than kept pace until the early years of the war with revolutionary France at the end of the century. Diets became more varied.

(a) There were marked differences from region to region.

Source: Sir F. M. Eden, *The State of the Poor* (1797), vol. I, pp. 496ff.

There is not only a remarkable difference in the proportion of earnings appropriated to the purchase of subsistence by labourers in the North and South of England; but their mode of preparing their food is no less dissimilar. In the South of England, the poorest labourers are habituated to the unvarying meal of dry bread and cheese from one week's end: and in those families, whose finances do not allow them the indulgence of malt liquor, the deleterious produce of China [tea] constitutes their most usual and general beverage. If a labourer is rich enough to afford himself meat once a week, he commonly adopts the simplest of all culinary preparations; that of roasting it; or, if he lives near a baker's, of baking it; and if he boils his meat, he never thinks of forming it into a soup, that would not only be as wholesome, and as nourishing, but, certainly, more palatable than a plain boiled joint.

In the North of England, and in Scotland and Wales, on the contrary, the poorest labourers can, and actually do, regale themselves with a variety of dishes that are wholly unknown to the Southern inhabitant of this island. . . . To begin with one of the simplest articles of diet, 'the healsome porritch, chief of Scotia's food', hasty-pudding . . . is extremely nutritious. . . . *Crowdie* is not so generally used as hasty-pudding. It is, however, a very common dish in the North, among labourers of all descriptions, but particularly miners, as it is soon made ready, and without much trouble. The process is extremely simple; and consists in pouring boiling water over oat-meal and stirring it a little. [Broth or corned beef may be added]. . . .

(b) Arthur Young complained that the poor had misused their earnings in the early part of the century when prices were lower.

Source: A. Young, *The Farmer's Letters to the People of England* (1771 edn.).

Some years ago they [the poor] could buy bread and beer and cheese [the foundations of their diet] &c. &c. much cheaper than they can *at present*, while their earnings were the same. What was the effect of such cheapness? If the present *dearness* is so afflicting them, were the former good times attended with no trifling effects? Instead of laying up three or four pounds; they then, doubtless, saved twice as much! No such matter; whatever was gained by such cheapness was constantly expended by the husband in a proportionable quantity of idleness and ale, and by the wife in that of tea.

(c) Eden gave details of village labourers' budgets in 1792.

Source: Eden, *The State of the Poor* (1797), vol. III, pp. ccc-xliv.ff. (*See* table on p. 282.)

(d) There was a sharp increase in prices in the later 1790s, with 1795 a year of great scarcity (see above, p. 35). The increase in the price of food over a larger period is well brought out in the following table of housekeeping expenses, drawn up in Bury St. Edmunds.

Source: The *Annual Register* (1800), p. 94. (*See* table on p. 283.)

(e) Artisans' budgets are more difficult to come by than those of farmers, but it is clear that artisans lived far better than village labourers.

Source: Note on Sheffield in *Ibid.,* p. 873.

Wheaten bread is, universally, used here: malt liquor, and butcher's meat, form part of the diet of all ranks of people. The tradesman, artisan, and labourer all live well; and in general, industry is a more prominent feature in their conduct than economy.

(f) The standard of life of the country gentleman was high.

Source: Letter of Matthew Bramble to Dr. Lewis in T. Smollett, *Humphrey Clinker* (1771).

At Brambleton Hall . . . I drink the virgin lymph, pure and crystalline as it gushes from the rock, or the sparkling beverage

T

BUDGETS OF VILLAGE LABOURERS' FAMILIES (each of 4 persons) IN 1792

	LINCS.	LEICESTER-SHIRE	NORFOLK	CUMBER-LAND
Earnings (weekly)				
Man	10– 6	8– 6	9– 0	7– 6
Wife	—	1– 6¾	8	1– 4
Children	—	1–10	—	—
Total	10– 6	11–10¾	9– 8	8–10
Expenditure on Food (weekly)				
Bread, flour, oatmeal	2– 8	3– 9	2–10	3– 4
Yeast and salt	2	3	1½	1½
Bacon, pork and other meat	1– 9	1– 4	—	–10
Tea, sugar and butter	1– 5	7½	5½	–10
Cheese	—	6½	2¾	—
Milk	4	2½	3½	6
Potatoes	6¾	3	3	5
Small Beer	5½	1	—	3¾
Soap	1¾	2	1¾	2¼
Candles	2	2¾	1¼	1¾
Thread and Worsted	1½	2¼	1½	1½
Total	7– 9	7–7½	4– 6	6– 9¼
YEARLY EARNINGS	27– 6– 0	30–17– 6	23–16– 8	22–19– 4
YEARLY EXPENSES (as above)	20– 3– 0	19–16– 9	11–17– 3	17–12– 1
YEARLY TOTAL on RENT	1–10– 0	1–11– 3	2–10– 0	2–10– 0
YEARLY TOTAL on FUEL	1–19– 0	1–10– 0	1–10. 0	2– 0– 0
YEARLY TOTAL on CLOTHES	3– 3– 0	4–17– 7¼	2– 7– 6	2– 0– 0
YEARLY TOTAL on BIRTHS, SICKNESS, BURIALS etc.	1– 1– 0	2– 6	8– 6	—
YEARLY TOTAL EXPENSES	27–16– 0	27–17– 1¼	20– 2– 6	24– 2– 1
SURPLUS OR DEFICIENCY	10– 0D	3–0– 4¾s	3–14– 2s	1– 2– 9D

(i) In Lincolnshire, the man was 30 and the woman 25. Their children were 4 and 6. At the end of 1795, they were free from debt. They never had assistance from the parish

(ii) In Leicestershire, the man was 41 and the woman 31; the children were 11 and 8.

(iii) In Norfolk, the man was 33 and the woman 30. Their children were 3 and 1. The man was 'industrious' and the woman 'frugal'.

(iv) Cumberland. The man was 35 and the woman 30; both children were under 7; and the family was described as 'decent', 'reckoned to live well, and, notwithstanding their deficiency, to manage economically.'

	1773 £ s. d.	1793 £ s. d.	1800 £ s. d.
Comb [4 bushels or half a quarter] of Malt	0 12 0	1 3 0	2 0 0
Chaldron of Coals	1 11 6	2 0 6	2 11 0
Comb of Oats	0 5 0	0 13 0	1 1 0
Load of Hay	2 2 0	4 10 0	7 0 0
Meat	0 0 4	0 0 5	0 0 9
Butter	0 0 6	0 0 11	0 1 4
Sugar (loaf)	0 0 8	0 1 0	0 1 4
Soap	0 0 6	0 0 8	0 0 10
Window lights, 30 windows	3 10 0	7 10 0	12 12 0
Candles	0 0 6	0 0 8	0 0 10½
Poor rates, per Quarter	0 1 0	0 2 6	0 5 0
Income Tax on £200	—	—	20 0 0
TOTAL	8 4 0	16 2 8	45 14 1½

home-brewed from malt of my own making; or I indulge
with cider, which my own orchard affords; or with claret of
the best growth . . . my bread is sweet and nourishing, made
from my own wheat, ground in my own mill, and baked in
my own oven; my table is, in a great measure, furnished from
my own ground; my five-year old mutton, fed on the fragrant
herbage of the mountains, that might vie with venison in
juice and flavour; my delicious veal, fattened with nothing
but the mother's milk, that fills the dish with gravy; my
poultry from the barn door . . . ; my rabbits panting from the
warren; my game fresh from the moors; my trout and salmon
struggling from the stream; oysters from their native banks;
and herrings, with other sea-fish, I can eat in four hours after
they are taken. My salads, roots, and pot-herbs, my own
garden yields in plenty and perfection; the produce of the

natural soil, prepared by moderate cultivation. The same soil affords all the different fruits which England may call her own so that my dessert is every day fresh-gathered from the tree; my dairy flows with nectareous tides of milk and cream, from whence we derive abundance of excellent butter, curds and cheese; and the refuse fattens my pigs, that are destined for hams and bacon.

(g) Orders for food, however, were often sent to London.

Source: Letter of 6 Feb. 1747 in *The Purefoy Letters*, p. 69.

Mr Willson/

I desire you will send mee
One pound of the best Bohea Tea
Half a pound of the best green Tea
Two pounds of the best Coffeeberries
A quarter of a pound of nutmegs
Two ounces of mace
A quarter of an hundred of the best treble refined Loaf sugar
A quarter of an hundred of Household sugar about 6 pence a pound
Half a quarter of an hundred of Polish starch
Half a quarter of an hundred of Rice

Send these by ye Buckingham carrier . . . send your Bill with them & will order you payment. The last Bohea Tea was so ordinary I could not drink it, my neighbours had as good for six shillings a pound. The last hundredweight of Raisins you sent were so bad they spoiled the Liquor they were made on. I hope you will send no more bad Goods, I have had no reason to complain till now, tho' I have dealt at yr shop these forty years & am

Your humble servt
E. P.

p.s. If you can't conveniently send them on Tuesday Mr Jones ye carrier sets out of London on Saturday mornings early.

(h) There were great food markets in London. Billingsgate, opened in 1699, followed Covent Garden and Smithfields: there were also large numbers of open street markets.

Source: Sophie v. la Roche, *Sophie in London in 1786* (1933), p. 143.

We left early for Covent Garden to visit Mr. Forster and view the fruit and vegetable market, remarkable both for its constant fresh supply of fruit, vegetables and flowers, as for the order reigning there. We were told that London consumes annually 2,957,000 bushels of wheaten flour, 100,000 oxen, 700,000 sheep and lambs, 195,000 calves, 238,000 pigs, 115,000 bushels of oysters, 14,000,000 mackerel, 16,000,000 pounds of butter, and 21,000,000 pounds of cheese annually, exclusive of game and poultry; that a fat ox costs 20 pounds sterling, a sheep 2, a pig 3; that 5s. pays a goose, 3s. a fowl, 2s. three pigeons, and 1s. buys 20 eggs; thus the millions of millions necessary for general circulation can be roughly calculated. You will laugh, children, when you hear that calves are bled so as to keep their meat white; it is a proof, however, of the enormous luxury. 140,000,244 quarts of beer, a most nourishing beverage, are brewed annually in London

(i) London, like the country, had great contrasts. Quite apart from the very poor, even batchelor clerks could find the going difficult.

Source: Considerations on the Expediency of Raising, at this Time of General Dearth, the Wages of Servants that are not Domestic, particularly Clerks in Public Offices (1767).

'That Fifty Pounds a Year is abundantly sufficient for the Subsistence of Clerks in Public Offices' . . . is as absurd and impudent [a statement] as it is false and malignant. I have made the following Estimate [to show so].

BREAKFAST

	£	s.	d.
Bread and Cheese, and Small Beer, from the Chandler's Shop,			2

DINNER

	£	s.	d.
Chuck-Beef, or Scrag of Mutton, or Sheeps Trotters, or Pig's Ear soused; Cabbage, or Potatoes, or Parsnips; Bread, and Small Beer, with half a Pint of Porter,			7

SUPPER

	£	s.	d.
Bread and Cheese, with Radishes, or Cucumbers, or Onions,			3

Small Beer, and half a Pint of Porter,   1½

	1	1½
Multiplied by 7	7	10½
An additional Repast on Sunday		4
	8	2½
LODGING in a ready-furnished room . . .		2 6
WASHING . . .		10
SHAVING and Combing a Wig twice. . . .		6
PLEASURES. Saturday-Night's Club, One Tankard of Porter		3½
	12	4
Multiplied by 52	32	1 4
APPAREL, COALS, CANDLES . . .	16	4 9
SOAP, BLACKING, PEPPER, VINEGAR, AND SALT		10 0
CHURCH EXPENSE (if he is not an avowed enemy to the Christian Faith. . . .)		10 0
THE LADY'S MAID AT CHRISTMAS		1 0
	49	7 3
Balance Saved		12 9
	50	0 0

. . . For the common Entertainments of Life, such as almost all People partake of, I have left him wholly dependent upon the Bounty of others; not allowing him, at his own Cost, one Night at Sadlers-Wells, one Drop of Wine or Punch, one Dish of Tea or Coffee, one Pennyworth of Fruit, one Pipe of Tobacco, or one Pinch of Snuff; and the Ten Shillings Church-expences include the Sum-Total of his yearly Bounty to the Poor. I have driven him to the dirtiest and meanest Parts of the Town, to seek for a cheap Lodging; I have cloathed him in the plainest and coarsest Manner; I have scarcely allowed him to be clean enough for the Place of his stated Appearance; I have fed him with the Refuse of the Market. . . . and I have granted him no Indulgence but his Saturday Night's Club of Three-pence half-penny, that he may forget for a few Hours, the Toils and Cares of the past Week. . . .

(j) Rich Londoners or even the comfortably off could dine well. Dinner was eaten early in the century at 5 or 6 o'clock and supper was taken so late that in the words of *The Tatler* (1710) the meal was in danger 'of being entirely confounded and lost in breakfast'. Later in the century 2 to 3 and 7 to 8 o'clock became main meal times, with afternoon tea growing in popularity among the rich. More attention was paid to styles of cooking, and French fashions influenced traditional habits.

Source: A Lady, *The Art of Cooking Made Plain and Easy* (1747).

In the Days of good Queen *Elizabeth*, when mighty Roast Beef was the *Englishman's* Food; our Cookery was plain and simple as our Manners; it was not then a Science or Mistery, and required no Conjuration to please the Palates of our greatest Men. But we have of late Years refined ourselves out of that simple Taste, and conformed our Palates to Meats and Drinks dressed after the *French* Fashion. The natural Taste of Fish or Flesh is become nauseous to our fashionable Stomach; we abhor anything that should appear at our Tables in its native Properties; all the Earth, from both the Poles, the most distant and different Climates, must be ransacked for Spices, Pickles and Sauces, not to relish but to disguise our Food.

(k) Many other attacks were made on 'luxury' in eating.

Source: D. Defoe, *The Complete English Tradesman* (1725), pp. 322–3.

'Tis surprising, what a swarm of gardeners, poulterers, pastry-cooks, &c. are supported by the mere extraordinaries of eating; raising plants by mere violence, and, as it were, a rape upon the earth; forcing her to produce things before her time, and, as it were, in spite of seasons, climates, forward or backward springs, and the most obstinate opposition of natural causes?

What Rapes are committed upon nature in the production of Animals as well as Plants? making the ewes bring lambs all the winter, fatting calves to a monstrous size, using cruelties and contrary diets to the poor brute, to whiten its flesh for the palates of the Ladies, and to gorge the dainty stomachs of those who lay up their felicity in eating fine, as they call it? [But will any body say, that most of these people might not

be better and more usefully employ'd, for the good of the
Commonwealth?

(l) As food habits diverged, the pleasures of simpler foods were
often sung. Yet there had always been striking differences in food
preferences.

Source: J. Gay, *The Shepherd's Week* (1715).

> In good roast beef my landlord sticks his knife,
> The capon fat delights his dainty wife,
> Pudding our Parson eats, the Squire loves hare,
> But white-pot thick is my *Buxoma's* fare;
> While she loves white-pot, capon ne'er shall be,
> Nor hare, nor beef, nor pudding, food for me.

(m) During the French Wars at the end of the century attempts
were made to discipline food habits and to minimize ostentation,
rather along the lines of Defoe.

Source: Note in *The Times*, 23 July 1795.

THE WAY TO PEACE AND PLENTY.
Rules for the Rich
1. Abolish gravy soups, and second courses.
2. Buy no starch when wheat is dear.
3. Destroy all useless dogs.
4. Give no dog, or other animal, the smallest bit of bread or
   meat.
5. Save all your skim-milk carefully, and give it all to the
   poor, or sell it at a cheap rate.
6. Make broth, rice pudding, &c., for the poor, and teach
   them to make such things.
7. Go to church yourselves, and take care your servants go
   constantly.
8. Look into the management of your own families, and visit
   your poor neighbours.
9. Prefer those poor who keep steadily to their work, and go
   constantly to church, and give nothing to those who are
   idle, and riotous, or keep useless dogs.
10. Buy no weighing meat, or gravy beef: if the rich would
    buy only the prime pieces, the poor could get the others
    cheap.

Rules for the Poor

1. Keep steadily to your work, and never change masters, if you can help it.
2. Go to no gin-shop, or alehouse: but lay out all your earnings in food, and cloaths, for yourself, and your family: and try to lay up a little for rent and rainy days.
3. Avoid bad company.
4. Keep no dogs: for they rob your children, and your neighbours.
5. Go constantly to church, and carry your wives, and children, with you, and God will bless you.
6. Be civil to your superiors, and they will be kind to you.
7. Learn to make broth, milk pottage, rice-pudding, &c. One pound of meat, in both, will go further than two pounds boiled or roasted.
8. Be quiet, and contented, and never steal, or swear, or you will never thrive.

2. BREAD

Bread was the staple food in the South, and the standard of life of the poor depended on bread. White bread was in general demand, and the cultivation of wheat greatly increased at the expense of other cereals. There were frequent complaints in London about the adulteration of bread. In the North, many other cereals were grown, and in some cases bread was not a staple. Parliament authorized the sale of 'standard bread' containing a higher proportion of bran in 1756–58, 1772–74 and 1795–1800: it was never popular.

(a) *Source:* Note in *The Gentleman's Magazine* (1776), quoted in J. Drummond and A. Wilbraham, *The Englishman's Food* (1958 edn.), p. 174.

The ploughman, the shepherd, the hedger and ditcher, all eat a white bread as is commonly made in London, which occasions the great consumption of wheat.

(b) This remark was not true of the North of England.

Sources: Samuel Bamford, *Early Days* (1893 edn., ed. H. Dunckley), pp. 98–9.

The mode of living at my uncle's was of the simplest country style. At breakfast, a brown earthen dish being placed on a low beaufet [buffet] near the middle of the floor, a boiling of water porridge was poured into the dish, hot from the pan. A mess-pot of the same material as the dish was placed for each one about to partake of the breakfast, a quantity of milk and a spoon were placed in each pot, my uncle took a seat and asked a blessing, each of the children of the family standing around; we then took our several messes of milk, and helped ourselves to the steaming porridge as quickly as we chose, and mixing and eating in the manner we liked best, not a word being spoken all the time. The porridge being scraped up . . . each would take a piece of hard oaten cake and eat it to the remainder of his milk, after which a little butter, or a small piece of cheese, with more oaten bread, would finish the meal, and in a few minutes work was resumed. . . . Our dinners consisted generally of butcher's meat and potatoes, or potato-pie, or meat and broth, or barm dumplings, or drink porridge, or hasty pudding, and in each case the food was partaken in the same primitive manner. . . . When we had potato pie for dinner an allowance of the crust was given to each; the potatoes were then eaten out of the dish as before, and the crust, as being the most dainty, was eaten afterwards. . . .

Our bagging, or afternoon lunch, consisted of half an oaten cake, with butter, treacle, cheese, or milk, as circumstances rendered most convenient, and our supper was generally the same as breakfast. On Sunday mornings we had mint or balm tea, sweetened with treacle, and oaten cake and butter; on Sunday afternoons we had tea of the same kind, and a slice of buttered loaf was added, which was an especial dainty.

(c) For people in a different section of society, bread and butter began to assume a different significance in the weekly diet.

Source: C. P. Moritz, A Journey to England (1782).

The slices of bread and butter, which they give you with your tea, are as thin as poppy-leaves—But there is another kind of bread and butter usually eaten with tea, which is toasted by the fire, and is incomparably good. This is called toast.

(d) There were many complaints about the adulteration of bread in eighteenth-century London, and sharp controversies ensued about bakers' practices.

Source: T. Smollett, *Humphrey Clinker* (1771).

The bread I eat in London is a deleterious paste, mixed up with chalk, alum and bone-ashes; insipid to the taste and destructive to the constitution. The good people are not ignorant of this adulteration; but they prefer it to wholesome bread, because it is whiter than the meal of corn. Thus they sacrifice their taste and their health, and the lives of their tender infants, to a most absurd gratification of a misjudging eye; and the miller or the baker, is obliged to poison them and their families, in order to live by his profession.

(e) Ancient rules about the size and distribution of bread were always invoked at times of shortage.

Source: Report in *The Times*, 8 July 1795.

Monday, in consequence of an information, Mr. Justice ADDINGTON, attended by several officers, went to a Baker's shop, in Holborn, where they found 70 loaves, short of the standard weight, 181 ounces. The Magistrate fixed the penalty of 5s. per ounce, which amounted to £45, 5s., but which was mitigated to £40.

(f) The 'Speenhamland system' of poor relief (see above, p. 172) depended on fixing the level of poor relief in terms of bread prices.

Source: Report in the *Reading Mercury*, 20 April 1795.

[The Magistrates] very earnestly recommend to the Farmers and others throughout the county to increase the Pay of the Labourers in proportion to the present Price of Provisions; and . . . have unanimously Resolved, That they will, in their several divisions, make the following calculations and allowances for the relief of all poor and industrious men and their families, who, to the satisfaction of the Justices of their parish, shall endeavour (as far as they can), for their own support and maintenance, that is to say, when the gallon loaf of second flour, weighing 8 lbs. 11 oz. shall cost one shilling, then every poor and industrious man shall have for his own support 3s.

weekly, either produced by his own or his family's labour or an allowance from the poor rates, and for the support of his wife and every other of his family 1s. 6d. When the gallon loaf shall cost 1s. 4d. then every poor and industrious man shall have 4s. weekly for his own, and 1s. 10d. for the support of every other of his family. And so in proportion as the price of bread rises or falls (that is to say) 3d. to the man and 1d. to every other of the family, on every penny which the loaf rises above a shilling.

3. POTATOES

The potato has a social history of its own. Rarely cultivated at the beginning of the century, except in big gardens and in some districts of the North-West, it became commonplace first in the North and then in the South. Its nutritional value was well-known at the time, and has been confirmed since. None the less, it was attacked as 'inferior food', and was associated with war-time scarcity, Irish labour and 'the miseries of the poor'. It offered the cheapest subsistence diet.

(a) *Source:* Note from *The Report of the Board of Agriculture, concerning the Culture and Use of Potatoes* (1795), p. 84.

It is also a fact, and one of the greatest importance, that potatoes and water alone, with common salt, can nourish men completely; but other mealy substances, though the principal food of millions of the human race, who never taste animal substances, are always mixed with some other kind of alimentary matter; such as, with oil, fruits, whey, milk, sour milk &c.

(b) The Board of Agriculture did much to spread propaganda about the potato. Eden also sang its praises.

Source: Sir F. M. Eden, *op cit.*, vol. I., p. 501.

Potatoes are not only particularly good in the North of England, but used in various ways. They are sometimes roasted, or boiled, and eaten with butter, as in the South; but are more commonly boiled (sometimes with the skin on, and sometimes with it taken off,) chopped into small pieces, and eaten with butter, (either cold or melted,) or bacon fried . . . but the principal way in which this useful root is dressed in the North by labourers' families is, by being peeled, or rather scraped, raw; chopped, and boiled together with a small quantity of meat cut into very small pieces. The whole of this mixture is then formed into a hash, with pepper, salt, onions &c. and forms a cheap and nutritive dish; which being common also in ships, is called by sailors *lobscouse*. No vegetable is, or ever was, applied to such a variety of uses in the North of England as the potatoe: it is a constant standing dish, at every meal, breakfast excepted, at the tables of the Rich, as well as the Poor.

(c) The consumption of potatoes rose sharply during the French Wars, meeting with violent criticism from William Cobbett.

Source: W. Cobbett, *Rural Rides* (Everyman, edn., 1957), vol I., p. 18.

The labourers [at Cricklade] seem miserably poor. Their dwellings are little better than pig-beds, and their looks indicate that their food is not nearly equal to that of a pig. . . . Yesterday morning was a sharp frost; and this had set the poor creatures to digging up their little plots of potatoes. In my whole life I never saw human wretchedness equal to this.

4. OTHER FOODS

If potatoes were often regarded as symbols of wretchedness, the roast beef of England was a traditional symbol of national pride (see above, p. 287). Meat figured in most diets, though often only in the form of bacon or cheap pork. The quality of livestock greatly improved. Vegetables also increased in size and variety throughout the eighteenth century, but milk consumption was patchy. Some new luxury products were introduced.

(a) *Source:* Sir Richard Weston, *A Treatise concerning the Husbandry and Natural History of England* (1742).

Some old men in *Surrey*, where it flourishes very much at present, report. That they knew the first Gardeners that came into those parts, to plant *Cabbages* and *Cauliflowers*, and to sow

Turnips, Carrots and *Parsnips*; to sow Raith (or early ripe) *Rape, Pease*; all which at that time were great rarities, we having few or none in *England,* but what came from *Holland* or *Flanders.*

(b) *Source:* J. Hanway, *Letters on the Importance of the Rising Generation* (1767).

The food of the poor [at Stevenage] is *good bread,* cheese, pease, and turnips in winter, with a little pork or other meat, when they can afford it; but from the high price of meat, it has not lately been within their reach. As to milk, they have hardly sufficient for their use.

(c) *Source:* T. Smollett, *Humphrey Clinker* (1771).

The milk itself [in London] should not pass unanalyzed, the produce of faded cabbage leaves and sour draff, lowered with hot water, frothed with bruised snails; carried through the streets in open pails, exposed to foul rinsings discharged from doors and windows, spittle, snot, and tobacco quids, from foot-passengers, overflowings from mud carts, spatterings from coach-wheels, dirt and trash chucked into it by roguish boys for the joke's sake. . . .

(d) In the country there was game, although enclosure reduced it in quantity and the game laws removed it from the diet of most of the poor.

Source: F. G. Stokes (ed.), *The Blecheley Diary of the Rev. William Cole* (1931), p. 174. The year is 1767.

Frid. 9. Excessive sharp Frost & some Snow. Will Grace brought me a wild Goose: I asked him to Dinner. Mr Cartwright & his Neice Bet Lord dined & supped with me. . . . Will Grace, Tom & John Holdom went out at 8 o'clock at Night on Horseback between here & Stoke to shoot Wild Geese where were near an Hundred: they brought Home one. I was ill in the Night with Wind in my Stomach.

(e) Among the new products introduced in the late eighteenth century was rhubarb. Oranges and lemons were obtainable throughout the century, even locally. There was a national market for oysters. The sardine made its debut in 1801.

Source: Advertisement in the *Morning Post,* 10 Aug. 1801.

SARDINIAS, a Fish cured in a peculiar manner, are highly esteemed as a Sandwich, and deemed of superior flavour to the Anchovy.

5. FOOD RIOTS

Throughout the century there were local riots to protest against food shortages or high prices. There was a pattern in the riots which tended to follow regular procedures and rituals. Conflicts in the eighteenth century centred more, indeed, on food than on wages.

(a) To Arthur Young 'agitators' were to blame for such disturbances.

Source: A Young, *A Six Weeks Tour Through the Southern Counties of England* (1772 edn.).

In all occupations, there will be idle, drunken, unsettled and disorderly persons; a few of these getting together, and talking over the *dearness of provisions* (which presently becomes a cant term among them), inflame each other.

(b) *Source:* An Account by local magistrates of a Yorkshire Food Riot of April 1740 in the Public Record Office, SP/36/50.

My Lord,

We think it our Duty to Inform your Grace, that last Saturday Morning, Several Persons, Men and Women to the Number of about 400, did Riotousely & Tumultuously assemble together at Dewsbury about four Miles from this Place; having a Drum beat before them; Carrying a Sort of Ensigne or Colours with designe to prevent any Corn Ground into Meal or Flower, being carried by Badgers and such dealers, from these parts Westwards, & into Lancashire on Pretence that such practice much Inhanced the Price of Corn here; to the oppression of the Poor.

Their first Attempt was to Stop & Seize certain Sacks, which they Suppos'd to be full of such Flower belonging to one John Willson who was carrying the same from Dewsbury to some Place Westward; But he having some notice, of such their designe, had fill'd these Sacks only with Bran which they took out and threw into the Highway.

Being thus disappointed and Supposing the Meal & Flower to have been left in the Miln at Dewsbury, they attempted to break into the farm. But the doors thereof being well Secured & Barrocaded on the Inside, they were then prevented in that design.

And that night about 400 of the Rioters as was Supposed rested in a Wood near Dewsbury, and on Sunday (being the Day following) they pulld down Dewsbury Miln, and what Corn they co'd not Carry away they threw into the River.

From thence they went to another Miln in Thornhill Parish where they likewise broke open the Doors, pull'd down the Bolting Milln, cutt the Sacks of Corn, carryed part of it away, and pull'd the Slate off of the Miller's House, out of which they took the Corn and cut the Sacks.

From thence they return'd to Dewsbury where they broke into another Miln and attempted to destroy it in the same manner; But the High Sherriffe having notice of the Tumult, apply'd to S.^{ir} Jn.^{e} Kaye being the next Justice of Peace and they two went with their Servants to Dewsbury where they met a great Number of Persons said to amount to the Number of 400, or upwards upon being asked the Occasion of their meeting they told the High Sherriffe and Sir John that it was to prevent Corn being carried out of the Country, which they pretended occasioned a great Scarcety amongst them; upon this the High Sherriffe & Sir John endeavoured to persuade them to disperse, telling them the dangerouse Consequences of Continuing together in so Riotous a Manner; and upon their refusal the High Sherriffe read the Proclamation during which Time Stones and other things were thrown at the High Sherriffe & Sir John but in about an hour's time after the Proclamation was read they dispers'd and being told by Sir John that if they had any just grounds of Complaint, if some few of them wo'd repair to his House the next Morning he wo'd send to some Neighbouring Justices of the Peace to meet there to hear them.

That on Monday Morning about nine o'clock Several of these Persons and others to the Number of near 1000, who began to assemble that Morning by five o'clock by beat of Drum came to Sir John Kaye's House and after some short Stay there went from thence with Uzza's & Beat of Drum to a

Milln in the Parish of High Hogland, which they broke into, wound the Miller & took away a great Quantity of Meal & Flower.

That some Short time after the Mobb was gone from Sir John Kaye's House the High Sherriffe and one Mr. Burton a Neighbouring Justice of Peace came thither, where they agreed to Send an Express to the Commanding Officer of General Barrill's Regiment Quartered at York, to desire he wo'd send over, such a detachment as he thought might be proper for suppressing such a Riot, which Express coming to him about one o'clock on Tuesday Morning, he Immediately Ordered about, 100, Men with proper Officers to March hither, who arrived here about four o'Clock in the afternoon of the same Day.

After the Rioters had left the last mentioned Miln, they proceeded in the same Riotous manner to a Miln in Sandal Parish, where they did no Damage but broke into a Gentleman's House and took out a Bolting Miln and broke it in Pieces.

And from thence they proceeded to the House of one Joseph Pollard at Criggleston, and broke into his Barn, where he had lodged his Flower of which they took and destroy'd to the Value of Ten pounds, whereupon the said Joseph Pollard to save the rest, gave them notice that if they did not desist he intended to fire upon them which upon their refusing he did Several times with Hail Shott; & wounded some of them five of which he took, who were Secured in the Town by a Neighbouring Justice of Peace all night & Conducted to Wakefield the next Morning.

Before they left Pollard's House they threatened to return that night and destroy, him, his House and Family, and Continued their menace all that Day.

On Tuesday Morning in the Town of Wakefield, a great Number of People Attended the Door of the House where the Prisoners were lodged, appearing to have a designe, to rescue them; Upon which the Proclamation was read.

About two o'Clock in the afternoon of the same Day Several Hundreds with beat of Drum entred the West end of the Town, and being asked by Mr. Burton the Reasons of their coming,

U

one of them told him he was come to release his Prisoners, upon which Mr. Burton Seized him and three more, whereupon the rest dispersed Seven others were taken and Secured with those before mentioned are now Confined in the House of Correction. ... We are now taking their Examination and Intend to Committ them to the Castle at York.

We think it Necessary for the Preservation of the Peace, that the Troops we now have, sho'd be continued here for some time and humbly desire they may have Orders accordingly.

(b) Rioters were often heavily punished.

Source: Letter from Darby, the ironfounder, to Earl Gower, 23 Aug. 1757, printed in A. Raistrick, *Dynasty of Ironfounders* (1953), p. 79.

The Riots that we have unfortunately had in this County [Shropshire] under pretence of the High price of Corn, made it prudent and necessary for Government to proceed with severity against the Ringleaders, promoters of those disorders for the sake of Example and to prevent the like Tumults for the future; with this view several of the Rioters were prosecuted last year two of whom out of the number of 10 were capitally convicted, & have been hanged. The other 8 were reprieved till the last assizes, when they were ordered to be transported for 14 years. In the number to be transported are included Rd Corbett, Wm. Cadman, John Cock, & Saml. Barker who till they were drawn into the said Riots at the Instance and threatenings of others, & perhaps with a view to procure sustenance for their starving families, always behaved as honest Industrious and most laborious Workmen; and as such deserve pity and compassion, and the rather as they are truely sensible of the high offence they have comitted and hope his Majesty will extend his Mercy to them for the sake of their distressed Familys.

The characters of these four Men till this unfortunate affair happened, makes me feel greatly for their distress, and solicitous to obtain their pardon, and for that purpose I have presumed to trouble thee with the state of their case, earnestly entreating thee to apply to our king for their pardon.

Examples have been made by hanging two of the said

Rioters, and if the King shall be graciously pleased to shew Mercy to the 4 I have mentioned, I am persuaded it will have a good effect upon the minds of the people of this County in general, and be considered as a shining instance of that Humanity Mercy and Compassion which the King always wishes to shew to the moans of his distressed subjects.

(d) There were particularly fierce food riots in London in 1800. Birmingham, Nottingham, Coventry, Norwich, Sheffield and Oxford were other centres of disturbance. By then new radicalism overlapped with more traditional expressions of discontent. Placards appeared in the streets on Saturday and Sunday, September 13th and 14th urging people to take direct action. The price of corn did fall, but the riots continued.

Source: Placard quoted in J. Ashton, *The Dawn of the Nineteenth Century in England* (1906), p. 19.

Bread will be sixpence the Quartern if the People will assemble at the Corn Market on Monday. FELLOW COUNTRYMEN, how long will ye quietly and cowardly suffer yourselves to be imposed upon, and half starved by a set of mercenary slaves and Government hirelings? Can you still suffer them to proceed in their extensive monopolies, while your children are crying for bread? No! let them exist not a day longer. We are the sovereignty; rise then from your lethargy. Be at the Corn Market on Monday.

6. BANQUETS AND FEASTS

Food riots provide ample evidence of eighteenth-century hunger. The great banquets of the century, private or public, offer another remarkable eighteenth-century contrast.

(a) *Source:* Letter from Lord Hervey to the Prince of Wales, July 1731, printed in the Earl of Ilchester (ed.), *Lord Hervey and His Friends* (1950), p. 73.

Our company at Houghton [Sir Robert Walpole's house] swelled at last into so numerous a body that we used to sit down to dinner, a little snug party of thirty odd, up to the chin in beef, venison, geese, turkeys, etc.; and generally over the chin in claret, strong beer and punch. We had Lords spiritual and temporal, besides commoners, parsons and freeholders innumerable.

(b) Walpole's outlay on food was over £1,000 per annum, and he put in orders for 100 pounds of chocolate costing £17 at one time.

Squib writers satirized the dishes served at his table: for a critique of French cooking, see above, p. 287.

Source: A passage from *The Norfolk Congress*, printed in J. H. Plumb, 'Sir Robert Walpole's Food' in *Men and Places* (1963), p. 157.

There was one dish that shocked many of the spectators which was an English collar of brawn, stuck with French lilies, instead of rosemary. At this many were offended, and said the times were hugely changed with our Land-lord and his taste, and way of living strangely altered: For they remembered when he had like to have overturned the whole table, upon seeing some French kickshaws upon it, which he said was poison to an English constitution. But now forsooth nothing but French sauces will go down.

(c) A ten-year old boy attended a children's ball in 1733 at Devonshire House.

Source: A. H. Tipping, 'Wentworth Castle' in *Country Life*, 25 Oct. 1924.

We had a very handsome supper, viz. at the upper end cold chickens, next to that a dish of cake, parch'd almonds, sapp biskets, next to that tarts and cheesecakes, next to that a great custard and next to that another dish of biskets, darch'd almonds and preserved apricocks, and next a quarter of lamb.

(d) On 10 June 1784 Parson James Woodforde ate a 'very genteel dinner'.

Source: *The Diary of a Country Parson. By James Woodforde* (ed. J. Beresford) World's Classics, p. 227.

We had a very genteel Dinner, Soals and Lobster Sauce, Spring Chicken boiled and a Tongue, a piece of Rost Beef, Soup, a Fillet of Veal rosted with Morells and Truffles, and

Pigeon Pye for the first course—Sweetbreads, a green Goose and Pease, Apricot Pye, Cheesecakes, Stewed Mushrooms and Trifle.

7. COOKS AND RECIPES

Many cookery books were published during the century, many of them dealing with 'traditional' recipes, using fresh water fish and game, others showing French influence. One of the most famous, often reprinted, was Elizabeth Raffald's *The Experienced English Housekeeper, For the Use and Ease of Ladies, Housekeepers, Cooks, etc.* (1769).

(a) *Source:* 'How to Stew Carps' from *Mrs Elizabeth Slany's Book of Receipts* (1715).

Take your carps and kill them under the gills or tails with a penknife and as they bleed you must keep the blood stirring with a little white wine that it clots not together. Then take your carps and scour them with some salt. Then open them and scour them well and put them in your stew-pan or dish and cover them with claret and put in a bunch of sweet herbs, 2 or 3 whole onions and some salt, whole pepper and some large mace and half a nutmeg sliced. Cover them close and let them stew; and when they are about half stewed turn them and then put in the blood, stir it in the liquor they were stewed in and put in a basin and set it over a chafing-dish of coals with 6 yolks of eggs well beaten and a shallot or two and 2 or 3 anchovies. Let them be dissolved in your sauce; then set it over the fire with the eggs stirring it all the while for fear lest it should curdle them; pour it to your carps and send it in.

(b) *Source:* 'How to make a Rich, Great Cake', from *The Lady's Companion. . . . Containing Upwards of Three Thousand Receipts in Every Kind of Cookery* (6th edn., 1753), vol. II, p. 214.

Take a peck of Flour well dried, an Ounce of Cloves and Mace, Half an Ounce of Nutmegs, as much Cinnamon; beat the Spice well, and mix them with your Flour, and a Pound and Half of Sugar, a little Salt, and thirteen Pounds of Currants, well washed, picked, and dried, three Pounds of Raisins of the

Sun stoned, and cut into small Pieces; mix all these well together; then make five Pints of Cream almost scalding hot, and put into it four Pounds of fresh Butter; then beat the Yolks of twenty Eggs, three Pints of good Ale-yeast, a Pint of Sack, a Quarter of a Pint of Orange-flower-water, three Grains of Musk, and six Grains of Ambergrease; mix these together, and stir them into your Cream and Butter, and mingle all in the Cake: Set it an Hour before the Fire to rise, before you put it into your Hoop. Mix your Sweetmeats in it, two Pounds of Citron, and one Pound of candied Orange and Lemon-peel, cut in small Pieces. You must bake it in a deep Hoop; butter the Sides, and put two Papers at the Bottom, and flour it; then put in your Cake. It must have a quick Oven, four Hours will bake it; when it is drawn, ice it over the Top and Sides: Take two Pounds of double-refined Sugar, beat and sifted, and the Whites of six Eggs beaten to a Froth, with three or four Spoonfuls of Orange-flower-water, and three Ounces of Musk and Ambergrease together; put all these into a Stone Mortar, and beat them with a wooden Pestle till it is as white as Snow, and with a Brush, or Bunch of Feathers, spread it all over the Cake, and put it in the Oven to dry, but take Care the Oven does not discolour it; when it is cold, paper it, and it will keep five or six Weeks.

8. BILLS OF FARE

Some of the best English food was to be enjoyed in the country. Already, eating out in London was less satisfactory than eating in a club.

(a) *Source:* M. Misson, *Memoirs and Observations* (1719), p. 146.

It is very certain, that an *Englishman*, who has twelve or fifteen hundred Pound Sterling a Year, does not make such a Rout with it, as a *Frenchman* that has but the tenth Part of it. One Word more about the Cooks Shops, to give a full Idea of the Thing. Generally four Spits, one over another, carry round each five or six Pieces of Butcher's Meat, Beef, Mutton, Veal, Pork, and Lamb; you have what Quantity you please cut off, fat, lean, much or little done; with this, a little Salt and Mustard upon the Side of a Plate, a Bottle of Beer, and a Roll; and there is your whole Feast. Those who would dine at one or two Guineas *per* Head, are handsomely accommodated at our famous *Pontac's*; rarely and with difficulty elsewhere.

(b) *Source:* Letter from H. Purefoy to D. Baxter, the landlord of the Lord Cobham Arms in Buckingham, 4 Nov. 1750, printed in *The Purefoy Letters*, vol. I, p. 417.

Mᴿ Baxter,

I propose to dine at your house too morrow & desire you will get a couple of ffowlls killed too night & boyled with bacon, & a small shoulder of mutton roasted, to be on yᵉ Table at one o'clock. Pray be at home yourself because of paying you the 10s., & let us have yᵉ Ground room on the left hand as wee come into your house, wᶜʰ will oblidge

Your freind to serve you

H. P.

(c) *Source:* C. P. Moritz, *A Journey to England* (1782).

[They eat] a piece of half-boiled or half-roasted meat; and a few cabbage-leaves boiled in plain water; on which they pour a sauce made of flour and butter, the usual method of dressing vegetables in England.

9. INSTITUTIONAL EATING

Because of easily available surviving sources, there is plentiful evidence about eating in prisons, hospitals, schools, barracks and workhouses. The following extracts are drawn from this kind of literature, which also illuminates eighteenth-century theories of nutrition.

(a) *Source:* R. H. Nichols and F. A. Wray, *The History of the Foundling Hospital* (1935), which gives the diet sheet for children in November 1747. Vegetables were not added to the diet until 1762. (*See* upper table on p. 304.)

(b) *Source:* Sir F. M. Eden, *The State of the Poor* (1797), vol. III, p. 849, gives the diet of the inmates of Leeds Workhouse. (*See* lower table on p. 304.)

	Breakfast	Dinner	Supper
Sunday	Broth	Roast Pork or Beef	Bread
Monday	Gruell	Potatoes	Milk and Bread
Tuesday	Milk Porridge	Boiled Mutton or Beef	Bread
Wednesday	Broth	Rice Pudding or Rice-milk	Bread and Cheese
Thursday	Gruell	Boiled Pork or Mutton	Bread
Friday	Milk Porridge	Dumplins or Sewett Puddings	Milk and Bread
Saturday	Gruell	Hasty Puddings	Bread and Cheese

	Breakfast	Dinner	Supper
Sunday	Milk-pottage and bread	Mutton, potatoes, bread, broth, beer	Bread and broth
Monday	ditto	Rice-milk, bread, beer	Milk-pottage and bread
Tuesday	ditto	Flour dumplings, beer	ditto
Wednesday	ditto	Bread, cheese, beer	ditto
Thursday	ditto	Potatoes, bread, broth, beer	Bread and broth, or beer only
Friday	ditto	Rice-milk, bread, beer	Milk-pottage and bread
Saturday	ditto	Drink-pottage, bread	ditto

(c) *Source:* J. Howard, *The State of the Prisons in England and Wales* (1777).

I have before said, that I am no advocate for luxury in prisons; for I would have no meat diet for criminals in houses of correction, or at most, only on Sundays. Yet I would plead that they should have, at least, a pound and a half of good household bread a day, and a quart of good beer; besides twice a day a quart of warm soup made from pease, rice, milk or barley. For a change they might sometimes have turnips, carrots, or potatoes. It may be said this diet will starve those who work in houses of correction; but I am persuaded of the contrary, by what I have seen abroad, in the galleys, in the houses of correction, and among the most robust labourers.

10. TEA

Coffee and chocolate were very popular drinks in the early eighteenth century, but the tea-drinking habit spread rapidly from the aristocracy to the middle classes and finally to working people. Many moral defects were attributed directly to it, and few accounts of diet were complete without references to it. By the end of the century (leaving smuggling on one side) over 20 million pounds of tea were being imported, about 2 pounds per head of population.

(a) *Source:* J. Hanway, *Journal* (1757), vol II, p. 220.

The use of tea descended to the *Plebaean* order, among us, about the beginning of this century; but it was not before the year 1715, that we began to buy large quantities of *green tea* of the *Chinese*, having been till then contented with *bohea*.

In 1720, the consumption was so much augmented, that the *French*, who had hitherto brought home only raw-silk, porcelain, and silken manufactures from *China*, began to import considerable quantities of tea into *France;* and by establishing the trade of running it into this island, have found their *profit* in *our folly* ever since.

From 1717 to 1726, we imported annually about 700,000 pounds. The quantities run in upon us, however, must have been prodigious, for it was calculated in 1728, that 5,000,000 pounds were imported into Europe, of which we were much the greatest consumers. . . . Where will this Evil stop?

(b) *Source: Ibid.*, pp. 35–6.

Madam,

Though habit reconciles *us* to the use of *tea*, as it does the *Turks* to *opium*, may we not with great propriety ask the following questions?

Is it not disturbing the operations of nature, to *drink* when neither thirst nor heat provokes?

Do we not often *sip tea* when we have already drank too great a quantity of water, or other diluting liquors?

Would not *cold* liquids sometimes relieve nature better than *hot?*

Is it not the polite question, 'have you drank your tea,' and supposed that *every body* drinks tea *every* evening, and *every* morning?

Are not physicians generally agreed, that we have many choice and medicinal herbs of our own growth, better than tea?

Are they not also agreed, that tho' tea is proper for some persons, under particular circumstances, that it is in general hurtful to the constitution in the manner we use it? . . .

Will the *sons* and *daughters* of this happy isle, this reputed abode of *sense* and *liberty*, for *ever* submit to the bondage of so *tyrannical* a custom as drinking tea?

Must the *young* and *old*, and *middle aged*, the *sickly* and the *strong*, the *poor* and *rich*, in *warm* weather and *cold*, in *moist* and *dry*, with one common consent, employ so many precious hours, in *so low* a gratification as *drinking tea?*

Arc we to be bread up from *generation* to *generation* to this vast expence?

Is not this a *want* which nature does not make, and are not many *unhappy*, if it is not *regularly* supplied? etc. etc.

(c) *Source:* T. Alcock, *Observations on the Defects of the Poor Laws* (1752), pp. 45ff.

Several poor persons, who received Charity have their Tea once, if not twice a Day. . . . To run daily into such idle Extravagances, is certainly a very ridiculous Piece of Management: For the Expence of the whole Apparatus of Tea, Sugar, Cream, Bread and Butter, etc. must now be treble to that of Milk or Broth, or any other common wholesome Breakfast.

11. GIN

Whatever the merits of tea, the merits of gin were still more dubious. 'Drunk for 1d., dead drunk for 2d, straw for nothing' is a phrase that has passed into popular history. There was heavy gin drinking, particularly in London, and in 1725 it was reckoned that in one parish gin was sold retail in every fifth house. An act of 1736 aimed at prohibition, but it was so unpopular that it was repealed in 1743 and a milder act substituted for it. Gin drinking was at its height in the 1740s (see Hogarth's *Gin Lane,* part of a successful campaign against it), but new legislation from 1751 onwards curbed excesses. Gin consumption fell in the last years of the century, although there was a sharp upward move in 1785. There was heavy consumption of alcoholic drinks, however, and this was a factor, as Fielding saw, in the background of London crime. (See below, p. 373.)

(a) *Source:* An anonymous pamphlet of 1736, *Distilled Liquors the Bane of the Nation* in the Place Papers, British Museum, Add. MSS. 27,825, p. 178.

Every one who now passes through the streets of this great Metropolis and looks into the distillers' shops . . . must see, even in shops of a creditable and wholesome appearance, a crowd of poor ragged people, cursing and quarrelling with one another over repeated glasses of these destructive liquors. . . . In one place not far from East Smithfield . . . a trader has a large empty room backwards where, as his wretched guests get intoxicated, they are laid together in heaps, promiscuously, men, women, and children, till they recover their senses, when they proceed to drink on, or, having spent all they had, go out to find wherewithal to return to the same dreadful pursuit.

(b) *Source:* H. Fielding, *An Inquiry into the Causes of the Late Increase of Robbers* (1751).

Wretches are often brought before me, charged with theft and robbery, whom I am forced to confine before they are in a condition to be examined; and when they have afterwards become sober, I have plainly perceived from the state of the case, that the *Gin* alone was the cause of the transgression, and have been sometimes sorry that I was obliged to commit them to prison. . . . Gin is the principal sustenance (if it may be so called) of more than an hundred thousand people in this metropolis. Many of these wretches there are, who swallow pints of this poison within the twenty four hours; the dreadful effects of which I have the misfortune every day to see, and to smell too.

(c) The Act of 1751 increased duties on gin and forbade its sale in chandlers' shops.

Source: Extracts from the Preamble of the 1751 'Act for granting a duty to his Majesty to be paid by distillers upon licences to be taken out by them for retailing spirituous liquors'.

WHEREAS the immoderate drinking of distilled spirituous liquors by persons of the meanest and lowest sort, hath of late years increased, to the great detriment of the health and morals of the common people; and the same hath in great measure been owing to the number of persons who have obtained licences to retail the same, under pretence of being distillers, and of those who have presumed to retail the same without licence, most especially in the cities of *London* and *Westminster*, the borough of *Southwark*, and other places within the weekly bills or mortality, contrary to the good and wholesome laws heretofore made for preventing thereof: and whereas we your Majesty's dutiful and loyal subjects the commons of *Great Britain* in parliament assembled, ever attentive to the preservation and health of your Majesty's subjects, have taken this great evil into our serious consideration, and proposed such laws and provisions as appear to us to be more likely to put a stop to the same. . . .

(d) In the 1780s there was a general tightening up of licensing regulations, particularly in the manufacturing districts. The new policy was related to Evangelical views on morality (see above, p. 276) and to recognition of the need to maintain factory discipline (see above, pp. 50ff.).

Source: Note in the *Leeds Intelligencer,* 26 June 1787.

At the Brewster Sessions held at Sheffield yesterday s'en night, before the Justices of Peace for this Riding, a total suppression was ordered of the numerous dram-shops in that town, by withholding from them ale licences, which, according to the Act in that respect made, restrains them from selling less than two gallons of any kind of spirituous liquors.

(e) Despite the increase in population, the total number of publicans' spirit licences fell between 1779 and 1790.

Source: Appendix 32a of the *First Report of the Commissioners of Inland Revenue* (1857), the table from which is printed in S. and B. Webb, *The History of Liquor Licensing in England* (1903), p. 87.

1779	37,172
1781	36,033
1783	34,329
1785	35,697
1787	36,675
1789	33,349
1790	32,850.

12. ALE AND WINE

Ale had always been a staple drink, and the sale of ale and beer had been under control, like the sale of bread, from the middle ages. In the eighteenth century beer was a patriotic drink, and Hogarth's Beer Street idealized beer while his Gin Lane was a study in degradation. Moreover, malt produced in England had obvious patriotic advantages over grapes produced in France. The favourite form of beer in the eighteenth century was porter, and a large-scale brewing industry began to emerge, with a few large firms dominating the market.

(a) *Source:* H. Jackson, *An Essay on Bread* (1758).

Beer, commonly called Porter, is almost become the universal Cordial of the Populace, especially since the necessary Period of prohibiting the Corn-Distillery; the Suppression presently advanc'd the Price of that common Poison Gin, to near three times its former Price, and the Consumption of Beer has kept pace with such advance.

(b) There were complaints about the quality of beer and experiments to improve it.

Source: Letter from T. Greenall (of St. Helens) to J. Hill, 1787, printed in T. C. Barker and J. R. Harris, *A Merseyside Town in the Industrial Revolution* (1954), p. 100.

We have took the liberty of sending you 2 half Barrels of a second sort of Beer (it is sold at Bolton at 6d. pr. Qt.) we have charg'd it you only 44/- per Barrel and wish you to make trial of it, it is good Beer but *rathere* [*sic*] slenderer than our Strong Beer, however if it will not sell by itself, it will mix very well with the strong Beer; and make your profit more advantageous —Shou'd it (the second sort of beer) meet your approbation we should be glad to send you a Load, as it would in some measure save your strong Beer; and we are rathere scarce of that *Article*, at this *Season* of the year than any other.

(c) In the 1780s the attempt to control gin drinking was accompanied by an attempt to control beer drinking also.

Source: Report in the *Chelmsford Chronicle*, 10 Aug. 1787.

At a Vestry held at the parish church of Wanstead . . . it was resolved that the . . . parish officers and police officers be required to pay particular attention to the conduct of the several keepers of public-houses within this parish, and that they make their report to the Vestry concerning them; whether they keep good order; whether they suffer gambling or tippling at unseasonable hours . . . and especially whether they keep their houses open for the entertainment of their guests in the time of Divine Service on the Lord's Day . . . [It was also resolved that] the constables be required to visit the public-houses within this parish at ten o'clock every night, and see that the publican dismiss his guests and shut up his house at that hour; and that they take into their custody all such persons as shall refuse quietly to depart when called upon by the constables and publicans to do so.

(d) *Source:* Report in *The Times*, 4 Oct. 1797.

In the City of London, and within the Bills of Mortality, there are at present 5,204 licensed Public Houses, and it is calculated that [the] consumption of Ale, and Porter, annually, in the metropolis, and its environs, is stated to be 1,132,147 barrels, equal to 36,625,145 gallons, making 158,400,580 pots at 3½d. £2,311,466 15 10

(e) Wine drinking was a middle-class as well as an aristocratic habit. At the beginning of the century French wines, including claret and champagne, were in demand, but as the century went by the consumption of port—along with sherry and madeira—greatly increased. Brandy also was a favourite drink, even though it came from France: rum from the West Indies was another late eighteenth-century drink. The following extract is a wine account for one year, 1735–36, from the Mildmay Archives.

Source: Lord Fitzwalter's Wine Account, printed in Edwards (ed.), *English History from Essex Sources*, vol. I, pp. 158–9.

			£	s.	d.
Jan.	11	For one hogshead of white port sent in Feb. 16 1733, £19; April 12 to one hogshead of red port sent to Moulsham Hall, £20: to one hogshead of white port at the same time to Moulsham, £14; to one hogshead of white port, Sept. 20, sent also to Moulsham, £15; and in full of all accounts to this day	65.	0.	0
Jan.	15	Came in one hogshead of white port wine bottled off at Mr. Vanderstegen's, which run 21 dozen 2 bottles, for which I am to pay him. Bottled off a hogshead of claret this Jan., which run 20 dozen and three bottles, and began to drink it Jan. 17. N.B. This hogshead of claret lasted to May 17.			
Feb.	13	Mr. Lyon his bill in full for claret I had of him by dozens last summer, and in full of all accounts	27.	17.	5
June	7	Bottled off by Turner my butler, one hogshead of claret imported from Boulogne. . . .			
June	17	Pd. Alexander Gordon . . . for a hogshead of claret, £21 . . . and in full of all accounts	22.	10.	0

Aug. 22   Bottled off a hogshead of white Lisbon
had of Mr. Vanderstegen, which run 19
dozen; but there was three dozen and ½
drunk from the hogshead, so that it
contained in the whole 22 dozen, ½.

Nov. 20   To Capt. Gilbey for a hogshead of claret,
Monsr. Pigualt, £15. 0. 6, and for duty
on landing, £13. 6. 6, and for freight
and primage, 11s. 0, in all   28.   8. 0

PLATE 17

PLAY

A Theatre Ticket

Sadler's Wells

PLATE 18

MANNERS AND STYLES

Farmer and Man

PLATE 19

MANNERS AND STYLES

A Coffee House

'Selling a Wife'

PLATE 20

MANNERS AND STYLES

The anxious Mother, with a Parents Care,
Presents our Labours to her future Heir,
"The Wise, the Brave, the Temperate, and the Just,
Who love their Neighbour, and in God who trust,
Safe through the Dang'rous paths of Life may Steer,
Nor dread those Evils we exhibit "Here".

Advice for the Young

PLATE 21

FOOD AND DRINK

A Gentleman's Kitchen

PLATE 22

FOOD AND DRINK

An Election Entertainment

PLATE 23

RELIGION

The Sermon

PLATE 24

RELIGION

St Paul's, Sheffield

A Quaker Meeting

PLATE 25

EDUCATION

'Pious Tuition'

PLATE 26

CRIME AND PUNISHMENT

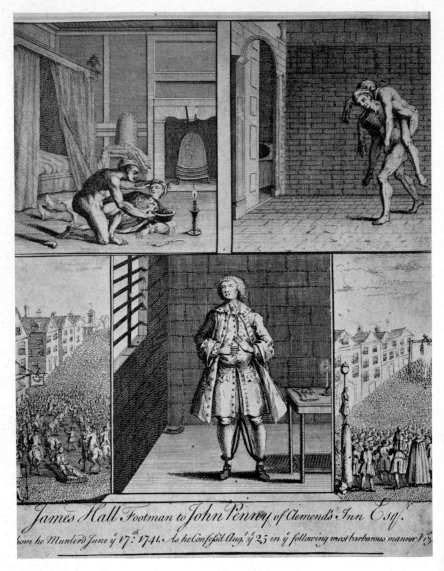

James Hall Footman to John Penny of Clement's Inn Esq.

whom he Murderd June y 17th 1741. As he Confess'd Aug.t y 25 in y following most barbarous manner Viz

The Story of James Hall

PLATE 27

CRIME AND PUNISHMENT

'Free Choice' as seen by Gillray

The Press Gang

PLATE 28

GOING TO WAR

Waterloo

PLATE 29

THE PURSUIT OF THE ARTS AND SCIENCES

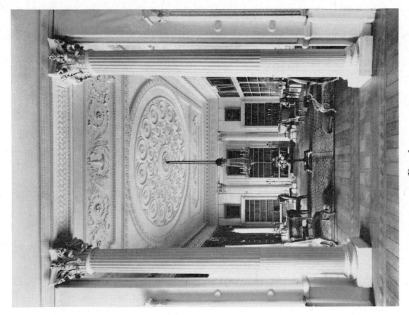

Books

Sculpture

PLATE 30

THE PURSUIT OF THE ARTS AND SCIENCES

The Royal Academy

PLATE 31

THE PURSUIT OF THE ARTS AND SCIENCES

An Experiment

PLATE 32

POLITICS

The House of Commons

Politics in the Street

CHAPTER X

Religion

Though I am a poor person, I will be bold to say I am an honest man, and would not do an ill thing to be made a bishop.
(Abraham Adams in HENRY FIELDING'S
The Adventures of Joseph Andrews, 1742)

ENTHUSIASM, a vain belief of private revelation, a vain confidence of divine favour or communication.
(SAMUEL JOHNSON, *Dictionary*, 1755)

It is monstrous to be told that you have a heart as sinful as the common wretches that crawl on the earth.
(The DUCHESS OF BUCKINGHAM to LADY HUNTINGDON, 1741)

Ungodliness is our universal, our constant, our peculiar character . . . a total ignorance of God is almost universal among us. . . . High and low, cobblers, tinkers, hackney coachmen, men and maid servants, soldiers, tradesmen of all rank, lawyers, physicians, gentlemen, Lords are as ignorant of the Creator of the World as Mohametans or Pagans.
(JOHN WESLEY, *Estimate of Manners at the Present Time*, 1782)

The necessity of going to church in procession with us on the anniversary, raises an honest ambition to get something decent to wear, and the churches on Sundays are now filled with very clean-looking women.
(HANNAH MORE, Letter to WILLIAM WILBERFORCE, 1791)

1. SIR ROGER DE COVERLEY AT CHURCH

Joseph Addison (1672–1715), who had introduced the readers of the *Spectator* to Sir Roger de Coverley, 'a gentleman of Worcestershire, of ancient descent, a baronet' and a batchelor, in March 1711, went on to describe in a later number (24 March) the division of the clergy into 'generals, field officers, and subalterns', the latter 'not to be numbered'. The pattern of rural religion described below persisted for most of the rest of the century.

Source: The *Spectator*, 9 July 1711.

I am always very well pleased with a country Sunday, and think, if keeping holy the seventh day were only a human institution, it would be the best method that could have been thought of for the polishing and civilising of mankind. It is certain the country people would soon degenerate into a kind of savages and barbarians, were there not such frequent returns of a stated time, in which the whole village meet together with their best faces, and in their cleanliest habits, to converse with one another upon indifferent subjects, hear their duties explained to them, and join together in adoration of the Supreme Being. Sunday clears away the rust of the whole week, not only as it refreshes in their minds the notions of religion, but as it puts both the sexes upon appearing in their most agreeable forms, and exerting all such qualities as are apt to give them a figure in the eye of the village. . . .

My friend Sir Roger, being a good Churchman, has beautified the inside of his church with several texts of his own choosing: He has likewise given a handsome pulpit-cloth, and railed in the communion table at his own expense. He has often told me, that at his coming to his estate he found his parishioners very irregular; and that, in order to make them kneel and join in the responses, he gave every one of them a hassock and a common prayer-book; and at the same time employed an itinerant singing-master, who goes about the country for that purpose, to instruct them rightly in the tunes of the psalms. . . .

As Sir Roger is landlord to the whole congregation, he keeps them in very good order, and will suffer nobody to sleep in it besides himself; for, if by chance he has been surprised into a short nap at sermon, upon recovering out of it he stands up and looks about him, and if he sees anybody else nodding, either wakes them himself, or sends his servants to them. . . .

As soon as the sermon is finished, nobody presumes to stir till Sir Roger is gone out of the church. The knight walks down

from his seat in the chancel between a double row of his
tenants, that stand bowing to him on each side; and every
now and then inquires how such as one's wife, or mother, or
son, or father do, whom he does not see at church; which is
understood as a secret reprimand to the person that is absent.

2. BISHOPS

(a) *Source:* Historical Manuscripts Commission, *Egmont MSS.,
Diary of Viscount Percival, 1st Earl of Egmont* (1920), vol I, p. 100.
Percival is noting in his Diary of 1730 his approval of Bishop
Joseph Willcocks of Gloucester. (Note the close link between
religion and politics.)

He resides as much as any bishop in his diocese, at least four
months in the year, and keeps a very generous and hospitable
table; which makes amends for the learning he is deficient in.
However, though no great scholar, nor a deep man, he is a
very frequent preacher, and this, with his zeal for the Government, good humour, and regular life, makes him very well
liked by the Government and all that know him.

(b) *Source:* H. C. Foxcroft, *Supplement to Burnet's History of his own
Time* (1902). Bishop Gilbert Burnet, author of the famous *History
of his own Times* is reminiscing in 1710 about the spiritual side of
his diocesan work.

I resolved to go round my diocese about three weeks or a
month each year, preaching and confirming every day from
church to church. . . . I continued still to go about preaching
and confirming, so that I have preached and confirmed in
275 churches of my diocese, and ten or twelve times in all the
market towns and considerable places. I look upon confir-
mation, if rightly managed, as the most effective means
possible for reviving Christianity, but I could never prevail with
the greater part of my clergy to think of any other way of
preparing their youth to it but to hear them repeat their
catechism; they did not study to make them consider it as the
becoming a Christian by an act of their own. I have now
settled on a method in which I intend to continue as long as

God continues my strength to execute it. I stay a week in a place where every morning I go and preach and confirm in some church within six or seven miles of the place; and then at 5 o'clock after evening prayer I catechise some children and explain the whole catechism to them, so that I go through it all in six days and confirm the next Lord's day; and make presents to the value of about a crown a day to all whom I catechised, and I have them all to dine with me on the Lord's day.

3. PARISH PRIESTS

Among the many diaries of eighteenth-century parish priests, that of James Woodforde, the Somerset priest, is outstanding. There was, of course, great variety in parish size and organization, as there was in the status, stipend and outlook of the priest.

(a) *Source:* J. Beresford (ed.), *The Diary of a Country Parson* (1924–31), entries for May to November 1769.

29 May. I read Prayers this morning at C. Cary, being 29 of May, the Restoration of King Charles II from Popish Tyranny. . . .

21 June. I played with Mr. James Clarke at Battledor and Shuttlecock, and we kept the cock up once upwards of 500 times. . . .

22 Sept. Great rejoicings at Cary today being the Coronation Day. Bells ringing all day . . . a very large bonfire on the top of the hill and very grand fireworks were sent from London and were Sky-Rocketts, Mines, Trees, Crackers, Wheels, and divers Indian fireworks. . . . We did not break up till nearly two in the morning. . . .

23 Sept. Great doings again at Cary in the Park. At one o'clock there was a shift run for by women. There were five that started for it, and won by Willm. Francis's daughter Nan of Ansford—her sister Pegg was second and therefore had ribbands. I never saw the Park so full of people in my life. The women were to run the best of three half mile Heats: Nan Francis run a Heat in three minutes. . . .

1 Oct. I read Prayers, churched a woman and read the Act of Parliament against profane swearing as directed by Law. . . .

18 Oct. After breakfast went with Mr. Creed in his Chair to Wells with a great possy from Cary to attend at the County Meeting to consider of a proper Petition to his Majesty in the present crisis of Affairs.[1] We went to the Swan, where we dined with upwards of a hundred Gentlemen of the first rank in the County. We had a very respectable meeting on this occasion. . . . Britons never will be slaves was played during the dinner. . . .

12 Nov. I read Prayers and preached this morning at C. Cary Church. I was disturbed this morning at Cary Church by the Singers. I sent my Clerk some time back to the Cary Singers, to desire that they would not sing the Responses in the Communion Service, which they complied with for several Sundays, but this morning after the first Commandment they had the Impudence to sing the Response, and therefore I spoke to them out of my desk, to say and not sing the Responses which they did after, and at other places they sang as usual. . . .

13 Nov. We had news this morning of Mr. Wilkes gaining his point against Lord Halifax and 4,000 pound damages given him. Cary and Ansford bells rung most part of the day on the occasion. . . .

(b) Henry Crookes was a vicar of an urban parish, Hunslet, near Leeds.

Source: Extracts from his Manuscript Diary for 1758 in Leeds Reference Library.

Easter Sunday 26. . . . Went to Chapel at 9. Read prayers and expounded the 2nd Lesson and went to Leeds to assist at a Sacrament where were 12 Clergymen. . . . Dined at the Vicar's. Went to Chapel Quarter past 3 Read prayers and preached from John 20 v 9. . . .

[1] The Petition concerned John Wilkes and the freedom of election. See below, pp. 499ff. The year 1769 was important in relation to the development of concerted extra-parliamentary action in the counties.

Monday 27. . . . About 10 rode up to Middleton to buy a Cow and Calf of Joseph Walker but did not. . . .

Friday 31. . . . At 3 went to the Funeral of Mr. Bilton and got Home between 7 and 8. The Vicar read the Office and I stood at the Door, (till the persons invited were got into the Chapel) to keep out the Mob, which was excessive great and very rude. There were an Hearse and two Mourning Coaches, the Recorder's Coach Sir Harry Ibbotson's Coach and a Chaise. The Bearers, the Vicar the Apothecary the Family (for Mr. Bilton died in London March 14) and Self had Scarfs and Hatbands and the other Gentlemen had Scarfs. . . . The Discourse was altogether trifling. After the Funeral 5 of the Reverend Mr. Colby's Daughters (own Nieces to the Deceased) came to our House, (they were there before the Funeral) and went away presently afterwards. After Supper smoked a pipe. A little past 9 called the Family in sung two Hymns, had prayer and to Bed 10 Minutes before 10.

Saturday 8 April. . . . I left Home a little before 6 [in the evening] to go to see Anne Daughter of Benjamin Gomersail. Benjamin keeps a bad House, and am afraid (by the Reports I hear) that his Wife is little better than a common prostitute, training up her Daughter too much like herself. May the Lord have Mercy upon that wicked Family, and may they all have a saving Interest in the Blood of Jesus. The poor young Woman calls out for Mercy, which I pray God She may obtain. . . .

Friday 5 May. . . . After Dinner went to see Hannah Wife of Benjamin Armitage, a poor unhappy Soul, despairs of God's Mercy, and has twice intended to destroy herself, once by a Razor and another by a Rope, and I pray God She may not put that bloody Design into Execution at some Time or other, for She confesses, when the Rope was taken from Her, that another Method of Self murder was impressed upon her Mind, but would not tell me what it was. Went to prayer with Her and came away. . . .

Wednesday 8 November. . . . I spent an agreeable Afternoon with Mr. and Mrs. Armitage (lately Miss Hales of Liverpool) old Mrs. Armitage Mrs. Featherstone and Miss Armitage. Mr. Hales of Liverpool the Father of young Mrs. Armitage had a Son (Neddy Hales) whom He despised for his

Seriousness. Neddy was a preacher among the Methodists, and perhaps one of the most heavenly Youths in this part of the world. His Father could not bear with his uncommon Holiness, and was so exasperated because He could not bring [Him] from preaching among the Methodists that He turned Him (as it were) out of Doors and disowned Him for his Son. But behold what strange Things the providence of God brought about. For, the same Mr. Hales, notwithstanding his Usage of his Son became so surprisingly altered in his Temper (or what You please to call it) that He has given his only Daughter of who He was extravagantly fond, to Mr. James Armitage, as deep in Methodism as his Son was and what is more strange, He gave Orders to Mr. Newton of Liverpool to write to Mr. Armitage to fetch his Daughter away on the same Month and the same Day of the Month this year on which He turned his Son out of Doors last year. We have this Day been to pay a Bride Visit, and an happy Visit it was to my Soul. . . .

Thursday 9. . . . I walked to Francis Weatherheads to see Him. Had some serious Discourse with Him concerning his Soul, which so gravelled Him He could not contain but broke out against me as a preacher of nothing but Hell and Damnation. I bless God my haughty heart did not rise, and I heartily trust it never may. In his Heat Francis upbraided me with the Want of a meek and humble Spirit, which I ingenuously confessed, being too conscious of the pride of my heart, and it pleased God to make my Confession the Means of quelling his Anger. While I was talking with Him the G[l]azier came to mend his Windows and prevented me going to prayer. From Him I went to see Mary Wife of Joseph Crowther with whom and her Daughter Matty I had about ½ an Hours serious Conversation before prayer. Poor Woman, She has been 10 Weeks down of a Fever and a Miscarriage and their Goods are to be sold toMorrow by a hard hearted Landlord. From them I went to see Mr. Hollingworth where I met with Mr. Martin Brown junior and Harry Moore and presently afterwards Mr. Stoney came in. I smoked a pipe with Mr. Brown, and had some Discourse with Him concerning the Folly of Hunting, but to no purpose, for they were all against me. I came away between 6 and 7. . . .

(c) Crookes was not typical of all the clergymen of his time, and in rural parishes there were many laymen whose private opinions of their clergymen were highly critical. In East Sussex, for example, Thomas Turner clearly had a mind of his own.

Source: Entry for 20 Jan. 1757, in the *Diary* of Thomas Turner.

In the even I read a pamphlet, entitled *Primitive Christianity Propounded*, which I imagine was written by a Baptist preacher, in favour of preaching without notes. I must say I can find no harm consequent on our method or reading, as the author is pleased to call it; but I must acknowledge that the idle, lazy way of preaching which many of our clergy are got into, seems rather to prove self-interest to be the motive of the exercising of their profession, than the eternal happiness and salvation of mankind.

4. CHURCH MAINTENANCE

The Church was an economic as well as a religious interest. The clergy farmed their own glebe land and relied on tithes. Church repairs were often a severe burden on the parish.

(c) *Source:* An Account of the Parish of Quatt Malvern in *Shropshire Parish Documents* (1903), p. 270.

The Rectory House consists of about five Bays of Building; ye Barn Stable and Cow House are ten Bays. All ye Land belonging to ye Rectory is ye Church-yard Garden Orchard Fold-yard and Barnyard, which consists of betwixt two and three Acres or thereabout.

All tithes are due to ye Rector in kind . . . and if any Land produces two Crops in one year ye tithes of both are by Special custom due.

The Custom for tithing Hay Clover and Rye-grass is ye Eleventh cock, and ye eleventh Mow of Wheat Mon' corn and Rye, and ye tenth cock of Pease Barley Oats and Vetches, and ye tenth bottle of Hemp and Flax if ye land it grows upon be less than a Statute Acre; and ye time for tithing these aforesaid sorts of Grain Hay &c. is when they are sufficiently fielded and made ready to carry.

The Rector has a tithe Lamb at Seven and allows three pence for each Lamb under ten, but if they be under seven ye owner pays him three pence for each Lamb. . . . If Sheep are wintered in ye Parish there is a penny due for ye herbage of each Sheep and three pence for ye fall of each Lamb. . . .

For a Cock there is due three Eggs, for a Hen two Eggs, for a Pullet one Egg, and ye same for Drakes Ducks Turkeys and all other sorts of fowls.

The Surplus Fees are for a Marriage with a Licence five shillings, for a Marriage by Banns one Shilling and Six pence, and one shilling for publishing; for a Burial Six pence, and for Churching four pence.

For Easter offerings, as Communicants ye custom is for a Man and his wife to pay two pence, and a Single person two pence, which is all paid by ye Master or Mistress of the family, for a Garden is paid a penny, and for Smoke a farthing.

The Clark's wages by Ancient custom is four pence ye Yard-land through out the Parish.

(b) *Source:* Letter from Henry Purefoy to James Perkins, 30 March 1748, in *The Purefoy Letters*, vol. I, pp. 21–2.

Our Church at Shalstone is so much out of Repair & one of the main Beams broke wch is now forced to be propt to prevent its falling on the People, & unlesse there is a new Beam ye Revd Mr Haws can't Repair his Chancell. The Pews of the Church are likewise out of repair & must be repaired soon & the Church floor must be new paved with stone, & likewise the Church windows must be new glazed; there must also be a new Church Bible. I consider ye Tennants have great losses in their Cattle & 't is hard Times with them, so entreat you will let Mr Taylor know that if hee will condescend to give an Oak Tree to repair the Church Pews & three Guineas towards glazing the Church windows, I will give an Oak Tree for a beam for the Church & a Church Bible. Then there will be the Paving of the Church left for the Parish to do which will come to about four pounds besides ye workmanship. . . .

5. METHODISM

Dissatisfaction with the limits of formal religion encouraged the growth of 'vital religion' or 'the religion of the heart'. John Wesley

(1702–1791) spread the new message among the crowds. John Nelson, described below, was a stone mason and a dedicated early convert.

(a) *Source:* J. Wesley's *Journal* (Everyman edn., 1906), pp. 134ff, 176ff.

I set out early in the morning, and *Wednesday 26* [May 1742] in the evening, reached Birstall, six miles beyond Wakefield.

John Nelson had wrote to me some time before, but at that time I had little thought of seeing him. Hearing he was at home, I sent for him to our inn, whence he immediately carried me to his house, and gave me an account of the strange manner wherein he had been led on from the time of our parting at London.

He had full business there and large wages. But from the time of his finding peace with God it was continually upon his mind that he must return (though he knew not why) to his native place. He did so about Christmas in the year 1740. His relations and acquaintances soon began to inquire, 'What he thought of this new faith?' And whether he believed there was any such thing as a man's knowing that his sins were forgiven? John told them point blank, that 'this new faith, as they called it, was the old faith of the Gospel; and that he himself was as sure his sins were forgiven as he could be of the shining of the sun.' This was soon noised abroad. More and more came to inquire concerning these strange things. Some put him upon the proof of the great truths which such inquiries naturally led him to mention. And thus he was brought unawares to quote, explain, compare and enforce several parts of the Scripture. This he did, at first, sitting in his house, till the company increased so that the house could not contain them. Then he stood at the door, which he was commonly obliged to do in the evening as soon as he came from work. God immediately set his seal to what was spoken; and several believed and therefore declared that God was merciful also to their unrighteousness and had forgiven all their sins. . . .

I preached at noon, on the top of Birstall Hill, to several hundreds of plain people, and spent the afternoon in talking severally with those who had tasted of the grace of God. At eight I preached on the side of Dewsbury Moor. . . .

Thursday 12 [August 1745].—I came to Leeds, preached at five, and at eight met the Society; after which the mob pelted us with dirt and stones great part of the way home. The congregation was much larger the next evening, and so was the mob at our return, and likewise in higher spirits, being ready to knock out all our brains for joy that the Duke of Tuscany was Emperor. What a melancholy consideration is this? That the bulk of the English nation will not suffer God to give them the blessings he would, because they would turn them into curses.

Wednesday, 18.—About five we came to Newcastle, in an acceptable time. We found the generality of the inhabitants in the utmost consternation, news being just arrived that, the morning before, the Pretender had entered Edinburgh. A great concourse of people were with us in the evening, to whom I expounded the third Chapter of Jonah, insisting particularly on that verse, 'Who can tell if God will return, and repent, and turn away from his fierce anger, that we perish not?'

Thursday, 19.—The Mayor summoned all the householders of the town to meet him at the Town Hall, and desired as many of them as were willing to set their hands to a paper, importing that they would, at the hazard of their goods and lives, defend the town against the common enemy. Fear and darkness were now on every side, but not on those who had seen the light of God's countenance. We rejoiced together in the evening with solemn joy, while God applied these words to many hearts: 'Fear not, ye; for I know that ye seek Jesus which was crucified.'

Friday, 20.—The Mayor ordered the townsmen to be under arms and to mount guard in their turns, over and above the guard of the soldiers, a few companies of whom had been drawn into the town on the first alarm. Now, also, Pilgrim Street Gate was ordered to be walled up. Many began to be much concerned for us, because our house stood without the walls. Nay, but the Lord is a wall of fire unto all that trust in Him.

Saturday, 21.—[There] came the news of General Cope's defeat [at Prestonpans]. Orders were now given for the doubling of the guard and for walling up Pandon and Sally-Port Gates.

Sunday, 22.—The walls were mounted with cannon and all things prepared for sustaining an assault. Meantime our poor neighbours on either hand were busy in removing their goods, . . . and more and more of the gentry every hour rode southward as fast as they could.

All this week the alarms from the North continued, and the storm seemed nearer every day. Many wondered we would stay without the walls. Others told us we must remove quickly, for if the cannon began to play from the top of the gates, they would beat all the houses about our ears. This made me look how the cannons on the gates were planted, and I could not but adore the providence of God, for it was obvious, 1. They were all planted in such a manner that no shot could touch our house. 2. The cannon on Newgate so secured us on one side, and those upon Pilgrim Street Gate on the other, that none could come near our house without being torn in pieces.

On *Friday and Saturday (27 & 28)* many messengers of lies terrified the poor people of the town, as if the rebels were just coming to swallow them up. Upon this the guards were increased and abundance of country gentlemen came in with their servants, horses and arms.

Sunday, 29.—Advice came that they were in full march southward, so that it was supposed they would reach Newcastle by Monday evening. At eight I called on a multitude of sinners in Gateshead to seek the Lord while he might be found.

On *Monday and Tuesday* I visited some of the Societies in the country, and on *Wednesday, October 2*, returned to Newcastle, where they were just informed that the rebels had left Edinburgh on Monday, and were swiftly marching toward them. But it appeared soon that this also was a false alarm. . . .

On *Thursday and Friday* I visited the rest of the country Societies. On *Saturday [5]* a party of the rebels (about a thousand men) came within seventeen miles of Newcastle. This occasioned a fresh alarm in the town, and orders were given by the General that the soldiers should march against them on Monday morning. But these orders were countermanded.

Wednesday, 9.—It being supposed that the danger was over for the present, I preached at four in Gateshead, and then taking horse with Mr. Shepherd, in the evening reached Sandhutton.

Thursday, 10.— . . . We lay at Doncaster, nothing pleased with the drunken, cursing, swearing soldiers who surrounded us on every side. Can these wretches succeed in anything they undertake? I fear not, if there be a God that judgeth the earth.

(b) The next two extracts bring out the vigour and drive of Methodist laymen. Thomas Lee was converted to 'vital Christianity' by Rev. William Grimshaw, Vicar of Haworth, near Keighley, a great Anglican friend of the Methodists. Lee was a textile worker, but in 1751 or 1752 gave up his trade, bought a horse and became a full-time itinerant preacher.

Source: 'The Autobiography of Thomas Lee' in *The Lives of Early Methodist Preachers* (1837), vol. IV, pp. 157–9.

After I had preached some time at Greenough Hill [in Yorkshire], I was invited to Pateley Bridge. Here I was called to an exercise of my faith which I had not hitherto known. The first time I was there, Mr. . . . had prepared and encouraged a numerous mob, who spared neither mud nor stones, with many strokes besides, so that they themselves owned, 'We have done enough to make an end of him.' I did indeed reel to and fro, and my head was broken with a stone. But I never found my soul more happy, nor was ever more composed in my closet. It was a glorious time; and there are several who date their conversion from that day. After I was a little cleaned, I went to a neighbouring town, where, when my head was dressed, I preached abroad to abundance of people, many of whom had followed me from Pateley Bridge. Some of the mob also followed, but as the wretched minister was not present to head them, and as they were greatly outnumbered, they behaved peaceably, and the Lord blessed us much. . . .

6. PREACHING TO THE POOR

One of Wesley's contemporaries, George Whitefield (1714–1770) was also a highly successful preacher, appealing to the same kind of people and drawn into similar controversies. As a Calvinist, however, he disagreed with Wesley on doctrine.

(a) *Source:* Entry for 30 March 1739 in *George Whitefield's Journal* (1960 edn.), p. 241.

Preached this afternoon near Coal-Pit Heath, seven miles from Bristol, a place to which I was earnestly invited, and where great numbers of colliers live. I believe there were above two thousand people assembled on this occasion. The weather was exceedingly fair, the hearers behaved very well, and the place where I preached being near the maypole, I took occasion to warn them of misspending their time in revelling and dancing. Oh, that all such entertainments were put a stop to. I see no other way to effect it, but by going boldly, and calling people from such lying vanities in the Name of Jesus Christ. That reformation which is brought about by a coercive power, will be only outward and superficial; but that which is done by the force of God's Word, will be inward and lasting. Lord, make me meet by Thy grace for such a work, and then send me.

(b) Sunday Schools spread after the 1760s, Robert Raikes usually being regarded, mistakenly, as their pioneer. Methodists were prominent in the movement, which also brought in Anglicans and Nonconformists.

Source: S. Bamford, *Passages in the Life of a Radical* (1893 edn.), vol. I, pp. 100–1.

Every Sunday morning at half-past eight o'clock was this old Methodist school open for the instruction of whatever child crossed its threshold. A hymn was first led out and sung by the scholars and teachers. An extempore prayer followed, all the scholars and teachers kneeling at their places; the classes, ranging from those of the spelling-book to those of the Bible, then commenced their lessons, girls in the gallery above, and boys below. Desks which could either be moved up or down, like the leaf of a table, were arranged all round the school, against the walls of the gallery, as well as against those below, and at measured distances the walls were numbered. Whilst the Bible and Testament classes were reading their first lesson the desks were got ready, inkstands and copy-books numbered, containing copies and pens, were placed opposite corresponding numbers on the wall; and when the lesson was concluded the writers took their places, each at his own number, and so continued their instruction. When the copy was finished, the book was shut and left on the desk, a lesson of spelling was gone through, and at twelve o'clock singing and prayer again took place, and the scholars were dismissed. At one o'clock there was service in the chapel, and soon after two the school reassembled, girls now occupying the writing desks, as boys had done in the forenoon, and at four or half-past the scholars were sent home for the week.

7. CRITICS OF METHODISM

Many pamphlets appeared attacking the Methodists and their sympathizers both as deluded 'enthusiasts' and as agents of subversion.

(a) *Source:* Anon, *Observations upon the Conduct and Behaviour of a Certain Sect, Usually distinguished by the Name of Methodists* (1740?). The pamphlet was probably written by Edmund Gibson, Bishop of London.

Besides the many *Irregularities* which are justly charged upon these Itinerant Preachers, as Violations of the Laws of Church and State; it may be proper to enquire, Whether the Doctrines they teach, and those Lengths they run, *beyond* what is practised among our *Religious Societies*, or in any other Christian Church; be a Service or a Disservice to Religion. . . . Whether Notions in Religion may not be heighten'd to such *Extremes*, as to lead *some* into a Disregard of Religion itself, through Despair of attaining such exalted Heights. . . . Whether a due and regular attendance on the publick Offices of Religion, paid by good men, in a serious and composed Way, does not better answer the true Ends of Devotion, and is not a better Evidence of the Co-operation of the Holy Spirit, than those sudden Agonies, Roarings and Screamings, Tremblings, Droppings-down, Ravings and Madnesses; into which their Hearers have been cast; according to the Relations given of them in the Journals referr'd to? . . . Whether in a Christian Nation, where the Instruction and Edification of the People is provided-for, by placing Ministers in *certain Districts*, to whom the care of the Souls within those Districts is regularly committed; It can be for the Service of Religion, that Itinerant Preachers run up and down from Place to Place, and from County to County, drawing after them confused Multitudes of People, and leading them into a Disesteem of their own Pastors. . . . All the while, for the sake of those Schemes, and in Pursuance of them, violating the wholesome Rules, which the Powers Spiritual and Temporal have wisely and piously established, for the preservation of Peace and Order in the Church.

(b) Whitefield, like Wesley, had to face bitter opposition, as his correspondence with the Mayor of Basingstoke shows.

Source: Entries in *George Whitefield's Journal*, pp. 307ff.

'*Basingstoke*, July 19, 1739.

Sir,—Being a civil magistrate in this town, I thought it my duty, for the preservation of the peace, to forbid you, or, at least dissuade you, from preaching here. If you persist in it, in all probability, it may occasion a disturbance, which I think it is your duty, as a clergyman, as well as mine, to prevent. If any mischief should ensue . . . I am satisfied it will fall on your own head, being timely cautioned by me, who am, sir, your most humble servant,

JOHN ABBOT.

P.S. The Legislature has wisely made laws for the preservation of the peace; therefore, I hope, no clergyman lives in defiance of them.'

To this I immediately sent the following answer:—

'Honoured Sir,—I thank you for your kind letter, and I humbly hope a sense of your duty, and not a fear of man, caused you to write it.

If so, give me leave to remind you, honoured sir, as a clergyman, that you ought to be not only a terror to evil-doers, but a praise to them that do well. I know of no law against such meetings as mine. If any such law exists, I believe you will think it your duty, honoured sir, to apprise me of it, that I may not offend against it. If no law can be produced, as a clergyman, I think it my duty to inform you that you ought to protect, and not in any way to discourage, or permit others to disturb an assembly of people meeting together purely to worship God. . . .

I am, honoured sir, your humble servant,

GEORGE WHITEFIELD.'

Friday, July 20. After breakfast I waited in person on the mayor, to see what law could be produced against my meetings. As soon as I began to talk with him, I perceived he was a little angry. He said, 'Sir, you sneered at me in the letter you sent last night. Though I am a butcher, yet sir,' said he, 'I———' I replied, I honoured him as a magistrate, and only desired to know what law could be produced against my preaching; in my opinion, there could be none, because there was never any such thing as field-preaching before. I then instanced the trial of P . . . , the Quaker, where the jury, notwithstanding they were so hardly used, gave a verdict in favour of him. 'Sir,' said he, 'you ought to preach in a church.' 'And so I would,' I replied, 'if your minister would give me leave.' 'Sir,' said he, 'I believe you have some sinister ends in view; why do you go about making a disturbance?' I answered, 'I make no disturbance. It was hard I could not come into your town without being insulted. It was your business, sir, to wait, and if there was any riot in my meetings, then, and not till then, to interpose.' . . . I then pressed him to shew me a law against meetings, urging, that if there had been any law, they would have been stopped long since. He answered, 'It was an odd way of preaching. But sir, I must go away to a fair; before you came I had written you another letter, which I will send you yet, if you please.' Upon this, I thanked him, paid him the respect due to a magistrate, and took my leave. Soon after I had returned to my company, he sent me the following letter:—

'*Basingstoke*, July 20, 1739.

Rev. Sir,—I received your extraordinary letter, and could expect no other from so uncommon a genius.

I apprehend your meetings to be unlawful, having no toleration to protect you in it. My apprehension of religion always was, and I hope always will be, that God is to be worshipped in places consecrated and set apart for His service; and not in brothels, and places where all manner of debauchery may have been committed; but how far this is consistent with your actions, I leave you to judge. . . .

Your appearing against me as a swift witness, at the day of judgment, I must own, is a most terrible thing, and may serve

Y

as a bugbear for children, or people of weak minds; but, believe me, reverend sir, those disguises will have but little weight amongst men of common understanding.

Yours,

JOHN ABBOT.

P.S. I told you I had a letter written. I make bold to send it.'

To this I sent the following answer:—

'*Basingstoke*, July 20, 1739.

Honoured Sir,—Does Mr. Mayor do well to be angry? Alas! what evil have I done? I honour you as a magistrate; but, as a minister, I am obliged to have no respect of persons. Your *apprehending* my meetings to be unlawful, does not make them so. There is no need of a toleration to protect me, when I do not act unconformable to any law, civil or ecclesiastical. Be pleased to prove that my meetings are schismatical, seditious, or riotous, and then I will submit.

But you say they are upon unconsecrated ground. Honoured sir, give me leave to inform you, that God is not now confined to places, but seeketh such to worship Him, who worship in spirit and in truth. Where two or three are gathered together in Christ's Name, there will Christ be in the midst of them. The Church, by our ministers in their prayer before their sermons, is defined to be, not the church walls, but a congregation of Christian people. Such is mine.

As for judging me, to my own Master I stand or fall. At His dreadful tribunal I will meet you; and then you shall see what is in the heart of, honoured sir, your very humble servant,

GEORGE WHITEFIELD.'

About eight o'clock I went into a field, lent my by Mr. H . . . ; and though one said, I should not go out of Basingstoke alive if I preached there, and another said, the drum should beat just by me, yet I had little or no interruption, and God gave me power to speak against revelling; and those few scoffers that were there, were not able to gainsay or resist it.

8. EVANGELICALISM

Despite protests of this kind, there was a powerful Evangelical movement working within the eighteenth-century Anglican Church. By the end of the century it had captured a large number of parishes, particularly in growing centres of population, for example, in the West Riding of Yorkshire. Crookes's Diary (see above, pp. 317ff.) reflects it. The Methodists, despite John Wesley's dislike of separation, became a religious sect and soon a series of related religious sects. Evangelicalism within the Church remained, however, as one of the powerful strands in religious life. It directly influenced social and political life also, tightening moral 'discipline', particularly during the wars against revolutionary France and Napoleon, imposing rigorous codes of conduct, and providing driving force for the anti-slavery campaign.

(a) *Source:* I. Milner (ed.), *Works of the Late Rev. Joseph Milner* (1870), vol. VIII, pp. 190–1.

Practice has grown as corrupt as principle. This must be the case. The preaching of morality is not God's appointed way of making men holy in their lives. It has a place, an extremely necessary place in doctrine, but not a prominent one. Christ crucified is the chief Gospel theme. Who does not see what an increase of wickedness has prevailed among us! Look at the Clergy! I would be tender in speaking of my brethren; but is there not a loud call for it, in charity? That sermons should be sold to them by a person advertising in the newspapers, is a flaming proof of the low state of their religious views and studies. . . . That we are a selfish, profane, licentious people, is evident. *The whole head is sick, and the heart weak.*

(b) *Source:* William Wilberforce, *Practical View of the Religious System of Professed Christians Contrasted with Real Christianity* (1797). 7,500 copies of this work sold within six months. It had run through 15 editions by 1826.

To the decline of Religion and Morality our national difficulties must both directly and indirectly be chiefly ascribed: . . . my only solid hopes for the well-being of my country depend not so much on her fleets and armies, not so much on the wisdom of her rulers, or the spirit of her people, as on the persuasion that she still contains many, who in a degenerate age, love and obey the Gospel of Christ; on the humble trust that the intercession of these may still be prevalent, that for the sake of these, Heaven may still look upon us with an eye of favour.

(c) *Source:* Extract from the *Royal Proclamation against Vice* (1787). This Proclamation enjoined the enforcement of 'laws of conduct'. Wilberforce, who declared that he had been chosen by God to secure the reformation of his country's manners, was also responsible for the formation of the Society for the Reformation of Manners, known at first as the Proclamation Society. There had been an earlier society with this name in existence from 1692 to 1738. (See above, p. 275.)

We do hereby strictly enjoin and prohibit all our loving subjects, of whatever degree of quality soever, from playing on the Lord's Day at dice, cards, or any game whatsoever, either in public or private houses. . . . Our further pleasure is, and we strictly charge and command all our judges, mayors, sheriffs, justices of the peace, and all other our officers and ministers, both ecclesiastical and civil, and all other subjects, to be very diligent and strict in the discovery and effectual prosecution and punishment of all persons who shall be guilty of excessive drinking, blasphemy, profane swearing and cursing, lewdness, profanation of the Lord's Day, or other dissolute, immoral, or disorderly practices; and that they take care also effectually to suppress all public gaming houses, and also all unlicensed public shows, interludes and places of entertainment, using the utmost caution in licensing the same; also to suppress all loose and licentious prints, books and publications, dispensing poison to the minds of the young and unwary, and to punish the publishers and vendors thereof.

9. PREACHING TO THE RICH

Evangelicals were often accused—e.g. by William Cobbett—of interfering with the 'liberties of the poor' in the name of religion. (See above, p. 277.) At the same time, the Evangelicals made fervent appeals to the rich and well-connected. Arthur Young was a convert in the 1790s. Note the fear of the French Revolution.

(a) *Source:* A. Young, *An Enquiry into the State of the Public Mind* (1798), p. 25.

The true Christian will never be a leveller; will never listen to French politics, or to French philosophy. He who worships God in spirit and in truth will love the government and laws which protect him without asking by whom they are administered. But let it not be imagined that such characters will abound among the lower classes while the higher by their Sunday parties, excursions and amusements and vanities; by their neglect of public worship and their families show that they feel not themselves, what perhaps they talk of, or recommend for the poor.

10. CHRISTIANITY AND SOCIAL ORDER

Underlying Evangelicalism, indeed, there were profound value judgements relating not only to religion but to society and its structure. Wilberforce's picture of a 'practical Christian' brings this to the surface.

Source: W. Wilberforce, *Practical Christianity* (1797).

[With a practical Christian] there will be no capricious humours, no selfish tempers, no moroseness, no discourtesy, no affected severity of deportment, no peculiarity of language, no indolent neglect, no wanton breach, of the ordinary forms or fashions of society. . . . If he give offence, it will only be where he dares not do otherwise; and if he falls into dis-esteem or disgrace it shall not be chargeable to any conduct which is justly dishonourable, or even to any unnecessary singularities on his part, but to the false standard of estimation of a misjudging world. . . . In whatever class or order of society Christianity prevails, she sets herself to rectify the particular faults, or if we would speak more distinctly, to counteract the particular mode of selfishness to which that class is liable. Affluence she teaches to be liberal and beneficent; authority to bear its faculties with meekness, and to consider the various cares and obligations belonging to its elevated station, as being conditions upon which that station is conferred. Thus, softening the glare of wealth, and moderating the insolence of power, she renders the inequalities of the social state less galling to the lower orders, whom also she instructs, in their turn, to be diligent, humble, patient: reminding them that their more lowly path has been allotted to them by the hand of God; that it is their part faithfully to discharge its duties, and contentedly to bear its inconveniences; that the present state of things is very short; that the objects about which worldly men conflict so eagerly, are not worth the contest; that the peace of mind, which Religion offers to all ranks indiscriminately, affords more true satisfaction than all the expensive pleasures which are above the poor man's reach; that in this view, however, the poor have the advantage, and that if their superiors enjoy more abundant comforts, they are also exposed to many temptations from which the inferior classes are happily exempted . . . finally, that all human distinctions will soon be done away, and the true followers of Christ will all, as children of the same father, be alike admitted to the possession of the same heavenly inheritance.

11. DISSENTERS

Outside the ranks of Evangelicals and Methodists were the old dissenters or nonconformists, descendents of the Puritan sects of the seventeenth century, suffering civil disabilities, sometimes severe ones. They were always liable to be unpopular and to suffer persecution, as in Anne's reign or as in the last decade of the century, when many of them sympathized with the French Revolution.

(a) *Source:* Sir William Blackstone, *Commentaries on the Laws of England* (1775 edn.), vol. IV, pp. 52ff.

Non-conformists are of two sorts: first, such as absent themselves from divine worship in the established church, through total irreligion, and attend the service of no other persuasion. . . . The second species of non-conformists are those who offend through a mistaken or perverse zeal. . . . All persons who will approve themselves no papists or oppugners of the trinity, are left at full liberty to act as their consciences shall direct them, in the matter of religious worship. And, if any person shall wilfully, maliciously, or contemptuously disturb any congregation, assembled in any church or meeting-house, or shall misuse any preacher or teacher there, he shall be bound over to the sessions of the peace and forfeit twenty pounds.

(b) *Source:* J. White, *Letter to a Gentleman Dissenting* (1746), p. 10, p. 91.

The main body of Dissenters are mostly found in cities and great towns among the trading part of the people [and] their ministers are chiefly of the middle rank of men, having neither poverty nor riches. . . . If I had a son brought up in any trade and had no consideration either for him or myself in another world, I should be ready to say to him at setting up—*my son, get Money, and in order to do that, be a Dissenter.*

(c) The Unitarians, who gained in strength during the century, did not believe in the trinity. They included many outstanding individuals both in intellect and culture. They were interested in government, and were drawn naturally to the viewpoint, considered dangerous after 1789, that 'the people [are] the origin of power' and that 'the enjoyment of life, liberty and property [are] the right of all mankind'. The Quakers, for the most part withdrawn from politics, were a highly distinctive dissenting group.

Source: B. Faujas de St. Fond, *A Journey Through England in 1788,* pp. 113ff.

I love the Quakers, and I have great pleasure in seeing them in private, in society, and in their religious assemblies. They inspire me with an involuntary veneration.

Clothed with all that is most simple, plain, and modest, but at the same time, most neat, finished, and perfect, it has seemed to me that their mind shares in the whiteness of their beautiful linen, and must be as pure and as carefully tended as their clothes. . . . The places where the Quakers assemble for worship, or rather for meditation, where they descend into their own thoughts, and await the inspirations of virtue in their hearts, are calculated to awaken respect.

This kind of temples, like those of the nations of antiquity, admits the light only from the roof. The walls are of a dazzling white; . . . the seats are simple benches, placed in parallel rows. In vain would one look here for paintings, statues, altars, priests, and acolytes. All these accessories are considered by the quakers as excrescences, devised by man, and foreign to the Supreme Being. They prefer to offer up to him pure hearts, and acts of virtue and beneficence. They are persuaded that nothing can be more agreeable to him than that mild philanthropy which induces them to regard all men as brothers and real friends, with whom they travel, in common, the short, but difficult road of life, in which they reciprocally stand in need of assistance.

They, accordingly, hold in abhorrence those cruel and sanguinary persons, who, from motives of ambition or vengeance, provoke war. . . .

When the quakers are assembled in their churches, the men occupy a place apart from that of the women, and have their heads covered with a black hat, of a broad half-cocked brim, without loop or button. Their eyes are humbly bent on the ground, and often entirely shut, to avoid any distraction in the midst of their contemplative meditations.

The women also have their heads covered with bonnets, made of silk, velvet, or straw, but very plain. They, in general, conceal their faces; at least they do so in this place of meditation. . . . They are attired in the most decent taste. . . .

At the farther end of the church there is a kind of platform, a little raised, and surrounded with a wooden balustrade. It is not a pulpit; it is rather a large and long tribune from which to harangue. Here it is that those (including the women) who are animated by heavenly inspiration, take their place, to communicate in a loud voice to their brethren the transports of their souls, and the impressive thoughts which the Eternal has sent to them.

(d) *Source:* J. Godber (ed.), *The Diary of Elizabeth Brown of Ampthill,* printed in *Some Bedfordshire Diaries* (1959), pp. 113–14.

23 Oct. 1778. This day passed in assisting M[ercy] E[xton] at ironing. . . .

24th. At home employed in the family. In the evening read part of an old history, which was entertaining as also informing. . . .

25th. Employed whilst Meeting time in cookery. After Meeting had to dine with us M.A., G[eorge] E[xton] and M.E., with whom the afternoon was agreeably spent, and the evening at J. Humphreys'.

26th. Passed the morning at home, employed in family affairs. [In] the afternoon took a pleasant walk and went to assist M.E. in the evening. Read of Philip, King of Macedon, a great warrior who conquered many nations and was guilty of some acts of cruelty. . . .

27th. First of the week at Meeting. J.T. appeared in the morning; he reminded that 'Blessed is the man that feareth always', inferring that nothing short of that can preserve. . . . The Meeting concluded with a prayer. In the afternoon no public Friends. Went after Meeting to drink tea at G.E.'s in company with uncle, aunt, and R.B., as also some more. The conversation turned in part on American affairs. There seems not much probability of reconcilement at present; and news [was] brought of the English fleet being dispersed the second time in a storm, and one if not more ships wrecked, wherein 80 perished, and upwards of 400 taken prisoners by the Americans. The French fleet suffered no damage that we heard of. It seems as if there was need of chastisement, if we may be favoured to profit by it. In the evening read in Purver's Bible.[1] What a mercy and favour that we enjoy the privilege of that valuable book!

28th. Busied at home in family affairs. In the evening read the *News*, which gives account of the arbitrary proceedings of the Americans, those that pretend to be such advocates for liberty, under whom our fellow professors suffer greatly.

29th. Spent the morning in necessary business, and copied from the *Northampton Mercury* a hymn for that called Christmas Day, which breathed a heartfelt gratitude for the wonderful condescension of our dear Lord in coming into the world to redeem poor lost mankind. . . . The evening was spent in pleasant conversation, having at

[1] Purver's Bible was an annotated edition prepared in 1702-07.

our house H.C., a poor but honest well-disposed Friend, far beyond many of those in higher station. . . .

31st. Assisted at the shop to-day, a pleasant employ, of which I have been deprived of late through an indisposition. . . . The evening was in company with a person professing Quakerism, but whose conduct had so much politeness in it as cannot be quite consistent with that of the true Quaker. . . .

(e) One Quaker, John Woolman—from America—was very worried about the state of the Friends.

Source: John Woolman, *Journal* (Everyman edn., 1906), pp. 149–50.

I have felt great Distress of Mind, since I came on this Island, on Account of the Members of our Society being mixed with the World in various Sorts of Business and Traffick, carried on in impure Channels. Great is the Trade to *Africa* for Slaves! and, in loading these Ships, abundance of People are employed in the Factories; amongst whom are many of our Society. Friends, in early Times, refused, on a religious Principle, to make, or trade in, Superfluities; of which we have many large Testimonies on Record; but, for Want of Faithfulness, some gave way; even some, whose Examples were of Note in our Society; and from thence others took more Liberty. Members of our Society worked in Superfluities, and bought and sold them; and thus Dimness of Sight came over many: At length, Friends got into the Use of some Superfluities in Dress, and in the Furniture of their Houses; and this hath spread from less to more, till Superfluity of some Kinds is common amongst us.

In this declining State, many look at the Example one of another, and too much neglect the pure Feeling of Truth.

12. ROMAN CATHOLICS

There were not many Roman Catholics in eighteenth-century England, although there were pockets of strength, particularly in Lancashire, where they were protected by recusant landed families.

Many of them had to face charges of Jacobitism early in the century, and throughout the whole period anti-Papalism never died out as a popular force.

(a) *Source:* Nicholas Blundell, *Diary and Letter Book* (1952), pp. 77–9. Blundell is asking the Provincial of the Jesuits in 1706 to find him a good priest.

Sir,

Tho you be a Stranger to me yet I presume to address myself to you, being you are not ignorant of ye Subject I writ about wch is to desire you will, with what convenient Speed you can, furnish us with one of yours, that you think will be propper. You have formerly been informed how we desire he should be qualifyed, so shall be breef on that. Subiect, only say in few words that we desire a Man of Wit and Conversasion, one that can preach well and is willing to take Pains among ye poore Catholicks, of which we have a great Many and onc that is of a good Humour and will be easy contented with tollerable good Fair. . . . Sir your speedy Answer to this would much oblidge.

Your Humble Servant

Nicholas Blundell.

Barnes recommended a priest called Aldred, who became one of Nicholas's closest friends. He soon left the Hall, however, for a cottage. Blundell thanked Barnes for his choice.

To Mr. Barns. Feb. 17th. 1707/8.

I ought long since to have returned you thanks for the good Man you sent us viz: Mr. Aldred who is qualified according as desired and is extreamley to my liking and gives very great Satisfaction to the Catholicks hereabouts who are very numerous, but cannot say my Wife carries to him as sivilly as she ought, which causes him to be dissatisfied and not willing long to continue in my Famoly. However he being so well approved of both by myself and all the Neighbourhood, I am not willing he should part far, so have taken care that another Hous not far distant be hence provided for him . . . the Neighbours have not only Petissioned for his stay, but have on their own Accord promised considerably towards his Maintonance which, with what I shall do, will I hope, maintain him Sufficiently. . . .

CHAPTER XI

Education

I now plainly perceive that a man may be of much more consequence by improving his mind in various kinds of knowledge, than by all the finery and magnificence he can acquire.

> (THOMAS DAY, *Sandford and Merton*, 1783)

> From the coffee-house then I to Tennis away
> And at five I post back to my College to pray:
> I sup before eight, and secure from all duns,
> Undauntedly march to the *Mitre* or *Tuns*:
> Where in punch or good claret my sorrows I drown,
> And toss off a bowl 'To the best in the town':
> At one in the morning, I call what's to pay,
> Then home to my College I stagger away.
> (From the *Lounger's Diary* in the *Oxford Sausage*, 1760)

Our misfortune is that there is too much business here, so that some can spare little time for learning.

> (Letter from the Vicar of BRADFORD to the Society for Promoting Christian Knowledge, 1721)

Those parents who . . . obstinately refuse to send their children to the Sundays' School shall be deemed improper Objects to receive any Charity that shall in future be distributed in the parish of Curry Rivel.

> (Ordinances for the Founding of a Sunday School at Curry Rivel, 1786)

If any trust can be said to be of God and as such ought not to be relinquished at the command of men, it is that which we have of the education of our children.

> (JOSEPH PRIESTLEY, *First Principles of Government*, 1771)

1. EDUCATION—FOR AND AGAINST

Opportunities for education depended directly on social rank, yet even upper-class education was often haphazard and disorganized.

There was an intermittently lively debate about whether the poor should be educated at all, and women's education was almost always viewed with suspicion.

(a) *Source:* P. Grosley, *A Tour to London* (1772), p. 167.

Education, the aim of which should be to direct, and to temper the natural disposition, has little or no influence upon the English. It begins with teaching to read and write at home. The principal object of this groundwork of education is, not to put any constraint upon the tempers of children, nor any bias upon the operations of nature, in unfolding the faculties either of the body or mind. ...

In pursuance of the same principle, children are sent from their father's house to public schools, in which there are a great number of boys, and which are supported and maintained by handsome foundations. After the young people have, in these schools, been taught the elements of the learned languages, they are sent to the universities of Oxford and Cambridge.

The public schools and universities, by bringing together persons of all ranks and conditions in life, put them, in some measure, upon a level. A spirit of emulation reigns there, which is excluded by domestic education: connexions are formed, which often lay the foundation of the greatest fortunes. Such, say the English, was the education at Sparta, calculated to form men, and not *petits maitres*.

(b) *Source:* C. B. Andrews (ed.), *The Torrington Diaries* (1934), vol. II, p. 371. The passage refers to the year 1791.

When tradesmen, farmers and yeomen brought up their children to business, to attend to agriculture, and to assist in their fathers' fortunes, why then truth, society and honesty dwelt in the land: for the sons were honest, hearty fellows and the girls unaffected, notable housewives.—But now, from false pride, and idle hope, parents educate their children in fashionable folly, the misses sent to French boarding schools, or convents, and the boys are to become bishops, or generals. Of such blindness what must be the result? Why, such misery and distress of the old folks, that the farm (for ages in the family) must be sold; the sons turn'd out into the world, (to make their fortune, as the term is) sink into debauchery, disappointment, and end in a jail, whilst the fine misses, vain, pert and ignorant, quickly degenerate into harlots, take lodgings in Wardour Street and perish;—we hope repentant sinners.

(c) *Source:* J. Fawel, *The Principles of Sound Policy* (1785).

The Ignorance of the Poor affords their masters the best security of their unremitting Utility, Faithfulness and Obedience. That to instruct them in Reading and Writing generally puffs them with Arrogance, Vanity, Self Conceit and . . . unfits them for the menial stations which Providence has allotted for them.

(d) *Source:* Adam Smith, *The Wealth of Nations* (1776), Book V, Part III.

The education of the common people requires, perhaps, in a civilised and commercial society the attention of the public more than that of people of some rank and fortune. People of some rank and fortune are generally eighteen or nineteen years of age before they enter upon that particular business, profession, or trade, by which they propose to distinguish themselves in the world. They have before that full time to acquire, or at least to fit themselves for afterwards acquiring, every accomplishment which can recommend them to the public esteem, or render them worthy of it. Their parents or guardians are generally anxious that they should be so accomplished, and are, in most cases, willing enough to lay out the expense which is necessary for that purpose. If they are not always properly educated, it is seldom from the want of expense laid out upon their education, but from the improper application of that expense. . . . It is otherwise with the common people. They have little time for education. Their parents can scarce afford to maintain them even in infancy. As soon as they are able to work, they must apply to some trade by which they can earn their subsistence. That trade, too, is generally so simple and uniform as to give little exercise to the understanding. . . . But though the common people cannot, in any civilised society, be so well instructed as people of some rank and fortune, the most essential parts of education, however, to read, write and account, can be acquired at so early a period of life that the greater part even of those who are to be bred to the lowest occupations have time to acquire them before they can be employed in those occupations. For a very small expense the public can facilitate, can encourage, and can even impose upon almost the whole body of the people the necessity of acquiring those most essential parts of education.

2. CHARITY SCHOOLS

The Charity School movement was inspired above all else by the desire to promote 'social discipline' along with 'godly discipline'. It represented, in Richard Steele's phrase, one of the 'greatest instances of public spirit the age had produced'. By 1730 there were nearly 1,500 Charity Schools in England with over 22,000 pupils. The main sponsor was the Society for the Promotion of Christian Knowledge, founded in 1695. In 1800 there were 2,000 Schools.

(a) *Source:* Isaac Watts, *An Essay Towards the Encouragement of Charity Schools* (1728), p. 26.

I would persuade myself that the masters and mistresses of these schools among us teach the children of the poor which are under their care to know what their station in life is, how mean their circumstances, how necessary 'tis for them to be diligent, laborious, honest and faithful, humble and submissive, what duties they owe the rest of mankind and particularly to their superiors.

(b) *Source:* St. Margaret's Parish Charity School, Westminster, *Minute Book*, 1698. Quoted in M. G. Jones, *The Charity School Movement* (1930), pp. 44–5. The School was later known as the Grey Coat Hospital.

Several of the inhabitants of Westminster, having taken into their serious consideration the great misery that the poor children of the parish do generall suffer, by reason of their Idle and Licentious Education; their Nurses, or those that provide for them, generally suffering if not encouraging, them to wander about and begg, by which Means the Evil Customs and Habits they contract thereby become, for the most part, the Curse and Trouble of all places where they live, and often, by their Wicked Actions, are brought to Shameful and Untimely Death; to prevent the like miseries for the future, in the said Parish, where 40 of the greatest objects of charity they could find should, from time to time, be educated in sober and virtuous principles, and instructed in the Christian Religion. And for their Incouragement in their Learning they did propose that the said 40 children should be clothed, as hereafter directed, and when fit to go out Apprentices should be carefully placed out to Honest Masters, who should take care as well of their good Principles as instruct them how to get an honest livelyhood, by their labours and industry in the World.

(c) Each year from 1704 onwards (until 1877) there was an annual assembly of the London Charity Schools. There are many descriptions of this event.

Source: Sir Gilbert Elliot, first Earl of Minto, *Life and Letters* (1880), vol. I, pp. 303–4.

Under the dome were piled up to a great height all round, 6,000 children from the different charity Schools in the City, in their different habits and colours. This was by far the most interesting part of the show. You may see this any year for they are brought to St. Paul's and placed in the same order every year, and I think it will be worth your while if you ever come within sight of St. Paul's again. After the House of Commons and of Peers etc. were seated . . . and when the King approached the centre all the 6,000 children set up their little voices and sang part of the Hundredth Psalm. This was the moment I found most affecting and without knowing exactly why I found my eyes running over and the bone in my throat, which was the case with many other people.

(d) William Blake gave a poetic description of the same scene later in the century.

Source: A poem in *Songs of Innocence* (1789).

'Twas on a Holy Thursday, their innocent faces clean
The children walking two by two, in red and blue and green,

Grey-headed beadles walk'd before, with wands as white as
snow
Till into the high dome of Paul's they like Thames water flow
O what a multitude they seem'd, these flowers of London
Town!
Seated in companies they sit with radiance all their own.
The hum of multitudes was there, but multitudes of lambs,
Thousands of little boys and girls raising their innocent
hands.

(e) Discipline was strict, and humility and obedience were always
inculcated. (For attention to time, see also above, pp. 49ff.)

Source: Mrs. Sarah Trimmer, *The Charity Spelling Book: The
Part of a Plan of Appropriate Instruction for the Children of the Poor*,
vol. I, Lesson VIII, 'Moral Duties' (1808 edn.).

Instructor: There is one kind of dishonesty which is often
practised without thought by workmen, and that is wasting
the time for which they are paid and the materials belonging
to the Trade or Manufacture they work at. Of the same nature
with this is the crime of many household servants who take
every opportunity of being idle and who make no scruple of
wasting provisions or giving them away without leave. . . .
Question: Is it honest for workmen to waste and destroy the
materials and implements which they make use of?
Answer: No.
Question: Who do these things belong to?
Answer: Their Master.
Question: Whose eyes see you when your master is not by?
Answer: God's.

(f) Girls, in particular, were expected to be particularly 'good'.

Source: The Poor Girl's Primer used in the Sheffield Girls' Charity
School, 1789.

Opening Prayer: Make me dutiful and obedient to my benefactors, and charitable to my enemies. Make me temperate
and chaste, meek and patient, true in all my dealings and
content and industrious in my station. . . .

z

Lesson I

Be good,
Be a good Girl,
Be a good Girl, and God will love you
Be a good Girl, and God will love, and bless you. . . .

Lesson IV

Keep your Clothes clean,
Wash your Hands, and Face,
Comb your Head,
Tye your Shoes.

Lesson V

Learn to spin Wool and Linen.
Learn to sew Shifts and Shirts and Caps.
Learn to knit Hose.
Learn to bake and brew and wash.
Learn to clean Rooms and Pots and Pans.

Lesson VI

Do no wrong.
It is a sin to steal a Pin.
Swear not at all, nor make a Brawl.
Use no bad Words.
Live in Peace with all as much as you can.

(g) In addition to primers, there were formal rules, often copied from school to school.

Source: 'Rules to be observed by the Children' in *Rules and Orders Agreed upon by the Trustees of the late Mr. Scott's Charity School, Stourbridge.*

1. To attend School constantly at Nine in the Morning and Two in the Afternoon.
2. To attend School with Hands and Face clean, Hair combed and Shoes brushed.
3. On all occasions to speak the Truth.
4. To behave with particular and solemn reverent Quietness when reading the Holy Scriptures.
5. To behave with Solemnity in all Places of Public Worship.
6. To be obedient at Home to Parents and Friends.

7. To avoid all bad Company.
8. Never to use bad Words or ill Names.
9. To avoid all Quarrelling and Contention.
10. Never to mock lame or deformed Persons, and to be kind to all men.
11. To avoid Cruelty, and never tease or in any way harm brute Creatures.
12. To be silent in School.
13. To enter and leave School orderly.
14. To obey the Rules and Orders of the School.

Whenever a Boy is about to leave School, it is expected that he will inform the Master.

(h) There were also rules for the Trustees and Teachers.

Source: Society for Promoting Christian Knowledge, *The Methods Used for Erecting Charity Schools with the Rules and Orders by which they are Governed* (1715), p. 7.

VI. The Qualifications to be required in a School-Master.

1. That he be a Member of the Church of *England*, of a sober Life and Conversion, and not under the Age of 23 Years.

2. That he understand well the Grounds and Principles of the *Christian Religion*, and be able to give a good Account thereof to the Minister of the Parish, or Ordinary, on Examination.

3. That he be of a meek Temper and humble Behaviour.

4. That he have a good Government of himself and his Passions, and keep good Orders.

5. That he frequent the Holy Communion.

6. That he have a Genius for Teaching, write a good Hand, and understand Arithmetick.

7. That he be approved by the Minister of the Parish.

AND here it may be noted, That it will be adviseable for any new-elected School-Master to consult with some of the experienc'd Masters of these Schools, for the better Understanding of his Duty.

(i) Posts in schools were advertised. In the North of England some masters taught industrial skills.

Source: Advertisement in the *Leeds Mercury*, 14 Nov. 1750.

For the promoting Industry in our extensive Manufacture, and for the Benefit of the Poor in general; it is thought very requisite and necessary, that the Children educated in the CHARITY-SCHOOL here, should be enured to some easy Labour; in Order the better to qualifie them for Service when they go out Apprentices.

Any Person capable of teaching such Children to spin Worsted, Yarn, &c. may apply to the Trustees at the said CHARITY-SCHOOL, on Friday the 30th Instant, at Three o'Clock in the Afternoon.

The Person chosen Work Master, shall be accommodated with a good Dwelling House and reasonable Wages.

N.B. Such Inhabitants who are willing to promote so commendable an Undertaking, their Company will be very acceptable to the Trustees at the said Meeting.

3. GRAMMAR SCHOOLS

Four hundred old grammar schools existed at the beginning of the eighteenth century. Very few, however, were created during the century. Classical education was the basis of the system, and studies tended to become stereotyped. None the less, there were some attempts to modernize the curriculum, and some of the schools in commercial communities, like Manchester or Newcastle, catered for a broad cross section of the community.

(a) *Source:* S. Bamford, *Early Days* (1893 edn.), pp. 80–2.

After a time I was sent to the Free Grammar School (at Manchester). . . . The school was a large room of an oblong form, extending north and south, and well lighted by large windows. At the northern end was a fireplace, with a red cheerful fire glowing in the grate. The master's custom was to sit in an armed chair, with his right towards the fire and his left arm resting on a square oaken table, on which lay a newspaper or two, a magazine or other publication, a couple of canes with the ends split, and a medley of boys' playthings, such as tops, whips, marbles, apple-scrapers, nut-crackers, dragon banding, and such like articles. The scholars were divided into six classes, namely, accidence, or introduction to Latin, higher Bible, middle Bible, lower Bible, Testament, and spelling classes. . . . Each class sat on a strong oaken bench, backed by a panel of the same, placed against the wall, with a narrow desk in front, so that they all sat around the school in regular gradation. The spellers only had not a desk, they sat on forms outside the desk of the higher Bible class, they being considered as children among the boys. The boys of each class were placed according to their proficiency, and the first and second boys of the class exercised considerable authority over the others. The school hours were from 7 to 8.30 at morning, from 9.30 to 12 at noon, and from 2 till 5 afternoon. The master was seldom more than five minutes beyond the time, and on coming in, he first pulled off his hat, and his extra coat or handkerchief, if he brought such; he would then probably give his hands a warming at the fire, stamp the wet from his shoes, and turning his back to the pleasant warmth, he would take a survey of the muster already arrived. Every boy who now entered the school was bound to go up to the table and present his shoulders for a correction, and they in general got off with a slight cut or two of the cane, except frequent de-faulters, and those were hit more severely, being often sent off to their class writhing, to the amusement of their more orderly comrades. The mustering and flogging being over, the classes were severally called up, arranged round the table, and went through their lessons, the boy who in spelling or reading could readiest make out a word when those above him were at fault, moving up to their places, and thus the quickest spellers and readers were always towards the upper end of their class. When a boy had been at the head of his class some time, and especially if he happened to have some acquaintance amongst those of the next class above him and they wished to have him amongst them, their head boy would take him by the hand, and leading him to the master, would say, 'If you please, sir, must X (mentioning the surname) go into my class?' when a brief intimation, as a nod, a 'yes', or 'no', would decide the application, and the parties withdrew either elated with success or abashed by failure.

(b) Bamford went to the school at the end of the century. The following table gives a breakdown of the occupational background of fathers of boys at the school earlier in the period.

Source: A. A. Mumford, *History of Manchester Grammar School* (1919).

FATHERS	1740–45	1745–50	1750–55	1755–60	1760–65	TOTAL
Gentry	5	11	19	18	15	68
Clergy	2	5	12	27	19	65
Law	—	2	4	4	2	12
Medicine/Surgery	1	2	—	4	3	10
Freemen/Yeomen	8	7	4	10	6	35
Innkeepers	8	11	13	12	17	61
Tradesmen	9	12	14	17	7	59
Dyers	8	4	6	1	9	28
Hatters	3	3	5	4	5	20
Artisans, Shopkeepers etc.	36	59	64	68	87	314
TOTAL	80	116	141	165	170	672

Of the total, 196 were boarders. 84 of these proceeded to the universities, as against only 16 day boys. 160 entered the Church, 75 the Army and 11 the Navy. 72 became lawyers and 32 medical men. The majority entered industry and commerce.

4. PUBLIC SCHOOLS

While it was not until the nineteenth century that the special claims and privileges of the 'public schools' were fully expressed, nine schools (Eton, Westminster, Winchester, Harrow, St. Paul's, Shrewsbury, Rugby, Merchants Taylors and Charterhouse) are said to have supplied almost one-third of England's eighteenth-century *élite*, defined as those people whose careers are set out in the *Dictionary of National Biography*.

(a) Boarding was, of course, a feature of the system, although some boys, as at Sedbergh, boarded with landladies.

Source: Letter from William Cotesworth to his father, 7 April 1716, printed in E. Hughes, *North Country Life in the Eighteenth Century* (1952), pp. 344–5.

Honoured Father,

We arrived here on Wednesday night. . . .

Our Landlady is a very neat woman, and as far as we have

tried, does very well by us. We have always 2 Dishes of meat to dinner and there are three sorts of Bread set upon the table, and we have liberty to choose of which we will. As for our breakfasts, we have butter and bread and cheese, and as much milk as we desire, and if we be hungry betwixt meals she bids us call for what we want. We have a little room entire to ourselves where we have shelves for our books, and pins for our cloths, and there's a room almost as large as the Hall (at their home) which we have liberty to walk in. Mr. Saunders (the Headmaster) seems to be a very civil man and calls every day to see us. We gave him everyone a Guinea and my Uncle (according to the custom of the School) gave the Usher half as much. . . .

Your Dutyful son,
William Cotesworth.

(b) *Source:* A letter from William's younger brother, Robert, 15 April 1716, in *ibid.*, p. 345.

. . . My Landlady does very well by us and is very civil as likewise is every Body else. Mr. Sanders is not at all severe, but on ye contrary very good humour'd. . . . My brother gives his duty to you and my Aunt, his love to Hannah and service to all friends.

P.S. [by William] I have been forced to buy several Books since I came here which I never learned before. I desire that you would let Neddie buy me Madam Dacier's Homer, it's in either 2 octavo volumes or 5 twelves; it is a very good Book and will be a means to make me understand Homer perfectly. Mr. Sanders bought it very lately. Our seat is to-day making Latin verses upon one of our Scholars who is dead of the small pox; they are to be pinn'd upon the Pall.

(c) Not all schooldays were as happy as this.

Source: P. Gosse (ed.), *Dr. Viper, The Querulous Life of Philip Thicknesse* (1952), pp. 16–17.

I believe I could at this day shew upon the backs of my hands some marks of the favours frequently confer'd upon them by that truly beautiful nobleman the present Earl of . . . for as cash often ran low with me, and Nan Batchelor's tarts and custards were as grateful to my palate as to any lord's in the school, I did sometimes spend that money which was given me on the bougie account by my mother rather too hastily, so that I had no other means of light for the school than exposing the back of my hand to a yard and a half of double waxed candle, at so much a cut: and his lordship was of so generous a disposition that I was as sure of my night or morning's bougie from his lordship's bountiful hand, as a poor woman is, who goes to the humane pawnbroker with her last shift, to borrow a shilling upon, to buy bread for her children. . . .

5. CURRICULA: TOO MUCH LATIN?

In grammar schools, public schools and many of the newly founded private schools, Latin and Greek were the main subjects taught. By the end of the century a vigorous reaction had set in. Indeed even before 1700, there were 'academies' which offered a far wider (in some cases a 'comprehensive') curriculum.

(a) There were many reasons given for studying the classics.

Source: R. L. Edgeworth, *Essays on Professional Education* (1808), p. 372.

A knowledge and taste for classical literature is peculiarly ornamental and useful, indeed indispensably necessary to every Briton who aspires to distinction in public life, for in this country a statesman must be an orator. It is by eloquence, that he must bring himself into notice; by eloquence, that he must preserve this power, and accomplish by his influence in the senate what ever designs he may form for his own advantage or the good of the country.

(b) *Source:* J. Lowe, Article on *England* in the *Encyclopedia Britannica* (4th edn. 1816).

In regard to the mode of education in England, there is much both to commend and censure. Scotland has been for a century past in possession of a larger proportion of parish schools; but the utility of these is much lessened by an established routine of teaching Latin to almost all youths, whatever be their intended line of life. In England this absurdity is less prevalent, because most of the schools are private undertakings, the managers of which are necessarily guided by considerations of utility. The youth destined for a life of business are thus saved a serious waste of time; their education, if imperfect, is not supererogatory; but, on examining the higher seminaries of England, we find much ground for disappointment, and many marks of a blind adherence to ancient usage. . . . In a country of which commerce forms the strength, there are no teachers of political economy. Under a government which has so long borne the representative form, there are no classes for the study of modern history, or the principles of legislation. There are here hardly any of those public lectures, which, in the rest of Europe, constitute the grand characteristic of a university, and distinguish it from schools:—all, or nearly all, is done by private tuition.

(c) An Advertisement at the back of W. Foot, *An Essay on Education* (1750).

An Academy, where young gentlemen, intended for military employment, are instructed in Fortification, Gunnery, Surveying, etc., and every other part of knowledge necessary for that profession, as modern languages, Riding, Fencing, Drawing, etc. Those who incline to the Marine are taught every branch of Navigation etc. Those who would be formed for the Counting House, learn to write strong and free,—to compute with ease, expedition and demonstration—to enter Mercantile Transactions by double entry—to know the use of all the books kept by Merchants with their different methods—to draw all forms of business—the nature of foreign exchange and the proper style for correspondence. The intention of this undertaking being to perfect the instructed in any branch of knowledge as capacity and application will admit. . . . Poor pupils are made accountants gratis on proper recommendation.

6. METHOD: TOO MANY PUNISHMENTS?

Corporal punishment played a large part in the life of the public schools, while in most conventional schools, including the charity schools, learning by rote was a main form of instruction. Reformers talked of rewards as well as punishments, and experimented with ingenious methods of instruction.

(a) *Source:* J. Talbot, *The Christian Schoolmaster* (1721 2nd edn.), p. 79.

After they have gone through the Letters of the *Alphabet*, he must instruct them in the true Spelling of Words, and the Distinction of Syllables, by the Help of some proper *Spelling-Book* for that Purpose. From this they may proceed to the Reading of Words, as they are joined together in a Sentence: And great care must be taken from the Beginning, that each Syllable and every Word may be Pronounced very Plainly, Distinctly, and Audibly, without *Muttering* or *Stammering.* . . . These Things being thus Premised, it may be very proper to Appoint their first Lessons in such Parts of the *Church-Catechism* as they had not Learnt by Heart before they began to Read: That so by Repetition of the Words, while they are thus Practising to Read them, they may become Familiar with the Catechism.

(b) *Source:* E. Hobson (ed.), *The Diary of a West Country Physician* (1934). The physician was Dr. Claver Morris of Wells, Somerset. His son was a pupil at Sherborne School.

MARCH 5, 1724. I went about ten o'clock to Sherborne to be fully informed whether the report of Mr. Wilding's excessive severity to my son under his instructions was true. I found he had been often whipped since Christmas, but not above three lashes, not fourteen at a time as he was before I had desired him to be more moderate in his discipline. Mr. Wilding showed me his exercises in one of which there were thirty literal faults. but none of false concord or very improper words. He read about ten lines of English and made him piece by piece turn them into Latin off-hand which he did very well. He then examined him in Latin and Greek, being late put into the Greek Testament. He made him decline a Greek verb, conjugate it through all the moods . . . which he did exactly to the greatest satisfaction to me imaginable. At last Mr. Wilding said he would compare him with any boy in England of his standing and did not doubt but he should make him an incomparable scholar and the best that ever went from his school. He loved him heartily, for he had no fault but one, and that was he would not take pains, which he endeavoured by his often whipping him to break him of, and he had almost compassed his desire. If he would but search his dictionary they should never fall out. Mr. Wilding then bid him go out a little while and divert himself, and he would call him in again. Then he . . . professed he had not given him above three lashes at a time since I had talked with him about it. He said also that I should tell his mother that he would whip him no more. I answered him then, all would be spoilt that way; no, I did not desire that, but only moderate correction, which to him, a good-natured and flexible though lazy boy, I hoped would be effectual.

(c) *Source:* An Advertisement at the back of J. Rule, *Poetical Blossoms* (1766).

At this Academy [at Islington], no Saturday nor Thursday afternoon are observed and there are but two breakings-up in the year, of three weeks each, one at Christmas and the other at Whitsuntide; when premiums are bestowed on the most deserving to excite the necessary spirit of emulation.

(d) *Source:* L. Lochée, *An Essay on Military Education* (1773).

The members of this Academy [at Little Chelsea] constitute a military republic; the laws of which are so framed that the liberty and accommodation, as well as discipline and improvement of each individual, are inseparably connected with the order and good government of the whole. Of these laws there is a written code, which is regularly read over to the whole society every week. Every new member, after mature examination, declares his concurrence with the laws passed before his admission, and afterwards has an equal share in the enaction of new laws. . . . The rewards consist of tickets of temporary privilege, silver and gold medals, and superiority of station and honour lasting as the superiority of merit that gained it. The punishments are either pecuniary, corporal, viz. guards extraordinary, arrest, and the black-hole, or degrading . . . they are immediately inflicted. . . . The week is divided into theoretical and practical days. The theoretical days are Mondays, Wednesdays and Fridays, on which the study of the sciences and the attainment of all useful knowledge is pursued, such as languages, drawing, arithmetic, algebra, geometry, mechanics, fortification, artillery, chronology, geography, civil law and history. The practical days are devoted to the exercise of the body in dancing, fencing, riding and the manual exercise during the day; and in the evenings in sports for the improvement of agility and strength. . . . The money accumulated by fines is appropriated to the purchase of medals.

7. SCHOOLMASTERS

There was every variety of eighteenth-century schoolmaster, as the previous extracts show.

(a) Some got their posts by advertisement.

Source: The *Leeds Mercury*, 6 Jan. 1741.

This is to give Notice that at Rawcliffe, in the Parish of Snaith, there wants a School-Master, to teach the Children to read and write true English and Arithmetic. There's an Endowment of £11 or 12 a Year for teaching about fourteen Children, and attending on the Chappel as Clerk: It's a populous and improving Town, where an industrious Master may acquire a good School, and be well paid; . . . he must be approv'd on by the Trustees for the said Charity; they wou'd have a sober, and (willingly) a single Man.

N.B. If such Person understand the Latin and Greek Tongues, he'll find further Encouragement.

(b) Some got into difficulties.

Source: The *Diary* of Walter Gale, a Sussex schoolmaster.

26 October 1759. I was called into the little chamber over the club-room, and there I found Mr. Baker, Mr. Dowgate, old Sawyer, and old Kent, who said that 'I spent my time in reading printed papers to the neglect of the children; he said

that I was covetous, and undertook to do other persons' business to the neglect and detriment of the school; that the children did not improve, and that he would get an old woman for 2d. a week that would teach them better.' I answered that 'many of them were extremely dull, and that I would defie any person that should undertake to teach them better.' He then said 'that I got money so fast that I was above my business, and it made my saucy'.

Resolution of Meeting of 18 October 1771. That the schoolmaster, Mr. Walter Gale, be removed from the School for neglecting the duties thereof, and that he have notice to leave the same the next quarter day.

Resolution of Meeting of 10 April 1772. It was ordered that Mr. Gale, the old schoolmaster, be not paid his salary due, till he has absolutely put the Schoolhouse in such a condition to the form of it as it was at the time of his entering upon such house. Agreed *nem. con.*

(c) Many were under-paid.

Source: Article on 'Teachers' in the *Encyclopedia Britannica* (4th edn; 1800).

We will venture to say, that there is no class of men to whom a nation is so much indebted as to those employed in instructing the young: For if it be education that forms the only distinction between the civilized and the savage, much certainly is due to those who devote themselves to the office of instruction. It must be the duty therefore of every state to take care that proper encouragement be given to those who undertake this office. There ought to be such a salary as would render it an object of ambition to men of abilities and learning, or at least as would keep the teacher respectable. In Scotland, the office of a schoolmaster was formerly much more lucrative than at present, and most of that class had received liberal education; and this is the reason why the common people in Scotland have been famous even to a proverb, for their learning. But at present the salary of a country schoolmaster, independent of fees for scholars is not greater than a ploughman can earn, being seldom more than £8 6s. 8d., the consequence of which is that this, which is in fact an honourable, because an useful profession, is now

sinking into contempt. It is no longer an object to a man of
learning; and we must soon be satisfied with schoolmasters
that can read, write, and cast accounts, a little better than the
lowest of the people, or who from some natural deformity are
unable to exercise a trade. And what in this case must become
of the minds of the common people? They must be totally
uncultivated.

8. HOME EDUCATION

There was a lively debate in the eighteenth century about the
respective merits of home education versus school education.
Schools were sometimes compared with prisons, at other times with
crowded cities: both their scale and their system of relationships
seemed to be wrong.

(a) *Source:* E. Hamilton, *Letters on Elementary Principles of Education*
(1801).

The great seminaries, where hundreds of bad and good boys
are promiscuously mingled, where the time of boys is so entirely
at their own disposal, that of the four and twenty hours but
two or three at the utmost are spent under the master's eyes;
of the remainder, when we deduct what is employed in the
important business of purveying, in quarrelling and in
play, we shall find little left for the purpose of voluntary
improvement.

(b) Many famous men in the eighteenth century did not go to
school, and were brought up by private tutors in the society of the
home. William Cowper, the poet, educated at Westminster, balanced
the merits of the two systems.

Source: W. Cowper, *Tirocinium* (1784).

Would you your son should be a sot or dunce,
Lascivious, headstrong, or all these at once;
That in good time the stripling's finished taste,
For loose expense and fashionable waste
Should prove your ruin, and his own at last;
Train him in public with a mob of boys,

Childish in mischief only and in noise . . .
There shall he learn, ere sixteen winters old,
That authors are most useful, pawned or sold;
That pedantry is all the schools impart,
But taverns teach the knowledge of the heart . . .
[yet]   Be it a weakness, it deserves some praise,
We love the play-place of our early days.

(c) There was another side to the picture, particularly when boys went to university very young.

Source: Vicesimus Knox, *Liberal Education* (1781), p. 35.

After all the confinement and trouble of a domestic education, it is probable that the boy will at last be sent to the University. There he will find the greater part of his associates to consist of young men who have been educated at schools; and if they have any vices he will now be in much greater danger of infection, and will suffer much worse consequences from it, than if he had not been secluded from boys at a boyish age.

9. UNIVERSITIES

Oxford and Cambridge, each based on a collegiate pattern, were the two English universities, although there were four more vigorous universities in Scotland, more closely linked to the educational systems of the continent, and one in Ireland.

(a) *Source:* E. D. Clarke, *Tour Through the South of England* (1791), pp. 397–9.

The approach to Oxford from Woodstock, is not marked by any particular beauty. The country, bleak, champaign and flat, consists of those features which *melancholize* the environs of its sister seminary. It is not in the power of nature to assume a visage more deformed that she wears in the neighbourhood of Oxford and Cambridge. Not one expressive line, not one interesting object, presents itself to the traveller's eye; and the desponding Freshman, as he sojourns a-cross the drear expanse, feels the full force of Johnson's assertion, when, speaking of Scotland, he says 'that, if the miserable aspect of the country should induce a man to hang himself, he would scarcely find a tree to swing from!'

I shall confine my remarks upon this city within a very small compass—it is foreign to my present purpose to record, in pompous detail, its colleges and the history of their founders; and those, who wish to acquire a more accurate knowledge of their buildings and benefactors, will find ampler sources of information in the *Oxford and Cambridge Guides* than in any laboured essay of mine.

In Oxford there seems, what may be styled, *a disease of buildings*. The traveller is presented with a profusion of edifices jumbled together with no great display either of taste or design. It is a kind of anarchy in stone and mortar, where every thing is confused; and architecture, in a high fever, seems to have stuck one edifice here and another there, varying the nonconformity of her work in proportion to her delirium. There is a *Mausoleum* for a *library*, and a *cock-pit* for *public disputants*. There is a *sepulchre* of *manuscripts*, and a long gallery, where heroes with ugly faces, and learned graduates in full bottomed wigs, are copiously displayed upon canvass. What shall be said of CHRIST-CHURCH? where neat little PECKWATER cements the dirty puddle and the leaden mercury that disgraces its neighbouring quadrangle—and of the boasted THEATRE? with its wrong side foremost, that turns its back upon the public and hides its fine front in a corner—and of ST. MARY's? with a low gothic spire, but of sufficient beauty for every one to wish it taller—and of the prospect from the top of RADCLIFF's empty LIBRARY? where the view of ALL-SOULS alone is a recompence for the fatigue of ascending.

After leaving Oxford, the prospect of the University on the London side is worth paying attention to. The country gradually improves towards HENLY.

(b) This was only one impression of the setting: there were others.

Source: Rev. Sir J. Peshall's edition of Anthony Wood's *The Antcient and Present State of the City of Oxford* (1773).

Oxford is better seen than described. The magnificent

Colleges, and other most noble Edifices, standing in, and giving an Air of Grandeur to the Streets: the many delightful Walks: elegant Gardens: rich Chapels: grand Libraries: the Beauty of the Meadows and Rivers, that on every side delight the Eye: the Sweetness of the Air: the Learning, and frequent public Display of it, and the Politeness of the Place: the Harmony and Order of Discipline: not to mention the great Number of Strangers that continually visit us and express their Satisfaction, conspire to render it the Delight and Ornament of the Kingdom, not to say of the World.

(c) One of the best-known accounts of Oxford is that of Edward Gibbon. Again his impressions were not universally shared. There were 'poor students' at Oxford and Cambridge who were there entirely for their brains. As one writer, Thomas Baker, put it in his *An Act at Oxford* (1704), 'the difference between us the servitors and Gentleman Commoners is this, we are men of wit and no fortune and they are men of fortune and no wit'. Gibbon, of course, had both. There is evidence that the absolute and relative numbers of 'poor students' at both Oxford and Cambridge declined in the late eighteenth century.

Source: E. Gibbon, *Autobiography*, written in 1792–93. Gibbon was an undergraduate at Magdalen College from 1752 to 1755. He was only fifteen years old when he arrived.

. . . My own introduction to the University of Oxford forms a new aera in my life, and at the distance of forty years I still remember my first emotions of surprize and satisfaction. In my fifteenth year I felt myself suddenly raised from a boy to a man; the persons whom I respected as my superiors in age and Academical rank entertained me with every mark of attention and civility; and my vanity was flattered by the velvet and silk gown which discriminate a Gentleman-Commoner from a plebeian student. A decent allowance, more money than a schoolboy had ever seen, was at my own disposal, and I might command among the tradesmen of Oxford an indefinite and dangerous latitude of credit. A key was delivered into my hands which gave me the use of a numerous and learned library; my apartment consisted of three elegant and well-furnished rooms in the new building, a stately pile, of Magdalen College; and the adjacent walks, had they been frequented by Plato's

AA

disciples, might have been compared to the Attic shade on the banks of the Ilissus. Such was the fair prospect of my entrance into the University of Oxford. . . .

The expression of gratitude is a virtue and a pleasure; [yet] to the University of Oxford *I* acknowledge no obligation: and she will as chearfully renounce me for a son, as I am willing to disclaim her for a mother. I spent fourteen months at Magdalen College; they proved the fourteen months the most idle and unprofitable of my whole life. . . .

The fellows or monks of my time were decent easy men, who supinely enjoyed the gifts of the founder; their days were filled by a series of uniform employments, the Chappel and the Hall, the Coffee-house and the common room, till they retired, weary and well-satisfied, to a long slumber. From the toil of reading, or thinking, or writing, they had absolved their conscience; and the first shoots of learning and ingenuity withered on the ground without yielding any fruit to the owners or the public. . . . Their conversation stagnated in a round of College business, Tory politics, personal anecdotes, and private scandal. . . .

The example of the senior fellows could not inspire the undergraduates with a liberal spirit, a studious emulation; and I cannot describe, as I never knew, the discipline of the College. Some duties may possibly have been imposed on the poor scholars, whose ambition aspired to the peaceful honours of a fellowship . . . but no independent members were admitted below the rank of a Gentleman-Commoner, and our velvet cap was the cap of liberty. A tradition prevailed that some of our predecessors had spoken Latin declamations in the Hall, but of this ancient custom no vestige remained; the obvious methods of public exercises and examinations were totally unknown; and I never heard that either the President or the Society interfered in the private economy of the Tutors and their pupils. . . . No plan of study was recommended for my use . . . and, at the most precious season of my youth, whole days and weeks were suffered to elapse without labour or amusement, without advice or account.

(d) For the don's life, there are many vivid portraits. This comes from Cambridge.

Source: Notes from *The Journal of a Senior Fellow or Genuine Idler* (1750).

Monday,   9. Turned off my bedmaker for waking me at eight. Consulted my weather-glass. No hope of a rise before dinner.

       10. After breakfast transcribed half a sermon from Dr. Hickman. N.B. never to transcribe any more from Calamy: Mrs. Pilcocks, at my Curacy, having one vol. of that author lying in her parlour-window.

       11. Went down into my cellar.

        1. Dined alone in my room on a sole. . . . Sat down to a pint of Madeira. Mr. H surprized me over it. We finished two bottles of port together and were very cheerful.

        6. Newspaper in the Common Room.

        7. Returned to my room, made a tiff of warm punch, and to bed before nine.

10. DISSENTING ACADEMIES

Dissenters were kept outside the old universities and developed academies of their own. Some of them, like the Warrington Academy, had a deservedly high reputation. Their curricula were often progressive, and included scientific subjects.

Source: J. Orton, *Memoirs of the Life, Character and Writings of the late Reverend Philip Doddridge* (1766), pp. 87–92.

As the Method of Education in the Seminaries of *Protestant Dissenters* is little known, it may be proper to give some general Account of his [Philip Doddridge's, first at Market Harborough (1729) and later at Northampton]; which bears a near Resemblance to others of the Kind. He chose to have as many of his Students in his own Family as his House would contain, that they might be more immediately under his Eye and Government. The Orders of this Seminary were such, as suited a Society of *Students*; in a due Medium between the Rigour of School-discipline, and an unlimited Indulgence. As he knew that Diligence in redeeming their Time was necessary to their Attention to Business, and Improvement of their Minds, it was an established Law, that every Student should rise at *Six o'Clock* in the Summer, and *Seven* in the Winter. A *Monitor* was weekly appointed to call them, and they were to appear in the public Room, soon after the fixed Hour. Those who did not appear were subject to a pecuniary Penalty, or, if that did not cure their Sloth, to prepare an additional academical Exercise; and the Monitor's Neglect was a double Fine. Their *Tutor* set them an Example of Diligence, being generally present with them at these early Hours. . . .

One of the first Things he expected from his *Pupils*, was to learn *Rich's* Short-hand, which he wrote himself, and in which his Lectures were written; that they might transcribe them, make Extracts from the Books they read and consulted, with Ease and Speed, and save themselves many Hours in their future Compositions. Care was taken in the first Year of their Course, that they should retain and improve that Knowledge of *Greek* and *Latin*, which they had acquired at School, and gain such Knowledge of *Hebrew*, if they had not learned it before, that they might be able to read the *Old Testament* in its original Language: A Care very important and necessary! . . . Those of them, who chose it, were also taught *French*. He was more and more convinced, the longer he lived, of the great Importance of a *learned*, as well as a *pious* Education for the Ministry. . . . Systems of *Logic, Rhetoric, Geography* and *Metaphysics* were read during the first Year of their Course, and they were referred to particular Passages in other Authors upon these Subjects, which illustrated the Points, on which the Lectures had turned. To these were added Lectures on the Principles of *Geometry* and *Algebra*. These Studies taught them to keep their Attention fixed, to distinguish their Ideas with Accuracy and to dispose their Arguments in a clear, concise and convincing Manner.—After these Studies were finished, they were introduced to the Knowledge of *Trigonometry, Conic-sections* and *celestial Mechanics*. A System of natural and experimental *Philosophy*, comprehending *Mechanics, Statics, Hydrostatics, Optics, Pneumatics*, and *Astronomy*, was read to them; with References to the best Authors on these Subjects.

But the chief Object of their Attention and Study, during three Years of their Course, was his *System of Divinity*, in the largest Extent of the World. . . .

11. WOMEN'S EDUCATION

Most women in the eighteenth century received no education, a fact which had provoked Defoe to write that he believed that it was 'one of the most barbarous customs in the world, that we deny the advantages of learning to women'. This was by no means a general view a hundred years later, as some of the following extracts show, yet there was no shortage of 'blue-stockings' in the eighteenth century, many of them women of exceptional learning. Girls were also educated (humbly) in charity schools (see above, p. 345) and (expensively) in private boarding schools.

(a) *Source:* Letter of Lady Mary Wortley Montagu, 10 Oct. 1753, printed in *Letters and Works* (1861), vol. II, p. 242.

There is no part of the world where our sex is treated with so much contempt as England. I do not complain of men for having engrossed the government . . . but I think it the highest injustice . . . that the same studies that raise the character of a man should hurt that of a woman. We are educated in the grossest ignorance, and no art omitted to stifle our natural reason; if some few get above their nurses' instructions, our knowledge must rest concealed, and be as useless to the world as gold in the mine. I am now speaking according to our English notions, which may wear out, some ages hence, along with others equally absurd.

(b) *Source:* Advertisement in the *Leeds Mercury*, 2 Aug. 1743.

This is to give Notice to all Ladies, and others, who have occasion for Gowns, or Petticoats, drawn for French Quilting, running Patterns or Sprigs, to be wrought in Silk or Worstead; also drawing upon Canvas for Chairs, Fire-Screens, or Stools; likewise she draws Pictures from any Copper-plate or Oil-Piece that shall be sent to her, without ever damaging them; She draws it upon silk or Canvas, to be wrought and then fram'd and glass'd; she also will teach any Person to paint upon

Glass, or Water Colours upon Cloth; she will likewise teach any Person to Draw and Work the above. Also she will teach all sorts of Tent-work, White-work, Marking and Plain-work, which is carefully and expeditiously performed at reasonable Rates; by MARY ENGLAND at the Charity-School House in *Wakefield*.

N.B. The Charity Children will be no Disturbance to any Person that learns with me, they being Taught in another Apartment by my Husband and his Mother.

(c) *Source:* J. Lackington, *Memoirs* (1791).

Many farmers, observing how some, in circumstances inferior to themselves, bring up their daughters, think that because they can better afford the expence, their girls ought to be brought up as genteelly as their neighbours; so that instead of having them taught to read and write, and do plain-work at a day-school, until they are ten or eleven years old, and then taken home to help milk the cows, &c. they are sent to a boarding-school, where they remain until they are fourteen, or older. There they are called ladies, and learn filigree, pride, and extravagance. When their education is completed, their infatuated parents find themselves despised by their own children, who think themselves ladies, and look with disdain on all they see going forward in the old farm-house. To see their father come in from the fields in his smock-frock, with a pick on his shoulder, is 'monstrous.' To see the butchers and pig-dealers about the house, and by the fireside, bargaining for calves, sheep, hogs, &c. is 'insupportable!' To see their mother with a serge petticoat, woollen-apron, mob-cap, and old hat milking the cows, making butter, cheese, &c. is 'prodigious monstrous.' And when any of their old schoolmates happen to call on them, O, they are ready to expire with shame and vexation, while they hear their mother apologize for her homely dress, &c.

Such girls, instead of being useful in the affairs of the farm-house, &c. are rendered good for nothing; instead of assisting, they expect to be waited upon; to have horses to make their idle visits; and a servant several times a week to exchange novels at the circulating library.

12. ADULT EDUCATION

There was no organized adult education in the eighteenth century, but there were many local and voluntary initiatives, some of them ambitious both in object and in name, as the first extract shows. Lecture courses were given, encyclopedias, 'repositories' and periodicals produced, philosophical and scientific societies formed, and at the end of the century evening classes organized for mechanics.

(a) *Source:* Advertisement of 31 March 1742.

At the East End of Exeter Change in the Strand, this evening at 6. o'clock will be opened the London University, where all liberal Arts and Sciences will be most usefully, critically and demonstratively taught in the mother tongue in proper courses of lectures, composed by men of the greatest learning and delivered with good address, so as to be entertaining to all and particularly improving to the ladies and such gentlemen as have not had an academical education, as more real learning will be exhibited thus in few months than in an equal number of years elsewhere. The opening lecture will be a rational view of the nature, reality, origin, extent, past and present state of all liberal Arts and Sciences with the means of improving them.

At midsummer next proper Schools will be opened in the centre of the town where very able Professors will teach all liberal Arts and sciences in the mother tongue.

(b) *Source:* H. Brougham, *Practical Observations upon the Education of the People* (1825), p. 17.

About the year 1800 he [Dr. Birkbeck] announced a course of lectures on National Philosophy, and its application to the Arts, for the instruction of mechanics. But a few at the first availed themselves of this advantage; by degrees, however, the extraordinary perspicuity of the teacher's method, the judicious selection of his experiments, and the natural attractions of the subject, to men whose lives were spent in directing or witnessing operations, of which the principles were now first unfolded to them, proved successful in diffusing a general taste for the study. . . .

CHAPTER XII

Crime and Punishment

One is forced to travel, even at noon, as if one was going to battle.

(HORACE WALPOLE to SIR HORACE MANN, 1752)

Elizabeth Walker, of Snowden, was sent to the House of Correction at Wakefield for fourteen days, and ordered to be publicly whipped for embezzling 3lb of combed wool.

(From the *Newcastle Journal*, 1 August, 1767)

Each wanton judge new penal statutes draw,
Laws grind the poor, and rich men rule the law

(OLIVER GOLDSMITH, 1764)

I now come to a fourth encouragement which greatly holds up the spirit of robbers, and which they often find to afford no deceitful consolation; and this is drawn from the remissness of prosecutors, who are often,

1. Fearful, and to be intimidated by the threats of the gang; or,
2. Delicate, and cannot appear in a public court; or,
3. Indolent, and will not give themselves to the trouble of prosecution; or
4. Avaricious, and will not undergo the expense of it; nay, perhaps, find their account in compending the matter; or,
5. Tender-hearted, and cannot take away the life of man;
   Lastly, Necessitous, and cannot really afford the cost, however small, together with the loss of time which attends it.

(HENRY FIELDING, *An Enquiry into the Late Increase of Robbers*, 1751)

The indiscriminate application of the sentence of death to offences exhibiting very different degrees of turpitude has long been a subject of complaint in this country, but it has still been progressive and increasing.

(SAMUEL ROMILLY, Speech in the House of Commons, 1810)

1. INSECURITY

Eighteenth-century England felt itself particularly vulnerable to crime. There was no adequate police force, and the increase in wealth in a society grounded in inequality widened the range of criminal opportunity. The privileged classes were sensitive (above all else) to crimes against property, but they were also gravely concerned, as were humanitarian reformers, by displays of brutality. In an attempt to protect themselves, new statutes imposing capital punishment were introduced at the rate of more than one a year between 1727 and 1810. At the same time English criminal procedure—methods of prosecution and trial—was far more liberal than that in most continental countries, as European travellers observed, and from the middle of the century there was a movement for reform.

(a) *Source:* The Duc de Lévis, *L'Angleterre au commencement du dix-neuvième siecle* (Paris, 1814), p. 35.

In a country where there are neither forests nor great mountains, you should have no more robbers than there are wolves; but why do you not have police to catch your robbers? . . . [My English friends reply] 'Such an institution is incompatible with liberty.'

(b) *Source:* Remarks of Dr. Primrose in O. Goldsmith, *The Vicar of Wakefield* (1766).

Government, while it grows older, seems to acquire the moroseness of age; and, as if our property were to become dearer in proportion as it increased—as if the more enormous our wealth the more extensive our fears—all our possessions are paled with new edicts every day, and hung around with gibbets to scare every invader.

2. COUNTRY CRIME

There were many complaints in the eighteenth century of rural crime, some of it highly organized, and among the crimes punished by death were maliciously cutting down trees and destroying the heads of fishponds. Transportation was a general punishment in the later century, applied to stealing sheep or even oysters. There were many anomalies in the law. To steal fruit already gathered was a felony: to gather it and then steal it was a trespass.

(a) *Source:* Letter of Lady Fermanagh, 4 Dec. 1710, printed in *The Verney Letters*, p. 285.

... The Dumb Boy is dead that was shott, & Jack Busby is dead. ... There is such robbing that I never heard on since I came into Buckingham. They robb between us and Dr. Busby's, I have the back dore locked, & the Key brought up to me as soon as it is dark.

(b) *Source:* Note in *Hertfordshire County Records*, Quarter Sessions Book, vol. 14, Epiphany Session, 1783.

This Court took into Consideration the numerous Roberies, Felonies, and Misdemeanors lately committed in this County and resolved as follows. ... That it is the Opinion of this Court (and this Court doth recommend to all other Justices of the Peace of this County) that, to prevent the Committing of such a Number of Felonies, Roberies, and Misdemeanors as have lately been committed in this County, it is necessary that frequent Petty Sessions should be held in the several divisions of the County, and all High and Petty Constables be summoned, and strict charges given them to apprehend and carry before the Magistrates all suspicions and disorderly Persons, to be examined and dealt with as the Nature of their Cases may require and as the Law directs; and in Parishes where there is only one Constable, another should be appointed, and in large and extensive Parishes, two Constables and two Head-boroughs, who should frequently visit the Publick Houses to see that good Order be observed, good Hours Kept, and the House shut up by nine o'clock in the Evening in Winter and ten in Summer, and that no gaming be permitted. ...

That it be recommended to all Parish Officers and other at their Vestry Meetings at Easter to make Choice of good Character, strong, decent and active, to execute the offices of Constables and Headboroughs. That it is recommended to all Lords of Courts best to direct their Stewards not to swear into the office of Constable or Headborough any other than Men of good Character, not keeping Publick Houses.

And that it be recommended to all Farmers and others not to Harbour or permit wandering Beggars to lodge and sleep in their outhouses, which has brought great inconvenience and charges upon many Parishes.

And it is ordered that the Foregoing Resolutions be advertised once in two daily Papers and once in two Evening Papers, and that they be printed and sent to the Chief Constables, to be distributed and put up in all Parishes and Places in the County, and also that they be sent to the acting Justices of the Peace for this County.

(c) *Source:* C. Vancouver, *General View of the Agriculture of the County of Devon* (1808), pp. 366–7.

The business (for as such in some parts of the county, it seems to be almost exclusively practised) of sheep-stealing, is carried on to a most atrocious extent, particularly in the vicinity of the forests of Exmoor and of Dartmoor. A well attested fact states, that one farmer lost in the course of five years, no less than 108 sheep from off the former of these wastes; and it is no uncommon case for farmers in the neighbourhood of these moors to lose 20 sheep in the course of a season. Not in depredations upon sheep only are these excesses carried, but to so great a height is thieving arrived at, that neighbours are frequently detected in robbing each other of potatoes whilst yet in the ground. To put some check to these enormities, an association has been formed in the neighbourhood of Bideford, and this will most probably be soon followed by others in the county.

3. LONDON CRIME

Serious, though scattered, rural crime might be, urban crime, particularly in the rich and bustling metropolis, posed far greater problems. London footpads were particularly dreaded, and pickpockets were present not only on all special occasions when great crowds assembled, but regularly in the shopping streets and in inns and theatres. 'London swarms with pickpockets, as daring as they are subtile and cunning', wrote P. J. Grosley in 1765. Many of the pickpockets were between the ages of twelve and fourteen.

It was often difficult to draw the dividing line between beggars and criminals: both belonged to a Brechtian underworld. Among the hidden criminals were fences and counterfeiters.

(a) *Source:* John Gay, *Trivia or the Art of Walking the Streets of London* (1716).

> When the Mob gathers, swiftly shoot along,
> Nor idly mingle in the noisy Throng;
> Here dives the skulking Thief, with practis'd sleight,
> And unfelt Fingers make thy Pocket light.
> Where's now thy Watch, with all its Trinkets, flown?
> And thy late snuff box is no more thine own.

(b) *Source:* Letter written by William Shenstone in 1743, printed in M. Williams (ed.), *The Letters of William Shenstone* (1939), vol. III, p. 73.

London is really dangerous at this time; the pick-pockets, formerly content with mere filching, make no scruple to knock down with bludgeons in *Fleet-street* and the *Strand*, and that at no later hour than eight o'clock at night: but in the Piazzas, Covent-garden, they come in large bodies, armed with *couteaus*, and attack whole parties, so that the danger of coming out of the play-houses is of some weight in the opposite scale, when I am disposed to go to them oftener than I ought.

(c) *Source:* King George II's speech to Parliament 1751, printed in *Journals of the House of Commons*, vol. XXVI, p. 3.

I cannot conclude without recommending you in the most earnest Manner, to consider seriously of some effectual Provisions to suppress those audacious Crimes of Robbery and Violence, which are now become so frequent, especially about this great Capital, and which have proceeded in a great Measure from the profligate Spirit of Irreligion, Idleness, Gaming, and Extravagance, which has of late extended itself, in an uncommon Degree, to the Dishonour of the Nation, and to the great Offence and Prejudice of the sober and industrious Part of my People.

(d) Henry Fielding, magistrate as well as novelist, had already drawn attention to the lurid social background of crime. In a fascinating tract of 1750, quoted below, he drew upon the evidence of one of his collaborators in detecting crime, the Bow Street magistrate, Welch. (For the effects of gin drinking, see above, pp. 307ff.).

Source: H. Fielding, *An Inquiry into the Causes of the Late Increase of Robbers* (1750).

That in the parish of St. Giles there are great numbers of houses set apart for the reception of idle persons and vagabonds, who have their lodgings there for twopence a night; that in the above parish, and in St. George Bloomsbury, one woman alone occupies seven of these houses, all properly accommodated with miserable beds from the cellar to the garret, for such twopenny lodgers; that in these beds, several of which are in the same room, men and women being strangers to each other, lie promiscuously; the price of a double bed being no more than threepence, as an encouragement to them to lie together; but as these places are thus adapted to whoredom, so are they no less provided for drunkenness, gin being sold in them all at a penny a quartern; so that the smallest sum of money serves for intoxication; that in the execution of search warrants, Mr. Welch rarely finds less than twenty of these houses open for the receipt of all comers at the latest hours; that in one of these houses, he hath numbered fifty-eight persons of both sexes, the stench of whom was so intolerable that it compelled him in a short time to quit the place.

(e) Some eighteenth-century crimes are no longer perpetrated.

Source: Report in *The Times*, 23 Dec. 1796.

Early on Tuesday Morning, some suspicion being entertained that the Pesthouse burial-ground, in Old-Street-Road, had been frequently violated, the parish watchmen were ordered to keep a good look out, when a hackney coach was observed, waiting near the spot. Upon the watchman's approaching it, he was assaulted, and beaten, by three men, who then made off: but afterwards, springing his rattle, the assistants took the coachman into custody, who had three sacks in his coach, two of them containing the body of a man each, and the other, three children. Several other bodies, which had been dug up for the purpose of carrying away, were found under the wall of the burying-ground: and, it is generally believed, that almost all the bodies deposited therein, for 5 weeks past, have been stolen, which, upon an average, must have been 15 per week. The hackney-coachman, who owned he was to have had ten guineas for his night's fare, was committed to the New Prison, Clerkenwell. This fellow, it should seem, was hardened to his business: for, though put into the cage with the bodies he was carrying off, he slept so sound that it was with some difficulty he was awakened by the visit of a brother-whip, previous to his going before a Magistrate.

4. HIGHWAYMEN

Highwaymen, like pirates, have passed into legend. Dick Turpin, who was hanged at York in 1739, did so at once. Their combination of violence and politeness reflects the eighteenth-century combination of these qualities. As the amount of road passenger traffic increased (see above, p. 102), the numbers of highwaymen increased, even in the immediate vicinity of London.

(a) *Source:* Mme. van Muyden (ed.), *A Foreign View of England in the Reigns of George I and George II*, written in French by C. de Saussure between 1725 and 1730.

Highwaymen are generally well mounted; one of them will stop a coach containing six or seven travellers. With one hand he will present a pistol, with the other his hat, asking the unfortunate passengers most politely for their purses or their lives. No one caring to run the risk of being killed or maimed, a share of every traveller's money is thrown into the hat, for were one to make the slightest attempt at self-defence the ruffian would turn bridle and fly, but not before attempting to revenge himself by killing you. If, on the contrary, he receives a reasonable contribution, he retires without doing you any injury. When there are several highwaymen together, they will search you thoroughly and leave nothing. Again, others take only a part of what they find; but all these robbers ill-treat only those who try to defend themselves. I have been told that some highwaymen are quite polite and generous, begging to be excused for being forced to rob, leaving passengers the wherewithal to continue their journey.

(b) *Source:* C. Williams (ed.), *Sophie in London, 1786* (1933), p. 235.

[Sophie describes how a party of ambassadors outside London broke their meeting because] they feared highwaymen, for they were all booked for the evening, and so had to leave for London much earlier than eleven; perhaps they needed their money for gaming, and hence could not afford to give it to the highwayman! So they decided to depart all together, as the robbers would hardly hold up four coaches at once.

(c) There was much popular admiration for highwaymen, as there was for other bold criminals. Turpin, according to the *Gentleman's Magazine*, gave £3 10s. to men who were to follow his cart as mourners, and the crowd snatched his body from the surgeon's dissecting knife and secured him a Christian burial.

Source: A Broadside Ballad in the Firth Collection, printed as an illustration to H. L. Beales's chapter on 'Travel and Communications' in A. S. Turberville (ed.), *Johnson's England* (1933), vol. I, p. 145.

O Rare Turpin

As I was riding over Hunslow Moor,
There I saw a lawyer riding before,
And I asked him if he was not afraid,
To meet bold Turpin that mischievous blade.
CHORUS.—I asked him if he was not afraid,
To meet bold Turpin that mischievous blade.

Says Turpin to the lawyer and for to be cute,
My money I have hid all in my boot,
Says the lawyer to Turpin they mine can't find,
For I have hid mine in the cape of my coat behind.
I rode till I came to a powder mill,
Where Turpin bid the lawyer for to stand still
For the cape of your coat it must come off,
For my horse is in want of a new saddle cloth.
Now Turpin robbed the lawyer of all his store,
When that's gone he knows where to get more.

And the very next town that you go in,
Tell them you was robb'd by the bold Turpin.
Now Turpin is caught, and tried and cast,
And for a game cock must die at last,
One hundred pounds when he did die,
He left Jack Ketch for a legacy.

5. GANGS

Much crime was organized not by individuals but by criminal
groups, some of them gangs. Jonathan Wild, for instance, has been
called 'Director-General of the United Forces of Highwaymen,
House-breakers, Footpads, Pickpockets, and private thieves'.
Gangs had their own slang and their own codes of behaviour.
Frequently, in the absence of police, citizens also banded themselves
together for protection.

(a) *Source:* John Gay, *The Beggar's Opera* (1728), Act. II. Scene,
A Tavern near Newgate.

Jemmy Twitcher, Crook-finger'd Jack, Wat Dreary, Robin
of Bagshot, Nimming Ned, Henry Paddington, Matt of the
Mint, Ben Budge, *and the rest of the Gang, at the Table, with Wine,
Brandy and Tobacco.*

Ben. But pr'ythee, *Matt,* what is become of thy Brother
Tom? I have not seen him since my Return from Transportation.

Matt. Poor Brother *Tom* had an Accident this time Twelvemonth, and so clever a made fellow he was, that I could not
save him from those fleaing Rascals the Surgeons; and now,
poor Man, he is among the Otamys at *Surgeons Hall.*

Ben. So it seems, his Time was come.

Jemmy. But the present Time is ours, and no body alive
hath more. Why are the Laws levell'd at us? are we more
dishonest than the rest of Mankind? What we win, Gentlemen,
is our own by the Law of Arms, and the Right of Conquest.

Crook. Where shall we find such another Set of Practical
Philosophers, who to a Man are above the Fear of Death?

Wat. Sound Men, and true!

Robin. Of try'd Courage, and indefatigable Industry!

Ned. Who is there here that would not die for his Friend?

Harry. Who is there here that would betray him for his Interest?

Matt. Shew me a Gang of Courtiers that can say as much.

Ben. We are for a just Partition of the World, for every Man hath a Right to enjoy Life.

Matt. We retrench the Superfluities of Mankind. The World is avaritious, and I have Avarice. A covetous fellow, for the sake of hiding it. These are the Robbers of Mankind, for Money was made for the Free-hearted and Generous, and where is the Injury of taking from another, what he hath not the Heart to make use of?

Jemmy. Our several Stations for the Day are fixt. Good luck attend us all. Fill the Glasses.

(b) *Source:* Newspaper cutting of the 1790s, printed in A. S. Turberville, *English Men and Manners in the Eighteenth Century* (1929), p. 167.

BATH GUARDIAN SOCIETY for the Prosecution of FELONS, FORGERS, RECEIVERS of STOLEN-GOODS etc. and to defray the Expences of Advertisements, Hand-Bills; all of which are paid out of the Public Stocks raised annually at Five Shillings each Member residing in the City of Bath; and Two Shillings and Sixpence additional for such as reside in the [Outer Parishes].

This Society has been established upon its present Plan Fourteen Years, and a great number of Offenders, who had robbed or defrauded the Members of this Society have been *apprehended, prosecuted,* and *brought to justice*; many of whom would prabably have escaped the punishment due to their crimes. . . . The Committee of this Society do therefore invite their Fellow-Citizens, and the neighbouring Inhabitants, to join in this laudable Undertaking, the good effects of which have been sensibly felt by the Public, not only in the Punishment of Offenders; but, it is presumed, in the Prevention of Crimes.

6. TRIALS

The method of trial of criminals in England, wrote one observer, 'is very singular, and different from other nations.' Once beyond

BB

the petty courts, where local justices had social as well as legal authority (see above, p. 370), there were 'numerous rules favourable to the person accused'. He was presumed innocent until found guilty, he could not be tortured to extract evidence, he was tried by jury, he could call witnesses to prove his innocence, and proceedings were for the most part oral. There was great public interest in trials during the eighteenth century, as later, and many publications devoted to describing them. The language quoted may well represent the natural spoken language of the period more faithfully than any other surviving evidence. There were weaknesses as well as strengths in trial procedures, however, and the very severity of punishments for minor crimes encouraged 'merciful interpretation' of some statutes in the courts and large-scale commuting of sentences later. This carried with it arbitrariness and indeterminacy, both of which were attacked by penal reformers.

(a) *Source:* J. Marchand (ed.), *A Frenchman in England, 1784* (1933), p. 117. The Frenchman was F. de la Rochefoucauld.

The administration of justice in England deserves the highest commendation. On two occasions I was myself a witness of the equitable way in which English criminal, as well as civil, cases are conducted and I can testify that almost against my will I was filled with respect and admiration.

(b) *Source:* Lord Campbell, *The Lives of the Chief Justices of England* (3rd. edn. 1874), vol. 4, pp. 21–2. Mansfield was not a lenient judge.

Trying a prisoner at the Old Bailey on a charge of stealing in a dwelling house to the value of forty shillings, when this was a capital offence, Lord Mansfield advised the jury to hold a gold trinket, the subject of the indictment, to be of less value. The prosecutor exclaimed, with indignation, 'Under forty shillings, my Lord! Why the *fashion* alone cost me more than double the sum.' Lord Mansfield calmly observed, 'God forbid, gentlemen, we should hang a man for *fashion's sake.*'

(c) The following account of a trial figures Jonathan Wild.

Source: J. Wilford (printer), *Select Trials for Murders, Robberies, Rapes . . . and other Offences at the Sessions House in the Old-Bailey* (1735), vol. II, p. 106.

Not long after this, *Jonathan* mist another very useful Hand. He had minuted down in his Books a Gold Watch, a Parcel of fine Lace, and several other Things of great Value, which this Rascal (whose Name was *Jack Butler*) had made upon the *Lodging Lay* at *Newington-Green*; and yet he wholly neglected coming to Account, and no News was to be heard of him for two or three Months. *Jonathan* swore he would be up with him for his Ingratitude, and accordingly spared no pains in hunting after him; but as *Jack* had retired from Business, it was no easy Matter to meet with him. However, hearing at last that he lodged at an Ale-house in *Bishopsgate-street*, he got a Warrant, and taking two or three to assist him, went thither betimes in the Morning, and gaining an easy Admittance at the Street-door he went foremost up Stairs with a Pistol in his Hand, tho' not so softly but *Butler* heard him, upon which he jump'd out of Bed, slipt on his Coat, Breeches and Shoes, and getting out of the Window (which was but one Story high) dropt into the Yard, climb'd over the Wall into the Street, and ran cross the Way into a *Dyer's* Shop, and so through to a Wash-house where some Women were washing. He told 'em he was pursued by Bailiffs, and begg'd they would let him hide himself. The good Women pitied his Case, and directed him to the Coal-hole. In the mean Time *Jonathan* had wrench'd open the Door, and found that *Butler* had given him the Slip, and what was more he knew not which Way to follow him. . . . At last he saw the *Dyer's* Door open, upon which he goes over, and meeting with the Man of the House, acquainted him with what had happen'd, and said he believed the Rogue must have run in there, because (it being early in the Morning) he saw no other Door open thereabouts. *He can't be here* (says the *Dyer*) *for I have not been out of the Shop above a Minute. Sir* (says *Jonathan*) *that must be the very Time he slipp'd in, and therefore I beg you would give me leave to search for him.* The *Dyer* bid him search and welcome.

Jonathan and his Assistants went in, and finding the Women in the Wash-house, enquir'd of them if they had seen such a Fellow: They deny'd it stiffly, till he satisfied them that the Man he wanted was a Thief, and then they advised him to look in the Coal-hole. *Jonathan* took a Candle and look'd all round, but to no purpose. He examined the Cellar, the Kitchen, the Shop, and every other Place where he thought it was possible for the Fellow to be hid, and yet all was Labour in vain. He was heartily vex'd, and swore he was never so foil'd in his Life before. He told the *Dyer* he believed the Rogue was got out again. *That's impossible*, said the Dyer, *for I have been in the Shop ever since, and if he went down Stairs he must be there still, for there's no other Way out but at this Door, and he could not come this Way without my seeing him, and therefore I'd advise ye to look in the Cellar again, and I'll go with ye.* Down they all went, and the *Dyer* turning up a large Tub which he used in his Trade, immediately *Butler* made his appearance. *So, Mr. Son of a Bitch! have I caught you at last?* says *Jonathan; What have you done with the Gold Watch, the Lace, and the other Movables that ye stole out of your Lodgings, ye runnagate Rascal? ye shall certainly swing for it: I'll take care of you, if there's never another Rogue in England.* But notwithstanding these Menaces, *Jack* knew the Secret of calming *Jonathan's* Wrath, and therefore calling him aside, *If you'll step to my Room again*, says he, *and look behind the Bed's Head, you may find something that will make you amends for your Trouble. Jonathan* went, and was well satisfy'd with what he found; but as *Butler* was apprehended in so publick a Manner, it was necessary to carry him before a Justice, and the Justice committed him to *Newgate*; and by good Management, instead of being hang'd, he was only transported.

7. PUNISHMENTS

Punishments were severe in the eighteenth century, and the authorities made every attempt to display to the public how severe they could be.

(a) *Source:* M. Misson, *Memoirs and Observations* (1719), p. 218.

This Punishment [the Pillory] is allotted for those who are convicted of any notorious Cheat, or infamous Imposture; of having publish'd defamatory Libels against the King or Government; of false Testimony, and of publick Blasphemy; They are expos'd in a high Place, with their Heads put thro' two Pieces of notch'd Wood; the uppermost whereof being made to slide down, shuts the Neck into the Notch. The Criminal's Hands are confin'd on each Side his Head in the same Manner; and thus he stands in this ridiculous Posture for more or less Time, or with more or fewer Repetitions, according to his Sentence. If the People think there is nothing very odious in the Action that rais'd him to this Honour, they stand quietly by, and only look at him; but if he has been guilty of some Exploit dislik'd by the Tribe of 'Prentices, he must expect to be regaled with a hundred thousand handfuls of mud, and as many rotten Eggs as can be got for Money. It is not lawful to throw Stones, but yet 'tis often done.

(b) *Source:* Note in *The Grub Street Journal*, 21 Oct. 1731.

The same day, at noon, the Sessions ended at the Old Baily, when the 2 following persons received sentence of death, viz. John Turner, for breaking into the apartments of Mrs. Turner, who was an intimate of his father's, near Queenhithe, and stealing from thence 1 guinea, £5 1s. in silver, and several wearing apparel; and Anne Palmer, alias Hinks, for stealing £8 1s. in money, and goods to the value of 38s., the property of Mr. Sam. Ruffel. . . . Five were burnt in the hand, and 30 were cast for transportation. . . . Seven were burnt in the hand, and about 20 ordered for transportation. . . . Eight were burnt in the hand.

(c) *Source:* Report in the *Morning Post*, 4 Nov. 1800.

This day, being hay-market day at Whitechapel, John Butler, pursuant to his sentence at the last General Quarter Sessions, held at Clerkenwell, is to be publicly whipped from Whitechapel Bars, to the further end of Mile End, the distance of two miles, for having received several trusses of hay, knowing them to have been stolen, and for which he gave an inferior price.

8. TYBURN

Prisoners sentenced to death in London went in slow procession from Newgate to Tyburn. They travelled in clothes of their own choice, and, when they were men of standing, in their own carriages.

Large crowds assembled, expressing their sympathy or reprobation; such was the sense of excitement that the execution days were known as 'Tyburn Fair' or the 'Hanging Match'. Around the gallows there were boxes, the hangmen were public personalities, there were sometimes theatrical speeches, and broadsides were on sale. Children were taken there, and all sections of society were represented. Many superstitions developed round the rituals of the occasion. In 1783, however, the place of execution was transferred from Tyburn to Newgate. The sheriffs felt that the procession defeated 'all the ends of public justice'. In fact, large and noisy crowds continued to gather at Newgate.

(a) *Source:* J. Swift, *Tom Clinch* (1727).

> As clever Tom Clinch, while the rabble was bawling,
> Rode stately through Holborn to die in his calling,
> He stopt at the George for a bottle of sack,
> And promised to pay for it when he came back.
> His waistcoat, and stockings, and breeches, were white;
> His cap had a new cherry ribbon to tie't.
> The maids to the doors and the balconies ran,
> And said, 'Lack-a-day, he's a proper young man!'
> But, as from the windows the ladies he spied,
> Like a beau in the box, he bow'd low on each side!
> And when his last speech the loud hawkers did cry
> He swore from his cart 'It was all a damn'd lie!'
> The hangman for pardon fell down on his knee;
> Tom gave him a kick in the guts for his fee:
> Then said I must speak to the people a little;
> But I'll see you all damn'd before I will whittle![1]
> My honest friend Wild (may he long hold his place)
> He lengthen'd my life with a whole year of grace.
> Take courage, dear comrades, and be not afraid,
> Nor slip this occasion to follow your trade;
> My conscience is clear, and my spirits are calm,
> And this I go off without prayer-book or psalm;
> Then follow the practice of clever Tom Clinch,
> Who hung like a hero, and never would flinch.

(b) *Source:* L. J. Ferri de St. Constant, *Londres et les Anglais* (1804), vol. I, pp. 303–4.

[1] To 'whittle' meant to confess at the gallows.

To show off favourably the humanity of the English their criminal laws and the way they are put into operation are often cited. Yet how can we reconcile such sentiments of humanity with the curiosity which draws a crowd of both sexes to the public executions? How can we explain this taste for cruel spectacles which recalls the barbarism of gladiatorial contests?

9. PRISON LIFE

For criminals who were sent to prison, conditions varied as much as they did for paupers placed in workhouses. There were two main types—common county or borough gaols and Bridewells or 'houses of correction' originally designed for the wantonly idle. All prisons were dirty and liable to epidemics, in many food was appalling and in most conditions were corrupting. Prison reformers, notably John Howard, did much to expose conditions and to encourage reforms.

(a) *Source:* J. Howard, *The State of Prisons in England and Wales* (1777). There were then, according to Howard, 4,084 prisoners in England and Wales, of whom 2,437 were debtors.

The gaol for this large populous town [Birmingham] is called the Dungeon. The court is only about 25 feet square. Keeper's House in front, and under it 2 cells down 7 steps. Straw laid on bedsteads. On one side of the Court 2 night rooms for women, 8 ft. × 5 ft. 9 inches and some rooms over them; on the other side the gaoler's stable and one small day room for men and women; no window. Over it another room or two.

In this small court, besides the litter from the stable, a stagnant puddle near the sink for the gaoler's ducks. Gaoler's poultry is a very common nuisance, but in so scanty a court is intolerable. The whole prison very offensive. Sometimes great numbers confined here. Over 150 prisoners in the winter of 1775.

(b) Howard's suggested reforms are summarized in a pamphlet published by the Society for the Enforcement of the Proclamation against Vice and Immorality.

Source: Model regulations set out in *An Account of the Present State of the Prisons* (1789).

I. That Rules be made by the Justices, and confirmed by the Judges, for the direction of the gaolers, and the conduct of the prisoners, and that the same be painted on a board in a legible manner, and hung up in one or more conspicuous parts of every prison.

II. That the act of [1774] and the clauses against drunkenness in the act of [1784] be in like manner hung up in the prisons.

III. That until the laudable example of the county of Sussex, and some few other places, in abolishing all fees, be generally adopted, a table of fees made by the Justices, and confirmed by the Judges, be also hung up in the prisons; and that no garnish, or any other fee but what is allowed as above, be permitted to be taken of any prisoner.

IV. That every prison be white-washed at least once in every year, and that this be done twice in prisons which are much crowded.

V. That a pump and plentiful supply of water be provided, and that every part of the prison be kept as clean as possible.

VI. That every prison be supplied with a warm and cold bath, or commodious bathing tubs, and that the prisoners be indulged in the use of such baths, with a proper allowance of soap, and the use of towels.

VII. That attention be paid to the sewers, in order to render them as little offensive as possible.

VIII. That no animals of any kind which render a prison dirty, be allowed to be kept in it, either by the gaoler, or any prisoner. The only exception to this rule, should be one dog kept by the gaoler.

IX. That great care be taken, that as perfect a separation as possible be made of the following classes of prisoners, *viz.* That felons be kept entirely separate from debtors; men from women; old offenders from young beginners; and convicts from those who have not been tried.

X. That all prisoners, except debtors, be clothed on their admission with a prison uniform, and that their own clothes be returned them when they are brought to trial, or are dismissed.

XI. That care be taken that the prisoners are properly

supplied with food, and their allowance not deficient, either in weight or quality.

XII. That no gaoler, or any person in trust for him, or employed by him, be permitted to sell any wine, beer, or other liquors, or permit or suffer any such to be sold in any prison; or on any pretence whatever, to suffer any tippling or gaming in the prison.

XIII. That a proper salary be given to the gaoler, in lieu of the profits which he formerly derived from the tap, from fees, and other perquisites.

XIV. That those prisoners who are committed to hard labour be not permitted to be idle, and that such other prisoners as are willing to work, be supplied with materials, and be allowed part of the profits of such work, as the act directs.

XV. That a clergyman be appointed, with a proper salary, and that divine service be regularly performed on Sundays and holydays: that on those days no persons be allowed to visit the prisoners; and that such prisoners as will not attend divine service be locked up, and not suffered to disturb others while it is performed.

XVI. That care be taken that no swearing, cursing, or profane conversation be permitted, that the keepers and turnkeys be cautioned against it, and strictly enjoined not to suffer the prisoners to be guilty of it.

XVII. That cells be provided for the refractory, and night-rooms for solitary confinement, but that no prisoner be kept in any dungeon, or room under ground.

XVIII. That a surgeon or apothecary be appointed (with a proper salary) to afford the necessary assistance to the sick, and that two rooms, one for men, and one for women, be set apart as infirmaries, and be furnished with proper bedding.

XIX. That great attention be paid to what concerns the debtors, as it is found that that part of the management of our prisons has hitherto been the most neglected.

XX. That wherever any legacies have been bequeathed, or any charitable donations given for the benefit of prisoners, an account of the same be hung up in the prison; and that care be taken that the sums of money so given, be employed to the purposes for which they were intended by the donors.

XXI. That agreeably to the act [1782], the keeper of every house of correction be obliged to deliver to the Chairman at the Quarter Sessions, a list of the prisoners in his custody, distinguishing their age and sex, and mentioning in what trade or business each person hath been employed, and is best qualified for; as also the behaviour of such person during his or her confinement.

XXII. That the prisons be frequently visited, that the visiters take notice whether the regulations which have been established are observed or neglected; that a report from the visiters be presented to the Justices at every Sessions, and that these reports be taken into consideration, at least once a year, *viz.* at the Michaelmas Quarter Sessions.

XXIII. That attention be paid to prisoners when they are discharged, and that, if possible, some means be pointed out to them, by which they may be enabled to gain a livelihood in an honest manner.

(c) There were many escapes from prisons.

Source: An account of the escape of John Shepherd, who was awaiting trial for burglaries in 1724 from J. Wilford (printer), *Select Trials* (1734), vol. I, p. 441.

On *Wednesday, October* 14. The Sessions begun at the *Old-Bailey*; and *Jack* knew that the Keepers would then have so much Business, in attending the Court, as would leave them but little Leisure to visit him; and therefore thought that this would be the only time to make a Push for his Liberty.

The next Day, about Two in the Afternoon, one of the Keepers carried *Jack* his Dinner, and as usual examined his Irons, and found all fast, and so left him. He had hardly been gone an Hour, before *Jack* went to work. The first thing he did, he got off his Hand-cuffs, and then with a crooked Nail, which he found upon the Floor, he open'd the great Padlock that fasten'd his Chain to the Staple. Next he twisted asunder a small Link of the Chain between his Legs, and drawing up his Feet-locks as high as he could, he made 'em fast with his Garters. He attempted to get up the Chimney, but had not advanced far, before his Progress was stopt by an Iron Bar that went a-cross within Side, and therefore descending, he fell to work on the Outside, and with a piece of his broken Chain pick'd out the Mortar, and removing a small Stone or two about six Foot from the Floor, he got out the Iron Bar, which was an Inch square, and near a Yard long, and this proved of great Service to him. He presently made so large a Breach, that he got into the Red Room over the Castle. Here he found a great Nail which was another very useful Implement. The Door of this Room had not been opened for 7 Years past; but in less than 7 minutes he wrenched off the Lock, and got into the Entry leading to the Chappel. Here he found a Door bolted on the other Side, upon which he broke a Hole thro' the Wall, and push'd the Bolt back. Coming now to the Chappel-Door, he broke off one of the Iron Spikes, which he kept for further Use, and so got into an Entry between the Chappel and the lower Leads. The Door of this Entry was very strong, and fastened with a great Lock, and what was worse, the Night had overtaken him, and he was forced to work in the dark. However, in half an Hour, by the help of the great Nail, the Chappel Spike, and the Iron Bar, he forced off the Box of the Lock, and open'd the Door, which led him to another yet more difficult; for it was not only lock'd but bar'd and bolted. When he had try'd in vain to make this Lock and Box give way, he wrench'd the Fillet from the main Post of the Door, and the Box and Staples came off with it. And now *Sepulchre's* Chimes went Eight. There was yet another Door betwixt him and the lower Leads; but it being only bolted within Side, he open'd it easily, and mounting to the Top of it, he got over the Wall, and so to the upper Leads.

His next Consideration was how to get down; for which Purpose looking round him, and finding the Top of the *Turner's* House adjoining to *Newgate*, was the most convenient a Place to alight upon, he resolved to decend thither; but as it would have been a dangerous Leap, he went back to the Castle the same way that he came, and fetch'd a Blanket he used to lie on. This he made fast to the Wall of *Newgate*, with the Spike he stole out of the Chappel, and so sliding down, dropt upon the *Turner's* Leads, and then the Clock struck Nine.

Luckily for him the *Turner's* Garret-Door on the Leads happen'd to be open. He went in and crept softly down one

Pair of Stairs, when he heard Company talking in a Room below. His Irons giving a Clink, a Woman started, and said, *Lord! What Noise is that?* Somebody answer'd, *The Dog or the Cat;* and thereupon *Sheppard* returned up to the Garret, and having continued there above two Hours, he ventured down a second Time, when he heard a Gentleman take Leave of the Company, and saw the Maid light him down Stairs. As soon as the Maid came back, and had shut the Chamber-Door, he made the best of his way to the Street-Door, unlock'd it, and so made his Escape, about Twelve at Night.

10. PRISON BUILDING

(a) By the early nineteenth century, improvements in prison building and planning were sometimes visible.

Source: J. J. Gurney, *Notes on a Visit made to some of the Prisons in Scotland and the North of England* (1819), pp. 94–7.

This jail [York City] is a new, and in some respects a commodious building, and is kept in a state of great cleanliness by George Rylah, the jailor, and his wife, who also bear the character of real benevolence towards their prisoners.

There is a good day-room, and an airy court-yard for men and women prisoners respectively; but no further classification is attempted. There were at this time but four criminals in the prison; one woman and three men. No regular provision exists in this jail for the employment of the prisoners; but the woman was engaged in needle-work; and one of the men, who was placed in a small room by himself, was carrying on the business of a watch-maker.

The sleeping-cells were well ventilated, and the bedding sufficient. The allowance of food is much too scanty, consisting only of one pound and a half of bread and a pennyworth of milk per day. No firing is allowed, and clothing only in cases of particular necessity. The prisoners have been permitted, at their own request, to sleep two in a cell; but there is abundant accommodation for single sleeping; and we were given to understand that it would be enjoined for the future. The male criminals are ironed.

The debtors' apartments in this prison are remarkably pleasant and commodious, far more so than is usually the case. The chaplain gives attendance twice in the week.

THE HOUSE OF CORRECTION, which we visited on the same day, and in company with the same gentlemen, also belongs to the City and Liberties of York, and is a place of confinement for petty offenders before trial, as well as for those who have been sentenced to a term of imprisonment. . . . All parts of [this] prison are kept in a state of much neatness and cleanliness.

The prisoners meet for worship twice in the week. They are never ironed. Their allowance of food is the same as that of the prisoners in the jail. . . .

A Committee of Ladies has been formed, with the sanction of the Lord Mayor and Aldermen of York, for the purpose of superintending the females in the two prisons, which I have now described; and it may be hoped that a similar care will be extended over the male prisoners. When this object is effected, and sufficient employment provided, there will be little to prevent either of these prisons from becoming places of reform—prisons tending to the diminution of crime.

11. PENAL REFORM

Prison reform was merely one aspect of a new attitude to crime and to punishment. The position of debtors, indeed, encouraged the Society for the Discharge and Relief of Persons imprisoned for Small Debts (founded in 1772) to examine general abuses, and the harshness (and ineffectiveness) of the laws relating to capital punishment led many reformers, most influenced either by religion or by the ideas of the Enlightenment, to urge drastic changes in the law. Jeremy Bentham was one reformer; Samuel Romilly another. Wilberforce, too, backed their attacks on 'the barbarous system of hanging'. Yet the arguments of other eighteenth-century writers, like the philosopher clergyman, William Paley, were used by opponents of reform. All suggested changes were resisted, and the fruits of the ideas of the reformers belong to the nineteenth century.

(a) *Source:* Letter from Samuel Romilly, 22 May 1781, printed in the introduction to his *Speeches* (1820), vol. L, p. 29.

It [Howard's *State of the Prisons*] is not a book of great literary merit—but it has a merit infinitely superior—it is one of those books which have been rare in all ages of the world—being written with a view only to the good of mankind. The author ... made a visit to every prison and house of correction in England with invincible perseverance and courage; for some of the prisons were so infected with diseases and putrid air that he was obliged to hold a cloth steeped in vinegar to his nostrils during the whole time he remained in them, and to change his clothes the moment he returned. After having devoted so much time to this painful employment here, he set out on a tour through a great part of Holland, Germany and Switzerland, to visit their prisons. What a singular journey!—not to admire the wonders of art and nature—not to visit courts and ape their manners,—but to compare the misery of men in different countries, and to study the arts of mitigating the torments of mankind! What a contrast might be drawn between the painful labour of this man, and the ostentatious sensibility which turns aside from scenes of misery, and with the mockery of a few barren tears, leaves it to seek comfort in its own distresses.

(b) Romilly published his *Observations on the Criminal Law as it Relates to Capital Punishments* in 1810. He received a letter from the distinguished Scottish economist, Dugald Stewart, a leading representative of the Scottish Enlightenment.

Source: Romilly's sons, *Memoirs of the Life of Samuel Romilly* (1840), Vol. II, p. 134.

Kinneil House, June 28, 1810.

My dear Sir,

I have yet to thank you for the very great pleasure I received from your Observations on the Criminal Law of England. On every point which you have there touched upon, your reasonings carried complete conviction to my mind; and however unsuccessful they may have been in accomplishing your object in Parliament, I am satisfied that they must have produced a very strong impression on public opinion. I hope that nothing will discourage you from the prosecution of your arduous undertaking, in which you cannot fail to be seconded by the good wishes of every man of common humanity, whose understanding is not altogether blinded by professional or by political prejudices. . . .

12. THE BILL OF CRIME

Statistical information about eighteenth-century crime is patchy and inadequate. It is possible, however, to obtain information from writers like Howard and Colquhoun and from early nineteenth-century retrospective enquiries.

(a) *Source:* Parliamentary Papers, *Report of the Select Committee on Criminal Laws* (1819), pp. 135ff. (See table on p. 392.)

(b) The following is the breakdown of the 1785 totals of 97 executions. Note how they confirm foreigners' impressions that the number of murders in England was very small, far lower than on the continent.

Source: Ibid., p. 148.

Burglary and Housebreaking	43
Forgery	4
Horse stealing	4
Larceny on a navigable river	5
Murder	1
Personating others to obtain prize money	2
Robbery on the highway and other places	31
Unlawfully returning from transportation	4
Various	3
Total	97

(c) Patrick Colquhoun, a London magistrate, tried to make an estimate of the indigent and criminal population.

Source: P. Colquhoun, *Treatise on Indigence* (1806), pp. 38–43.

1. *Indigent persons* already stated to be the objects of parochial relief   1,040,716

2. *Mendicants,* comprising *indigent and distressed beggars, sturdy beggars, trampers,* persons pretending to have been *in the army and navy,* lame

NUMBER OF PERSONS CAPITALLY CONVICTED AND EXECUTED
IN LONDON AND MIDDLESEX, 1749–99

	Capital Convictions	Executions		Capital Convictions	Executions
1749	61	44	1776	80	38
1750	84	56	1777	63	32
1751	85	63	1778	81	33
1752	52	47	1779	60	23
1753	57	41	1780	94	50
1754	50	34	1781	90	40
1755	39	21	1782	108	45
1756	30	13	1783	173	53
1757	37	26	1784	153	56
1758	32	20	1785	151	97
1759	15	6	1786	127	50
1760	14	10	1787	113	92
1761	22	17	1788	83	25
1762	25	15	1789	97	26
1763	61	32	1790	67	33
1764	52	31	1791	83	34
1765	41	26	1792	89	24
1766	39	20	1793	58	16
1767	49	22	1794	71	7
1768	54	27	1795	49	22
1769	71	24	1796	93	22
1770	91	49	1797	81	10
1771	60	34	1798	82	19
1772	79	37	1799	72	24
1773	101	32			
1774	87	32			
1775	74	46			

and maimed, travelling all over the country, and using many devices to excite compassion, estimated, including their children at about 50,000

3. *Vagrants*, under which description are to be included gypsies, and another race of vagabonds who imitate their manners . . . wandering about the country with jackasses, sleeping in the open air under hedges, and in huts and tents, loving idleness better than work, and stealing wherever opportunities offer. . . . 20,000

4. *Idle and immoral persons*, who are able to work, but who work only occasionally, who neglect their families, and either desert them totally, or loiter away their time idly in alehouses and half support them leaving the deficiency to be scantily made up by the parishes—this class of depraved characters are pretty numerous. . . 10,000

5. *Lewd and immoral women*, who live wholly or partly by prostitution. . . . 100,000

6. *Persons described in the statute of 17 Geo. II as rogues and vagabonds*, comprising *wandering players* of interludes at fairs, *mountebanks, stage dancers* and *tumblers* . . . *showmen, ballad singers, minstrels* with hurdy gurdies and hand organs, etc., *vagabonds* with dancing bears and monkeys, *low gamblers* with E O tables, wheels of fortune, and other seductive implements of gaming; *duffers* with waistcoat pieces and other smuggled goods, and *petty chapmen* and *low Jews* . . . pretended *horse dealers* without licences exposing stolen horses for sale. All these different classes of vagabonds visit almost every fair and horse-race in the country and live generally by fraud and deception. Foreign vagabonds, who also wander around the country, pretending to sell pictures, but who are also dealers in obscene books and prints, which they introduce into boarding schools,

CC

on pretence of selling prints of flowers, whereby the youth of both sexes are corrupted, while at the same time some of these wanderers are suspected of being employed by the enemy as spies. . . .   10,000

7. *Lottery vagrants*, or persons employed in procuring insurances during the drawing of the lotteries. . . .   10,000

8. *Criminal offenders*, comprising highway robbers, foot pad robbers, burglars, house breakers, pick pockets, horse stealers, sheep stealers, stealers of hogs and cattle, deer stealers, common thieves, petty thieves, occasional thieves who cannot resist temptations   80,000

Total number presumed to live chiefly or wholly on the labour of others   1,320,716

CHAPTER XIII

Going to War

Colonel Southwell has sold his regiment for £5000 to Colonel Hansom of the Guards.

(G. F. LUTTRELL's *Diary*, 12 June 1708)

Like other amphibious animals, we must come occasionally on shore; but the water is more properly our element, and in it, like them, as we find our greatest security, so we exert our greatest force.

(HENRY ST. JOHN, Viscount BOLINGBROKE,
Idea of a Patriot King, 1749)

Reason frowns on War's unequal game.

(SAMUEL JOHNSON, *Reason Frowns on War*, 1748)

Come cheer up, my lads, 'tis to glory we steer,
To add something new to this wonderful year.

(DAVID GARRICK, *Harlequin's Invasion*, 1759)

The progress of wealth and the application of productive labour must indispose the lower orders from entering into a military life.

(General MAITLAND, 1804)

1. RECRUITMENT

The Royal Navy was very much the senior service during the eighteenth century. Great pride in its achievements did not mean, however, that the method of recruitment by impressment was not extremely unpopular on occasion. There was no conscription for the Army, and in peace-time recruitment was by promise of bounty and sometimes threat of kidnapping. In time of war, bounties increased and magistrates were often given power to enlist idle or disorderly persons. The idea of a regular standing army remained extremely unpopular, and there was also (see below, pp. 419ff.) marked civilian dislike of billeting troops.

(a) *Source:* Note in the *Daily Courant*, 4 March 1703.

Hull, 1 March. Last week a Lieutenant came hither with a Press Gang, and had so good Success, that he soon Glean'd up a considerable number; but having no vessel to put them on board, he turn'd them into an upper Room in the Town Gaol, and on Saturday they broke out through the top of the House and Escap'd.

(b) *An Apology for the life of Bampfylde—Moore Carew* (n.d.). Carew was born in 1693, the son of the Rector of Bickley, Devon. Impressment of a rough kind was used to secure merchant seamen also.

Bampfylde then return'd back to *Torrington*, and calling on several Friends in his Way, steers directly for *Exeter*, where, having visited his old Friends, he leaves his Wife, and takes a Walk to *Topsham*. *Alas! little did he think this Walk would end in a long and cruel Separation from his Friends and Country, little did he imagine that in the Land of Freedom and Justice, he should be siezed upon by the cruel Grasp of lawless Power; tho' poor he thought himself under the Protection of the Laws, and as such, liable to no Punishment till they inflicted it.* How far he thought right in this let the Sequel tell: Going down to *Topsham*, and walking upon the Key there, enjoying the Beauties of a fine Evening meditating no Harm, and unsuspecting Danger, he was accosted by Merchant *D- - - - -y*, accompanied with several Captains of Vessels, in some such Words as these, *Ha! Mr.* Bampfylde *you are come in a right Time, as you came Home for your own Pleasure you shall go over for mine.* They then laid Hands on *Bampfylde*, who found it it in vain to resist, as he was overpower'd with Numbers, he, therefore, desir'd to be carried before some Magistrate, but this was not hearkened to, for they forc'd him aboard a Boat without the Presence or Authority of any Officer of Justice, not so much as suffering him to take Leave of his Wife, or acquaint her with his Misfortune, tho' he begg'd the Favour almost with Tears.

(c) Report in *St. James's Chronicle*, 4–6 May 1790.

The report of the number pressed in the river on Tuesday night was delivered to the Lords of the Admiralty yesterday morning, which amounted to about 1500 taken in Wapping, and in Southwark, &c., more than 600; amounting in the whole to upwards of 2100 men, besides those at the different seaport towns, reports of which were not received.

Four tenders went down the river yesterday morning, crowded with impressed men, to be shipped on board a vessel of war lying in Long-reach, ready to receive them. The same tenders were expected up again with the return of the tide, upon the same errand.

(d) *Source:* Recruiting Order and Notice of Bounty (1715), printed in C. M. Clode, *The Military Forces of the Crown* (1869), vol. II, pp. 580–1.

THESE are to authorise you by Beat of Drum or otherwise to raise Volunteers in any County or part of this Our Kingdom of Great Britain, for a Regiment of Foot under your Command for Our Service, to consist of Ten Companies, of Two Sergeants, Two Corporals, One Drummer, and Forty Private Soldiers, including the Widows' Men in each Company. And when you shall have listed twenty Men fit for Service in any of said Companies, you are to give noticc to two of Our Justices of the Peace of the Town or County wherein the same are, who are hereby authorised and required to view the said Men and certify the day of their so doing; from which day the said Twenty Men and the Commissioned and Non-Commissioned Officers of such Companies are to enter into Our pay.

(e) *Source:* A Recruiting Order of 1782, printed in M.S. Atholl Forbes (ed.), *Curiosities of a Scots Charter Chest* (1897), p. 302.

HIS MAJESTY'S FIRST ROYAL REGIMENT
OF
FOOT GUARDS

The greatest OPPORTUNITY *ever known for* YOUNG SCOTCHMEN *to raise themselves and Families.*

YOUR Duty is a constant Pleasure, being only to attend and Guard his MAJESTY's Person at the Palace, and to the Theatres, Opera-Houses, Masquerades, and Reviews of different Regiments.

When off Duty, you are under no Restraint; there is no Roll-calling; you may dress as you please, go where you please any where within 10 miles round London, and follow any Profession you please; which being constantly in London, is of great consequence to you, the Wages there being about three times more than anywhere else.

Your Pay is 10d. *per* day, and Subsistence 4s. *per* week, and 15s. a-year of QUEEN's Bounty, with excellent Quarters, a good Room to yourself, with a Lock and Key, with the full Use of the House, Coal and Candle, and 5 Pints of choice Beer or good Cyder every Day, which the Landlord must furnish you by Act of Parliament.

It is well known you cannot be draughted to any other Regiment.

So great an Opportunity as this cannot be supposed to last long; therefore, before it is too late, let all handsome young Men, whose Hearts beat at the Sound of the Drum, and are above mean Employments, inquire after the Party commanded by Captain DICK, where you shall have the Honour of being made one of His MAJESTY's own First Regiment of FOOT GUARDS.

The BOUNTY *is* THREE GUINEAS *and a* CROWN.

Lads from 16 to 19 are taken 5 Feet 5 inches and an Half; from that to 25 years of Age, at 5 feet 6 Inches and an Half.

N.B. *The Bringer of a good Recruit shall receive* ONE GUINEA, *by applying to Serjeant* SMITH *at the Sign of the Marquis of Granby's Head, Lady Milton's Dike, Canongate, Edinburgh.*

2. OFFICERS AND MEN

During the eighteenth century, Army commissions could be bought for cash and were frequently held for social reasons by the most unsuitable persons. Discipline was often harsh, and other ranks were treated toughly. Punishment was severe. In the Royal Navy it was easier to secure promotion, given ability, and many eighteenth-century admirals (Hood and Nelson, for instance) started as midshipmen. At the same time, 'influence' was the main factor guiding the chances of promotion, and life at sea was often hard.

(a) *Source:* An account of the rank-and-file in the Army from *The London Spy* (1703).

A Foot Soldier is commonly a Man, who for the sake of wearing a Sword, and the Honour of being term'd a Gentleman, is coax'd from a Handicraft Trade, whereby he might Live comfortably to bear Arms for his King and Country, whereby he has the hopes of nothing but to Live Starvingly. His Lodging is as near Heaven as his Quarters can raise him; and his Soul generally is as near Hell as a Profligate Life can sink him. Scars tho' got in Drunken Quarrels, he makes Badges of his Bravery; and tells you they were Wounds receiv'd in some Engagement, tho' perhaps given him for his Sawciness. He's one that loves Fighting no more than other Men; tho' perhaps a dozen of Drink and an Affront will make him draw his Sword. . . . If he spends Twenty years in Wars, and lives to be Forty, perhaps he may get a Halbert; and if he Survives Three Score an Hospital. The best end he can expect to make is to Die in the Bed of Honour; and the greatest Living Marks of his Bravery, to recommend him at once to the World's Praise and Pity are Crippled Limbs, with which I shall leave him to beg a better Lively Hood.

(b) Officers raised their own regiments when they could. The following extract describes Henry William Paget's (later Marquess of Anglesey) reaction to the news of the outbreak of war with revolutionary France in 1793.

Source: Memorandum by Paget, quoted in The Marquess of Anglesey, *One Leg* (1961), p. 41.

The moment I heard it, I jumped upon my horse and galloped to Ivy Bridge, from whence I rode post all night without stopping to Hertford Bridge. Then I dined and by chaise into London. I instantly wrote to Mr. Pitt [the Prime Minister] to beg to see him. He appointed the next day. I told him my anxiety to raise a Regiment of Cavalry. He received me most kindly, but told me Cavalry was not then wanted; that I might raise a Battn. of Infantry and have the rank of Lieut.-Colonel. I instantly closed with him [and] got my father's leave, who generously contributed everything that was necessary to effect the object. . . . Contrary to the practice of the day, my father was put to great expense in raising the Regiment. Many Commissions were given away, which in other hands would have been sold.

(c) One of the most vivid accounts of the life and duties of a non-commissioned officer is that of William Cobbett, who served in this capacity in Canada.

Source: W. Reitzel (ed.), *The Progress of a Ploughboy to a Seat in Parliament* (1933), pp. 31ff.

While I was Corporal I was made clerk to the regiment. In a very short time, the whole of business in that way fell into my hands; and, at the end of about a year, neither adjutant, paymaster, or quarter-master, could move an inch without my assistance. . . . Then I became Sergeant-Major to the regiment, which brought me into close contact at every hour, with the whole of the epaulet gentry, whose profound and surprising ignorance I discovered in a twinkling. The military part of the regiment's affairs fell under my care. In early life, [I] contracted the blessed habit of husbanding well my time. To this more than any other thing, I owed my very extraordinary promotion in the army. I was always ready. . . . My custom was this: to get up, in summer, at daylight, and in winter, at four o'clock; shave, dress, even to the putting of my sword over my shoulder and having my sword lying on the table before, me, ready to hang by my side. Then I ate a bit of cheese, or pork, and bread. Then I prepared my report, which was filled up as fast as the companies brought me in the materials. After this I had an hour or two to read, before the time came for any duty out of doors, unless when the regiment or part of it went out to exercise in the morning. When this was the case, and the matter was left to me, I always had it on the ground in such time as that the bayonets glistened in the rising sun, a sight which gave me delight. . . . If the officers were to go out, eight or ten o'clock was the hour, sweating the men in the heat of the day, breaking in upon the time for cooking their dinner, putting all things out of order and all men out of humour. When I was commander, the men had a long day of leisure before them. . . . About this time, the new discipline, as it was called, was sent out to us in little books, which were to be studied by the officers of each regiment, and the rules of which were to be immediately conformed to. Though any old woman might have written such a book; though it was excessively foolish from beginning to end; still, it was to be complied with, it ordered and commanded a total change. To make this change was left to me, while not a single officer in the regiment paid the least attention to the matter;

so that, when the time came for the annual review, I had to give lectures of instruction to the officers themselves, the Colonel not excepted; and, for several of them, I had to make out, upon large cards, which they bought for the purpose, little plans of the regiment, together with lists of the words of command, which they had to give in the field. . . . But I had a very delicate part to act with those gentry; for, while I despised them for their gross ignorance and their vanity, and hated them for their drunkenness and rapacity, I was fully sensible of their power.

(d) Cobbett's attitudes may well have been quite distinctive. More frequently, officers complained about the inferiority of their men. Wellington's despatches, for instance, reveal how difficult it was to control other ranks in the Army; the extract which follows shows how reluctant some other ranks were to serve.

Source: Letter to Viscount Castlereagh, 31 May 1809, printed in J. Gurwood, *Selection from Wellington's Despatches* (1841), p. 263.

The army behaved terribly ill. They are a rabbble who cannot bear success any more than Sir J. Moore's army could bear failure. I am endeavouring to tame them; but if I should not succeed, I must make an official complaint of them, and send one or two corps home in disgrace. They plunder in all directions.

(e) On the social distinctions between officers and men in the Royal Navy and the relations between them, there is a prodigious literature. The following extract dealing with the last part of the period covered in this book has more general reference: it refers to 'social space' on a frigate, not one frigate, but, in the author's words, to 'all the frigates that ever were built, or ever will'.

Source: Passage in the *Navy at Home* (1831) quoted by C. N. Parkinson, *Portsmouth Point* (1948), an indispensable book for further reading.

The deck then was just five feet five inches high to the beams . . . by some thirty-six or forty feet wide from side to side, and required a sort of reverential position when walking. . . . Those next the main-mast (opposite to which was situate the berth, parlour or drawing-room of the mids) might be seen thick-studded with the hats and belts of the marines in all stages of

pipe-claying polishing, and brushing, together with their other
accoutrements, *dangling in mid air* from their batons, while the
soldiers themselves filled up the space beneath, busy as bees in
the said operation; two exact rows of hanging tables garnished
either side; and the rest of more irregular jacks filled up a
confused distance into the very bows. Opposite the table of the
marines lay a gulf called the main hatchway—this yawned
terrible, displaying huge cables coiled in their tiers, and winding
upwards to daylight . . . in the middle, amidships, just before
the spot, stood, filing and hammering, two grim personages,
who might have passed for a pair of the cyclops. . . . Immediately behind all this, and on the opposite side, balancing
the *parlour* of the midshipmen, lay constructed the cabin of the
captain's steward—a person of infinite consequence. . . . Behind
this temple, on the same side, lived two quiet creatures, of
little note in the neighbourhood, and considered a couple of
old bores by the whole set of bloods . . . the *gunner* and the
carpenter of the ship—warrant officers and men of note and
authority on deck, but wholly insignificant at home. . . . They
never gained ground . . . except [with] the good-natured
scribe Toby, considered an amphibious animal whose bureau or
office, lay exactly opposite, and separated only from the mids
by the cabin of the boatswain. . . . We have now comprehended
the whole of the steerage—of that space included between
the hallowed partition, or *bulkhead*, which separated the awful
cabins of the lieutenants, and the foremost verge of the mids,
and captain's stewards' cabins on each side, between which
came down in mighty volume, the mainmast, and all the
pumps, great shores or stanchions, etc., forming a sort of thick
wood or forest—the scene of many skirmishes between the
belligerents in night attacks.

(g) There are many pictures of captains. The following extract
satirically describes an early eighteenth-century captain.

Source: Ned Ward, *The Wooden World Dissected* (1706).

He's a *Leviathan,* or rather a Kind of Sea God, whom the
poor Tars worship as the *Indians* do the Devil, more through
Fear than Affection. . . . The great Cabin in the *Sanctum
Sanctorum* he inhabits; from this all Mortals are excluded by a

Marine, with a brandish'd Sword. . . . It must be a great
change of Weather indeed, when he deigns to walk the Quarter-
Deck; for such a Prostitution of his Presence, he thinks, weakens
his Authority, and makes his Worship less reverenc'd by the
Ship's Crew. . . . Once in a Moon, he invites some Marine
Lieutenant to taste of his Bounty; but the poor Gentleman
finds his Dinner bestow'd rather as a Charity than an honourable Entertainment for upon his Entry he finds him aforehand
seated at Table, with as stiff an Air, as if he expected your
coming to kiss his Toe, for no Pope on Earth can look greater.

3. SERVICE

The extracts which follow do no more than pick out certain
aspects of military and naval service, emphasizing contrasts of
experience—boredom and valour; comfort and hardship; security
and danger. They are supplemented by extracts in later sections,
dealing with specific campaigns.

(a) *Source:* An account of the Royal Naval Hospital at Greenwich
in the *Diary of Sophie in London, in 1786,* pp. 250ff.

To-day we went to Greenwich. . . . At the outset the weather
was lovely, but changed to heavy rain during the journey, so
that there was a dense curtain of fog on both sides of the coach.
. . . To our joy it cleared up a little around Greenwich, so
that the majestic pile was visible from afar, rising sheer above
quantities of ships' masts; but when we alighted it began
raining again, so that my walk through the great peristyle
was spoiled.

The six buildings of this hospital, which stand detached,
facing the Thames, are not only large and extensive in character,
but of grand and noble structure, creating the impression of
summer palaces, which so many great lords had planned to
build here, rather than of a residence of sick sailors.

The glorious river, where battleships and merchantmen,
built in the neighbouring Deptford, always lie at anchor, and
the Woolwich cannon foundry adjacent, must bring back to
the two thousand old seamen supported here pleasant memories

of early days, about which they spin yarns to the one hundred and forty boys being trained for marine service.

Their dormitories are very pleasant; large, light and lofty, with cubicles containing glass windows on the side, where each has his own bed, small table, chair, wardrobe, tea and smoking outfit which he can lock up. No humanitarian with a philosophical turn of mind could be indifferent to the way in which they decorate their cubicles: a number of them have sea and land charts, with the voyages they have made marked out on them, or spots where storms have been overcome or battles fought, where they have lost an arm or a leg, or conquered an enemy ship, and so on; others have stuck figures of every nationality on cardboard, others of strange beasts in foreign lands, while a number have collected books in several languages with which they amuse themselves. . . .

Everything is spotless. Each man has two white shirts weekly, and a hundred and four women are employed to do the laundry and keep the place clean.

(b) A letter from the Lower Deck (1805), printed in C. Lloyd (ed.), *The Englishman and The Sea* (1946), pp. 121–2.

HONOURED FATHER,

This comes to tell you I am alive and hearty except three fingers; but that's not much, it might have been my head. I told brother Tom I should like to see a great battle, and I have seen one, and we have peppered the Combined rarely (off Trafalgar); and for the matter of that, they fought us pretty tightish for French and Spanish. Three of our mess are killed, and four more of us winged. But to tell you the truth of it, when the game began, I wished myself at Warnborough with my plough again; but when they had given us one duster, and I found myself snug and tight, I set to in good earnest, and thought no more about being killed than if I were at Murrell Green Fair, and I was presently as busy and as black as a collier. How my fingers got knocked overboard I don't know, but off they are, and I never missed them till I wanted them. You see, by my writing, it was my left hand, so I can write to you and fight for my King yet. We have taken a rare parcel of ships, but the wind is so rough we cannot bring

them home, else I should roll in money, so we are busy smashing
'em, and blowing 'em up wholesale.

Our dear Admiral Nelson is killed! so we have paid pretty
sharply for licking 'em. I never set eyes on him, for which I
am both sorry and glad; for, to be sure, I should like to have
seen him—but then, all the men in our ship who have seen
him are such soft toads, they have done nothing but blast their
eyes, and cry, ever since he was killed. God bless you! chaps
that fought like the devil, sit down and cry like a wench.

(c) Early scenes of army life began, as in the twentieth century,
with a visit to the barber, but the recruits were much younger.

Source: J. Shipp, *Memoirs of the Military Career of John Shipp* (1843).

On the following morning I was taken to a barber's, and
deprived of my curly brown locks. My hair curled beautifully,
but in a minute my poor little head was nearly bald, except
a small patch behind, which was reserved for a future operation.
I was then paraded to the tailor's shop, and deprived of my
new clothes—coat, leathers, and hat—for which I received in
exchange, red jacket, red waistcoat, red pantaloons, and red
foraging-cap. The change, or metamorphosis, was so complete,
that I could scarcely imagine it to be the same dapper little
fellow. I was exceedingly tall for a boy of ten years of age;
but, notwithstanding this, my clothes were much too large, my
sleeves were two or three inches over my hands, or rather
longer than my fingers; and the whole hung on me, to use a
well-known expression, like a purser's shirt on a handspike.
My pride was humbled, my spirits dropped, and I followed the
drum-major, hanging my head like a felon going to the place
of execution.

(d) If that was how army life began, it could end with a different
kind of misery.

Source: Petition from the Essex Justices to Lord Godolphin, 1709,
printed in Edwards (ed.), *English History from Essex Sources*, (1952),
vol. I, p. 128.

During the war with France many poor, sick, lame, maimed
and disabled soldiers have been weekly brought over in the
packet-boats from Holland to Harwich, which have been

relieved and conveyed with horses, carts and waggons from there to Bow in the County of Middlesex, being about three score miles. The charges of relieving and conveying these passengers hath been annually so very great that the monies yearly raised in the said county, pursuant to the said statutes, have not been sufficient to bear the charge. . . . We petitioners humbly pray that such future provision may be made for relief and conveying such poor soldier passengers as should be necessary for their subsistence.

4. FIGHTING IN BRITAIN

So long as there were disputes about the Hanoverian succession to the throne, there was always a threat to national stability from inside the country. The last great Stuart challenge reached its climax with an invasion of England (on 'Black Friday' the Prince reached Derby) and ended with the savage battle of Culloden in April 1746. In the late century there were threats of a different kind from Ireland (the United Irishmen's Rebellion, 1798), and in 1803 as in 1759, there was an invasion threat to England itself, which never materialized.

(a) *Source:* A letter of 16 April 1746 in the Mildmay Archives, printed in *English History from Essex Sources*, Edwards (ed.), vol. I, p. 147.

The Duke attacked near Culloden House, which is a small distance from Inverness. The rebels were upwards of 8,000 men, the King's army not exceeding 7,000. The rebels made a furious attack on one wing of the King's army, but that not succeeding they immediately turned their back and fled with the utmost precipitation. Of them there was killed and taken prisoners about 4,000; on the King's side not one hundred men killed. By my Lord Robert Ker, brother to my Lord Ancram, was there killed gallantly for the King and in defence and the laws and liberties of his country. So fell the handsomest and finest young fellow in Great Britain by the hands of the execrable villains. The same day my Lord Ancram killed four of my rebels with his own hand, and had his pistol at the head of my Lord Kilmarnock, who fell down on his knees and begged his life, so he took him prisoner.

(b) Punishment of the Stuart supporters in 1745 and 1746 was harsh, and a patriotic note was struck in all the broadsides.

Source: 'A New Song', printed in A. S. Turberville, *English Men and Manners in the Eighteenth Century* (1929), p. 37.

> He [Cumberland] cross'd the River Spey
> a battle did Ensue
> but few were left alive
> Rebellion to pursue. . . .
> Now Peace and Plenty
> amongst us all will Reign,
> *In* spite of a Pretender, Dupe
> to France and Spain,
> French Soupes we do dispise
> it suiteth not our blood,
> Brown bear and good rost beef
> is holsome British food

(c) At the time of the Irish Rebellion, there was perhaps a little more evidence of compassion.

Source: G. B., *Narrative of a Private Soldier in one of His Majesty's Regiments of Foot* (1819).

As our regiment had not been in the country during the outbreaking of the rebellion, we had received no injury to provoke our resentment. . . . The only loss the regiment sustained during this service, occurred one morning, when we were pursuing a body of rebels among the mountains. One of our men having fallen behind through weakness, was met by two or three rebels in women's clothes, carrying pails of milk on their heads, as if returning from milking. They offered him a drink, and while he was drinking, one of them seized his musket, and after threatening to kill him, they allowed him to proceed to the regiment, with the loss of his musket and ammunition. The sight of so many houses and villages, and parts of towns, burned and destroyed, and the great number of women and children who were in a destitute state, because their husbands and fathers were either gone with the rebels, or were fled for safety, touched most powerfully the sensibilities of our hearts, and diffused a feeling of generous sympathy through the regiment. It so happened at that time, that we had newly received a more than ordinary balance of arrears of pay, so that every man was in possession of money, less or more; and although we were very fond of milk, because we had been living long on salt provisions, before our arrival in Ireland, yet there were none, who would accept of a draught of milk for nothing, but would pay its price. And if the people of the house would not take payment, they would give the value of what milk they received, to the children.

(d) The threat of invasion of England in 1803 produced far sharper and more primitive reactions. Patriotism was everywhere the order of the day.

Source: Handbill in the British Museum collection of squibs, printed in J. Ashton, *The Dawn of the Nineteenth Century in England* (1906), pp. 80–1.

FELLOW CITIZENS, Bonaparte threatens to invade us; he promises to enrich his soldiers with our property, to glut their lust with our Wives and Daughters. To incite his Hell Hounds to execute his vengence, he has *sworn* to permit everything. Shall we Merit by our Cowardice the titles of sordid Shop-keepers, Cowardly Scum, and Dastardly Wretches, which in every proclamation he gives us? No! we will loudly give him *the lie*: let us make ourselves ready to shut our Shops, and march to give him the reception his malicious calumnies deserve. Let every brave young fellow instantly join the *Army* or *Navy*; and those among us who, from being married, or so occupied in business, cannot, let us join some Volunteer Corps, where we may learn the use of arms, and yet attend our business. Let us encourage recruiting in our neighbourhood, and loudly silence the tongues of those whom Ignorance or Defection (if any such there be) lead them to doubt of the attempt to invade or inveigh against the measures taken to resist it. By doing this, and feeling confidence in ourselves, we shall probably prevent the attempt.

5. FIGHTING IN EUROPE

There were many battles in Europe in the eighteenth century even after Marlborough's campaigns were over and a reaction had set in against far-reaching European commitments.

(a) *Source:* An account of the battle of Dettingen (1743) by James Wolfe in a letter to his father. This was the last battle in which a British king (George II) took part. Printed in C. H. Gardiner, *Centurions of a Century* (1910).

Höchst, 4 July 1743

This is the first time I have been able, or have had the least time to write. . . . The fatigue I had the day we faught, and the day after, made me very much out of order, and I was obliged to keep to my tent for two days. Bleeding was a great service to me, and I am now as well as ever. The enemy was drawn out this se'n night between a wood and the river, near a little village called Dettingen, in five lines—two of foot and three of horse. The cannons on both sides began to ply about till one o'clock in the morning, and we were exposed to the fire of them (said to be above fifty pieces) for near three hours, a great part of which planked us terribly from the other side of the water. The French were all the while drawn up in sight of this side. About twelve o'clock we marched towards them; they advanced likewise, and, as near as I can guess, the fight began about one. . . . [There were three attacks.] The third and last attack was made by the Foot on both sides. We advanced towards one another, our men in high spirits, and very impatient for fighting, being elated with beating the French Horse, part of which advanced towards us, while the rest attacked our Horse, but were driven back by the great fire we gave them. The Major and I (for we had neither Colonel nor Lt-Colonel) before they came near, were employed in begging and ordering the men not to fire at too great a distance, but to keep it if the enemy should come near us; but to little purpose. . . . [Eventually] the French . . . marched close to us in sore disorder and made us give way a little, particularly ours and two or three more regiments, which were in the hottest of it. However, we soon rallied again, and attacked them with great fury, which gained us a complete victory and forced the enemy

DD

to leave in great haste. . . . His Majesty was in the midst of
the fight; and the Duke behaved as bravely as a man could do.
He had a musket shot through the calf of his leg. I had several
times the honour of speaking with him just before the battle
began and was often afraid of his being dashed to pieces by
cannon balls. He gave his orders with a great deal of calmness,
and seemed quite unconcerned. The soldiers were in high
delight to have him near them. . . . I sometimes thought that
I had lost poor Neb when I saw arms, legs and heels cut off
close by him. He is called the 'old Soldier' and very deservedly.
. . . They talk of a second battle soon. . . . Your dutiful and
affectionate son, J. Wolfe.

(b) The most prolonged fighting in Europe was carried on during
the bitter struggle against Napoleon, which ended at Waterloo.

Source: An account of a campaign in the Peninsular War by a
young soldier, Kincaid, printed in W. H. Fitchett (ed.), *Wellington's
Men, Some Soldier Autobiographies* (1900), pp. 49ff.

March 15 [1811]—We overtook the enemy a little before
dark this afternoon. They were drawn up behind the Ceira, at
Fez d'Aronce, with their rearguard, under Marshal Ney,
imprudently posted on our side of the river, a circumstance
which Lord Wellington took immediate advantage of; and,
by a furious attack, dislodged them in such confusion that they
blew up the bridge before half of their own people had time
to get over. Those who were thereby left behind, not choosing
to put themselves to the pain of being shot, took to the river,
which received them so hospitably that few of them ever
quitted it.

About the middle of the action, I observed some inexperi-
enced light troops rushing up a deep roadway to certain
destruction, and ran to warn them out of it, but I only arrived
in time to partake the reward of their indiscretion, for I was
instantly struck with a musket-ball above the left ear, which
deposited me at full length in the mud.

I know not how long I lay insensible, but, on recovering,
my first feeling was for my head, to ascertain if any part of it
was still standing, for it appeared to me as if nothing remained
above the mouth; but, after repeated applications of all my

fingers and thumbs to the doubtful parts, I at length proved to myself satisfactorily, that it had rather increased than diminished by the concussion; and jumping on my legs, and hearing, by the whistling of the balls from both sides, that the rascals who had got me into the scrape had been driven back and left me there, I snatched my cap, which had saved my life, and which had been spun off my head to the distance of ten or twelve yards, and joined them a short distance in the rear, when one of them, a soldier of the 60th, came and told me that an officer of ours had been killed a short time before, pointing to the spot where I myself had fallen, and that he had tried to take his jacket off, but that the advance of the enemy had prevented him. I told him that I was the one that had been killed, and that I was deucedly obliged to him for his kind intentions, while I felt still more so to the enemy for their timely advance, otherwise, I have no doubt, but my friend would have taken a fancy to my trousers also, for I found that he had absolutely unbuttoned my jacket.

There is nothing so gratifying to frail mortality as a good dinner when most wanted and least expected. It was perfectly dark before the action finished, but, on going to take advantage of the fires which the enemy had evacuated, we found their kettles in full operation, and every man's mess of biscuit lying beside them, in stockings, as was the French mode of carrying them; and it is needless to say how unceremoniously we proceeded to do the honours of the feast. . . .

(d) Kincaid was present also at Waterloo.

Source: Account of the last stages of the battle in *ibid.* pp. 134ff.

I shall never forget the scene which the field of battle presented about seven in the evening. I felt weary and worn out, less from fatigue than anxiety. Our division, which had stood upwards of five thousand men at the commencement of the battle, had gradually dwindled down into a solitary line of skirmishers. The 27th Regiment were lying literally dead, in square, a few years behind us. My horse had received another shot through the leg, and one through the flap of the saddle, which lodged in his body, sending him a step beyond the pension-list. The smoke still hung so thick about us that we could see nothing. I walked a little way to each flank, to endeavour to get a glimpse of what was going on; but nothing met my eye except the mangled remains of men and horses, and I was obliged to return to my post as wise as I went.

I had never yet heard of a battle in which everybody was killed; but this seemed likely to be an exception, as all were going by turns. We got excessively impatient under the tame similitude of the later part of the process, and burned with desire to have a last thrust at our respective *vis-à-vis*; for however desperate our affairs were, we still had the satisfaction of seeing that theirs were worse. . . .

Presently a cheer, which we knew to be British, commenced far to the right, and made every one prick up his ears—it was Lord Wellington's long-wished-for orders to advance; it gradually approached, growing louder as it drew near—we took it up by instinct, charged through the hedge down upon the old knoll, sending our adversaries flying at the point of the bayonet. Lord Wellington galloped up to us at the instant, and our men began to cheer him; but he called out, 'No cheering my lads, but forward, and complete your victory!'

This movement had carried us clear of the smoke; and, to people who had been for so many hours enveloped in darkness, in the midst of destruction, and naturally anxious about the result of the day, the scene which now met the eye conveyed a feeling of more exquisite gratification than can be conceived. It was a fine summer's evening, just before sunset. The French were flying in one confused mass. British lines were seen in close pursuit, and in admirable order, as far as the eye could reach to the right, while the plain to the left was filled with Prussians. The enemy made one last attempt at a stand on the rising ground to our right of La Belle Alliance; but a charge from General Adams's brigade again threw them into a state of confusion, which was now inextricable, and their ruin was complete. Artillery, baggage, and everything belonging to them fell into our hands. After pursuing them until dark, we halted about two miles beyond the field of battle, leaving the Prussians to follow up the victory.

This was the last, the greatest, and the most uncomfortable heap of glory that I ever had a hand in . . . . We were, take us all in all, a very bad army. Our foreign auxiliaries, who constituted more than half of our numerical strength, with some exceptions, were little better than a raw militia—a body without a soul. . . .

If Lord Wellington had been at the head of his old Peninsula army, I am confident that he would have swept his opponents off the face of the earth immediately after their first attack; but, with such a heterogeneous mixture under his command, he was obliged to submit to a longer day.

The field of battle next morning presented a frightful scene of carnage; it seemed as if the world had tumbled to pieces and three-fourths of everything destroyed in the wreck.

6. FIGHTING FOR EMPIRE

Despite the loss of American colonies in the wars which ended in 1783, Britain added substantially to her overseas possessions in the eighteenth century. Both soldiers and sailors had to fight in strange conditions, often against strange foes, sometimes against European adversaries.

(a) *Source:* Memoirs of the Sergeant-Major of General Hopson's Grenadiers, printed in the Appendix of Part II of A. G. Doughty, *The Siege of Quebec and the Battle of the Plains of Abraham* (1901).

8 July 1759. The 8th, we landed on Quebeck-Shore, without any Interception, and marched up the River about two Miles; when the Louisbourg Grenadiers being order'd out to get Fascines, they had scarce set down to take a small Refreshment, and detach'd a small Party of Rangers to guard the Skirts of the Wood, before a large party of Indians surrounded them, kill'd and scalp'd 13, wounded the Captain-Lieutenant and 9 Privates; they likewise kill'd and wounded 14 of the Royal American, wounded 2 of the 22d and one of the 40th Regiment: we got only 3 Prisoners, and kill'd 2 of the Savages.

(b) Campaigns in India took place on both a large and a small scale.

Source: J. Shipp, *Memoirs of the Military Career of John Shipp* (1843).

About the 18th of December [1804] we took up a position

before the fort of Deig, and in two days after broke ground against it. The two companies to which I belonged led the column, carrying tools for working. The night was as dark as pitch, and bitterly cold. Secrecy was the great object of our mission, and we slowly approached the vicinity of the fort, steering our course towards a small village about eight hundred yards from the spot, where we halted under shelter from their guns. This village had been set on fire two days before, and its inmates compelled to take shelter in the fort. Small parties were dispatched in search of eligible ground for trenches, and within breaking distance. I was dispatched alone through the desolate village to see what was on the other side. I was yet but a novice in soldiering, and . . . I had no great fancy for this job; but an order could not be disobeyed; so off I marched, my ears extended wide to catch the most distant sound. I struck into a wide street, and, marching on tiptoe, passed two or three solitary bullocks, who were dying for want of food. These startled me for the moment, but not another creature could I see. I at one time thought I heard voices, and that I could see a blue light burning on the fort, from which I inferred that I was getting pretty close to it. Just as I had made up my mind that this must be the case, I distinctly heard a voice calling out 'Khon hie' in English, 'Who is there?' I was riveted to the spot, and could not move till the words were repeated; when I stole behind one of the wings of a hut close on my right. Soon afterwards I heard the same man say, 'Quoi tak mea ne deckah' which is 'I am sure I saw somebody'. Another voice answered 'Guddah, Hogah', which signifies 'A Jackass, I suppose', for there were several wandering about. I fully agreed with the gentleman who spoke last, but I was determined to throw off the appellation as quickly as possible, as endeavoring to find my way back . . . I can venture to say that I never ran so fast before in my life.

7. THE HAZARDS AND PRIZES OF SERVICE

War had many hazards—sickness as well as wounds, imprisonment as well as death. It also had prizes, particularly for sailors, and bounties were offered to persuade men to join the Army.

(a) *Source:* S. Ancell, *A Circumstantial Journal of the Long and Tedious Blockade of Gibraltar, from the Twelfth of September, 1779, to the Third Day of February, 1783.*

Yesterday and today they fired incessantly. Our batteries made but a trifling return, as it is almost madness to fire at their works, they being so thickly covered with sand, that our shot finds very little penetration. The enemy continue firing, and seem determined if possible, to batter down all our works. . . . We are really in a dismal situation—between the land and sea fire, we scarce dare close our eyes. On your part you must not expect correct letters, the hurry of times, the noise of mortars, howitzers, cannon and the busting of shells, render the mind so confused that it would be a task; let it suffice that I am alive; That shot and shells are my near companions, that smoke, and wounded brothers, soldiers, are constantly in view; that we have heavy duty, hard watchings, and little rest; that our comforts are groans, that our nightly repose is turned to harassing alarms, that our pastimes are destruction, that every hour, we or the enemy are inventing some horrid strategem; and that the next we behold each other plunged thereby into the most excruciating anguish.

(b) G. B., *Narrative of a Private Soldier in one of His Majesty's Regiments of Foot* (1819). [G.B. was fighting at this time in Egypt.]

The part of my wound where the ball entered healed in about sixteen days; but the part where it was extracted became inflamed, and the foot and ankle swelled considerably. I was suspicious that the dirty water with which it was sometimes washed was the occasion of the inflammation. An erroneous opinion was entertained, that salt water would smart the wounds; and as fresh water was not in plenty on board the ship, only a small quantity of it was allowed for washing them. . . . By the end of three weeks, my wound began to mortify. I was then put into a boat to be taken to the hospital at Aboukir, along with a number more whose cases were considered bad. Two were so weak that they were unable to sit, and were laid upon gratings in the bottom of the boat; one of them died before we reached the shore, and the other died upon the beach. These cases made little impression upon my mind; death was becoming familiar to me, and I looked at it with a careless indifference.

(c) *Source:* A Captain in the Navy, *The Life of a Sailor* (1832), quoted in C. N. Parkinson, *Portsmouth Point* (1948), p. 112.

We were cruising off the coast of Italy and had been very unsuccessful in the way of captures; our martial ardour, or empty pockets, had called into existence the desire of glory or gain. No doubt glory is a very fine thing but honour will not mend a broken leg, whereas gain will pay the apothecary's bill. I merely mention this, because we hear a great deal about honour and glory, and such like, and no one is candid enough to say that lucre—vile, filthy lucre, has anything to do with the business; but we 'sea attorneys' know better. I have known the prize-money shared in imagination, previous to the capture, and honour and glory never mentioned in the calculation.

8. MUTINY

Just as there were many signs of conflict in eighteenth-century society, so there were many examples of mutiny at sea and disturbances in the army. The most important of these were the Naval Mutinies at Spithead and the Nore in 1797.

(a) *Source:* Report in *The Times,* 13 Dec. 1794.

The mutiny which existed several days on board the *Culloden* of 74 guns, and which, it is said, originated in the wish of the crew to have the ship docked, previous to her sailing for the West Indies, was, on Wednesday, settled by an order from the Admiralty in the following manner:—'That several Captains were to go on board and inform the crew, unless they immediately returned to their duty, the *Royal George* of 110 guns, and *Queen* of 98 guns, would directly be laid alongside them.' They were allowed half an hour to consider the matter. The officers, and others, who chose to leave the ship, were at liberty so to do. The ship's company several times wanted to make terms, which could not possibly be complied with: in about twenty minutes they all agreed to return to their duty; 12 of the ringleaders were instantly seized, and put in irons, and will no doubt be tried by a Court Martial for the same. During the time the ship was in this mutinous state, the crew flogged several marines because they would not join them, and would have punished the whole, had they gone below.

(b) *Source:* Report in the *Annual Register* (1797).

The suppression of the disturbances among the seamen at Portsmouth, without recurring to violent measures, and by granting their petitions, occasioned universal satisfaction, and it was hoped that the causes of their discontent being thus effectually removed, no further complaints would arise to spread alarm throughout the nation. But these reasonable expectations were in a short time wholly disappointed by a fresh mutiny that broke out in the fleet at the Nore, on the twenty-second of May.

The crews on that day took possession of their respective ships, elected delegates to preside over them, and to draw up a statement of their demands, and transmit them to the lords of the admiralty. . . .

The principal person at the head of this mutiny was one Richard Parker, a man of good natural parts, and some education, and of a remarkably bold and resolute character. Admiral Buckner, the commanding officer at the Nore, was directed by the lords of the admiralty to inform the seamen, that their demands were totally inconsistent with the good order and regulations necessary to be observed in the navy, and could not for that reason be complied with; but that on returning to their duty, they would receive the king's pardon for their breach of obedience. To this offer Parker replied by a declaration, that the seamen had unanimously determined to keep possession of the fleet, until the lords of the admiralty had repaired to the Nore, and redressed the grievances which had been laid before them. . . . [Eventually] Parker was seized and imprisoned, and after a solemn trial, that lasted three days, on board of the *Neptune*, he was sentenced to death. He suffered with great coolness and intrepidity, acknowledging the justice of his sentence, and expressing his hope, that mercy might be extended to his associates. But it was judged necessary to make public examples of the principal and most guilty, who were accordingly tried, and, after full proof of their criminality, condemned and executed. Others were ordered to be whipped; but a considerable number remained under sentence of death till after the great victory obtained, over the Dutch fleet, by Admiral Duncan: when his majesty sent a general pardon to those unhappy men; who were, at that period, confined on board a prison ship in the river Thames.

(c) *Source:* Report in *The Times*, 31 July 1799.

LEWES.—Last week the Volunteers for regular Service from the Derby, Westminster, North Gloucester, and Surrey regiments of Militia, marched into this town, from their respective stations, on their routes to the grand depot, at Horsham. The large bounties which these men have received, enable them to keep up a scene of drunkenness, and insubordination, which it is very difficult to restrain. After parade here, on Saturday evening, Sir Joseph Mawbey, and other Officers, commanding the Surrey Volunteers, were compelled to have recource to their drawn swords, to enforce order, and maintain their command, which was for some time powerfully resisted, on their ordering a man to the guard-house. And, on dismissing the parade, yesterday evening, a similar disturbance took place. No swords were then drawn, but the clamour demanded the interference of General Hulse, who, in consequence, ordered out a piquet guard of infantry, and a patrole of horse, by which tranquillity was restored, and preserved. Others who have passed through this town, in their drunken frolics, distinguished themselves by swallowing Bank-notes between slices of bread and butter, and lighting their pipes with them, to the no small advantage of the Bankers.

9. SOLDIERS AND CIVILIANS

The Revolution of 1688 established a standing army, yet Englishmen were loath to admit it. Billeting of troops was usually unpopular, and there were many petitions against the presence of soldiers, even in war time.

(a) *Source:* Report in the *Journals of the House of Commons* (1759), vol. XXVIII, p. 600.

A Petition of the Inn keepers and Public-house Keepers within the City of *Winchester*, and Suburbs of the said City, was presented to the House, and read; complaining of the several Hardships, which the Petitioners allege they have laboured under ever since the *French* Prisoners came there; and alleging, that not less than Twenty-six Public Houses, in the said City and Suburbs, have lately given off, on Account of having so great a Number of Soldiers quartered in the said City and Suburbs as have been necessary to guard the said Prisoners, which has reduced the Number of Public Houses to Four Inns and Thirty-two small Public Houses; and further alleging, that the Petitioners, if not speedily redressed, must be obliged to give up their Houses, or be totally ruined; and that the Petitioners apprehend, that, if the Soldiers necessary to guard the said *French* Prisoners were put into Barracks in the Palace there, where the Petitioners are informed there is sufficient Room for that Purpose, it would be, as they are advised, the most speedy and effectual Method to remedy their great Grievances: And therefore the Petitioners implore the House to take their hard Case under Consideration, and give them such Relief in the Premises as the House shall think meet.

Ordered, That the said Petition do lie upon the Table.

(b) The events of 1745 continued to cast their shadow late in the century.

Source: Note in C. B. Andrews (ed.), *The Torrington Diaries* (1935), vol. II, p. 62.

This town [Preston] is over run by the drunken militia: ... being brought from home to be let loose upon their country men in fights, and insults, of which we saw various instances,— as well as their (*steady*) Rollcalling!!—

Being in all the distress that idleness and a great town occasion, we had only to saunter about the streets, where I made much enquiry about the Pretenders abode here in 1745; and enter'd the house, and saw the parlour where in these hasty, misguided adventurers quarell'd so fiercely, before their return. To me it appears strange that in a bad season he shou'd suffer his whole army to march on foot; and did not press the country for horses—for their forward march—or quick retreat—: but probably the want of breeches, and ignorance of riding, might prevent it.

They still speak of the rudeness of this army, and of their plunder of the town.

10. NEWS OF WAR AND PEACE

The number of people taking part in eighteenth-century wars was small, and most Englishmen had to register to news coming from great distances. Here are a few reactions. News from America influenced the whole pattern of eighteenth-century politics.

(a) *Source:* Note for 5 May 1765 in the *Diary* of Thomas Turner.

This was the day appointed by authority for a general thanksgiving for the late peace. No service at our church in the morn, Mr. Porter being on a journey. We have had no kind of rejoicing in this place, tho' it is the day for the proclamation of peace. I think almost everyone seems to be dissatisfied with this peace, thinking it an ignominious and inglorious one.

(b) *Source:* Letter from Henry Shiffner to George Shiffner, 25 October 1777 in the Shiffner MSS, 964, East Sussex Record Office.

We are in daily expectation of important News from America. Reports say that there has been a General Engagement & that the Rebels have been totally defeated & Washington killed, but till we have it under the Authority of the Gazette, there is no dependence on the truth of Report. Our Frigates have taken several foreign ships laden with Ammunition & I believe have orders to take all they meet with suspected of being destined for America. . . .

(c) There were many critics of war.

Source: Josiah Tucker, *Seventeen Sermons* (1776).

The love of country hath no place in the catalogue of Christian virtues. The love of country is, in fact, a local affection and a parental attachment; but the Christian covenant is general, comprehending all mankind within its embraces. . . . So far as the love of country means no more than a principle of self defense against invaders, so far it is justifiable, and so far hath Christianity provided for due exertion of it, by inculcating obedience to the respective powers set over us. But as to the ideas of honour and glory and conquest and dominion and the other fine things usually implied in the love of country, they are so foreign to the Christian plan that in this sense the love of country neither is, nor ought to be, a part of the Christian scheme of universal love and benevolence.

(d) There was certainly sharp criticism of the long wars against France, not least among middle-class manufacturers in the critical years from 1810 to 1812.

Source: An article in the *Manchester Gazette*, 17 March 1797.

We seduce every peasant from agriculture, extort wealth from the artisan and give it only to the man of blood; and then lament that the harvest is bad and industry is languishing. . . . While there is a guinea left in the country, or Bank notes current, and while bread can be got at any price, we will go on in the war; to gain what?—that we have never discovered.

(e) *Source:* An article in the *Monthly Repository* (1809).

Why rejoice in the midst of rivers of blood, while the burden of taxation presses so heavily on the middle classes of society, so as to leave the best part of the community little to hope and everything to fear?

CHAPTER XIV

The Pursuit of the Arts and Sciences

I am persuaded that to be a virtuoso (so far as befits a gentleman) is a higher step towards the becoming a man of virtue and good sense than the being what in this age we call a scholar. For even rude nature itself in its primitive simplicity is a better guide to judgement than improved sophistry and pedantic learning.

(LORD SHAFTESBURY, 1711)

Q. In what particular Manufactures, Arts or Sciences are the *English Nation* chiefly deficient?
A. They are said to be outdone by Foreigners in most of the higher or politer Arts, such as Painting, Engraving, Statuary and Music. And our Reason seems to be that neither the Religion, nor the Political Constitution of the Country give that Encouragement to those Studies, which is to be met with Abroad; our Church, for example, admitting of little more than elegant Neatness; and our Situation as an Island ... preventing our Artists from taking Models, or trying their Ingenuity in the Palaces of Foreign Princes.

(DEAN TUCKER, 1758)

The Enquiry in England is not whether a Man has Talents and Genius, but whether he is Passive and Polite and a Virtuous Ass and obedient to Noblemen's Opinions in Art and Science.

(WILLIAM BLAKE, c. 1808)

He lived through an age of memorable events and changes, and was an active and anxious contemporary. He was ... an effective ameliorator of a stern and uncharitable criminal code and the inventor of the interrogative system of education by which new impulses were given to the intelligence of society. He also placed natural philosophy on the basis of common sense, and developed the laws of nature on immutable principles which will always be co-extensive with the respect of mankind for truth. . . . He wrote and published more original works than any of his contemporaries, and in all of them advocated civil liberty, general benevolence, ascendancy of justice and the improvement of the human race. . . .

(From the Epitaph of SIR RICHARD PHILLIPS in the Churchyard of Brighton Old Parish Church, 1767–1840)

1. BUILDINGS AND TASTE

From the beginning of the eighteenth century, the pursuit of the arts—painting, sculpture, architecture and music—was directly related to the life of the Court, the aristocracy and the gentry. It was centred on London and the country house, with creativity and taste in one art influencing creativity and taste in another. There were marked but overlapping shifts of taste from one generation to another—rococo, neoclassical, picturesque, exotic, romantic— with influences from abroad being set first by Paris, then by Rome, and with the English themselves serving as the main initiators of the 'picturesque'. There were many English writers on taste, whose critical views express changing eighteenth-century canons of style and judgement.

(a) *Source:* D. Defoe, *Tour* (1724), Letter III.

But the beauty of *Stamford* is the neighbourhood of the noble palace of the Earl of *Exeter*. . . . This house, built all of free-stone looks more like a town than a house, at which avenue soever you come to it. . . . The late Earl of Exeter, father of his present lordship, had a great genius for painting and architecture, and a superior judgement in both, as every part of this noble structure will testify, for he changed the whole face of the building; he pulled down great part of the front of the garden and turned the old Gothic windows into those spacious sashes which are now seen there, and though the founder or first builder, who had an exquisite fancy also (as the manner of building then was) had so well ordered the situation and avenues of the whole fabric, that nothing was wanting of that kind, and had also contrived the house itself in a most magnificent manner, the rooms spacious, well directed, the ceilings lofty and the decorations just, yet the late Earl found room for alterations, infinitely to the advantage of the whole, as particularly, a noble staircase, a whole set of fine apartments, with rooms of state, fitting for the entertainment of a prince. . . . As this admirable gentleman, *the late Earl*, loved paintings, so he had infinite advantage in procuring them, for he not only travelled three times into Italy . . . but he was entertained at the Court of Tuscany . . . . The staircase, the ceilings of all the fine lodgings, the chapel, the hall, the late Earl's closet, are all finely painted by Varrio, of whose work I need say no more than this, that the Earl kept him twelve years in his family, wholly employed in painting those ceilings and staircases etc., and allowed him a coach and horses and equipage, a table and servants and a very considerable pension.

(b) There were many eighteenth-century treatises on architecture. The following extract is taken from a widely read mid-century book designed 'to serve as a library on this subject to the gentleman and the builder': it still serves as a mine of information about the application of mid-century conceptions of balance and proportion.

Source: I. Ware, *A Complete Body of Architecture* (1756), pp. 293–5.

The extent of ground being determined, the materials chosen, and the weight of the roof, and thickness of the wall, settled in the builder's mind, he is next to consider the article of proportion.

Here is a space to be covered with building: and the great consideration is its division into parts, for different uses; and their distribution. In this regard is to be had to two things, the convenience of the inhabitant, and the beauty and proportion of the fabrick. Neither of these should be considered independently of the other, because if it be, the other will not fail to be sacrificed to it; and this, which would be very disagreeable, is never absolutely necessary.

If the house be for a person in trade, the first principal attention must be shewn to the article of convenience; but with this the builder should always carry in his mind the idea of beauty, proportion, and a regular distribution of the parts. In the same manner, when the house is for a person of fashion, the beauty and proportional disposition of parts is to be principally considered; yet the great and needful article of convenience must not be disregarded. . . .

When convenience has been thus far considered in the plan, the next regard is to be shewn to proportion.

This is a thing of more strict concern than the other, and must be managed with the greatest accuracy. The matter of convenience falls under the direction of fancy, but proportion is established upon rule. . . .

Whatever the false taste of any particular time may adopt, the builder, though he complies with it from the orders he receives, yet he must never suppose that the caprice, or fashion, can change the nature of right and wrong. He must remember that there is such a thing as truth, though the present mode will not follow its steps; and establish it as a maxim in his own mind, that proportion and regularity are real sources of beauty, and always of convenience.

(c) The Adam brothers believed that architecture must be 'informed and improved by a correct taste', yet they experimented with varied forms and stressed 'movement' as well as proportion. They noted the change since the beginning of the century, referred to the relationships between the arts, and believed that everything in a room should 'match'—carpets, ceiling, fireplace, even paintings.

Source: R. and J. Adam, *Works* (1778), p. 35.

Movement is meant to express, the rise and fall, the advance and recess, with other diversity of form, in the different parts of a building, so as to add greatly to the picturesqueness of the composition. For the rising and falling, advancing and receding, with the convexity and concavity, and other forms of the great parts, have the same effect in architecture, that hill and dale, foreground and distance, welling and sinking have in landscape: That is, they serve to produce an agreeable and diversified contour, that groups and contrasts like a picture, and creates a variety of light and shade, which gives great spirit, beauty and effect to the composition.

(d) They also welcomed changes in styles of interior decoration which made for greater variety.

Source: ibid, p. 3.

A remarkable improvement in the form, convenience, and relief of apartments; a greater movement and variety in the

EE

outside composition; and in the decoration of the inside, an almost total change. The massive entablature, the ponderous compartment ceiling, the tabernacle frame, almost the only species of ornament formerly known in this country, are now universally exploded, and in their place, we have adopted a beautiful variety of light mouldings, gracefully formed, delicately enriched, and arranged with propriety and skill. We have introduced a great diversity of ceilings, friezes and decorated pilasters, and have added grace and beauty to the whole by a mixture of grotesque stucco and painted ornaments together with the painted rainceau with its fanciful figures.

(e) The Adam brothers drew much of their inspiration from classical styles, although they made a highly distinctive contribution of their own. Thomas Chippendale, who lived in the same London street as the painter, Sir Joshua Reynolds, worked in many styles, including Chinese and Gothic. His *Gentleman and Cabinet Maker's Directory* (1754) had an impressive list of subscribers and went through many editions. The descriptions of his furniture almost speak for themselves.

Source: Account of a lady's dressing table, quoted by O. Brackett in A. S. Turberville (ed.), *Johnson's England*, (1933), vol. II, p. 144.

A Design of a Dressing-Table for a Lady; the Drawer above the Recess hath all Conveniences for Dressing, and the Top of it is a Dressing-Glass, which comes forward with folding Hinges. On each Side is a Cupborad with Glass Doors, which may be either transparent or silvered; and in the Inside, Drawers or Pigeon Holes. Two Dressing-Tables have been made of Rosewood, from this Design, which gave an entire Satisfaction: All the Ornaments were gilt.

(f) By the end of the century Hepplewhite styles, as described and illustrated in *The Cabinet Maker and Upholsterer's Guide*, represented good taste, although Thomas Sheraton noted a 'decline' in the designs and called Chippendale's designs 'wholely antiquated and laid aside'. Carlton House, the Prince of Wales's residence, was a showplace of taste.

The lesser arts were also highly developed in England itself. Thus, the Chelsea porcelain factory, opened about 1743 and in operation until about 1770, produced vases, potpourri jars and small figures, some in imitation of those produced at Sèvres and

Meissen. There was excellent English silverware and some magnificent miniature paintings and portraits.

Source: Entry of 23 Oct. 1812 in J. Farington, *The Farington Diary* (1927), vol. VII, p. 122.

At breakfast we had conversation about taste in choosing furniture. Lady Beaumont said that the splendour of the furniture at Carlton House is so great that let the company who go there be ever so finely dressed they are not seen, the eyes of all being drawn off by the gorgeous decoration of the apartments. Sir George said that it was not so at Lord Grosvenor's where the furniture has a fine solemn effect, & when the apartments are filled with company the effect is like that of a Venetian picture.—Lord Lonsdale said Mr. Thos. Hope's house resembled a museum.

2. GARDENS AND LANDSCAPES

Changing tastes in gardens and landscapes reveal much about the attitudes of eighteenth-century men of property. Not surprisingly, alongside the serious literature, there is a rich literature of satire.

(a) *Source:* Note by Alexander Pope in *The Guardian*, 29 Sept. 1713.

I lately took a particular friend of mine to my house in the country, not without some apprehension that it would afford little entertainment to a man of his polite taste, particularly in architecture and gardening, who had so long been conversant with all that is beautiful and great in either. But it was a pleasant surprise to me to hear him often declare, he had found in my little retirement that beauty, which he always found wanting in the most celebrated seats, or if you will villas, of the nation. . . . There is certainly something in the amiable simplicity of unadorned nature that spreads over the mind a more noble sort of tranquillity, and a loftier sense of pleasure, than can be raised from the nicer scenes of art. . . . How contrary to this simplicity is the modern practice of gardening. We seem to make it our study to recede from nature, not only in the various tonsures of greens into the most regular and formal shapes, but even in monstrous attempts beyond the reach of the art itself. We run into sculpture, and are yet better pleased to have our trees in the most awkward figures of men and animals, than in the most regular of their own.

(b) Tastes changed.

Source: W. Gilpin, *Three Essays* (1792), Essay I.

Why does an elegant piece of garden ground make no figure on canvas? The shape is pleasing, the combination of the objects harmonious, and the winding of the walk in the very line of beauty. All this is true; but the *smoothness* of the whole ... offends in a picture. Turn the lawn into a piece of broken ground; plant rugged oaks instead of flowering shrubs; break the edges of the walk; give it the rudeness of a road; mark it with wheel tracks; and scatter round a few stones and brushwood—in a word, instead of making the whole *smooth*, make it *rough*, and you also make it picturesque.

(c) Appreciation of mountains was evidence of a change in taste. What previously had been thought of as 'considerable protuberances' became sources of awe and inspiration.

Source: T. Gray, *Journal* (1769), entry for 3 Oct.

A heavenly day. rose at seven, and walk'd out under the conduct of my landlord to *Borrowdale*. the grass was covered with a hoar-frost, wch soon melted, & exhaled in a thin bluish smoke. cross'd the meadows obliquely, catching a diversity of views among the hills over the lake & islands, & changing prospect at every ten paces, left *Cockshut* & Castle-hill ... behind me, & drew near the foot of *Walla-crag* whose bare & rocky brow, cut perpendicularly down 400 feet, as I guess, awefully overlooks the way ... opposite lie the thick hanging woods of Ld Egremont, & *Newland*-valley, with green and smiling fields embosom'd in the dark cliffs; to the left the jaws of *Borrowdale*, with that turbulent Chaos of mountain behind mountain roll'd in confusion; beneath you, & stretching far away to the right, the shining purity of the Lake. ...

(d) *Source:* E. Burke, *A Philosophical Enquiry into the Origin of our Ideas of the Sublime and the Beautiful* (1756), Part II, Section 1.

The passion caused by the great and sublime in *nature*, when those causes operate most powerfully, is astonishment: and astonishment is that state of the soul in which all its motions are suspended, with some degree of horror. In this case the mind is so entirely filled with its object that it cannot entertain any other, nor by consequence reason upon that object which employs it. Hence arises the great power of the sublime.

3. PAINTING

Eighteenth-century portrait painting leads back to the drawing room. It provided the staple livelihood of the painter, and many painters achieved social distinction themselves. 'The personal conceit of the sitter', Sir Osbert Sitwell has written, 'was only equalled by the technical conceit of the artist.' The personalities of the individual artists within the period—for example, Reynolds, Gainsborough and Romney—can be properly appreciated only from a detailed study of their work, yet Reynolds, in particular, was also a fluent writer on styles and tastes. Landscape painting won recognition more slowly—although there was an interesting East Anglian school—and the works of Constable, Bonington and Turner in the early nineteenth century derived from a living tradition of painting inherited from the Flemish studios.

(a) *Source:* Letter from the Duke of Bedford's agent to Thomas Gainsborough, 4 Jan. 1765, printed in M. Woodall (ed.), *The Letters of Thomas Gainsborough* (1961), p. 35.

Sir,

From the expectations you gave me when I saw you before I left Bath in November, I supposed before this time you wo'd have sent home the Pictures you painted for the Duke & Duchess of Bedford.

Her Grace now directs me to acquaint you that she desires you will immediately send her Picture & that of Lady Mary Fitzpatrick's, & that they need not wait for His Grace's Picture if you have not yet finished the Copies you were to make of it, but if they are done that the original can be spared you will please to send it with the two beforementioned.

Her Grace orders me to add that if it is agreeable to you

to come to London & will keep to your usual prices she will be answerable for its paying the expenses of the journey.

(b) Gainsborough's letters are full of interesting detail.

Source: Letter from Thomas Gainsborough to Henry Bate, 11 March 1788, printed in *ibid.*, p. 35.

Mr. Boydell bought the large landscape you speak of for seventy-five guineas last week at Greenwood's. It is in some respects a little in the *schoolboy stile*—but I do not reflect on this without a secret gratification; for as an early instance how strong my inclination stood for Landskip, this picture was actually painted at Sudbury in the year 1748; it was begun *before I left school*;—and was the means of my Father's sending me to London.

It may be worth remark that though there is very little idea of composition in the picture, the touch and closeness to nature in the study of the parts and *minutiae* are equal to any of my latter productions. In this explanation I do not wish to seem vain or ridiculous, but do not look on the Landskip as one of my riper performances.

It is full forty years since it was first delivered by me to go in search of those who had *taste* to admire it! Within that time it has been in the hands of twenty picture dealers, and I once bought it myself during that inverval for *Nineteen Guineas*. Is not that curious?

4. COLLECTORS

During the middle and late eighteenth century there was great enthusiasm for collecting pictures, statuary and antiquities from Europe, particularly Italy, and similar objects—and ancient poems and manuscripts—from England itself. English artists at Rome made money by buying, restoring and selling ancient 'masterpieces', but excavations at Herculaneum and Pompeii (profoundly influencing current tastes, including Wedgwood's pottery) the researches of Winckelmann, and the activities of the Dilettanti Society, founded in 1732, greatly widened the range. The great collectors of the early century like Dr. Meade, who died in 1754, were followed by new generations of explorer-collectors. In 1762, for instance, the antiquities of Athens were held up as a model and the purportedly ancient Celtic poems of Ossian were being discussed. In 1765 Thomas Percy published his *Reliques of Ancient English Poetry*. Throughout the last decades of the century museums, like zoos, were always popular.

(a) *Source:* Reminiscence of the artist Joseph Nollekens, quoted in J. T. Smith, *Nollekens and His Times* (1828), vol. I, p. 251.

I got the first and best of my money by putting antiques together. Hamilton and I, and Jenkins, generally used to go shares in what we bought. And as I had to match the pieces as best I could, and clean 'em, I had the best part of the profits. ... Jenkins followed the trade of supplying the foreign visitors with intaglios and cameos made by his own people that he kept in a part of the ruins of the Coliseum fitted up for 'em to work in slyly by themselves. ... Bless your heart! He sold them as fast as they made 'em.

(b) Reynolds did buying for the Duke of Rutland.

Source: Historical Manuscripts Commission, *MSS of the Duke of Rutland* (1900), vol. III, p. 310.

July 19, 1785, London. I set out to-morrow morning for Brussels. .... I have but just received a catalogue of the pictures which are now on view at Brussels. The Emperor has suppressed sixty-six religious houses, the pictures of which are to be sold by auction. Le Comte de Kageneck informs me the Emperor has selected for himself some of the principal pictures; however, there is one altar-piece which belonged to the Convent of the *Dames Blanches* at Louvain, which is to be sold. The subject is the Adoration of the Magi, ten feet by seven feet eight inches, which I take to be about the size of your picture of Rubens. ... This picture, I suspect, is the only one worth purchasing if your Grace has any such intention, or will honour me with discretionary orders in regard to other pictures. ...

Aug. 22, London. ... I was much disappointed in the pictures of the suppressed religious houses; they are the saddest trash that ever were collected together. The adoration of the Magi & St. Justus, by Rubens, & a Crucifixion by Vandyck, were the only tolerable pictures, but these are not the best of those masters. I did not like St. Justus as well [as] I did before, but I think of sending a small commission for it; the two others I dare say will not go to above £200 each. . . . I was shown some of the pictures which were reserved by the Emperor, which were not a jota better than the common run of the rest of the collection.

Though I was disappointed in the object of my journey, I have made some considerable purchases from private collections. I have bought a very capital picture of Rubens of Hercules & Omphale, a composition of seven or eight figures, perfectly preserved, & as bright as colouring can be carried. The figures are rather less than life. . . . I have likewise a Holy Family, a Silenus & Baccanalians, & two portraits, all by Rubens. I have a Virgin & Infant Christ & two portraits by Vandyck, & two of the best hunting of wild beasts, by Snyders & De Vos, that I ever saw.

Sept 22, London. I am sorry to accquaint your Grace that there is nothing bought at the sale. I have enclosed Mr. Gree's letter, by which it appears they went much above even the commission you wished me to send. I cannot think that either the Rubens or Vandyck were worth half the money they sold for. The Vandyck was an immense picture very scantily filled; it had more defects than beauties, & as to the Rubens, I think your Grace's is worth a hundred of them.

1785, Sep. 26, London. Immediately on the receipt of your Grace's letter I wrote to Mr. De Gree to make enquiry to whom the pictures were sold, & whether they would part with them at a certain profit, at the same time, I am confident if your Grace saw them you would not be very anxious about purchasing them.

(c) Source: T. Percy, Reliques of Ancient English Poetry (1765).

The old minstrel ballads are in the northern dialect, abound with antique words and phrases, are extremely incorrect, and run into the utmost licence of metre; they have also a romantic wildness, and are in the true spirit of chivalry.—The other sort are written in exacter measure, have a low or subordinate correctness, sometimes bordering on the insipid, yet often well adapted to the pathetic; these are generally in the southern dialect, exhibit a more modern phraseology, and are commonly descriptive of more modern manners.

(d) Space could induce the same feelings as time.

Source: Note on the collection of stuffed birds, animals and anthropological exhibits at the Leicester House Museum in the *European Magazine,* Jan. 1782.

The objects before him [the visitor] make his active fancy travel from pole to pole through torrid and through frigid zones. He beholds the manners of men in the forms of their habits. . . . He sighs to recollect the prevalent power of fear and superstition over the human mind, when he views the rude deformity of an idol carved with a flint, by a hand incapable of imitating the outline of nature. . . . [He must express] gratitude to the public-spirited proprietor, who has thus given his countrymen an opporunity of surveying the works of nature, and contemplating the various beings that inhabit the earth.

5. THE EXOTIC AND THE GOTHIC

Interest in the exotic (e.g. Chinese) or the Gothic (at first a term of contempt and then thought of as suitable a diversion or only for minor works and gardens) encouraged men of the later eighteenth century to deviate from symmetry and eventually to cultivate irregularity for itself. As some of the earlier passages have shown, there was a transition by the end of the century from antiquarian or sentimental or playful interest in the Gothic to the appreciation of the picturesque and the romantic. In the process taste and feeling were transformed.

(a) *Source:* T. Warton, *Pleasures of Melancholy* (1747).

O lead me, Queen Sublime, to solemn glooms
Congenial with my soul; to cheerless shades,
To ruin'd seats, to twilight cells and bowers . . .
Beneath yon ruin'd abbeys moss grown piles
Oft let me sit at twilight hour of eve,
When through some western window the pale moon
Pours her long-levelled rule of streaming light.

(b) *Source:* J. Shebbeare, *B. Angeloni, Letters on the English Nation* (1755), vol. II, p. 261.

The simple and the sublime have lost all influence, almost everywhere, all is Chinese or Gothic. Every chair in an apartment, the frames of glasses, and tables must be Chinese: the walls covered with Chinese paper fill'd with figures which resemble nothing of God's creation, and which a prudent nation would prohibit for the sake of pregnant women. . . . Nay, so excessive is the love of Chinese architecture become, that at present foxhunters would be sorry to break a leg in pursuing their sport in leaping any gate that was not made in the eastern taste of little bits of wood standing in all directions. The gothic, too, has its advocates; you see a hundred houses built with porches in that taste, such as are belonging to many chapels; not to mention that rooms are stuccoed in this taste, with all the minute, unmeaning carvings, which are found in the most Gothic chapels of a thousand years standing.

(c) Horace Walpole's Strawberry Hill, which he bought in 1747, kept him busy 'battlementing, pinnailing, fenestrating' for the rest of his life: he also wrote *The Castle of Otranto*, a Gothic story, in 1764.

Source: Letter from Walpole to Sir William Cole, 9 March 1765, printed in *Letters* (1914), vol. VI, p. 195.

I had time to write but a short note with the *Castle of Otranto*. . . . Your partiality to me and Strawberry have, I hope, inclined you to excuse the wildness of the story. You will even have found some traits to put you in mind of this place. . . . Shall I even confess to you, what was the origin of this romance? I waked one morning in the beginning of last June, from a dream, of which all I could recover was, that I had thought myself in an ancient castle (a very natural dream for a head filled like mine with Gothic story), and that on the uppermost banister of a great staircase, I saw a gigantic hand in armour. In the evening I sat down, and began to write, without knowing in the least what I intended to say. . . . Though I write romances, I cannot tell how to build all that belongs to them. . . . I have decided that the outside will be of *treillage* [trellis], which, however, I shall not commence, till I have again seen some of old Louis's old-fashioned *galanteries* at Versailles. Rosamond's bower, you, and I, and Tom Hearne [the antiquary] know, was a labyrinth, but as my territory will admit of a very short clew, I lay aside all thoughts of a mazy habitation; though a bower is very different from an arbour, and must have more chambers than one. In short, I both know, and don't know what it should be. I am almost afraid I must go and read Spenser, and wade through his allegories, and drawling stanzas to get at a picture. . . .

(d) Novelists could create the Gothic without inhibitions. It dominated their imagination, and there was whole genre of terror novels.

Source: Mrs. Radcliffe, *Udolpho* (1794).

As they crossed the first court, the light showed the black walls around them, fringed with long grass and dark weeds that found a scanty soil among the mouldering stones, the heavy buttresses, with here and there between them a narrow grate, the mossy iron gates of the castle, whose clustering turrets appeared above, opposite the huge towers of the portal itself.

(e) The imagination affected attitudes towards people as well as towards landscapes, qualifying eighteenth-century attitudes towards economics and morals (cf. 'Brechtian' attitudes to crime and squalor in the towns; see above, p. 372).

Source: A. Young, *Tour to the Lakes* (1761), vol. II, pp. 44ff.

In a moral view, the industrious mechanic is a more pleasing object than a loitering peasant. But in a picturesque light, it is otherwise. The arts of industry are rejected; and even idleness, if I may so speak, adds dignity to a character. Thus the lazy cowherd resting on his pole; or the peasant lolling on a rock may be allowed in the grandest scenes. . . . The characters that are most *suited to these scenes* of grandeur are such as impress us with some idea of greatness, wildness or ferocity; all of which touch on the sublime.

(f) With Wordsworth (see also below, p. 443) simplicity was in vogue again—simplicity imbued with romantic feeling. The 'natural' and the artificial were placed in sharp contrast. Lakeland characters were conceived of as being as far away from artificial life as noble savages.

Source: W. Wordsworth, Preface to the third edition of the *Lyrical Ballads* (1802).

The principal object . . . proposed in these Poems was to choose incidents and situations from common life, and to relate or describe them, throughout, as far as possible in a selection of language really used by men, and, at the same time, to throw over them a certain colouring of imagination, whereby ordinary things should be presented to the mind in an unusual aspect; and, further, and above all, to make these incidents and situations interesting by tracing in them, truly though not ostentatiously, the primary laws of our nature: chiefly as far as regards the manner in which we associate ideas in a state of excitement. Low and rustic life was generally chosen, because in that condition, the essential passions of the heart find a better soil in which they can attain their maturity, are less under restraint, and speak a plainer and more emphatic language; because in that condition of life our elementary feelings co-exist in a state of greater simplicity . . . and, lastly, because in that condition the passions of men are incorporated with the beautiful and permanent forms of nature.

6. MUSIC

Eighteenth-century English music was dominated by Handel, although the reception of his work was neither universally favourable nor consistent. Public concerts had been first established in England in the late seventeenth century in the form of musical evenings arranged in drawing rooms with admission by subscription for a series, and the first concert hall, the Holywell Music Room in Oxford, opened in 1748, remained a curiosity for the rest of the century. Opera was very much of a foreign import.

(a) *Source:* P. Grosley, *A Tour to London* Vol. II. (1772 edn.), pp. 113–14.

Queen Elizabeth's taste for music caused that art to make some progress in England, by giving it some of the improvements which it had before received in Italy.

In the present age Handel, a German by birth, brought about the same revolution in England, which Lully the Italian had effected in France in the last century. Since that æra the English flatter themselves that they have a national music: but it is nothing more than a dialect of the German, as the latter is itself a dialect of the Italian.

The grand concert at St. Paul's for the benefit of the sons of the clergy, those of Vaux-hall and Ranelagh, and some private ones to which I was admitted, were said to be English compositions. The symphony was half German, half Italian: with regard to the vocal performance, Englishmen have assured me that the just accent of their language was much murdered by the performers, as that of the French tongue is mauled in the burlesque operas, which are imitations or parodies of the Italian.

The London opera is entirely Italian, both with regard to the words and the music; but is much less frequented than the other theatrical entertainments. No expence is spared to procure fine singers; œconomy is observed only in the articles of machines and dances. With regard to both of these it is not half so well supplied as the French comedy at Paris is at present.

(b) *Source:* Preface to C. Burney, *An Account of the Musical Performances in Westminster Abbey and the Pantheon, 1784, in Commemoration of Handel* (1785), pp. iii–v.

HANDEL whose genius and abilities, have lately been so nobly commemorated, though not a native of England, spent the greatest part of his life in the service of its inhabitants: improving our taste, delighting us in the church, the theatre and the chamber; and introducing to many among us species of musical excellence, that, during more than half a century, while sentiment, not fashion, guided our applause, we neither wanted nor wished for any other standard. He arrived among us at a barbarous period for almost every kind of music, except that of the church. . . . The English, a manly, military race, were immediately captivated by [his] grave, bold, and nervous style, which is congenial with their manners and sentiments. And though the productions of men of great genius and abilities have, since his time, had a transient share of attention and favour; yet, whenever any of the works of Handel are revived by a performer of superior talents, they are always heard with a degree of general satisfaction and delight, which other compositions seldom achieve. . . . And it was perhaps, at the late performance in Westminster Abbey, that the compositions of this great master were first supplied with a band, capable of displaying all the wonderful powers of his harmony.

7. PATRONAGE

During the eighteenth century there was a shift in literature from dependence on patronage (already patronage had moved from the royal family to the aristocracy) to communication with a broader reading public. At the same time, patronage did not disappear even in literature, and it remained dominant in the organization of the other arts. The Prince Regent was a notable patron of the arts. The Exhibitions of the Society of Artists founded in 1760 (see below, p. 444) ensured, however, that artists were no longer completely dependent on patronage for a living.

(a) This dedication of a play to Lady Wortley Montagu is a characteristic eighteenth-century dedication of a work of art.

Source: H. Fielding, *Love in Several Masques* (1728).

MADAM,—Your Ladyship's well-known goodness gives my presumption the hopes of a pardon, for prefixing to this slight work the name of a lady, whose accurate judgment has long been the glory of her own sex and the wonder of ours: especially, since it arose from a vanity to which your indulgence, on the first perusal of it, gave birth. I would not insinuate to the world that this play passed free from your censure; since I know it is not free from faults, not one of which escaped your immediate penetration. Immediate indeed for your judgment keeps pace with your eye, and you comprehend almost faster than others overlook.

This is a perfection very visible to all who are admitted to the honour of your conversation; since, from those short intervals you can be supposed to have had to yourself, amid the importunities of all the polite admirers and professors of wit and learning, you are capable of instructing the pedant, and are at once a living confutation of those morose schoolmen, who would confine knowledge to the male part of the species, and a shining instance of all those perfections and softer graces, which nature has confined to the female.

But I offend your ladyship, whilst I please myself and the reader; Therefore I shall only beg your leave to give a sanction to this comedy by informing the world that its representation was twice honoured with your ladyship's presence, and am with the greatest respect,

Madam,
Your Ladyships' most obedient
Most humble servant
HENRY FIELDING

(b) Dr. Johnson was an acute critic of patronage.

Source: A conversation with Johnson in St. Andrews, 1773, reported in J. Boswell, *A Journal of a Tour to the Hebrides with Samuel Johnson* (1785).

Dr. Watson observed, that Glasgow University had fewer home-students, since trade increased, as learning was rather incompatible with it.

JOHNSON: 'Why, Sir, as trade is now carried on by subordinate hands, men in trade have as much leisure as others; and now learning itself is a trade. A man goes to a bookseller, and gets what he can. We have done with patronage. In the infancy of learning we have some great man praised for it. This diffused it among others. When it becomes general, an author leaves the great, and applies to the multitude.'

BOSWELL: 'It is a shame that authors are not now better patronised.'

JOHNSON: 'No, Sir. If learning cannot support a man, if he must sit with his hands across till somebody feeds him, it is as to him a bad thing, and it is better as it is. With patronage, what flattery! What falsehood! While man is in equilibrio, he throws truth among the multitude, and lets them take it as they please: in patronage he must say what pleases his patron, and it is an equal chance whether that be truth or falsehood.'

WATSON: 'But is it not the case now, that instead of flattering one person, we flatter the age?'

JOHNSON: 'No, Sir! The World always lets a man tell what he thinks, his own way. I wonder, however, that so many people have written, who might well have left it alone.

(c) A bookseller was in a strategic position to survey the rise of a general reading public.

Source: Memoirs of the Life of James Lackington (1792 edn.), pp. 388–91.

The sale of books in general has increased prodigiously within the last twenty years. According to the best estimation I have been able to make, I suppose that more than four times the number of books are sold now that were sold twenty year since. The poorer sort of farmers, and even the poor country people in general, who before that period spent their evenings in relating stories of witches, ghosts, hobgoblins &c., now shorten the winter nights by hearing their sons and daughters read tales, romances &c., and on entering their houses you may see *Tom Jones, Roderick Random,* and other entertaining books stuck up on their bacon racks &c.

8. ARTISTS AND WRITERS

Artists and writers played a prominent part in eighteenth-century life, and their interests crossed at many points. There were many varieties of art, including the fierce satire of Dean Swift (1667–1745), the pioneer dramatic art of William Hogarth (1697–8) and the rich and profound art of William Blake (1757–1827). Their work must be set alongside that of Pope or Gainsborough or Reynolds or Sheridan. The development of romantic ideas about art and artists transformed late eighteenth-century art as a whole.

(a) *Source:* Voltaire, *Letters Concerning the English Nation* (1733 translation), pp. 224–6.

The *English* have so great a veneration for exalted talents, that a man of merit in their country is always sure of making his fortune. Mr. *Addison* in *France* would have been elected a member of one of the Academies. . . . or else might have been imprisoned in the *Bastile*.... Mr. *Addison* was raised to the post of Secretary of State in England. Sir *Isaac Newton* was made Warden of the Royal Mint.... But the circumstance which mostly encourages the arts in *England*, is the great veneration which is paid them. The picture of the Prime Minister hangs over the chimney of his own closet, but I have seen that of Mr. *Pope* in twenty noblemen's houses.

(b) Hogarth, like Fielding, who greatly admired his influence, wanted art to have a direct impact.

Source: W. Hogarth, Note appended to *The Four Stages of Cruelty* (1751).

The leading points in these, as well as in *Beer Street* and *Gin Lane* were made as obvious as possible, in the hope that their tendency might be seen by men of the lowest rank and the fact is that the passions may be more forcibly expresst by a strong bold stroke, than by the most delicate engraving. To expressing them as I felt them, I have paid the utmost attention, and as they were addresst to hard hearts, have rather preferred leaving them hard.

(c) For the variety of commitments of an established writer, the following letter from Oliver Goldsmith, dated 7 Sept. 1772, is particularly interesting. It was written to Bennet Langton, a distinguished Greek scholar and a member of a literary club founded by Dr. Johnson. The other members included Boswell, Garrick, the actor, Burke, the politician and philosopher, and Sir Joshua Reynolds, the painter. The comedy referred to in the first paragraph was *She Stoops to Conquer*, first produced at Covent Garden in March 1773.

Source: K. C. Balderston (ed.), *Collected Letters of Oliver Goldsmith* (1928), pp. 102ff.

Since I had the pleasure of seeing you last, I have been almost wholly in the country at a farmer's house, quite alone, trying to write a comedy. It is now finished; but when or how it will be acted, or whether it will be acted at all, are questions I cannot resolve. I am, therefore, so much employed upon that, that I am under the necessity of putting off my intended visit to Lincolnshire for this season.

Reynolds is just returned from Paris, and finds himself now in the case of a truant that must make up for his idle time by diligence. We have, therefore, agreed to postpone our journey till next summer, when we hope to have the honour of waiting upon Lady Rothes and you, and staying double the time of our late intended visit. We often meet, and never without remembering you.

I see Mr. Beauclerc very often both in town and country. He is now going directly forward to become a second Boyle; deep in chemistry and physics. Johnson has been down on a visit to a country parson, Dr. Taylor; and is returned to his haunts at Mrs. Thrale's. Burke is a farmer, *en attendant* a better place; but visiting about too. Every soul is visiting about and merry but myself. And that is hard, too, as I have been trying these three months to do something to make people laugh. There have I been strolling about the hedges, studying jests with a most tragical countenance.

The *Natural History* is about half finished, and I will shortly finish the rest. . . .

(d) A number of 'pre-romantic' poets, like Thomas Chatterton, who committed suicide in 1770, influenced Blake, who was bitterly hostile to the dominant philosophy of the Enlightenment, 'the unholy Trinity' of Bacon, Newton and Locke. Blake's unique vision lights up the last years of the century.

Source: W. Blake's notes to his engravings of 1788 in G. Keynes, *The Complete Writings of William Blake* (1957), pp. 97–8.

He who sees the Infinite in all things, sees God. He who sees the Ratio only, sees himself only.

(e) Chatterton remained more important as a symbol than as a writer. Keats dedicated *Endymion* to him, and Wordsworth called him 'the sleepless soul that perished in his pride'. Chatterton wrote of 'Bristol's narrow streets, Where pride and luxury with meanness meets'. His *Last Verses* clearly set out his own view of the artist and his fate in 1770.

Source: H. D. Roberts (ed.), *The Complete Poetical Works of Chatterton* (1906), vol. I, p. 221.

Farewell, Bristolia's dingy piles of brick,
Lovers of Mammon, worshippers of trick!

Ye spurned the boy who gave you antique lays,
And paid for learning with your empty praise.
Farewell, ye guzzling aldermanic fools,
By nature fitted for corruption's tools!
I go to where celestial anthems swell;
But you, when you depart, will sink to hell.

(f) At the end of the century William Wordsworth set forward his own idea of the role of the artist.

Source: W. Wordsworth, Preface to the *Lyrical Ballads* (1800).

The Poems in these volumes will be found distinguished by at least one mark of difference, that each of them has a worthy *purpose*. Not that I always begin to write with a distinct purpose formally conceived; but habits of meditation have, I trust, so prompted and regulated my feelings, that my descriptions of such objects as strongly excite those feelings, will be found to carry along with them a *purpose*. If this opinion be erroneous, I can have little right to the name of a Poet. For all good poetry is the spontaneous overflow of powerful feelings: and though this be true, Poems to which any value can be attached were never produced on any variety of subjects but by a man who, being possessed of more than usual organic sensibility, had also thought long and deeply.

(g) Yet the 'polite artist' more than held his own throughout the period, not only in letters.

Source: Note of 20 Aug. 1813 in J. Farrington, *The Farrington Diaries* (1927), vol. VIII, p. 199.

We had conversation upon the State of Artists in this country compared with what it was when Mr. West arrived in England, in respect of their personal manners and the degree of estimation in which they were and are held. Mr. West said that in 50 years they had become a different description of men, so much more decorous in their deportment and in their reception in Society. He observed that the establishment of the Royal Academy had done much in giving dignity to the Arts, and that too much could not be done to preserve its importance.

9. SOCIETIES

Most artists, scientists and men of letters initiated or developed societies during the eighteenth century, often for good practical reasons. The Royal Society, founded in 1662, had led the way as far as scientists were concerned, and its *Transactions* (see below, p. 452) included important scientific articles.

(a) The practically orientated Society for the Encouragement of Arts was founded in 1753.

Source: P. Grosley, *Observations on England* (1772), pp. 13–14.

The object of this Society, the most numerous, not in England only but in all Europe, is the encouragement of arts, manufactures and commerce. (The Society is not erected into an academy, a title reserved by the English for learned assemblies.) It at present consists of about 3000 members, amongst whom are a great many peers of Great Britain. Each of these members contributes two guineas a year: many, however, do not confine themselves to this sum, which they are proud to exceed in proportion to their rank or wealth. . . . They have their meetings upon fixed days and hours, in a large house occupied by the society in the Strand.

The finest room in this house, forming a salon, with sky lights, is consecrated to the arts: a gallery adjoining to it, contains all the new invented machines, for abridging labour in the different trades. Whether perfect or imperfect in their kind, they are amply paid for by the society, whose chief aim is to direct those who have a genius for mechanics, to their proper objects.

(b) It was in the rooms of the Society for the Encouragement of Arts that the newly founded Society of Artists held their first exhibition in 1760. In 1768, however, the Royal Academy was formed, with Joshua Reynolds as President. In 1780 the Academy obtained new rooms in Somerset House.

Source: Report in the *Morning Chronicle*, quoted by A. Shirley, 'Painting and Engraving' in A. S. Turberville (ed.), *Johnson's England*, 1933 vol. II, p. 54.

The exhibition of the artists at the Royal Academy was opened in the new buildings, Somerset Place, where a noble suite of rooms has been adapted for that purpose. The grand room is at the top. . . . The rooms beneath are appropriated for drawings, models, statues, busts, &c. At the end of one are the portraits of their Majesties by Sir Joshua Reynolds. . . . The *tout ensemble* of the present exhibition is allowed on all hands to do infinite honour to the British arts and certainly contains many pictures that will prove lasting monuments of the real genius of the several artists. The concourse of people of fashion who attended the opening of the Royal Academy exhibition yesterday was incredible. . . .

(c) There were flourishing local societies in the provinces by the end of the century, like the Society of Gentlemen at Spalding, and the Manchester Literary and Philosophical Society, founded in 1781. The most famous was the Lunar Society of Birmingham of which Priestley (see below, p. 451), Erasmus Darwin, Josiah Wedgwood, James Watt and Matthew Boulton were members. Priestley's house was destroyed by a Birmingham mob during the French Revolution, and he had to flee to London. His letter recalls his association with the Society, which unfortunately did not keep minutes of its meetings.

Source: Letter of Joseph Priestley to Dr. William Withering, 5 Nov. 1791, printed in H. C. Bolton, *Scientific Correspondence of Joseph Priestley* (1892).

It will be a considerable time, with every assistance that money can afford before I can be at work again, and hardly ever to so much advantage as at Birmingham. Such assistance from philosophical friends I should in vain look for here, and as long as I live I shall look back with pleasure and regret to our Lunar meetings, which I always enjoyed so much and from which I derived so much solid advantage. If I could find the same *intelligence* in any club of Philosophers here, I could not find the same *frankness*, which is the charm of all society. . . . Still hoping to have the satisfaction of seeing you and the rest of my friends of the Lunar Society, some time hence, and always to hear of your proceedings.

10. PHILOSOPHY

The eighteenth century has often been called 'the age of reason'. One of the main contrasts of the age was that between reason and superstititution, a contrast which explains the power of the term 'Enlightenment'. Yet the word 'reason' meant many things, and the reaction against certain conceptions of reason was itself an eighteenth-century process. The following extracts relate to eighteenth-century attitudes towards philosophy and philosophers. In the background were Newton and Locke, and much of the later movement of thought and feeling was European rather than particularly English. David Hume's *Treatise on Human Nature* (1738) reflected a spirit of scepticism: during the last years of the century other Scottish philosophers, far more creative and imaginative than their English counterparts, ensured that Scotland made a distinctive contribution to the European Enlightenment.

(a) *Source:* M. Mendelssohn, 'On the Question: What is Enlightening?' in *Berliner Monatschrift* (1784). This interesting article, of European range, was followed three months later by an article by the German philosopher, Kant.

The words Enlightenment, Culture, Cultivation are rather new in our language. So far they are bookish terms only. The common mass hardly understands them. Should this mean, however, that the substance of the terms is altogether new with us? I don't think so. It is said of a certain people that it has no specific word for virtue and none for superstition; yet one may rightly attribute to it a good measure of both these qualities.

However, common usage has not yet apportioned definite borderlines to these terms which are closely allied yet must be distinguished. Cultivation, culture, and enlightenment are modes of the social life, achievements of men's industry and efforts to improve their social condition.

The degree of cultivation in a people can be gauged from the degree in which its social condition, through art and industry, has been brought into harmony with the destination of man.

Cultivation consists of culture and enlightenment. Culture seems to be concerned with the practical: with quality and beauty in the handicrafts, arts, and manners; with aptitude and industry in the two former, and with inclinations, urges, and customs in the latter. . . .

Enlightenment on the other hand seems to refer rather to

the theoretical element: to logical knowledge and the capacity to think rationally about the concerns of human life, according to their relevance and influence on the destination of man.

A language achieves enlightenment through the sciences, and culture through social intercourse, poetry and eloquence. . . . Both together confer cultivation on a language. . . .

Enlightenment has the same relation to culture as theory to practice, as knowledge to morality, as criticism to virtuosity. Objectively they depend on each other though subjectively they are often separated.

You can say: the people of Nuremberg have more culture, those of Berlin more enlightenment; the French have more culture, the English more enlightenment; the Chinese much culture and little enlightenment. The Greeks had both culture and enlightenment. They were a cultivated nation, just as their language is a cultivated language. Altogether the language of a people is the best measure of its cultivation, of its culture as well as of its enlightenment, both in its extension and its intensity.

Moreover, the destination of man may be subdivided into

1. the destination of man as man (individual), and

2. the destination of man as citizen (social being).

As regards culture, these aspects coincide in as much as all practical accomplishments are valuable only in the social sphere and must therefore be in keeping only with man's role as a member of society. Man as man alone needs no culture; but he needs enlightenment.

A citizen's standing and calling determine his duties and rights, and accordingly require different abilities and accomplishments, different attitudes, urges, manners, and customs, different types of culture and appearance. The more these correspond, in all ranks, with their respective callings as members of society, the more culture a nation is said to have.

Equally they require different theoretical insights and abilities according to an individual's rank and calling, or, in other words, different degrees of enlightenment. The enlightenment, which is of interest to man as individual man, is universal without distinction of ranks; the enlightenment of man as a citizen is modified according to station and profession. The destination of man, in this context too, determines the measure and the ends of his activities.

Accordingly the measure of a nation's enlightenment may be taken from 1. the sum of knowledge; 2. The relevance of this knowledge to the destination (a) of the individual, and (b) of the citizen; 3. the spread of knowledge throughout the ranks; 4. according to callings. . . .

There is potential conflict between individual and civic enlightenment. Certain truths which serve man as man, may be obnoxious to him as citizen. . . . Such a conflict can arise between 1. essential or 2. accidental ends of the individual on the one hand, and 3. essential or 4. non-essential, accidental ends of the citizen. . . .

Unhappy the state in which there is no harmony between the essential destination of man and that of the citizen, in which the enlightenment which all need cannot spread through all ranks of the realm without endangering the constitution.

But where the non-essential ends of man clash with the essential or non-essential ends of the citizen, there rules must be devised to provide for exceptions and to adjudicate in cases of collision.

When unhappily there is discord between the essential and the non-essential ends of man, when it is impossible to spread certain useful and worthy truths without overthrowing the very principles of religion and morality—then the virtuous enlightener will proceed carefully and cautiously and will suffer prejudice rather than refute the truths which are connected with it. . . .

Where enlightenment and culture are in step with each other, there they offer the best protection against corruption. . . . For a cultivated nation there is only one danger left, namely the abundance of national happiness . . . (like the perfectly happy and healthy man) it may fall prostrate because it cannot rise any higher. . . .

(b) David Hume considered the relationship between custom and reason.

Source: D. Hume, *An Inquiry Concerning Human Understanding* (1748).

All inferences from experience . . . are effects of custom, not of reasoning. Custom then is the great guide of human life. It is that principle alone which renders our experience useful to us, and makes us expect for the future a similar chain of events with those which have appeared in the past. Without the influence of custom we should be entirely ignorant of every matter of fact beyond what is immediately present to the memory and senses. We should never know how to adjust means to ends, or to employ our natural powers in the production of any effect. There would be an end at once of all action, as well as of the chief part of speculation.

(c) At the beginning of the century the role of the thinker and the philosopher had been extolled as against the role of the king, the fighter, the hero.

Source: Letter in *The Spectator*, No. 662, 19 Nov. 1714.

When we look back upon the history of those who have born the parts of Kings, statesmen, or commanders, they appear to us stripped of those out-side ornaments that dazzled their contemporaries; and we regard their persons as great or little, in proportion to the eminence of their virtues or vices. The wise sayings, generous sentiments, or disinterested conduct of a philosopher under mean circumstances of life, set him higher in our esteem than the mighty potentates of the earth, when we view them both through the long prospect of many ages.

(f) The same kind of problem was discussed by one of the leading writers of the Scottish Enlightenment later in the century.

Source: A. Ferguson, *An Essay on the History of Civil Society* (1767), pp. 30–1.

It is peculiar to modern Europe, to rest so much of the human character on what may be learned in retirement, and from the information of books. A just admiration of ancient literature, an opinion that human sentiment, and human reason, without this aid, were to have vanished from the societies of men, have led us into the shade, where we endeavour to derive from imagination and thought, what is in reality matter of experience and sentiment: and we endeavour, through the grammar of dead languages, and the channel of commentators, to arrive at the beauties of thought and elocution, which sprang from the animated spirit of society, and were taken from the living impressions of an active life. Our attainments are frequently limited to the elements of every science, and seldom reach to the enlargement of ability and power which useful knowledge should give. Like mathematicians, who study the Elements of Euclid, but never think of mensuration, we read of societies, but do not propose to act with men: we repeat the language of politics, but feel not the spirit of nations: we attend to the formalities of a military discipline, but know not how to employ numbers of men to obtain any purpose by strategem or force.

But for what end, it may be said, point out a misfortune that cannot be remedied? If national affairs called for exertion, the genius of men would awake; but in the recess of better employment, the time which is bestowed on study, if even attended with no other advantage, serves to occupy with innocence the hours of leisure, and set bounds to the pursuit of ruinous and frivolous amusements. From no better reason than this, we employ so many of our early years, under the rod, to acquire what it is not expected we should retain beyond the threshold of the school; and whilst we carry the same frivolous character in our studies that we do in our amusements, the human mind could not suffer more from a contempt of letters, than it does from the false importance which is given to literature, as a business for life, not as a help to our conduct, and the means of forming a character that may be happy in itself, and useful to mankind.

(g) Goldsmith talked also of the value of experience.

Source: O. Goldsmith, *The Citizen of the World* (1762), Letter LXVII.

Books, my son, while they teach us to respect the interests of others, often make us unmindful of our own; while they instruct the youthful reader to grasp at social happiness, he grows miserable in detail, and attentive to universal harmony, often forgets that he himself has a part to sustain in the concert. ... The discontented being, who retires from society, is generally some good-natured man, who has begun life without experience, and knows not how to gain it in his intercourse with mankind.

(h) Most writers were preoccupied with the relationship between the individual and society, with 'interest' and happiness. Different answers were given.

Source: J. Priestley, *Institutes of Natural and Revealed Religion* (1782), vol. I, part I, ch. 2.

Since however, the divine goodness is general, and impartial; and he must, consequently, prefer the happiness of the *whole*, to that of any *individuals*, it cannot be his pleasure, that we should consult our own interest, at the expense of that of others. Considering ourselves, therefore, not as separate individuals, but as members of society, another object that we ought to have in view is the welfare of our fellow creatures, and of mankind at large. But still there is no real disagreement among these different rules of conduct, because we are so made, as social beings, that every man provides the most effectually for his own happiness, when he cultivates those sentiments, and pursues that conduct, which, at the same time, most eminently conduce to the welfare of those with whom he is connected. Such is the wisdom of this admirable constitution, that every individual of the system gains his own ends, and those of his maker, by the same means.

(i) Tom Paine pursued this main line of argument. For the political implications of this, see below, p. 468.

Source: T. Paine, *The Rights of Man* (1791), part II, ch. 1.

A great part of that order which reigns among mankind is not the effect of Government. It has its origin in the principles of society and the natural constitution of man. It existed prior to Government, and would exist if the formality of Government was abolished. The mutual dependence and reciprocal interest which man has upon man, and all the parts of a civilized community upon each other, create that great chain of connection which holds it together. The land-holder, the farmer, the manufacturer, the merchant, the tradesman, and every occupation, prospers by the aid which each receives from the other and from the whole. Common interest regulates their concerns and forms their law; and the laws which common usage ordains have a greater influence than the laws of Government. In fine, society performs for itself almost everything which is ascribed to Government.

To understand the nature and quantity of Government proper for man, it is necessary to attend to his character. As nature created him for social life, she fitted him for the station she intended. In all cases she made his natural wants greater than his individual powers. No one man is capable, without the aid of society, of supplying his own wants; and those wants, acting upon every individual, impel the whole of them into society, as naturally as gravitation acts to a centre.

But she has gone further. She has not only forced man into society by a diversity of wants which the reciprocal aid of each other can supply, but she has implanted in him a system of social affections, which, though not necessary to his existence, are essential to his happiness. There is no period in life when this love for society ceases to act. It begins and ends with our being.

11. SCIENCE

English science was generally respected in the eighteenth century, and there was some interest in science not only among the *litterati* (Johnson, for example, was 'very fond' of chemical experiments), but even at a popular level. At the beginning of the century, it was the work of Newton and the mathematical physicists which stood out: by the end of the century there was a renewed interest in chemistry and biology. There was also considerable discussion of the experimental method, and a recognition amongst some writers that the practical applications of science were likely to transform mind and environment.

(a) *Source:* Letter from the Vicar of Upminster to the Squire of Belhus, June 1704, printed in Edwards (ed.), *English History from Essex Sources*, vol. I, p. 157. (Both men were Fellows of the Royal Society.)

I here send you by this messenger your two books which I borrowed, for which I give you many thanks. I beg the favour of borrowing the next volume of your *Transactions*, and Dr Plot's *History of Staffordshire*, and Mr. Newton's *Optics* if you can spare them.

I was yesterday at London, where I saw Mr. Newton's new contrivance of reflecting glasses. They were to have been tried yesterday before the Royal Society in the presence of Lords Halifax and Somers etc., but the day did not favour us. We were however regaled by Mr. Hawksbee's experiments in the pneumatic engine, viz:

1. A very light feather descended as swiftly as a piece of lead in the exsucked receiver.
2. Tepid water first gently rose with small bubbles, and as the receiver was emptied of air the bubbles increased, till at last (when quite evacuated) it boiled with the greatest violence as if the greatest fire had been under.
3. A glass vial included (and by a certain artifice evacuated) within the receiver, was broken into thousands of pieces by the admission of the air into the receiver.

(b) *Source:* P. Grosley, *Observations on England* (1772), pp. 185–8. The conception of science broadened out from the natural sciences into the study of antiquity. Gilbert White's *Natural History and Antiquities of Selborne* (1789) was an outstanding work in these fringe territories.

England has maintained the reputation for the abstruse sciences, which it had formerly for the philosophy and theology of the schools, when the greatest geniuses were entirely engrossed by those studies. Those which have established themselves upon their ruin, are infinitely indebted to the plans, the discoveries, of Bacon, Gilbert, Boyle, Newton, Halley, &c. &c. In investigations concerning antiquity, what obligations do we not owe to Usher, Selden, Marsham, and the accurate and laborious lucubrations of the learned men, who have raised from their ruins Palmyra, Athens, with the monuments of Dioclesian at Spalatro? England presents us with many living examples of the perseverance of its inhabitants in their attachment to such objects as have once engaged their attention.

The disposition and turn of mind, which excites men to such enterprize and inspires them with the courage requisite for carrying them into execution, is precisely the sort of character required by ancient legislators in statesmen. It is the *atrox animus* ... which the Stoics endeavoured to instil [into] their followers.

(c) A full account of the experimental method is given by Sir Humphry Davy, best known for his invention of the safety lamp.

Source: Humphry Davy, *Researches Chemical and Philosophical, Chiefly Concerning Nitrous Oxide and its Respiration* (1800).

APRIL, 1799. In April I obtained nitrous oxide in a state of purity and ascertained many of its chemical properties. Reflections upon these properties and upon the former trials made me resolve to endeavour to inspire it in its pure form, for I saw no other way in which its respirability or powers could be determined.

I was aware of the danger of this experiment. I thought that the effects might be possibly depressing and painful, but there were many reasons which induced me to believe that a single inspiration of a gas apparently possessing no immediate action on the irritable fibre could neither destroy or materially injure the powers of life.

APRIL 11. I made the first inspiration of pure nitrous oxide. It passed through the bronchia without stimulating the glottis, and produced no uneasy feeling in the lungs. The result of this experiment proved that the gas was respirable, and induced me to believe that a farther trial of its effects might be made without danger.

APRIL 16. Dr. Kinglake being accidentally present, I breathed three quarters of nitrous oxide from and into a silk bag for more than half a minute without previously closing my nose or exhausting my lungs. The first inspirations occasioned a slight degree of giddiness. This was succeeded by an uncommon sense of fulness of the head, accompanied with loss of distinct sensation and voluntary power, a feeling analogous to that produced in the first stage of intoxication, but unattended by pleasurable sensation. Dr. Kinglake, who felt my pulse, informed me that it was rendered quicker and fuller.

This trial did not satisfy me with regard to its powers; comparing it with the former ones I was unable to determine whether the operation was stimulant or depressing.

APRIL 17. I communicated the result to Dr. Beddoes and he was present when the following experiment was made. Having previously closed my nostrils and exhaused my lungs I breathed four quarts of nitrous oxide from and into a silk bag. The first feelings were similar to those produced in the last experiment, but in less than half-a-minute the respiration being continued, they diminished gradually, and were succeeded by a sensation analogous to gentle pressure on all the muscles, attended by a highly pleasurable thrilling, particularly in the chest and the extremities. The objects around me became dazzling and my hearing more acute. Towards the last inspirations the thrilling increased, the sense of muscular power became greater, and at last an irresistible propensity to action was indulged in. I recollect but indistinctly what followed; I know that my motions were various and violent.

These effects very soon ceased after respiration. In ten minutes I had recovered my natural state of mind. The thrilling in the extremities continued longer than the other sensations. This experiment was made in the morning. No languor or exhaustion was consequent; my feelings throughout the day were as usual, and I passed the night in undisturbed repose.

APRIL 18. The next morning the recollections of the effects of the gas were very indistinct, and had not remarks written down immediately after the experiment recalled them to my mind I should even have doubted of their reality. I was willing indeed to attribute some of the strong emotion to the enthusiasm which I supposed must necessarily have been connected with the perception of agreeable feelings when I was prepared to experience painful sensations. Two experiments, however, made in the course of this day, with scepticism, convinced me that the effects were solely owing to the specific operation of the gas. In each of them I breathed five quarts of nitrous oxide for rather a longer time than before. The sensations produced were similar, perhaps not quite so pleasurable. The muscular motions were much less violent.

Having thus ascertained the powers of the gas, I made many experiments to ascertain the length of time for which it might be breathed with safety, its effects on the pulse, and its general effects on the health when often respired. I found that I could breathe nine quarts of nitrous oxide for three minutes, and twelve quarts for rather more than four. I could never breathe it in any quantity so long as five minutes. Whenever its operation was carried to the highest extent the pleasurable thrilling at its height about the middle of the experiment gradually diminished, the sense of pressure on the muscles was lost, impressions ceased to be perceived, vivid ideas passed rapidly through the mind, and voluntary power was altogether destroyed, so that the mouth-piece generally dropped from my unclosed lips. Generally, when I breathed from six to seven quarts muscular motions were produced to a certain extent. Sometimes I manifested my pleasure by stamping or laughing only; at other times by dancing round the room and vociferating.

MAY 3. To ascertain whether the gas would accelerate or retard the progress of sleep, I breathed at about eight o'clock in the evening 25 quarts of nitrous oxide in quantities of six at a time, allowing but short intervals between each dose. The feelings were much less pleasurable than usual, and during the consumption of the two last doses, almost indifferent. Indeed, the gas was breathed rather too soon after its production and contained some suspended acid vapour which stimulated the lungs so as to induce coughing. After the experiments, for the first time I was somewhat depressed and debilitated. My propensity to sleep, however, came on at the usual hour, and as usual was indulged in. My repose was sound and unbroken.

Between MAY and JULY. I habitually breathed the gas, occasionally three or four times a day for a week together; at other periods, four or five times a week only. The general effects of its operation upon my health and state of mind are extremely difficult of description, nor can I well discriminate between its agency and that of other physical and moral causes. I slept much less than usual, and previous to sleep my mind was long occupied by visual imagery. I had a constant desire of action, a restlessness and an uneasy feeling . . . analogous to the sickness of hope. But perhaps these phenomena in some measure depended on the interest and labour connected with the experimental investigation relating to the production of nitrous oxide by which I was at this time incessantly occupied.
. . .

[Davy continued his experiments.]
Between SEPTEMBER and the end of OCTOBER. I made but

few experiments on respiration, almost the whole of my time being devoted to chemical experiments on the production and analysis of nitrous oxide. At this period my health being somewhat injured by the constant labour of experimenting and the perpetual inhalation of the acid vapours of the laboratory, I went to Cornwall where new associations of ideas and feelings, common exercise, a pure atmosphere, luxurious diet and moderate indulgence in wine in a month restored me to health and vigour.

(d) The need for scientists to communicate with each other encouraged the exchange of scientific papers and the formation of societies.

Source: Article by John Playfair in the Supplement to 4th, 5th and 6th editions of the *Encyclopedia Britannica* (1816–24).

Frequent communication of ideas, and a regular method of keeping up such communication, are evidently essential to works in which great labour and industry are to be employed and to which much time must necessarily be devoted; when the philosopher must not always sit quietly in his cabinet, but must examine nature with his own eyes, and be present in the workshop of the mechanic, or the laboratory of the chemist. These operations are facilitated by the institutions now referred to, which, therefore, are of more importance to the physical sciences than to the other branches of knowledge. They who cultivate the former are also fewer in number, and being, of course, farther separated, are less apt to meet together in the common intercourse of the world. The historian, the critic, the poet, finds everywhere men who can enter in some degree at least into his pursuits, who can appreciate his merit, and derive pleasure from his writings or his conversation. The mathematician, the astronomer, the mechanician, sees few men who have much sympathy with his pursuits, or who do not look with indifference on the objects which he pursues. The *world*, to him, consists of a few individuals, by the censures or approbation of whom the public opinion must be finally determined; with them it is material that he should have more frequently intercourse than could be obtained by casual encounter; and he feels that the society of men engaged in pursuits similar to

GG

his own, is a necessary *stimulus* to his exertions. Add to this, that such societies become centers in which information concerning facts is collected from all quarters. For all these reasons, the greatest benefit has resulted from the scientific institutions which, since the middle of the seventeenth century, have become so numerous in Europe.

(e) In the meantime science was a growing mystery to most laymen. Throughout the century there were experiments with electricity, which thrilled and astonished contemporaries. Joseph Priestley wrote an interesting *History and Present State of Electricity* (1767) dealing with them. Wesley wondered whether diseases could be cured by electric shock treatment.

Source: Journal of Thomas Turner, 28 April 1761.

There being at Janes's a person with an electrical machine, my niece and I went to see it; and tho' I have seen it several years agoe, I think there is something in it agreeable and instructing, but at the same time very surprising. As to my own part, I am quite at a loss to form any idea of the phœinomina.

12. MEDICINE

There had been many brilliant discoveries in the medical history of the seventeenth century, but it took time for learning to be applied to regular medical practice. Folk remedies were employed despite the development of sophisticated medical 'systems', many of them reflecting the influence of the Enlightenment. One of the main European centres of medical education was Edinburgh, where important reforms were introduced in 1726, and a distinguished line of professors began to develop university studies. Among the new 'inventions' of the century were forceps: another innovation was 'inoculation' against smallpox, introduced from the East in 1717, and followed up by vaccination in 1796.

(a) *Source:* A Cure for the Gout in *The Lady's Companion* (1753 edn.), vol. II, p. 387.

Half an Ounce of Hiera-picra, and eight Grains of Cochineal, finely powdered, being put into a Pint of the best Red Port, let it stand at least twenty-four Hours, shake the Bottle well, and often, during that Time, but shake not the Bottle for three or four Hours before you draw off any of the Tincture for Use; take of this half a Quartern, according as you find yourself strong or weak; you must continue taking of this every second, third, or fourth Day, till you take the whole Pint; and if the Gout returns, take another Pint as before, and so do to every Fit. This Tincture, if taken in a Fit of the Gout, in a few Hours dissolves all the Particles in the Blood, which causes the Pain, and if pursued, as before directed, will, in Time, work them all out of the Blood.

(b) *Source:* F. Turner (ed.), *A Berkshire Batchelor's Diary* (1932), p. 33. A Rt. to Cure ye Bite of a Mad Dog.

Of ye leaves of Rue pick'd from ye Stalks, six ounces, garlic pick'd and bruis'd four ounces, Venice treacle four ounces, scrapings of Pewter four ounces, metidate four ounces. Boil these ingredients over a slow fire in 2 quarts of strong Ale till one Pinte is consum'd; then keep it in a Bottle close stop'd and give of it 7 spoonfuls to a man or woman, warm, seven mornings fasting, and six to a dog.

This the author believes will not by God's blessing fail, if it be given within 9 days after ye bite of ye dog. Apply some of ye ingredients from wch. ye liquor was strained to ye bitten place.

N.B. This Rect. was taken out of Cathrop [Calthrop?] Church in Lincolnshire; many of ye inhabitants being bitten by mad dogs. All who took this medicine did well and recovered. The others died mad. It has also been found effectual when applied to other animals.

(c) Doctors were more professionalized at the end of the century than at the beginning, but they remained divided and stratified. Apothecaries, once tradesmen, became practising doctors; surgeons finally ceased to be linked with barbers; and physicians, the only 'gentlemen' of the profession at the beginning of the century, were more numerous and more 'professionally' educated, although still only a small *élite*. Physicians saw their patients only rarely.

Source: Letter from Henry Purefoy to his surgeon, 7 Oct. 1742, printed in *Purefoy Letters* (1931), vol. I, p. 100.

Sir!/

Since you was so kind to desire to know what effect your medicines had on mee I can now acquaint you I have done taking what you prescribed mee last ffriday and I hope they will perform a cure on my Leg, and then I shall think my Journey to Bath very fortunate. I have kept the Plaister to my leg as you ordered & it is quite dryed without any soreness or Tendernesse. I have not yet had an Issue made in my Leg & should be glad to know if it could be avoided without danger, if not I will be sure to have it done out of hand when I have your answer. The swelling in my Leg is in a manner quite gone. I bound on a binder higher on my leg besides that which you bound on, which I thought helped to lessen the swelling thereof. I desire your Directions whether I must take your last Prescriptions any more or if you would order mee anything else I still continue your plaister on & to swath my Leg as usuall. . .

(d) There is an interesting account of the costs of medical care in 1742/4 in the Mildmay Archives. The extract is printed in Edwards (ed.), *English History from Essex Sources*, vol. I, pp. 165–6.

			£	s.	d.
1742:	Mar. 1	Longmore my butler having a violent cold and inflammation in his breast, I sent for Dr. Barker. Gave him	1.	1.	0
	Mar. 22	For the lodgings and diet of Luke one of my footmen at Chelsea after he had had the measles £0. 8. 6. and also for his nurse and lodgings in Town during the time he had them, £1. 1. 0	1.	9.	6
	July 3	Gave Dr. Barker for his advice, having been troubled for some days with a lightness in my head—he advised bleeding	1.	1.	0
	July 3	Gave Mr. Hawkins for taking away ten ounces of blood	1.	1.	0
1743:	Jan. 19 to 22	Gave to Dr. Barker for advising my Lady Fitzwalter in a fit of the gout	4.	4.	0
	Feb. 8,9	Gave Dr. Barker for attending my Lady Fitzwalter on a return of the gout in a violent manner in the same foot	2.	2.	0
	Apr. 16	Gave Dr. Barker for coming to me 3 times upon a complaint of a lightness in my head, having a great cold	3.	3.	0
	Apr. 13	Gave Mr. Hawkins for bleeding me N.B. the sixteenth I took physic	1.	1.	0
	July 7	To Dr. Barker, being troubled with a palpitation	1.	1.	0
1744:	Mar. 19	Gave Mr. Curedin for syringing both my ears	2.	2.	0

(e) A few doctors' diaries survive.

Source: E. Hobhouse (ed.), *The Diary of a West Country Physician* (1934). The writer was Dr. Claver Morris (1684–1726).

1719. Jan. 1. My son being Ill, and supposing it would come to the Measles, I gave him a gentle Purge just as I saw immediately some Breaking Out on the Skin. The Purge made him very sick, and work'd with him 3 or 4 times. About 5 in the Afternoon 5 Spoonfuls of his Cordial-Mixture were given. . . .

Jan 2. My Son was very likely to Die in the Measles; though they were come out. . . .

Oct. 21. I was taken sick betwixt 11 and 12 a clock, with a shivering and coldness, like an Ague, I could not dine. I continued Ill all the afternoon. Prescribed for myself.

Oct. 22. I took a Purging Bolus last night, and with drinking Bawm [balm] tea, I attended on it working this day, I had 5 Stools.

1720. March 17. Visited Mr. Shirley at Sherborn. He was very Ill of a Jaundice, & his Physician Dr. Bull not discerning rightly his Disease, & Prescribing very languid Medicines for what he thought it, He desired mine Assistance, & I prescribed.

(f) For smallpox and the fears it engendered, and inoculation as a somewhat alarming way of dealing with its dangers, there is much evidence.

Source: Letter from Sanderson Miller to T. Lennard Barrett, 1744, printed in L. Dickins and N. Stanton (eds.), *An Eighteenth-Century Correspondence* (1910), pp. 95–6.

Dear Sir,—There is no reason why you should make any apology for your letter which I look upon as the strongest mark of your Friendship. I have never had occasion to study the Controversy about Innoculation, and indeed I always thought it a matter of prudence only. I believe there is much less chance for the Child's dying now, than there is if she has it in the common way, and as her station will oblige her to be much in Town, it is very improbable that she will excape it entirely, besides if she should, the tears and anxieties that the thoughts of the distemper might give her some day may be as bad consequence as the distemper itself. You see there are sufficient reasons for people to innoculate their Boys, and I am sure the reasons are much stronger for innoculating Girls, because the Ladies are generally of a more timorous disposition, and therefore it is more dangerous and if they have it during pregnancy it is found to be very fatal. . . . But in this case I would not venture to advise without having the same regard for you as for the Child.

(g) Edward Jenner, a friend and pupil of the great medical professor John Hunter, won both friends and enemies for his experiments with vaccination.

Source: A Resolution recorded in the Minutes of the Essex and Herts. Benevolent Medical Society, 1801, reprinted in Brown (ed.), *English History from Essex Sources*, vol. II, p. 146.

That the thanks of this court be given to Dr Jenner for his invaluable treatise on the Variola Vaccina, wherein he has clearly and satisfactorily demonstrated that the inoculated cow pox is a certain preventive of the small pox.

That as men of humanity, associated for the purposes of benevolence, we should be wanting to the character we assume, did we neglect the present opportunity of bearing our testimony to the value of this providential discovery, which, if generally practised we are of opinion, would effectually eradicate the small pox, one of the severest scourges of the human race.

(h) Throughout the century there was increasing if intermittent concern for public health. 154 hospitals, infirmaries and dispensaries were opened between 1700 and 1825. There were only about 3000 patients in hospitals in 1800, however, and they were still unclassified. Standards of cleanliness had improved even if it did not always come next after godliness. Sir John Floyer's *Right Use of Hot, Cold and Temperate Baths*, which ran through six editions between 1697 and 1722, had made no mention of bathing for cleanliness.

Source: D. Defoe, *Tour* (1724), letter II.

The Hospitals in and about the City of *London*, deserve a little further Observation, especially those more remarkable for their Magnitude, as,

I. *Bethlem*, or *Bedlam:* This and *Bridewell*, indeed, go together, for though they are Two several Houses, yet they are Incorporated together, and have the same Governors; also the President, Treasurer, Clerk, Physician and Apothecary are the same; but the Stewards and the Revenue are different, and so are the Benefactions; but to both very great.

The Orders for the Government of the Hospital of *Bethlem* are exceeding Good, and a remarkable Instance of the good Disposition of the Gentlemen concerned in it, especially those that follow;

1. That no Person, except the proper Officers who tend them, be allowed to see the Lunaticks of a *Sunday*.

2. That no Person be allowed to give the Lunaticks strong Drink, Wine, Tobacco or Spirits, or to sell any such thing in the Hospital.

3. That no Servant of the House shall take any Money given to any of the Lunaticks to their own Use; but that it shall be carefully kept for them till they are recovered, or laid out for them in such things as the Committee approves.

4. That no Officer or Servant shall beat or abuse, or offer any Force to any Lunatick; but on absolute Necessity. The rest of the Orders are for the good Government of the House. . . .

II. The hospital of *Bridewell*, as it is an Hospital, so it is also a House of Correction. The House was formerly the King's City Palace;

. . . As Idle Persons, Vagrants, &c. are committed to this House for Correction, so there are every Year, several poor Lads brought up to Handicraft Trades, as Apprentices, and of these the Care is in the Governors, who maintain them out of the standing Revenues of the House. . . .

The other City Hospitals, are the *Blue-coat* Hospital for poor Freemen's Orphan Children, and the Two Hospitals for Sick and Maimed People, as St. *Bartholomew's* and St. *Thomas's*.

III. *Christ's* Hospital was originally constituted by King *Edward* VI, who has the Honour of being the Founder of it. . . . It is now so far increased in substance, by the Benefactions of worthy Gentlemen Contributors, they now maintain near a Thousand, who have Food, Cloathing and Instruction, useful and sufficient Learning, and exceeding good Discipline; and at the Proper Times they are put out to Trades, suitable to their several Genius's and Capacities, and near Five thousand Pounds a Year are expended on this Charity.

IV. St. *Bartholomew's* Hospital . . . from [a] small Beginning, rose to the Greatness we now see it arrived at, of which take the following Account for one Year, *viz.* 1718;

Cur'd and discharg'd, of Sick, Maimed and Wounded from all Parts }	3088
Buried at the Expence of the House	198
Remaining under Cure	513

V. St. *Thomas's* Hospital in *Southwark* . . . has received greater Benefactions than St. *Bartholomew's*; but then 'tis also said to have suffered greater Losses, especially by several great Fires in *Southwark* and elsewhere, as by the Necessity of expensive Buildings, which, notwithstanding the charitable Gifts of divers great Benefactors, has cost the Hospital great Sums. The State of this Hospital is so advanced at this Time, that in the same Year as above, *viz.* 1718, the State of the House was as follows:

Cur'd and discharged of Sick, Wounded and Maimed from all Parts, }	3608
Buried at the Expence of the House	216
Remaining under Cure	566

Adjoining to this of St. *Thomas's*, is lately laid a noble Foundation of a new Hospital, by the charitable Gift and single Endowment of one Person, and, perhaps, the greatest of its kind, next to that of *Suttons* Hospital, that ever was founded in this Nation by one Person, whether private or publick, not excepting the Kings themselves.

This will, I suppose, be called *Guy's* Hospital, being to be Built and Endowed at the sole Charge of one Mr. *Thomas Guy*, formerly a Bookseller in *Lombard-street*, who lived to see the said Hospital not only designed, the Ground purchased and cleared, but the Building begun, and a considerable Progress made in it, and died [in 1724] while these Sheets were in the Press.

CHAPTER XV

Politics in a Changing Society

Our house is every day so very full of Country People, that its like an Election time.

(Letter from LORD FERMANAGH to RALPH
VERNEY, 31 Dec. 1712)

You will be of the House of Commons as soon as you are of age, and first you must be a figure there if you would make a figure in your country.

(Letter from LORD CHESTERFIELD to his son,
5 Dec. 1749)

You ask me my sentiments upon the affair of Mr. Wilks . . . I don't love Riots and Turmults. But it is necessary that it should be known, that the Nation is not satisfied.

(The DUKE OF NEWCASTLE, April 1768)

The present extraordinary era . . . affords a noble opportunity for the contemplation of wisdom, and, in the improvement of legislative and political establishments, for the exercise of human ability. . . . The particular objects next in succession to these great universal attainments, is the colonial and domestic prosperity of the British Empire, to restore to the Constitution and the Laws their original spirit, to preserve them from visionary emendations, and to support every measure which Reason dictates for their improvement and perfection in Church and State.

(Address to the Public, announcing the
publication of *The Observer*, Dec. 1791)

To enlighten the people, to show the people the reason, the ground for all their sufferings.

(The Object of the London Corresponding
Society, as defined by a witness at the Trial of
THOMAS HARDY, 1793)

465

1. THE CONSTITUTION

There was no written constitution in eighteenth-century Britain, yet most Englishmen during the eighteenth century referred legal and political questions to *the* Constitution as it had been left after 'the Glorious Revolution' of 1688. The Constitution was admired. even venerated by lawyers like Blackstone, and extolled by foreigners. Even radicals talked not of altering the Constitution but of restoring it. There were, however, many conflicting interpretations of what the Constitution meant, particularly after the American War of 1775 to 1783, which unsettled much in English life and politics. The French Revolution marked an even bigger break.

(a) *Source:* T. Somerville, *Observations on the Constitution and Present State of Britain* (1793), p. 1.

It cannot be deemed necessary to use many words in endeavoring to prove the existence of the British Constitution, to which the following pages principally refer. The form of the British constitution has often been described and explained. Its essential, constituent parts; their coordinate, combined influence in the legislature; their separate functions and interests; are understood by every person instructed in the elements of domestic policy. The spirit and principles of our constitution, well-known and familiar, are the standard to which we appeal in all our political disputes; and by which we estimate the merits and utility of measures of state.

(b) *Source:* Edmund Burke, *On The Reform of Representation in the House of Commons* (1782).

A nation is not an idea only of local extent, and individual momentary aggregation; but it is an idea of continuity, which extends in time as well as in numbers and in space. And this is a choice not of one day, or one set of people, not a tumultuary and giddy choice; it is a deliberate election of the ages and of generations; it is a constitution made by what is ten thousand times better than choice, it is made by the peculiar circumstances, occasions, tempers, dispositions, and moral, civil and social habitudes of the people, which disclose themselves only in a long space of time.

(c) *Source:* Timothy Telltruth, *The Collected Wisdom of Ages, The Most Stupendous Fabric of Human Invention, the English Constitution* (Philadelphia, 1799), pp. v ff.

The present constitution of England . . . is, by no means, that constitution which laid the foundation of English grandeur and riches, and introduced into that country the arts; those arts which in the hands of Englishmen have been improved, so as to excel all nations, and give them the pre-eminence in every quarter of the globe. . . . No! The present constitution is not calculated to build up, but to destroy; to render ineffectual even the temperance and salubrity of the climate; the richness of the soil; and above all to cramp the inventive genius and enterprizing spirit of Englishmen. . . . The government of England is liable to great, though imperceptible revolutions, and . . . the sovereign power may be transferred from the cabinct council to the king, if he chance to be a man of strong intellects, and have sufficient knowledge of mankind, and the art of governing; and *vice versa* if he should be a man of weak parts, and the members of the council ambitious. . . . It is also probable that the house of commons, if assisted by the people might obtain the sovereignty, but this would be a more stormy revolution and difficult to accomplish, for every transfer of the sovereignty from one body to another is a revolution. The English constitution, as it is considered by foreigners, and contemplated in theory, is perfect only when the bodies politic are respectively afraid of, and kept in awe by each other. . . . [At present] what with a splendid establishment for a royal family, and the members of the executive or cabinet council; a standing army; an immense navy (useless in time of peace): an expensive church establishment, and above all an enormous national debt, the very interest of which is now equal to all the other expenses of government; the people groan under an excessive weight of taxes which ultimately fall upon the lower classes. . . . [Yet as now] the poor are reduced as low as possible, no other resource is left for Pitt but to tax the rich, which, it appears, he is sensible of, by his taxes upon income, carriages, hair powder etc. But it cannot be expected (because it never has been known in the history of man) that the rich will bear oppression as patiently as the poor, therefore, it may be naturally supposed that the middling class of people, or employers in England, feeling themselves oppressed, will instruct the working people in their rights and wrongs and stir them up to sedition and revolt.

(d) The principles of the 'Enlightenment' were used by some late eighteenth-century radicals to test government.

Source: T. Walker, *A Review of Some of the Political Events which have occurred in Manchester during the last Five Years* (1794), pp. 1–2.

Of late years . . . it has been suspected, that society and civil government originally were, or ought to have been, intended to promote and render permanent the happiness of individuals who thus connect themselves with each other. . . . It has become important to ascertain . . . how the *few* have permanently contrived to live in affluence and luxurious indulgence, while the *many* drag on an existence laborious and miserable, in ignorance and vice, in pain and poverty! It is not great wonder that any set of men should prefer their own interest and inclination to that of their neighbours. . . . But though a melancholy, it is a very instructive problem, to ascertain how it thus happened, that the great mass, not merely of a community, but of mankind, should have for ages submitted to this state of things.

2. INFLUENCE

There were frequent displays of strong feeling in eighteenth-century politics, although the distribution of power and influence between different social classes was not a major issue before the nineteenth century. Political power was based on property, with landed property being treated as the foundation of society. The landed interest dominated parliamentary and local life, and any study of 'party' labels must begin with the facts of family connexion and 'interest'. 'Influence' operated in relation to social life, business, appointments and, not least, elections. 'Crude pressure', in Sir Lewis Namier's phrase, shaded off 'by almost imperceptible degrees' into traditions of influence.

(a) In Chester, for example, the Grosvenor family, living four miles away at Eaton Hall, exercised persistent local influence. Between 1715

POLITICS IN A CHANGING SOCIETY

and 1874 they always held one of Chester's two seats in the House of Commons and for 42 years both seats. The following letter, among the Grosvenor papers, is from the Town Clerk to Sir Richard Grosvenor, M.P. for Chester, after the latter had informed him in Dec. 1760 that he expected to be made a peer.

Source: Sir Lewis Namier and J. Brooke, *The House of Commons, 1754–90* (1964), vol. I, p. 221.

At an assembly of our corporation held yesterday the favour of your obliging and kind letter was presented and read. I am directed by the unanimous voice of the house to express their true and sincere thanks for all your repeated and willing services to this city, at the same time to assure you that Mr. Bootle's offer to fulfill the trust you are soon to resign [and to become M.P.] is wholly pleasing to the body. I am further to inform you, Sir, that the citizens think themselves happy in having your wishes and intentions for their welfare. The obligations they have so long received from you and your ancestors so much command their inclinations to be grateful, that your approbation is in their minds a sufficient foundation for their acceptance, and for those expectations they have already formed of your intended successor.

On all occasions, Sir, the city will hereafter confide in possessing your patronage and esteem. On their parts they will be always ready to exert the most unalterable attachment and regard to you and your worthy family.

(b) It was not only landed aristocracy which exercised 'influence'. All other groups used influence naturally and un-selfconsciously whenever they could.

Source: Note on the West Indian 'interest' (about 40 members) in the House of Commons in 1764 from the *Gentleman's Magazine*, vol. XXXVI, p. 230.

In almost every contest between the West-Indians and North-Americans, the West-Indians gained their point: In a very few instances, national justice and good sense defeated the combined power of the West-Indian aristocracy; for, in short, they considered themselves entitled to double influence, as members of the House of Commons, and people of large property both at home and abroad.

(c) Yet there were many critics of 'influence'.

Source: Note in the pre-election number of the *Political Register,*
March 1768.

The power of the grandees is ... become more formidable
than ever. Their number, their privileges, their court-emolu-
ments, their *influence* in *elections,* their weight in the law, the
army, the navy, the church, and the public offices, are all to an
unexampled degree increased. ... It is not for nothing, that
the wisdom of our ancestors established it as a fundamental
maxim, which is to this day (for form's sake) a standing
resolution of the House of Commons, that no lord of parliament, or peer of the realm, ought to interfere in elections of
members of the lower house. But to observe how electioneering
is, in our times, carried on, one would imagine the law of this
land was, That no member of the House of Commons should
be elected, but in *consequence* of *quality-influence.* ...

(d) It was possible to catalogue and to generalize about different
aspects of patronage and influence.

Source: Note relating to elections in the *Report on the State of
Representation* (1792), p. 30.

The patronage your Committee have divided under two
heads—*Nomination,* and *Influence*; and attributed it to distinct
persons, under the descriptions of *Peers* and *Commoners.*

   With respect to this first division, your Committee desire to
have it understood, that by a Nomination, they would describe
that absolute authority in a borough which enables the patron
to command the return. ... These [boroughs] in general are
the private property of the patrons, or have the right of voting
vested in a small corporate body the majority of whom are
his immediate dependants. By Influence, your Committee
would describe that degree of weight acquired in a particular
county, city or borough, which accustoms the electors on all
vacancies to expect the recommendation of a candidate by the
patron, and induces them, either from fear, from private interest, or from incapacity to oppose, because he is so recommended,
to adopt him.

3. ELECTIONS

Elections were often noisy and 'corrupt', providing opportunities for riot and disturbance. They were also expensive. For these reasons alone—apart from the deliberate counter balancing of local interests—there were large numbers of electoral compacts and understandings. The number of contested elections was never more than a small fraction of the total. There was, however, no uniform borough franchise, and in a number of boroughs there were frequent open contests. The desire to become a Member of Parliament was strong. 'To be out of Parliament is to be out of the World', wrote Admiral Rodney in 1780.

(a) *Source:* Letter from Sir Thomas Cave to Lord Fermanagh, 23 April 1715 in Lady Verney (ed.), *The Verney Letters of the Eighteenth Century* (1930), pp. 332–3. The letter relates to a Leicestershire County Election.

From the proceedings in the election it was by most conjectured that our antagonists would not appear nor disturb us, but they contradicted by a demand in person for their poll. . . . Ashby and Byrd obstinately stood a poll of 3 days continually buying off our votes at three and a half crowns, £1 15s. 0d., & 5s. per vote, and asiduously endeavoured to procure all second votes for Sir Geffery which they could not make for one of them, that I'm surprised how I gott to the number of 2203—Sir G. 2251, Ashby 1630, Byrd 1639—yet I hear the busy Lord Harborrow made very sure of getting the better of Us, we kept ourselfes very quiett (though frequently provoked) and free from Bribery . . . that tis hop't no petition shall be preferred. Ld. Keeper Wright heard we were in town and lest tricks should be played we came to Leicester on Wednesday night, and stay'd during the whole Contest. He protests to spend his blood and Estate before this Country shall be nos'd by any Duke in Xendom, and sure the Ducke of Auckland and Harborrow must think Us very stubborn. Mrs. Packe was Agt. Us and I'le ask her no more. Esquire Digswell, my Brother-in-Law, showed his goodwill against me this second time, and the Shame returns to himself.

(b) The Duke of Somerset was prepared to extend the power of his influence in Marlborough.

Source: Notes of Lord Bruce's election agent, Beecher, 29 July and 6 Aug. 1712. MSS of the Marquess of Ailesbury, printed in *Pryings Among Private Papers* (1905), pp. 205–6.

. . . I came hither on Monday & went to Marlborough yesterday, where I found that the D[uke] himself had been driving very high bargains with the burgesses for the next mayor & Parliament men. . . . He offered Mr. Meggs to become his servant in the nature of a surveyor, & to settle 40li. upon him & wife for their lives & to make his place worth 40li a year more to him. To John Clarke he promised to put him into a place in the Bluecoat Hospital worth 50li. or 60li. per annum, to pay his debts & employ him in all business at his farm. This not prevailing, he offered Clarke 200li. ready money. To Solomon Clarke he proposed settling 20li. per annum on him & his wife for life, to give him 30li. in hand, & to lend him more to increase his present stock of money for pin making, to merchandise or take off all the pins he should make & pay his debts. To William Garlick he offered what ready money he would ask, & to pay all his debts, & in hopes to make him comply (or to rid him out of the way as some say) Mr. Piggott drank the poor old man to such a pitch that he was very near death & 'tis thought would have died had not Dr. Savery taken great pains with him, he is so well to go about again, but very weak. . . . All these have flatly refused the D[uke] & rejected his offers. . . .

[Aug. 6.] . . . Rogers says the Duke declares publicly he will give 50li. a man for as many as will desert your Lordship [Bruce] & come over to him. He has actually given John Smith 100li. down, & engaged to be at the charge of educating a son of Smith's of seven year old at school & University, & to present him to a good living when he is capable of it—a good distant prospect this—but however, with the 100li. ready money, it has prevaled with Smith to leave your Lordship. In the room of whom we have got Flurry Bowshire for 40 guineas &c. . . . I am very sorry for this expense, my Lord, but without it your Lordship's interest would have been entirely defeated for ever, should the point be gained as to mayor, for Rogers assures me they do intend to bring in a sufficient number of Whig burgesses to secure elections to themselves hereafter, in case they succeed in the mayor.

(c) At Northampton in 1768 there were about 1000 voters, two-thirds of the adult male population. On the eve of a great contest in 1768, when three earls battled for their candidates, a compact was drawn up concerning election procedures.

Source: Agreement of 23 Oct. 1767, in the Northamptonshire Record Office, quoted in Brooke and Namier, *The House of Commons, 1774–1790* (1966), vol. I, p. 345.

1. That mobbing of all kinds shall be discontinued and discouraged by the above Lords, and gentlemen and all their friends from this time until the election shall be over.
2. That no house be opened at any time or any ticket given for drink or liquor either by the above mentioned principals, their friends or agents from this time until the day of election, except on seven days notice to the gentlemen who sign this paper.
3. That if on any occasion houses should be opened after seven days notice, it shall be done by tickets for drink given to the men inhabitants, half a crown to drink to those who have promised one vote and a crown to drink to those who have promised two.
4. That it shall be recommended by the principals and agents on both sides to prevent any noise and riots in the clubs or public meetings from this time till after the day of election, that no torches on either side shall be delivered and that the master shoemakers and woolcombers be persuaded as much as possible to treat their own men on St. Crispin's night and on the 3rd February.
5. That the candidates agree not to walk the town in canvass or make a personal application in it for a vote from this time till the election, unless at the committee (except on 7 days notice).
6. That the expense be limited to 2 guineas in the house where the committee shall meet.
7. That the damage done to the windows of the George Inn be repaired at a joint expense.
8. That the committee shall not meet oftener than once a week.

(d) Sometimes, of course, the number of electors was very small. In most 'pocket boroughs' there were few elections: when there was one, the result was often very close.

Source: Report in *The Times*, 6 June 1796.

Election for Launceston, Cornwall. Candidates, Hon. Mr. Rawdon, Mr. Brogden. The numbers were as follows:—

Hon. Mr. Rawden and Mr. Brogden   .   .   .   12.
Dalkeith and Garthshore . . . . 11.

This contest here was a hard fought battle between the Duke of Northumberland and the Duke of Buccleugh. Both parties have spent a great deal of money: but the former has carried the day.

(e) Boroughs could be bought from their owners, as Sir Francis Burdett, later a radical leader, bought Boroughbridge from the Duke of Newcastle's trustees in 1795.

Source: M. W. Patterson, *Sir Francis Burdett and His Times* (1903), vol. I, pp. 38–9, letter from Burdett to his father-in-law, T. Coutts.

DEAR SIR,

I have no objection to accepting the offer of the Duke of Newcastle's Borough, if I have got the money which is more than I know. I forget how much it was you mentioned to me, but that's of no consequence if I have it.

Yours,

F. BURDETT.

The bargain took this precise form:

Memorandum.   3rd May, 1796.

That it is agreed between the Trustees of the lately deceased Thomas Duke of Newcastle & Mr Thomas Coutts—that on Francis Burdett Esq. being returned a member to serve in the ensuing Parliament & having sat fifteen days without any Petition or objection having been preferred against him, The said Mr Coutts shall pay the sum of Four Thousand Pounds by applying the same towards discharging the Debt due to him by the said lately deceased Duke—which £4000 is to be in full & to include all charges & expences whatsoever; & if such Parliament shall be disolved before its having sat for the period of six years, The Trustees promise & undertake to bring the said Mr Burdett in again to Parliament to sit for such time as (together with the time past) shall complete the period of six years in all, & no longer—At the end of which period Mr Coutts undertakes that Mr Burdett shall pledge his honour to vacate his seat if he should be called on so to do by the Trustees.

It is also agreed between the said Trustees & Mr Coutts that during the period of six years above mentioned if Mr Burdett's seat at any time should be vacated by his acceptance of any Office or otherwise, He shall be reelected, He Mr Burdett in that case paying any sum not exceeding Three Hundred Pounds that the Trustees may state to have been expended on the occasion.

J. G. KNIGHT.
G. W. MASON.

4. PATRONAGE

Although there were 'political parties' in some of the constituencies, these were, for most of the century, instruments of connexion. In Parliament also, it was not the tie of party which bound members together in the mid-eighteenth century so much as the tie of connexion and the strength of patronage. (For the early century, see J. H. Plumb, *The Growth of Political Stability in England* (1967).) Government itself depended on the regular service of 'placemen'. There were sharp debates about the numbers of 'placemen' and the influence of the Crown in the 1770s and 1780s. Patronage, however, like influence, was a fact not only of politics but of late-eighteenth-century life as a whole (see above, p. 438).

(a) *Source:* Letter from Sir John Rushout to the Duke of Newcastle, 24th Jan. 1756, printed in L. B. Namier, *The Structure of Politics*, vol. I, p. 18.

I have never troubled your Grace for any great, much less, for any lucrative employment . . . for my fortune is sufficient for me, in any station of life, but my whole ambition centers in the hopes of a peerage for my family.

(b) *Source:* J. Douglas, *Seasonable Hints from an Honest Man on the present important Crisis of a new Reign and a new Parliament* (1761), pp. 37–8.

I am very sensible, that there are many well-meaning persons who seem to think, that without corruption, there might be danger apprehended from democratical encroachments on prerogative.—But ... when we consider, in how many boroughs the Government has voters at its command; when we consider the vast body of persons employed in the collection of the revenue in every part of the kingdom; the inconceivable number of placemen, and candidates for places in the customs, in the excise, in the post office, in the dockyards, in the ordnance, in the salt office, in the stamps, in the navy and victualling offices, and in a variety of other departments; when we consider again the extensive influence of the money corporations, subscription jobbers, and contractors; the endless dependence created by the obligations conferred on the bulk of the gentlemen's families throughout the kingdom, who have relatives preferred or about to be preferred, or waiting to be preferred, in our navy, and numerous standing army; when, I say, we consider how wide, how binding a dependence on the crown is created by the above enumerated particulars, no lover of monarchy need fear any bad consequences from shutting up the Exchequer at elections; especially when to the endless means the crown has of influencing the votes of the electors, we add the vast number of employments which the fashion of the times makes the elected desirous of, and for the obtaining which, they must depend upon the crown.

(c) *Source:* Advertisement in *The Times*, 15 April 1793.

PLACE UNDER GOVERNMENT. To be disposed of, a Genteel Place under Government: present Salary £100 a year, with the chance of rising and other advantages: the next rise will be a considerable one.—Any Young Gentleman, who can command from 500 £ to 1000 £ will be treated with: and by addressing a line to A. Batson's Coffee-house, with real name and place of abode, will be informed of further particulars. N.B. No Brokers will be attended to.

(d) *Source:* Definition of 'Placemen' in C. Pigott, *Political Dictionary* (1795).

Mr. Pitt, and his heaven-born family, Mr. Rose, Henry Dundas, and others. A heavenly, disinterested, and honorable Administration! *Quere.* Is it the king that has made them rogues, or they who have made the king a r. . . .?

5. THE MONARCHY

George III was for most of his fellow-countrymen a popular king, and despite the political difficulties of his reign, a secure king. Yet from Queen Anne's death to the defeat of the Pretender in 1745 (see above, p. 406) there had been a potential and prolonged threat to the Hanoverian succession. During his long reign from 1760 George III consolidated the position of the monarchy despite both the sharp political divisions and his own illness and eventual madness.

(a) *Source:* Letter of Lady Mary Wortley Montagu, 9 Aug. 1714, printed in Lord Wharncliffe (ed.), *The Letters and Works of Lady Mary Wortley Montagu* (1837), vol. I, p. 86.

The Archbishop of York has been come to Bishopsthorpe but three days. I went with my cousin to see the King [George I] proclaimed, which was done . . . with greater crowds of people than I believed to be in York, vast acclamations, and the appearance of a general satisfaction. The Pretender afterwards dragged about the streets and burned. Ringing of bells, bonfires and illuminations, the mob crying Liberty and Property! and Long Live King George! This morning all the principal men of any figure took port for London, and we are alarmed with the fear of attempts from Scotland, though all Protestants here seem unanimous for the Hanover succession.

(b) *Source:* Lord Chesterfield, *Character of Eminent Persons of His Own Time* (1777), p. 9.

George the First was an honest and dull German gentleman, as unfit as unwilling to act the part of a King, which is, to shine and impress. Lazy and inactive even in his pleasures; which were lowly and sensual: He was coolly intrepid, and indolently benevolent. He was diffident of his own parts which made him speak little in public and prefer in his social, which were his favourite, hours, the company of waggs and buffoons. . . . His views and affections were singly confined to the narrow compass of his electorate—England was too big for him—If he had nothing great as a King, he had nothing bad as a Man— and if he does not adorn, at least he will not stain the annals of his country. In private life, he would have been loved and esteemed as a good citizen, a good friend and a good neighbour. —Happy were it for Europe, happy for the world, if there were not greater Kings in it.

(c) 'James III', the Pretender, had obvious weaknesses.

Source: A Rebel, *A True Account of the Proceedings at Perth* (1716), p. 20.

I must not conceal that when we saw the man whom they called our King, we found ourselves not at all animated by his presence, and if he was disappointed in us, we were tenfold more so in him. We saw nothing in him that looked like spirit. He never appeared with cheerfulness and vigour to animate us. His countenance looked extremely heavy. He cared not to come abroad among us soldiers, or to see us handle our arms or do our exercises. Some said, the circumstances he found us in dejected him; I am sure the figure he made dejected us; and had he sent us but 3,000 men of good hopes, and never himself come among us, we had done other things than we have now.

(d) *Source:* Lord Hervey, *Memoirs* (1931 edn., ed. R. Sedgwick), vol. I., pp. 145–6.

His [George II's] faults were more the blemishes of a private man than of a King. . . . He bore the ascendant of his Ministers, who seldom were his favourites, with more patience than he suffered any encroachment on his will from his mistresses. Content to bargain for the gratification of his two predominant passions, Hanover and money, he was almost indifferent to the rest of his royal authority, provided exterior observance was not wanting; for he comforted himself if he did not perceive the diminution of Majesty, though it was notorious to all the rest of the world. Yet he was not so totally careless of the affection and interests of his country as his father had been.

(c) The young George III was imbued with high ideals of monarchy: his early ministers, particularly Bute, were subject to the taunts of the crowds. The references in the last two lines of the following verse are to taxation (see below, p. 494).

Source: J. Freeth, *Political Songster* (1790), p. 9. Freeth was describing a visit to London in 1763.

The King was going to Parliament,
A numerous crowd was round him,
Some huzza'd him as he went,
And others cry'd—confound him!
At length a shout—came thundering out!
Which made the air to ring, Sir,
All in one voice—cry'd no excise,
No BUTE, no Cyder King, Sir.

(d) George III chose Weymouth as his favourite watering place (cf. George IV's choice of Brighton). He was assured of a very loyal welcome there. In 1789 he was recovering from his first bout of mental disorder.

Source: A Letter of Fanny Burney, the diarist, to her father, 13 July 1789, printed in Charlotte Barratt, *Diary and Letters of Fanny Burney* (1904), vol. III, p. 193.

His Majesty is in delightful health, and much-improved spirits. All agree he never looked better. The loyalty of this place is excessive; they have dressed out every street with labels of 'God save the King': all the shops have it over the doors; all the children wear it in their caps, all the labourers in their hats, and all the sailors *in their voices,* for they never approach the house without shouting it aloud, nor see the King, or his shadow, without beginning to huzza, and going on to three cheers. . . . Think but of the surprise of His Majesty when, at the first time of his bathing, he had no sooner popped his royal head under water than a band of music, concealed in a neighbouring machine, struck up 'God save great George our King'.

One thing, however was a little unlucky;—when the Mayor and burgesses came with the address, they requested leave to kiss hands. The Mayor did not kneel, although he was told to do so by an equerry. 'You should have knelt, sir', said the equerry. 'Sir', answered the poor Mayor, 'I cannot.' 'Everybody does, sir.' 'Sir, I have a wooden leg!' Poor man! 'twas such a surprise! and such an excuse as no one could dispute.

(e) This account of an assault on George III on 29 Oct. 1800 shows that the crowds were not always so deferential.

Source: An account in the *Annual Register* (1800).

On the occasion of His Majesty's going to the House of Lords, the Mall and the Parade of St. James's Park, and Parliament Street, were completely choked up with spectators. The crowd was by no means so great at the Coronation. . . . Several noblemen and Cabinet Ministers passed through the Park from Buckingham House about two o'clock. The Earl of Chatham, Duke of Gloucester, &c., were hissed, and the Duke of Portland was very much hooted.

About twenty minutes afterwards the King left Buckingham House, and was violently hissed and hooted and groaned at the whole way; but no violence was offered till he arrived opposite the Ordnance Office, when a small pebble, or marble, or bullet, broke one of the windows. In returning, the moment His Majesty entered the Park the gates of the Horse Guards were shut, for the purpose of excluding the mob who followed the carriage; at which, as it passed opposite Spring Gardens Terrace, another stone was thrown, but it fortunately struck the woodwork between the windows.

The crowd now pressed closely round the coach, and His Majestry, in considerable agitation, signified, by waving his hands to the Horse Guards on each side, his anxiety that the multitude should be kept at a distance. In this way he passed on through the Park, and round by the Stable Yard, into St. James's Palace, at the front gate, the bottom of St. James's Street. A considerable tumult took place when His Majesty was about to alight, and one of the horses in the state coach took fright, threw down an old groom of the name of Dorrington and broke one of his thighs, but it proved, fortunately, a simple fracture; his other thigh was considerably bruised, but not dangerously.

A few minutes after His Majesty had entered the palace, the mob attacked the state coach with stones, and did it great injury. In its way along Pall Mall to the Mews many things were also thrown at it. After a short time the King went, in his private coach, from St. James's to Buckingham House; but, on his way through the Park the mob surrounded the carriage, and prevented it from proceeding, crying out, 'Bread! Bread! Peace! Peace!'—The Guards were, however, speedily brought up, and they protected the carriage till His Majesty got safe into Buckingham House.

When His Majesty entered the House of Peers, the first words he uttered were these, to the Lord Chancellor: 'My Lord, I have been shot at!' This alluded to the substance which had broke the window while passing the Ordnance Office.

6. PARLIAMENT

Regular parliamentary sessions, with debate across the House, distinguished the British political system from that of France. According to Blackstone, 'executive power' was 'checked and kept within due bounds' by the two Houses of Parliament—Lords and Commons. Such statements need careful analysis. What was beyond doubt was that the House of Commons provided the key either to smooth government or to constitutional conflict.

(a) *Source:* P. Grosley, *Observations on England* (1772 edn.), pp. 106ff.

It is in parliament that real eloquence is displayed. There the most important interests are discussed by orators used to speaking, and animated by the love of their country, or at least by the spirit of party. I have had the pleasure of being present at several meetings of both houses, and though I did not understand, I at least saw the warm debates in which they were engaged.

I was deprived of the two greatest pleasures that London could procure me: that of seeing the celebrated Garrick act upon the stage, and the illustrious Mr. Pitt harangue in the house of commons. The nation, at that time, seemed to be in a dangerous situation, and Mr. Pitt was looked upon as the only person capable of saving it; yet he did not make his appearance, but was constantly deaf to the general voice which called upon him to engage in public affairs.

His place as an orator was supplied by Mr. Beckford, who was opposed by Mr. George Grenville; these two gentlemen, seconded by speakers of inferior abilities, headed in the house of commons the two parties which divided the nation; and there was equal laughing in both houses. I could observe nothing remarkable in the action of these orators. They stood up uncovered, and addressed themselves to the speaker, with their legs straddling, one knee somewhat bent, and one arm extended, as if they were going to fence; they harangued a long time, but scarce any body gave attention to what they said, except just at the moment when the members of their party cried out in chorus, Aye, aye.

(b) The House of Commons offered a place for ambitious young men.

Source: J. Mackenzie, *History of the Proceedings of the Parliament of 1784* (1785).

The opportunity which Parliament affords to the young, the bustling, and the ambitious, of canvassing public measures, is one of those salutary counterpoises which our Constitution affords against the weight of the Executive Power. The Opposition in Britain is a sort of public body, which, in the practice at least of our government, is perfectly known and established.

(c) There were many defenders of Parliament as it was constituted.

Source: W. Combe, *A Word in Season to the Traders and Manufacturers of Great Britain* (1792), pp. 14–15.

The House of Commons is chosen by the great bulk of the freeholders in counties, and by different cities and boroughs in the kingdom, according to the several forms which charters or ancient custom have established. It, therefore, not only represents the great mass of landed property, but it has an immediate connection with property of every description. It consists of a mixture of persons chosen by the monied and mercantile interests—by the manufacturers and the mechanics—of those whose fortunes have been originally acquired, or are still embarked in trade. From the manner in which the right of election is distributed, an opening is offered to every man, who rises to an eminence in his own time, whose situation makes him respectable, or whose talents render him useful to the public. Hence it is, that even the places which have no immediate and separate representative, can never be at a loss to find those who have a common interest with themselves. No part of the country, no corner of the kingdom, feels itself neglected or forgotten; a communication is established through all the classes of society, and not only every description of men, but every individual in this country, who feels himself aggrieved, may find his way to Parliament, and is sure of an advocate and a friend. Parliament will be guided, as it ought, by the steady current of public opinion, but it will neither yield to the cry of a misguided populace, nor shift and turn with every gust of the varying passions of the day. This it is which distinguishes the gravity, the consistency, the wisdom of deliberative bodies from the levity and inconsistency of republican assemblies.

(d) Members of Parliament were proud of their independence and unwilling to tie themselves too tightly to their constituents.

Source: A Statement of Lord North, 1784, printed in *Parliamentary History* (1784), vol. XXIV, p. 988.

Those gentlemen who hold that the instructions of the constitutuents ought on all occasions to be complied with do not know the constitution of their country. To surrender their own judgements, to abandon their own opinions, and to act as their constituents thought proper to instruct them, right or wrong, is to act unconstitutionally. . . . They were not sent there, like a states general, to represent a particular province or district, and to take care of the particular interest of that province; they were sent there as trustees, to act for the benefit and advantage of the whole kingdom.

7. POLITICIANS

There were 558 Members of Parliament, all men of property. Only a small number of them, however, considered themselves 'politicians'. Much of their business consisted of private and local legislation—Horace Walpole once complained that the House of Commons was becoming 'a mere quarter sessions, where nothing is transacted but turnpikes and poor rates'—but they also dealt with all key problems of commercial policy and foreign affairs.

In general, legislation was far less important a task of the late eighteenth-century Parliament than 'management'. The politicians organized groups, 'confederacies by which knots of men struggle in a body for places', or 'interests', though some members, like Edmund Burke, pressed the claims of 'party' with vigour and eloquence.

The following passages refer to only a few of the political leaders in the eighteenth-century gallery. Professor Plumb has picked out three political leaders, each of whom in turn impressed his personality on successive 'ages'—Walpole, Chatham and Pitt the Younger.

(a) Robert Walpole extricated the government from the scandals of the South Sea affair. Thereafter, with his outstanding ability to manage people and his great capacity for work, he dominated politics from 1722 to 1733 and stayed in power until 1742. Much of the political and social stability of mid-eighteenth-century politics can be traced back to 'the age of Walpole'.

Source: Lord Hervey, *Memoirs of the Reign of George II* (1848), vol. I, pp. 22–5.

He had a strength of parts equal to any advancement, a spirit to struggle with any difficulties, a steadiness of temper immoveable by any disappointments. He had great skill in figures, the nature of the funds, and the revenue; his first application was to this branch of knowledge; but as he afterwards rose to the highest posts of power, and continued longer there than any first minister in this country since Lord Burleigh ever did, he grew, of course, conversant with all the other parts of government, and very soon equally able in transacting them: the weight of the whole administration lay on him; every project was of his forming, conducting, and executing: from the time of making the Treaty of Hanover, all the foreign as well as domestic affairs passed through his hands: and, considering the little assistance he received from subalterns, it is incredible what a variety and quantity of business he dispatched; but as he had infinite application and long experience, so he had great method and a prodigious memory, with a mind and spirit that were indefatigable: and without every one of these natural as well as acquired advantages, it would indeed have been impossible for him to go through half what he undertook.

No man ever was blessed with a clearer head, a truer or quicker judgement, or a deeper insight into mankind; he knew the strength and weakness of everybody he had to deal with, and how to make his advantage of both; he had more warmth of affection and friendship for some particular people than one could have believed it possible for any one who had been so long raking in the dirt of mankind to be capable of feeling for so worthless a species of animals. One should naturally have imagined that the contempt and distrust he must have had for the species in gross, would have given him at least an indifference and distrust towards every particular. Whether his negligence of his enemies, and never stretching his power to gratify his resentment of the sharpest injury, was policy or constitution, I shall not determine: but I do not believe anybody who knows these times will deny that no minister ever was more outraged, or less apparently revengeful. Some of his friends, who were not unforgiving themselves, nor very apt to see imaginary faults in him, have condemned this easiness in his temper as a weakness that has often exposed him to new injuries, and given encouragement to his adversaries to insult him with impunity. . . .

In all occurrences, and at all times, and in all difficulties, he was constantly pleasant and cheerful . . . no man ever knew better among those he had to deal with who was to be had, on what terms, by what methods, and how the acquisition would answer. He was not one of those projecting systematical great geniuses who are always thinking in theory, and are above common practice: he had been too long conversant in business not to know that in the fluctuation of human affairs and variety of accidents to which the best concerted schemes are liable, they must often be disappointed who build on the certainty of the most probable events; and therefore seldom turned his thoughts to the provisional warding off future evils which might or might not happen; or the scheming of remote advantages, subject to so many intervening crosses; but always applied himself to the present occurrence, studying and generally hitting upon the properest method to improve what was favourable, and the best expedient to extricate himself out of what was difficult. There never was any minister to whom access was so easy and so frequent, nor whose answers were more explicit. He knew how to oblige when he bestowed, and not to shock when he denied; to govern without oppressing, and conquer without triumph. He pursued his ambition without curbing his pleasures, and his pleasures without neglecting his business; he did the latter with ease, and indulged himself in the other without giving scandal or offence. In private life, and to all who had any dependence upon him, he was kind and indulgent; he was generous without ostentation, and an economist without penuriousness; not insolent in success, nor irresolute in distress; faithful to his friends and not inveterate to his foes.

(b) Chatham (William Pitt the Elder) never held power like Walpole, yet he could strike notes in politics well beyond Walpole's range. Horace Walpole called him 'the Heaven-Born Minister', and wrote a good sketch of him.

Source: H. Walpole, Memoirs of the Reign of King George II (1847 edn.), vol. III, pp. 84–6, 176.

Pitt was now arrived at undisturbed possession of that influence in affairs at which his ambition had aimed, and which his presumption had made him flatter himself he could exert like those men of superior genius, whose talents have been called forth by some crisis to retrieve a sinking nation. He had said the last year to the Duke of Devonshire, 'My Lord, I am sure I can save this country, and no one else can.' It were ingratitude to him to say that he did not give such a reverberation to our stagnating Councils, as exceedingly altered the appearance of our fortune. He warded off the evil hour that seemed approaching; he infused vigour into our arms; he taught the nation to speak again as England used to speak to Foreign Powers; and so far from dreading invasions from France, he affected to turn us into invaders. . . .

Pitt's, [however], was an unfinished greatness: considering how much of it depended on his words, one may almost call his an artificial greatness; but his passion for fame and the grandeur of his ideas compensated for his defects. He aspired to redeem the honour of his country, and to place it in a point of giving law to nations. His ambition was to be the most illustrious man of the first country in Europe; and he thought that the eminence of glory could not be sullied by the steps to it being passed irregularly. He wished to aggrandize Britain in general, but thought not of obliging or benefiting individuals. . . .

Posterity, this is an impartial picture. I am neither dazzled by the blaze of the times in which I have lived, nor, if there are spots in the sun, do I deny that I see them. It is a man I am describing, and one whose greatness will bear to have his blemishes fairly delivered to you—not from a love of censure in me, but of truth; and because it is history I am writing, not romance.

(c) Chatham could certainly win the support of the crowds.

Source: An account in the *Annual Register* (1761). Pitt was then out of power.

But what was most remarkable were the prodigious acclamations and tokens of affection, shewn by the populace to Mr. Pitt, who came in his chariot, accompanied by Earl Temple. At every stop the mob clung about every part of the vehicle, hung upon the wheels, hugged his footmen, and even kissed his horses. There was a universal huzza: and the gentlemen at the windows and on the balconies waved their hats and the ladies their handkerchiefs. The same, I am informed, was done all the way along.

(d) Chatham's son, Pitt the Younger, dominated English politics after the American War had disturbed political patterns and forced Lord North out of power. Throughout his life, however, Pitt had to deal with one great rival, Charles James Fox. There was a complete contrast in their personalities and outlook.

Source: An account of the difference in the attitudes of Pitt and Fox, very heavily weighted in favour of Pitt, in J. Horne Tooke's *Two Pair of Portraits* (1788), pp. 7ff.

FOX	PITT
Entered early on the turf, at gaming clubs, &c. . . .	Pursuing early the painful study of the laws and constitution of his country. . . .

FOX	PITT
By every art, intrigue and contrivance, he studies to banish from the minds of men all public motives and public principles, in exchange for party and cabal, for political and family connexions.	With virtue and public principle, he dares, (as his his father before him nobly declared)—'*to look the proudest connexions of this country in the face*'.
In connexion and in OFFICE with Lord North's administration [1784] he vehemently vociferates in the House of Commons, that the people have *no voice* but only within the walls of St. Stephen's. He asks, 'Who are the People?' and answers 'The Parliament'.	Acknowledges a voice of the people distinct from that of parliament. And when two opposite factions corruptly, greedily, and infamously united to form a majority in Parliament, in order at once to overpower both King and People, he made a constitutional, honourable, and *effectual* appeal to that voice without the walls of the House of Commons. . . .
Engaged in a fruitless and impossible attempt, to raise the finances of his party to a level with their own boundless profusion and prodigality.	In spite of all factious opposition, has already, by an œconomical reform of abuses in the expenditure . . . raised the revenues of the nation so much above its frugal ordinary occasions, as to be able to apply some portion towards the discharge of the national debt; and at the same time to hold the country in such a formidable posture of defence, as to secure it from all hostile menace.

(e) Pitt went on to lead the government in time of war, becoming
in a phrase of one of his greatest admirers, Canning, 'the Pilot that
weather'd the storm'. Yet he had many detractors, some of whom
were his victims in a period of relentless repression of radicals.
Fox retained many admirers, who were in complete disagreement
with what Horne Tooke had written about him.

Source: W. Hazlitt, *The Eloquence of the British Senate* (1807).

Mr. Fox excelled all his contemporaries in the extent of his
knowledge, in the clearness and distinctness of his views, in
quickness of apprehension, in plain, practical commonsense,
in the full, strong, and absolute possession of his subject. A
measure was no sooner proposed than he seemed to have an
instantaneous and intuitive perception of its various bearings
and consequences; of the manner in which it would operate
on the different classes of society, on commerce or agriculture,
on our domestic or foreign policy; of the difficulties attending
its execution; in a word, of all its practical results, and the
comparative advantages to be gained either by adopting or
rejecting it. . . . If to this we add the ardour and natural
impetuosity of his mind, his quick sensibility, his eagerness
in the defence of truth, and his impatience of every thing that
looked like trick or artifice or affectation, we shall be able in
some measure to account for the character of his eloquence. His
thoughts came crowding in too fast for the slow and mechanical
process of speech. . . . Everything showed the agitation of his
mind. . . . He was lost in the magnitude of his subject. He
reeled and staggered under the load of feeling which oppressed
him. He rolled like the sea beaten by a tempest. Whoever,
having the feelings of a man, compared him at these times with
his boasted rival [Pitt]—his stiff, straight, upright figure, his
gradual contortions, turning around as if moved by a pivot,
his solemn pauses, his deep tones, 'whose sound reverbed
their own hollowness', must have said, 'This is a man; that is an
automaton.'

(f) During the course of the eighteenth century, 'popular' politicians
emerged, notably John Wilkes (see below, p. 499). Their appeal
was to the crowds. By the end of the century, other politicians had
begun to appear who stressed the need for radical reform of the

political system (see below, p. 500). The American War, followed as it was by the French Revolution, quickened public interest in politics.

Source: W. Cobbett, *The Life and Adventures of Peter Porcupine* (1796), recalling his childhood days.

As to politics, we were like the rest of the country people in England; that is to say, we neither knew nor thought anything about the matter. The shouts of victory, or the murmurs at a defeat, would now-and-then break in upon our tranquillity for a moment; but I do not remember ever having seen a newspaper in the house. . . . After, however, the American War had continued for some time, and the cause of nature of it began to be understood, or rather misunderstood, by the lower classes of the people in England, we became a little better acquainted with subjects of this kind.

(g) Nonetheless, throughout most of the century, most members of parliament preferred to steer clear of politics as much as possible, whether or not they succeeded in doing so.

Source: Letter of Charles Townshend to an un-named correspondent, 10 Nov. 1762, quoted in Sir Lewis Namier and John Brooke, *Charles Townshend* (1964), pp. 77–8.

It is my firm resolution to act the part of a man of business and a man of honour; to be decided by things and not men; to have no party; to *follow* no leader, and to be governed absolutely by my own judgement. . . . .

8. PUBLIC OPINION

There were many turbulent displays of popular feeling during the early and mid-eighteenth century, particularly in London; and later in the century, as public opinions were more freely expressed not only about particular measures but the merits of governments, the idea of 'public opinion' began to crystallize. It was associated with formal county and city meetings and later with reform 'associations' and societies, the latter often cutting through the aristocratic structure of politics. The movement was sustained by the growth of the press, which both reported meetings and diffused ideas, and was anticipated in some of its forms of organization by Quakers and other religious bodies.

(a) *Source: A Letter to The People of England on The Necessity of Putting an Immediate End to War* (1760).

Countrymen and Friends, It is inconceivable to Slaves of other Nations, in what Degree every Individual in this Kingdom may justly boast himself to have a Share, as well in giving Laws to this Country, as in the immediate Administration of its Government. The Sovereign, indeed, makes Choice of his Ministers, and the People have their Representatives in Parliament; but neither, by the Allegiance they pay the one, nor the Confidence they place in the other, do Britons give up this natural Right, to be still Masters of their own Properties, and Guardians of their own Liberties. The recent Experience of a few Years past may furnish us with striking Instances, how loud the Voice of the People is heard in *England*, both on the Throne and in the Senate; Instances, that prove the vast Importance of its being distinguished from the impetuous Clamour of a factious Multitude, by its Conformity to the more sober Dictates of Reason and Truth.

(b) One constitutional means of bringing opinion to bear on Parliament was through petitioning, an ancient custom. Dr. Johnson satirized the practice.

Source: Samuel Johnson, *The False Alarm* (1770).

The progress of a petition is well known. An ejected placeman goes down to his county or his borough, tells his friends of his inability to serve them, and his constituents of the corruption of the government. His friends readily understand that he who can get nothing, will have nothing to give. They agree to proclaim a meeting; meat and drink are plentifully provided; a crowd is easily brought together and those who think that they know the reason of their meeting undertake to tell those who know it not. Ale and clamour unite their powers; the crowd, condensed and heated, begins to ferment with the leaven of sedition. All see a thousand evils, though they cannot show them, and grow impatient for a remedy, though they know not what. A speech is then made by the Cicero of the day; he says much, and suppresses more, and credit is equally given to what he tells and what he conceals. The petition is read and universally approved. Those who are sober enough to write, add their names, and the rest would sign it if they could. The petition is then handed from town to town, and from house to house, and where-ever it comes the inhabitants flock together that they may see that which must be sent to the King. Names are easily collected. One man signs because he hates the papists; another because he has vowed destruction to the turnpikes; one because it will vex the parson; another because he owes his landlord nothing; one because he is rich; another because he is poor; one to show that he is not afraid; and another to show that he can write.

(c) The demand for parliamentary reform was raised in the 1760s.

Source: An article in the *Political Register*, Jan. 1768, pp. 40–2.

The state reformers at the Revolution were so intent on binding down our *kings* to their good behaviour, that they left the *grandees* in possession of powers inconsistent with the first principles of liberty. For what can be imagined more contradictory to the natural rights of mankind, than that . . . *two* or *three hundred* persons should have it, at any time, in their power to stop the whole business of the *nation*? . . .

Let us, in order to form just notions of the degree of liberty at present secure to us, consider a few other particulars respecting the *lower* house. First, with regard to the *representation* . . . what could blind chance have determined more *unequal*, *irregular*, and imperfect, than we see it at this day? First, as to the landed interest, there are two members for each county. But, on comparing the extent and value of the counties, you will find, that one county, as Yorkshire for instance, is of six times more value than another, as Rutlandshire. There are but six representatives for the immense contiguity of the metropolis, comprehending London, Westminster, and Southwark, in which the very number of *dwelling-houses* (to say nothing of the *wealth* of the inhabitants), is beyond computation. There are as many for Old Sarum, and one or two other rotten boroughs in that neighbourhood, the whole number of houses in which have been estimated below the value of £4000. . . .

The monied interest is not represented at all. One hundred millions and upwards of property wholly excluded from a share in the legislature! excepting where the proprietors have other qualifications. The case is much the same with the *commercial* interest. A merchant or manufacturer, who exports to the value of half a million every year, is not represented as a merchant or manufacturer: he has not the privilege of a beggar in a Cornish borough. Accordingly the great manufacturing towns of Manchester, Birmingham, Sheffield, &c., have no representation in parliament. And in most towns the *corporation*, which bears no proportion to the inhabitants, either in number, or property, are the only voters.

London, Westminster, and Southwark, pay eighty parts in five hundred and thirteen of the land-tax, and of the subsidy, one hundred and thirty-five; while they send only eight members to the house of commons. Cornwall and Devon, pay twenty-nine parts land-tax, and twenty-four subsidy, while they send no less than seventy members. . . . May not the interest of a few persons deputed by a twentieth part of the people, by a fiftieth part of the property, be, by an artful and corrupt court, made to appear to them quite *different* from that of the *nation*?

(c) The Yorkshire Association was a pioneer body in the mobilization of provincial opinion. It was founded at a county meeting in 1779, and corresponded with similar associations in other parts of the country.

Source: An Address of the Yorkshire Association in 1781, printed in C. Wyvill, *Political Papers* (n.d.), vol. I, pp. 305–15.

By the unspeakable infatuation of our councils . . . the national substance is wasting fast away by the profusion of expence in this rash and unfortunate war [in America]. . . . The system of corruption has reached to its maturity; and the crisis of our country is at length arrived. . . . In opposition to that mercenary phalanx, the efforts of a few solitary individuals, or even a few unconnected cities and counties would be too unequal to succeed. From the joint endeavours of the public a political deliverance can only be expected. . . . Whether Associations in the several districts of the kingdom, acting by their respective Committees, and by general deputation from the Associated Bodies, be the more advantageous mode of collecting and supporting the sense of the public, it is not their part to decide, but it is a feasible mode; it is a mode conformable to law.

(d) When during the French Revolution Pitt's government sought to suppress corresponding societies exchanging radical views, critics pointed to the fact that Pitt himself had been a supporter of the Association movement of the 1780s.

Source: A Letter in the *Manchester Courier*, 12 July 1794.

A Convention of Delegates . . . supported by Corresponding Societies all over the Kingdom is . . . said to be dangerous and unlawful. If it is so, it must be proper to know who first set the example. Leaving the notorious conduct of Mr. Pitt and the Duke of Richmond out of the question, I will show, that the very men who now condemn these measures were the original promoters of them. . . . In the year 1780, Associations were formed in most of the counties, cities, and towns throughout England for the purpose of petitioning the House of Commons to reform the expenditure of public money, and to reform Parliament . . . and all other branches of the State; and they were carried on in a tone far exceeding in boldness any thing of the present day.

9. TAXATION

Throughout the century, one of the main interests of the public was the level and character of taxation. As the national debt grew in size and government expenditure increased, governments were drawn more and more into difficult decisions about debt and tax policy. There were sometimes severe public disturbances, as in 1733, when the Lord Mayor and Corporation of London raised a formidable and exceptionally well-organized opposition to Walpole's tax measures. The Younger Pitt, who introduced the income tax in 1798, established his reputation as a fiscal reformer. Because of the character of government expenditure—on war, for example, or on patronage—radicalism became a creed of cheap government.

(a) *Source:* An account of the 1733 crisis in Lord Hervey, *Memoirs of the Reign of George II* (1848), pp. 59–63.

Faction was never more busy on any occasion; terrors were never more industriously scattered, and clamour never more universally raised.

That which gave rise to these commotions was a project of Sir Robert Walpole's to ease the land-tax of one shilling in the pound, by turning the duty on tobacco and wine, then payable on importation, into inland duties; that is, changing the Customs on those two commodities into Excises; by which scheme, joined to the continuation of the salt-duty, he proposed to improve the public revenue £500,000 per annum, in order to supply the abatement of one shilling in the pound on land, which raises about that sum.

The landed men had long complained that they had ever since the Revolution borne the heat and burden of the day for the support of the Revolution Government; and as the great pressure of the last war had chiefly lain on them (the land having for many years been taxed to four shillings in the pound), they now began to say, that since the public tranquility both at home and abroad was firmly and universally established, if ease was not at this time thought of for them, it was a declaration from the Government that they were never to expect any; and that two shillings in the pound on land was the least that they or their posterity, in the most profound peace and fullest tranquility, were ever to hope to pay.

This having been the cry of the country gentlemen and landowners for some time, Sir Robert Walpole thought he could not do a more popular thing than to form a scheme by which the land-tax should be reduced to one shilling in the pound, and yet no new tax be substituted in the lieu thereof, no new duty laid on any commodity whatsoever, and the public revenue improved £500,000 per annum, merely by this alteration in the method of management.

The salt-duty, which had been revised the year before, could raise only in three years what one shilling in the pound on land raised in one year; consequently, as that tax was an equivalent only to one-third of a shilling on land, if the remission of that shilling on land was further and annually continued, some other fund must be found to supply the other two-thirds.

This Excising of tobacco and wine was the equivalent projected by Sir Robert Walpole, but this scheme, instead of procuring him the popularity he thought it would, caused more clamour and made him even, whilst the project was only talked of and in embryo, more vilified and abused by the universal outcries of the people, than any one Act of his whole administration.

The art, vigilance, and industry of his enemies had so contrived to represent this scheme to the people, and had so generally in every county and great town throughout all England prejudiced their minds against it; they had shown it in so formidable a shape and painted it in such hideous colours, that everybody talked of the scheme as a general Excise: they believed that food and raiment, and all the necessaries of life, were to be taxed; that armies of Excise officers were to come into any house and at any time they pleased; that our liberties were at an end, trade going to be ruined, Magna Charta overturned, all property destroyed, the Crown made absolute, and Parliaments themselves no longer necessary to be called.

This was the epidemic madness of the nation on this occasion; whilst most of the boroughs in England, and the city of London itself, sent formal instructions by way of memorials to their Representatives, absolutely to oppose all new Excises and all extensions of Excise laws, if proposed in Parliament, though introduced or modelled in any manner whatsoever.

(b) To finance the American War, Lord North, the Prime Minister, had to raise new taxes, mainly luxury taxes, like those on carriages, cards and dice. In 1777 a tax was imposed on male servants.

Source: Statute of 1777, cap. 39, printed in *Statutes at Large*, vol XXXI.

Be it enacted by the King's most excellent Majesty, by and with the advice and consent of the lords spiritual and temporal, and commons, in this present parliament assembled, and by the authority of the same, That, from and after the fifth day of

July 1777 there shall be charged, raised, levied, and paid unto his Majesty, his heirs and successors, after the rate of twenty-one shillings *per annum* for every male servant, within the kingdom of *Great Britain*, who shall then have been, or shall afterwards be, retained or employed in the following capacities; (that is to say) of maitre d'hotel, house-steward, master of the horse, groom of the chamber, valet de chambre, butler, under-butler, clerk of the kitchen, confectioner, cook, house-porter, footman, running-footman, coachman, groom, postillion, stable-boy, and the respective helpers in the stables of such coachman, groom, or postillion, or in the capacity of gardener (not being a day-labourer), park-keeper, game-keeper, hunts-man, whipper-in. . . .

(c) There were no more noisy issues in politics. Pitt's shop tax of 1785 raised another storm of protest.

Source: J. Freeth, *The Political Songster* (1790), pp. 103–4.

> 'Twas when the odious shop-tax had
> To murmurs given vent,
> And through the kingdom want of trade
> Increased the discontent;
> Of worthy citizens a band,
> Who found themselves oppresst . . .
> [As] thus their minds exprest.
> The servant who his country's love
> So rapidly has lost
> Whose conduct reason must reprove,
> No longer dein to trust . . .
> Your ministry once more disband,
> Nor think it bad advice;
> The trading int'rest of the land
> Will at the cause rejoice;
> And may not those to public woes
> Who patiently submit,
> As well be worried by a FOX
> As swallow'd in a PITT.

(d) The greatest of all outcries against taxation came during the long and wearing wars against Napoleon.

Source: Speech of the Member of Parliament for Appleby, 28 May 1806, in *Hansard*, vol. VII, col. 398.

The fact is, I fear, that we have arrived at the final limit of taxation on consumption, or very near it. The multitude can pay no more, without crushing and confounding the gradations of society, when no distinctions of rank or fortune will be left.

10. RIOT

No account of eighteenth-century politics would be complete without reference to riots. In addition to food riots (see above, p. 295), turnpike riots (see above, p. 94), labour riots (see above, p. 156) and election riots, there were riots which had their origins in religious disturbance (e.g. 1710, 1746, 1780), in anti-militia act protests (e.g. 1757, 1761), and in politics (mainly the Wilkesite riots of the 1760s and 1770s). Recently riots have been submitted to careful analytical study.

(a) *Source:* An account given by Sir Robert Walpole to his brother of an anti-Irish riot of July 1736, printed in G. F. Rudé, ' "Mother Gin" and the London Riots of 1736,' in *The Guildhall Miscellany* (1959).

On Monday night last there was an appearance of numbers being assembled in a very disorderly manner at Shoreditch, near Spitalfields. Their cry and complaint was of being underworked, and starved by the Irish: *Down with the Irish*, &c. But that night the numbers were not very great, and they dispersed themselves without doing any mischief. . . . On Tuesday evening they assembled again in bodies, and were about 7 o'clock thought to be 2,000 in number. They now grew more riotous; they attacked a public house, kept by an Irishman, where the Irish resorted and victualled, broke down all the doors and windows and quite gutted the house. Another house of the same sort underwent the same fate. By this time . . . the Mayor and Deputy Lieutenant of the Tower Hamlets were assembled in order to disperse them. The proclamation was read; but the mob, wholly regardless of the proclamation, increased every minute, and were thought to be about 4,000 strong. The Magistrate upon this gave orders for raising the Militia; and in the Meantime the Deputy Lieutenant wrote to the Commanding Officer at the Tower to send to their assistance such a number of the Guards as they could spare, upon which an officer with about fifty men was sent by Major White. Upon the appearance of the Guards the mob retired, shifted from one street and alley to another, and gave no resistance, and by break of day all were dispersed.

(b) There are many eye-witnesses' accounts of incidents in the 1768 riots.

Source: This account was given by W. H. Hipgrave and is printed in G. Rudé, *Wilkes and Liberty* (1962), Appendix I.

About 6 to 7 p.m. on Tuesday 10th May, 'he was at the Baptist Head in the Old Bailey with Jas. Winchelow & hearing that there was firing in St. George's Fields they agreed to a walk there. Set forward to Blackfriars Bridge, took a boat there to the Falcon where they went into a house and had some [beer]. Set forward to St. George's Fields where they found a great Mob near the King's Bench Prison, went up to the Mob and were told that the *Justices had been reading something* & stayed there about one Hour. In that time were frequently drove with the Mob up Horsemongers Lane by the soldiers, often lost his Companion Whichelow but afterwards finding him about 9 they set forward from that Place to return Home and when they came to the Distiller's at the Bridge Foot [meaning Mr. Russell's] found the Mob breaking the windows. He . . . again lost Whichelow, staid and saw them break Mr. Russell's House by the help of an Iron Crane at the Door. Saw Thomas Greenwood about a quarter of an hour after 9 at night in the Mob who shewed him a Bayonet or some such Yard or Instrum[t] whi[ch] he had concealed under his Coat. . . . That the Mob after they broke into the House of Mr Russell drank spirituous liquors out of their Hats and they made use of his hat among others for that purpose; and then he went homewards, called in at the Baptist's Head in the Old Bailey on his way but did not stay & so went home.

(c) There are also vivid contemporary accounts of the Gordon Riots of 1780.

Source: Letter of Horace Walpole, 15 June 1780, printed in *Letters,* vol. xi, p. 224.

You may like to know one is alive, dear Sir, after a massacre and the conflagration of a capital. I was in it, both on the Friday and on the *Black Wednesday,* the most horrible night I ever beheld, and which, for six hours together, I expected to end in half the town being reduced to ashes. I can give you little account of the origins of this shocking affair. Negligence was certainly its nurse, and Religion only its god-mother. The ostensible author is in the Tower. Twelve or fourteen thousand men have quashed all tumults; and as no bad account is come from the country, except for a moment at Bath, and as eight days have passed—nay, more, since the commencement—I flatter myself the whole nation is shocked at the scene, and that, if plan there was, it was laid only in and for the metropolis. The lowest and most villainous people, and to no great amount, were almost the sole actors.

I hope your electioneering riotry has not, nor will mix in these tumults. It would be most absurd; for Lord Rockingham, the Duke of Richmond, Sir George Saville, and Mr. Burke, the patrons of toleration, were devoted to destruction as much as the ministers. The rails torn from Sir George's house were the chief weapons and instruments of the mob. For the honour of the nation I should be glad to have it proved that the French were the engineers. You and I have lived too long for our comfort—shall we close our eyes in peace? . . .

11. SOCIAL POLITICS

During the last decade of the eighteenth century, under the influence of the French Revolution, new emphasis began to be placed on social aspects of politics. The London Corresponding Society, founded in 1792, talked not only of recovering the lost, ancient constitution but of working-men's rights and needs. Against the background of economic hardship in the last phases of the wars against Napoleon, both middle-class and working-class people (the term 'class' was beginning to be more widely used) emphasized their social grievances, the latter most conspicuously through the activities of the Luddites, 'an army of redressers' (see above, p. 161).

(a) *Source:* T. Somerville, *Observations on the Constitution* (1793), pp. 58–9.

The late revolution in France has given rise to a spirit of political speculation, tending to depreciate our domestic privileges; and to explode that satisfaction and pride which have hitherto been excited by the supposed pre-eminence of our constitution.

(b) Thomas Hardy, the shoemaker secretary of the London Corresponding Society, described its first meeting.

Source: Account of a meeting in the Bell Tavern, off the Strand, in January 1792, printed in *Memoir of Thomas Hardy . . . Written by Himself*, p. 16.

After having had their bread and cheese and porter for supper, as usual, and their pipes afterwards, with some conversation on the hardness of the times and the dearness of all the necessaries of life . . . the business for which they had met was brought forward—*Parliamentary Reform*—an important subject to be deliberated upon and dealt with by such a class of men.

(c) Their enemies spied on their activities on behalf of the government which after 1793 followed a policy of repression.

Source: A Note from a spy, Groves, in the *Treasury Solicitor's Papers*, June 1794, quoted in E. P. Thompson, *The Making of the English Working Class* (1963), p. 156.

There are some [members] of decent tradesmanlike appearance, who possess strong, but unimproved faculties, and tho' bold, yet cautious. The delegates of this description are but few. There are others of an apparent lower order—no doubt journeymen, who though they seem to possess no abilities and say nothing, yet they appear resolute . . . and regularly vote for every motion which carries with it a degree of boldness. The last description . . . and which is the most numerous consist of the very lowest order of society—few are ever decent in appearance, some of them filthy and ragged, and others such wretched looking blackguards that it requires some mastery over that innate pride, which every well-educated man must necessarily possess, even to sit down in their company.

(d) Francis Place, who attended meetings of the L.C.S., came to feel that eighteenth-century ways of approaching politics were out-of-date and repugnant. He was to be a key man in the reconstruction of radical politics in London after 1807.

Source: A Note in the *Place Papers*, British Museum Add. MSS, 27.850, ff. 19–20.

My indignation was greatly increased [in 1806] when I saw the servants of the Duke of Northumberland, in their showy dress liveries, throwing lumps of bread and cheese among the dense crowd of vagabonds they had collected together [at Westminster]. To see these vagabonds catching the lumps, shouting, swearing, fighting, and blackguarding in every possible way, women as well as men, all the vile wretches from the courts and alleys in St. Giles and Westminster, the Porridge Islands, and other miserable places; to see these people representing, as it was said, the electors of Westminster, was certainly the lowest possible step of degradation, except, indeed, if it be possible, to hear it said, as it was said, that the 'electors of Westminster had been treated by the bounty of the Duke.' Some who mingled in the mob were ashamed of the proceedings, and as the mob pressed round the butts which contained the beer, suggested that the best way would be to knock in the heads as they stood up on end. This was done immediately. The heads were beaten in, and the coal-heavers ladled the beer out with their long-tailed, broad-brimmed hats; but the mob pressing on, the butts were upset, and the beer flowed along the gutters, from whence some made efforts to obtain it. . . . I was not only one who felt indignation. Almost every man I knew was much offended with the whole of the proceedings and with all who were concerned in them.

(e) Much of the social discontent was provincial. This was already clear to contemporaries during the 1790s, as the idea of Corresponding Societies spread: it became even more clear in 1811 and 1812, birth years of nineteenth-century politics.

Source: R. I. and S. Wilberforce, *Life of William Wilberforce*, (1838), vol. II, p. 2.

Considerable numbers in Barnard Castle have manifested disaffection to the constitution, and the words, 'No King',

'Liberty', and 'Equality' have been written there upon the Market Cross. During the late disturbances amongst the keelmen at Shields and Sutherland, General Lambton was thus addressed: 'Have you read this little work of Tom Paine's?' 'No!' 'Then read it—we like it much. You have a great estate, General; we shall soon divide it amongst us.'

(f) *Source:* J. Bowles, *Thoughts on the Late General Election* (1803), p. 63.

During a contest at Lancaster in the General Election of 1802, the Jacobinical mob was addressed by a *lady*, who told them that 'the contest was between shoes and wooden clogs, between fine shirts and coarse ones, between the opulent and the poor, and that the people were everything if they chose to assert their rights'.

(g) Radical forces were to be unleashed almost everywhere at the end of the Napoleonic Wars, when unemployment rose. The different threads of popular agitation were pulled together.

Source: Report of a Speech by Orator Hunt at Spa Fields, London, in 1816, printed in the *Examiner*, 17 Nov. 1816.

What was the cause of the want of employment? Taxation. What was the cause of taxation? Corruption. It was corruption that had enabled the borough-mongers to wage that bloody war which had for its object the destruction of the liberties of all countries but principally of our own. . . . Everything that concerned their subsistence or comforts was taxed. Was not their loaf taxed? Was not their bread taxed? Was not everything they ate, drank, wore, and even said, taxed? . . . [The taxes] were imposed by the authority of a borough-mongering faction who thought of nothing but oppressing the people, and subsisting on the plunder wrung from their miseries.

12. URBAN POLITICS

As large and growing centres of population, the large towns, particularly those with an industrial population, were also centres of political argument. The clash between conservative and radical forces in the 1780s and 1790s was often fierce and violent, but by 1815 conservatism was no longer the dominating philosophy of the middle classes. Much of the new energy of the nineteenth century was to come from the new industrial districts of the North and Midlands.

(a) *Source:* W. Coombe, *A Word in Season to the Traders and Manufacturers of Great Britain* (1792), pp. 26ff.

It really astonishes me, who have lived all my life among manufacturers, that anything like a levelling and equalising spirit, should have got the least footing in any of our manufacturing towns; because I conceive it to be essential to their progress and existence, that the rich inhabitants should be few, and the laborious many; and that the subordination of the different classes, to each other, is the life and soul of every species of manufactory. By way of example, let me suppose for a moment, that the working manufacturers of Manchester or Birmingham should be so far inflamed by these new-fangled doctrines of the rights of man, as to say to their masters, we have toil'd for you long enough, you shall now toil for us: it is by our skill and industry that you are become rich, we will, therefore, have our rightful share of the wealth acquired by our means. Of such an operation of the rights of man, what would be the consequence?—Ruin to all—to the rich, who would be despoiled of their property, and to the poor, who would, thereby, lose every means of future maintenance and support. Indeed, it appears to me, that, in places particularly devoted to trade, manufactures, and commerce, there can be no evil so much to be dreaded as popular commotions. A foreign enemy would repay submission with clemency: fire may be checked in its progress—but who shall say to the mad spirit of popular tumult, thus far shall thou go, and no farther.

(b) *Source:* Manifesto of the Manchester Constitutional Society, Oct. 1790, printed in T. Walker, *A Review of Some of the Political Events which have Occurred in Manchester, during the last Five Years* (1794), p. 17.

Resolution I.—That in every civil community, the legitimate authority of the *Governors*, can only be derived from the consent of the *Governed*.

II. That the happiness of the people governed ought to be the sole end and aim of all civil government.

III. That public honours and emoluments can only be due for services conferred on the state.

IV. That every person from the highest to the lowest, appointed to and accepting any office or trust for the benefit of the Community, is ultimately responsible to the people for the complete discharge of the duties of it.

V. That *Actions* only, and not *Opinions*, are the proper objects of civil jurisdiction.

VI. That no Law or Statute can be fairly made, which is not enacted by and with the consent of a majority of the people, given expressly by themselves, or by means of a full, fair, and adequate Representation.

VII. That the People of Great Britain are not fully, fairly and adequately represented in Parliament; and that the defective state of the representation of this country, and the extended duration of Parliament require a speedy and effectual reform, and are the objects to which the attention of this Society ought particularly to be directed.

(c) Yet there was resistance to such arguments.

Source: Manifesto of the Manchester Church and King Club, printed in *ibid.*, p. 17.

The Church and King Club, held at the house of Mr. Jonathan Foster, the Weaver's Arms, on Cockspit Hill, Manchester, think it necessary, openly in the following Declaration, to state their reasons for publishing their Principles.

DECLARATION

This Society beholds with infinite concern the many dangerous plots and associations that are forming in various parts of this kingdom, for the avowed purpose of disseminating discord, and for subverting the order of one of the most beautiful systems of government, that the combined efforts of human wisdom has ever yet been able to accomplish.

When we see such deadly *wounds* aimed at our glorious constitution, we consider it the duty of all good citizens,

KK

publicly to step forward, and express their abhorrence of the
malevolent and most wicked intentions of those disappointed
men, who are audaciously clamorous for a reform in parliament,
but whose real object is to excite civil commotion in this our
happy and well-governed State.

We are from believing, should they ever effect their purpose
(which Heaven forbid!) that the change would be for the
better, but must aways regard those persons as the bane of
civil society, who have given so many proofs of an innate
propensity for power, and of that restless ambition which has
long been their most dangerous characteristic.

PRINCIPLES OF THE CHURCH AND KING CLUB

It is a principle of this Society to revere the Constitution
and obey the King, according to the laws of that Constitution
... to reprobate the wild theories and seditious doctrines
respecting the Rights of Man, which have lately been pro-
mulgated by the enemies of our most excellent Constitution
in Church and State, as they are subversive of all civil authority;
and ..., if they were put into practice, would tend to nothing
but anarchy and confusion, which is contrary to all order. ...
It is a principle of this Society, that the Constitution of this
country was renovated and fixed at the time of the glorious
Revolution ... that the Constitution has not since that time
been essentially departed from ... that all other modes of
legislation, than by King, Lords and Commons have always
been found, by experience, repugnant to the genius of Englishmen ... that it is requisite in every good governed State, that
there must exist an established Church, and that no one is to
bear any office, either in Church or State, but such as will
conform and be in communion with that Church. It is a
principle of this Society that the Corporation and Test Acts
are the great bulwarks of our Constitution in Church and
State, therefore ought never to be repealed ... that toleration
in religious matters is to be extended to Dissenters of every
denomination. Finally; it is the fixed determination of this
Society, at all times and in all places, to avow and maintain
the above principles to be truly constitutional.

(d) The methods of nineteenth-century urban politics were anticipated at Liverpool in 1812 where Brougham and Canning fought a lively election.

Source: Letter of Harry Brougham to Lord Grey, printed in *The Life and Times of Lord Brougham, Written by Himself* (1871) vol. II, p. 62.

You can have no idea of the nature of a Liverpool election; it is quite peculiar to the place. You have every night to go to the different clubs, benefit societies, etc., which meet and speechify. This is from half-past six to one in the morning at least; and you have to speak to each man who polls, at the bar, from ten to five. It lasted eight days. I began my canvas three whole days before, and had nine nights of the clubs, besides a regular speech each day at close of the poll. I delivered in that time one hundred and sixty speeches and old; and yesterday and today, after being beaten I rallied and delivered regular speeches to the whole multitude. I had to close with one above an hour long, so you may guess how exhausted I am, especially as I never saw a popular election before.

(e) Much of the later history of the nineteenth century was anticipated in the manifesto of the Birmingham Chamber of Commerce (1813).

Source: G. H. Wright, *Chronicles of the Birmingham Chamber of Commerce* (1913), pp. 49ff.

The strong and immediate interest which the middle class feel in the commercial prosperity of the country, leads them to investigate and discriminate the bearings of public measures upon its commerce and manufactures: but the members of that class of society of which the legislature is composed have seldom a personal acquaintance with trade. . . . Hence it has frequently happened that the interests of the manufacturing districts have been unintentionally sacrificed to erroneous commercial and political regulations, whilst the landed, the shipping, the Colonial and other great and powerful interests have been protected by their advocates in Parliament.

(f) See also a speech by a Manchester manufacturer at a reform meeting in October 1816, reported in J. B. Smith, *Reminiscences 1819–1832* (manuscript, n.d.), p. 10.

He described in glowing terms the munificence of the Great Creator in providing corn and the precious fruits of the earth for all his creatures and the aristocracy standing between God and his people and impiously declaiming 'Thou shalt not eat'.

(g) Yet there was also another side to urban politics. Not all the conflicts in the towns were or were to be between middle classes and aristocracy. There were also social conflicts between employers and workers.

Source: A Note by 'A Churchman' in the *Manchester Observer*, 23 May 1818.

They (the manufacturers) call it 'promoting industry'. But I think it may with greater propriety be called the advancement of slavery.

INDEX OF NAMES AND PLACES